Cuban Tourist Poster - 1949

The Exciting Story of Cuba

by

Captain Hank Bracker

Understanding Cuba's Present by Knowing Its Past

www.CaptainHankBracker.com
www.AtoZPublishers.com
www.TheExcitingStoryofCuba.com

Heinrich W. W. Bracker, *The Exciting Story of Cuba – Understanding Cuba's Present by Knowing Its Past*, by Captain Hank Bracker,
1st edition
p. cm.
Includes historical references
ISBN-13: 978-1484809457
ISBN-10: 1484809459
Copyright 2015. Library of Congress Cataloging-In-Publication Data.
1. Bracker 2. History 3. Cuba 4. Caribbean 5. Florida 6. Stories 7. Maine Maritime Academy 8. Captain Hank

FIRST EDITION
Released for print and electronic reproduction 2015

Contents

Tribute to the *Cubano-Americanos*

This book is a salute to the stalwart Americans who trace their national origin to Cuba. There are almost a million of them living in South Florida alone, with another 200,000 living in Northern New Jersey and New York City.

Their journey to the United States began prior to the Louisiana Purchase, when many of them arrived in Key West and in Ybor City in the Tampa Bay area, where they worked for the tobacco industry, skillfully making cigars. More came during the second half of the 19th century when a number of Cuban cigar manufacturers moved their operations from Havana to Florida. With the continuing disruptions brought on as Cubans fought for their independence from Spain, others followed bringing their customs and traditions. José Martí, Cuba's respected national hero, recognized the importance of these Cuban-Americans by visiting and inspiring them on numerous occasions.

After the 1959 Cuban revolution, Castro allied himself with the Soviet Union and introduced communism to the proud island nation. This started an exodus of refugees that frequently used inner tubes and small boats to cross the treacherous Straits of Florida. Most of these Cuban-Americans came from Cuba's more-educated middle and upper classes. During the early 1960's more than 14,000 Cuban children arrived on the shores of the United States as part of what was called "Operation Peter Pan." With unbridled ambition, hard work and a cooperative spirit they became respected engineers, politicians, doctors, bankers and business people. Their culture has become part of the American fabric and has enriched the United States with its colorful art, epicurean delights, music, literature and cultural values.

"I believe in the promise of America. Being a Cuban refugee, having come here when I was eight, I know that this is a shining city on the hill."
Ileana Ros-Lehtinen, the first Hispanic woman to serve in Congress, U.S. Representative for Florida's 27th Congressional District

Preface

Acknowledgements

My thanks go to the people who assisted me in writing this book, as well as to my patient wife Ursula, who put up with my eccentric ways and my mysterious disappearing acts into the man-cave I use as an office, to think, research and write.

Thanks to my wonderful friend Lucy Shaw, for relentlessly helping me with this complicated apparatus called a computer, and for proofing the more than 138,000 words contained within this book. Although she has many outside responsibilities, Lucy has been much more than a proofreader and it gives me great pleasure to dub her "My learned copy editor!"

My enduring appreciation also goes to Jorge Fernandez, an exceptionally good friend, who arrived on the shores of Florida in 1962 at 18 years of age, looking for freedom and better opportunities than his homeland of Cuba could afford him. When he arrived, it was with empty pockets; however, he never lost his sense of heritage or the realization that in America anything is possible. His ambitious nature never failed him, as he first studied to become an aircraft mechanic and then became a Structural Engineer. As this book progressed, Jorge frequently took time from his work as the best Structural Engineer in the Tampa Bay area of Florida, to correct me when my historical insights became too fanciful or my views became skewed. Jorge diligently worked on the details of arranging and formatting this work.

This book would not have been possible without the generosity of dedicated time, donated by both Lucy and Jorge. Without them, this book would never have become a reality and I would probably still be floundering around out in the Gulf Stream, somewhere between Florida and Cuba! Figuratively speaking, I hope....

"The most difficult thing is the decision to act. The rest is merely tenacity." Amelia Earhart, American aviation pioneer and author

More than just Cuba

Although this book centers on Cuba, the tentacles of history have reached far beyond the island. It is not enough to know that Columbus discovered Cuba or that Julio Antonio Mella started the Communist Party. With every fact, there is always the question, "Why?" For those interested, it is not enough to discuss basic historical facts but rather to examine all the events leading up to what finally transpired. In this book, I have attempted to go far beyond the simplicity of just the basic occurrences by traveling down the twisted paths that surround them.

Do not be surprised when you find yourself reading about the Bering Straits, China during the Ming Dynasty, the Inca Empire or the Library of Alexandria. The expression that "No Man is an Island" by John Donne, holds true for Cuba just as much as any other place on our planet. It is comforting to know that our heritage contains a common bond that we all share.

Historical Accuracy

History can never be fictitious... or can it? The actual historical events will always adhere to past reality, however in time the memory of these happenings fade or can even, inadvertently, change. Things that have been told to me and appear in this book are only as reliable as the memory, political leanings, or honesty of that person allows it to be. Where possible, most of the accounts that I have written about have been researched and cross-referenced from several sources, and can be considered reasonably reliable. Cuban history is frequently seen through the prism of individual political or economic spectrums and since there are at least two sides to a story, I have attempted to ferret out fairness and truth in the narration of these accounts. Historical Bridges are infrequently used to flesh out a narrative where the basic facts are obvious but some of the finer details are speculative. Ultimately, readers are responsible for interpreting the issues and discerning for themselves, what is factual, or what may be considered conjured.

Chronology

Short narratives relating to important aspects of Cuban history occasionally interrupt the chronological sequence of this book. An example of this is Part 5, where the reader has the opportunity to deviate from the main course of sequential Cuban history, in order to view the introduction and expansion of Communism in Cuba to a greater depth. Part 6 continues by following the story of Julio Antonio Mella, who founded the Cuban Communist Party in the mid 1920's. Part 7 tells the anecdote of a specific event about a ship built out of cement that is still part of the seascape along the northern coast of the island. It is not until Part 8 that the book returns to the progressive course of Cuban history.

Pictures, Posters and Photographs

Edward Henry Weston took the photographs of Tina Modotti during the early 1920's. The same, and additional photographs, can be found in *Tina Modotti Photographs* by María Caronia or in Mildred Constantine's *Tina Modotti, A Fragile Life*. See the Recommended Research Material section near the back of the book.

Paintings, maps and photographs are mostly in the public domain, and have been acquired from The Library of Congress, Wikimedia, or were otherwise available on the internet. They are used only to illustrate the narrative, and are to be considered "fair use" for educational purposes in this book.

The posters are indicative of the many travel posters that were seen in the pre-Castro era. It is with great appreciation to the artists, most of whom are now deceased, that I use the illustrations contained within.

"A colony of mice playing in a field decided that in order to remain safe from a marauding cat, they would have to hang a bell around its neck. The plan was applauded, until one mouse asked who would volunteer to place the bell around the cat's neck, at which time they all made excuses..." Thought from a fable attributed to Aesop, "The Mice in Council." As recalled by Jorge Fernandez as a commonly-known story from his childhood days in Cuba

Introduction

This book is a very different way to view Cuban history. Instead of just being focused on the facts of what happened on this island nation, it takes a wide-angle view and follows the trail of what occurred before and after a given event. The narrative of this book takes the reader from Greenland to Europe and South America, uncovering the colorful stories that illustrate why things happened the way they did. Bringing Cuban history to life in the context of World events makes its history exciting and relevant to current and future happenings.

While writing my book *Seawater One*, I came to a section regarding my earlier voyages to Cuba, which was during the onset of Castro's Revolution. Although very little of *Seawater One* concerns itself with the history of Cuba, the historical aspects of it caught my attention. I suddenly grasped that I had been in Santiago de Cuba just five months after Fidel Castro and his brother Raúl were convicted for attacking the Moncada and Bayamo Barracks. I realized that I was there during the time of the revolution that changed this island nation so drastically. Moreover, I have always had a fascination for the culture of our closest neighbor across the Florida Straits in the Caribbean.

It was in 1953 that I first set foot on Cuban soil, and the following year I found myself in Havana for their Mardi Gras, a celebration that emphasized the extreme but delightful decadence during the Batista era. It was a celebration I mischievously enjoyed and certainly will never forget. However, it also accented all that was wrong with the régime in power.

Towards the back of this book, I have included a quick reference of people who helped shape Cuba. Although there have been many others, in my judgment these people exercised the greatest amount of influence, directly or indirectly, in bringing the nation to where it is today.

In writing this historical narrative of stories, I tried not to judge or take sides. I tell the events as they happened and attempt to take a neutral or reasonable political position; however I am also convinced that both sides will disagree with some of my views. Hopefully this is not just one more dry history book, but rather a presentation of interesting stories of Cuba.

Unfortunately, Cuba is still a divided country with extreme political leanings and loyalties. Cubans, in both the United States and on the island, are a proud people who frequently find it difficult to reach a middle ground. Research into recent history demonstrates that the people who fled from Castro, and those who still support him, see things in a very different light. It is said that, "To the victor go the spoils," and in this case, both sides have experienced both victory and defeat. Thus, events are recorded in two very different ways. Americans have also played a major role in Cuban history. However, to be very clear, not everything America has done was right, nor was it always wrong, since special interest groups frequently influenced events in Washington. The consequential actions of the United States as they pertain to Cuban affairs reflect this.

In the end, it is the reader's conclusion that counts, but my attempt is to separate the wheat from the chaff and to clarify the brine as much as possible, but always with a sense of responsibility mixed with humor. The nature of this book is definitely historical and therefore can be used as a reference source that, although not footnoted, can easily be cross-referenced with standard textbooks as well as historical novels. It contains photographs, stories and information not readily found in other books about Cuban history.

Repetition of events is only used as a tool to demonstrate continuity, to view the event from another perspective, or to emphasize its importance.

My information came from numerous reliable sources and some personal accounts. Living in Florida gives me a better perspective on Cuban history than I could expect to have if I lived elsewhere. My thanks go to many, although in some cases to give specific credit may identify their political position, put people in harm's way, or unnecessarily create undue anxiety for them. It should be noted that there are still those that can be seen as extreme activists and would not hesitate to resort to violence, directed against what they consider their opposition.

The United States is a country that has fought in more wars than most, and most frequently for honorable reasons. The United States usually leaves the countries it fought against in better shape than they were previously, and before long returns to having peaceful, productive relations with them. Unfortunately, that has not been the case with its neighboring country Cuba, where wounded feelings, the economic relationship, and special interests, have prevented things from normalizing. If reason prevails, the relationship between Cuba and the United States can and should improve....

"History will be kind to me for I intend to write it." Winston Churchill, Prime Minister of Great Britain

The Exciting

Story of Cuba

José Martí

José Martí, Hero of Cuban Independence
Restored and modified by John M. Kennedy

Works of José Martí

Duty of a Man

"The first duty of a man is to think for himself."

~~~

"I always Dream with Open Eyes"

Day and night
I always dream with open eyes
And on top of the foaming waves
Of the wide turbulent sea,
And on the rolling Desert sands,
And merrily riding on the gentle neck
Of the mighty lion
Monarch of my heart,
I always see a floating child
Who is calling me!

Men are like the stars

"Men are like the stars; some generate their own light while others reflect the brilliance they receive."

"I Cultivate a White Rose"

I cultivate a white rose
In July as in January
For the sincere friend
Who gives me his hand freely.

And for the cruel person who tears out
the heart with which I live,
I cultivate neither nettles nor thorns:
I cultivate a white rose.

Cultivo Una Rosa Blanca

Cultivo una rosa blanca
En julio como en enero
Para el amigo sincèro
Que me da su mano franca.

Y para el cruel que me arranca
El corazón con que vivo,
Cardo ni ortiga cultivo,
Cultivo una rosa blanca

Talent is a gift

"Talent is a gift that brings with it an obligation to serve the world, and not ourselves, for it is not of our making."

Socialist Ideology

"Socialist ideology, like so many others, has two main dangers. One stems from confused and incomplete readings of foreign texts, and the other from the arrogance and hidden rage of those who, in order to climb up in the world, pretend to be frantic defenders of the helpless so as to have shoulders on which to stand."

A Hill of Foam from Simple Verses

If you see a hill of foam
It is my poetry that you see:
My poetry is a mountain
And is also a feather fan.
My poems are like a dagger
Sprouting flowers from the hilt;
My poetry is like a fountain
Sprinkling streams of coral water.
My poems are light green
And flaming red;
My poetry is a wounded deer
Looking for the forest's sanctuary.
My poems please the brave:
My poems, short and sincere,
Have the force of steel
Which forges swords.

The Girl of Guatemala

At a wing's shade, I want to tell
This story, like a flower:
The girl from Guatemala,
The girl that died of love.
The flowers were lilies,
And mignonette ornaments
And jasmine: we buried her
In a silk casket.
She gave to the forgetful A perfumed sachet:
He came back, came back married:
She died of love.
She was carried in a procession
By bishops and ambassadors:
Behind were the town's people in groups
They were all carrying flowers.
She wanted to see him again,
She stepped out to the balcony:
He came back with his wife:
She died of love.
She went into the river at dusk,
She was dead when the doctor pulled her out:
Some say she died of coldness:
But I know she died of love.

La niña de Guatemala

"Quiero, a la sombra de un ala,
Contar este cuento en flor:
La niña de Guatemala,
La que se murió de amor.
Eran de lirios los ramos,
Y las orlas de reseda
Y de jazmín: la enterramos
En una caja de seda.
...Ella dio al desmemoriado
Una almohadilla de olor:
El volvió, volvió casado:
Ella se murió de amor.
Iban cargándola en andas
Obispos y embajadores:
Detrás iba el pueblo en tandas,
Todo cargado de flores.
Ella, por volverlo a ver,
Salió a verlo al mirador:
El volvió con su mujer:
Ella se murió de amor.
Se entró de tarde en el río,
La sacó muerta el doctor:
Dicen que murió de frío:
Yo sé que murió de amor."

The Vote

"After seeing it rise, quake, sleep, prostitute itself, make mistakes, be abused, sold and corrupted; after seeing the voters turn into animals, the voting booths besieged, the ballot boxes overturned, the results falsified, the highest offices stolen, one still must acknowledge, because it is true, that the vote is an awesome, invincible and solemn weapon; the vote is the most effective and merciful instrument that man has devised to manage his affairs."

Liberty

Man loves liberty, even if he does not know that he loves it. He is driven by it and flees from where it does not exist.

Maps and Charts
Historical Maps

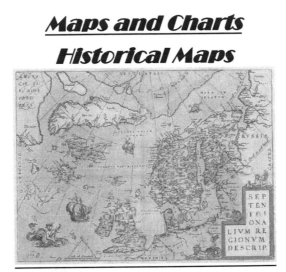

Early Chart of the North Atlantic Ocean

Early Map of Spain and Portugal

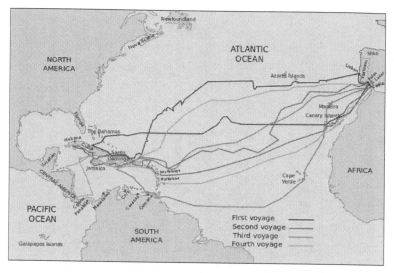

Starting dates for Columbus' four voyages:
1492, 1493, 1498 and 1502

Cuba and the West Indies, c 1700's

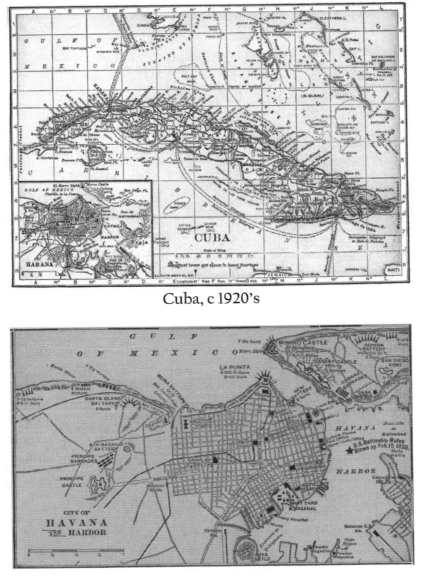

Cuba, c 1920's

Havana, c 1900

Ocean Currents

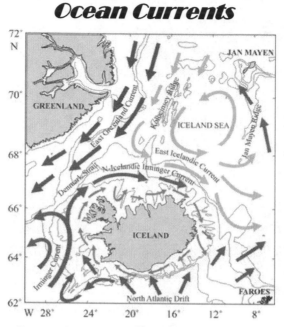

Ocean Currents affecting the Vikings

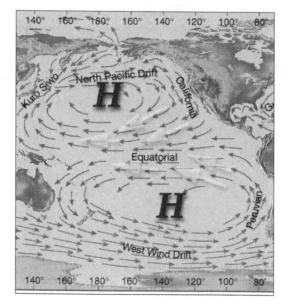

Pacific Ocean Currents re: the Discovery of America

Ocean Currents around the Caribbean Sea

Current Maps

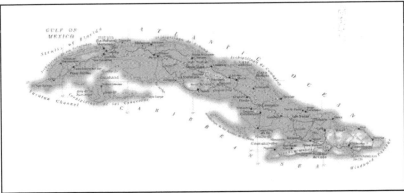

Present day Cuba

The Exciting Story of Cuba

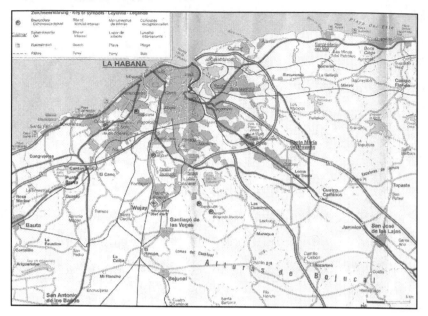

Havana

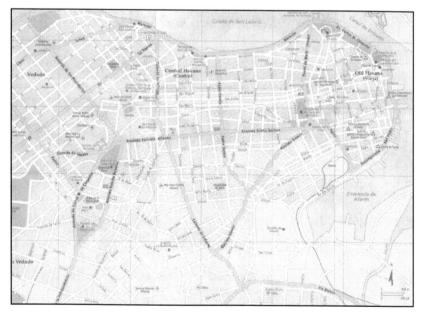

Havana Street Map

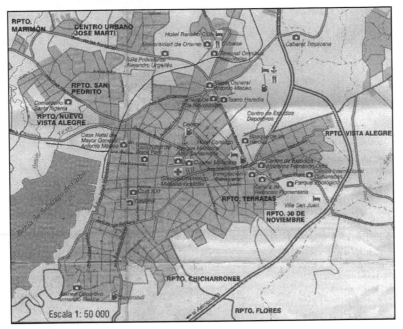

Santiago de Cuba

Fidel Castro's Rebel Stronghold in the
Sierra Maestra Mountains - 1958

"Che" Guevara's Bolivian Insurgence

Bolivian Highlands

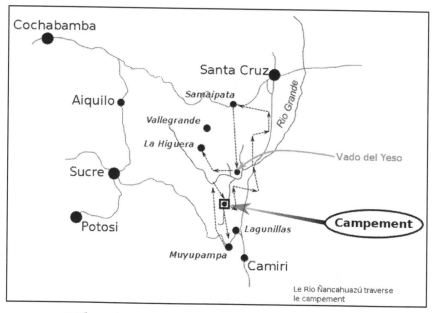

"Che" Guevara's Bolivian Campaigns - 1967

The Exciting Story of Cuba.... Part 1

The Early Years

It's a Small World After All....

Nothing, other than perhaps our universe, started in a vacuum and neither did the discovery of the Americas, which of course included the island of Cuba. To find a starting point, a little background regarding the Iberian Peninsula is helpful, since that is where it all began. Why did Columbus want to sail for parts unknown? What was going through his mind when he turned his small fleet of three ships in a westerly direction and headed towards the edge of the world? Surely, he didn't have a death wish, so what was it that he knew that the rest of the 15th century world didn't?

In the days prior to Christ, when the Roman Empire was ruled by the heathen Caesars in Rome, there were forces at work and other centers of power that greatly affected history. The Roman Empire, which followed the classical Greek civilization, expanded and reached its greatest potential when Julius Caesar ruled, just 44 years prior to the birth of Christ. At that same time, there was a grand library in Alexandria, Egypt, that contained as many as 500,000 scrolls. These were the records of human endeavors, and the shared knowledge known to the people of that era. Many of these scrolls concerned themselves with science, history and the earthly wisdom that scholars wanted to share with others. Unfortunately, everything in the library was lost, when this magnificent structure burned to the ground in 48 BC. It could have been an accident, however there are many who blame Julius Caesar directly for this intellectual travesty. The fact remains that much of the knowledge concerning our earth, and the events of the time, was lost forever in that roaring inferno.

In spite of this setback, the Roman Empire continued to flourish and the Christian religion began to spread. The "Edict of 313" allowed Christianity to flourish in Rome and by the year 800 AD, Charlemagne had created the Holy Roman Empire through extensive land grabs. It was only a few hundred years prior to this time that Mohammed was born in Mecca and unified Arabia into a single religious community under Islam. Thus, without any harmful intention, Charlemagne created a huge theological split between the people of the known world. No one felt it more than those on the Iberian Peninsula. The Moors, consisting primarily of Arabs and Berbers, invaded Spain from Morocco in 711 AD. At the time, the Arabs controlled the Iberian Peninsula, but were stopped from advancing into Western Europe at the Pyrenees by a Christian army during the Battle of Tours, led by Charles Martel. By 790 AD, these aggressive Islamic hordes ruled most of the Iberian Peninsula, and it was not until 1212 that a number of Christian kings drove out most of the Muslims at the Battle of Las Navas de Tolosa. It took another 280 years, when finally on January 2, 1492, the last of them were assimilated or driven out of Granada.

Forced by the Roman Church and the Pope, those few Jews and Muslims that remained, were coerced into converting to Catholicism. Individual freedom of thought or expression was definitely frowned upon and failure to conform, subjected those offenders to the torture of the Spanish Inquisition, which incidentally was conveniently approved of by Queen Isabella and King Ferdinand.

Portugal, which had a significant percentage of the total population on the Iberian Peninsula, broke away and became a separate country in 868. In 1139 after the battle of Ourique, Christians, having won the battle against the Muslims, created the "Kingdom of Portugal." At that time Afonso Henriques, also known as Afonso I, and referred to as "the Conqueror," "the Founder," and "the Great" by his followers, was unanimously elevated from Count to King.

Discovering Asia

Marco Polo's father, Niccolò Polo, traded with the Persians who were known to the early Europeans. These early Persians came from the province of Fârs, sometimes known in Old Persian as *Pârsâ*, located in the southwestern region of Iran. As a people, they were united under the Achaemenid Dynasty in the 6th century BC, by Cyrus the Great. In 1260, Niccolò Polo and his brother Maffeo lived in Constantinople, now Istanbul, Turkey. After the Mongol conquest of Asia Minor, the Polo brothers liquidated their assets into tangible valuables such as gold and jewels and moved out of harm's way.

Having heard of advanced eastern civilizations the brothers traveled through much of Asia, and even met with the Kublai Khan, the grandson of Genghis Khan, who later became emperor of China and established the Yuan Dynasty. Not being the first to travel east of Iran, they had heard numerous stories regarding the riches to be discovered in the Far East.

Twenty-four years later in 1295, after traveling almost 15,000 miles, they returned to Venice with many riches and treasures.

The Polo brothers had experienced a quarter century of adventures on their way to Asia that were later transcribed into *The Book of Marco Polo* by a writer named Rustichello, who came from Pisa in Tuscany, Italy. This was the beginning of a quest that motivated explorers, including Christopher Columbus, from that time on.

In 1383, after having experienced the Black Plague, the House of Aviz, led by King John I, became the ruling house in Portugal and opened up the newly formed country for economic expansion. Ten years prior, Portugal had entered into an alliance with England, which still happens to be in effect, and has become the most enduring alliance in existence. The people living on the west coast of the Iberian Peninsula were in an ideal position to look across the horizon and position themselves for future exploration. In the early part of the 15th century, Portugal took a decided lead in the Age of Discovery.

In the Far East, following the fall of the Mongol-led Yuan Dynasty, the Ming Dynasty came into power. It was founded in 1368 by the rebellious peasant leader Zhu Yuanzhang and became the ruling dynasty of China for 276 years. The Ming Dynasty made great achievements in cultural restoration and expansion. China was experiencing a renaissance and for their "chosen few" made significant advances. In many ways, China made considerable progress in Science, Medicine, Literature, Seafaring, Geography and Cartography. It was also during this period that the Great Wall of China was completed, protecting the Chinese empire from their enemies, the Mongols and then the Manchus. Some years later, the Portuguese and the Dutch became their foes. The less informed Chinese actually believed that the Portuguese ate babies, when in fact they took children to sell as slaves. The Dutch held Taiwan before surrendering the island to a Ming general after being besieged for a number of months. The Qing Dynasty followed and was China's last great imperial dynasty. Starting in 1644 this new régime lasted nearly 300 years until 1912.

"Morals are in all countries the result of legislation and government; they are not African or Asian or European: they are good or bad." Denis Diderot, a French philosopher, art critic and writer

The Age of Discovery

Infante Dom Henrique de Avis, Duke of Viscu, better known as Prince Henry the Navigator of Portugal, was the fifth child of King John I. The prince was a responsible ruler and is remembered for developing Portugal's trade routes with foreign countries, exploring the islands along the central spine of the Atlantic Ocean and sailing along the western coast of Africa in search of new trade routes to the Far East.

The 15th century was exciting as well as dangerous. It was a time when exploring meant going to sea and discovering new lands inhabited by many people that were previously unknown to Europeans. The explorations started in about 1418, when two Portuguese ships were inadvertently driven off-course by a storm. The vessels grounded onto the island now known as Porto Santos. The captains, João Gonçalves Zarco and Tristão Vaz Teixeira, who had been commissioned by Prince Henry the Navigator, saw heavy clouds in the distance, under which lay the island of Madeira. Eight years later, Diogo de Silves discovered islands north of Madeira, now known as the Azores.

Legend has it that King Juba, an ancient Lybian prince, discovered the Canary Islands during the 1st century AD. These islands were also known as the "Fortunate Islands" by early Roman seafarers.

Along the western coast of the Sahara desert, about half way between the Canary Islands and the Cape Verde Islands, lies a sand spit called Cape Barbas. In 1441, ships attached to Estêvão da Gama's fleet were sent by Prince Henry to explore the coastline south of Cape Barbas, which, five years earlier, was the farthest point reached by any of Prince Henry's captains. Although there are some conflicting stories regarding the discoveries of the mid-Atlantic islands, it is safe to assume that in 1501 João da Nova discovered Ascension Island. The desolate island remained deserted until it was rediscovered two years later on Ascension Day by Alfonso de Albuquerque. He was also the first European to discover the Red Sea and the Persian Gulf.

The island Saint Helena was most likely discovered by João da Nova. In 1506, the island Tristan da Cunha was discovered another 1,243 miles farther south, and it is considered the most remote inhabited archipelago in the world. The archipelago is made up of four islands including Inaccessible Island, which is now accessible and lies 1,491 miles from the southernmost point in Africa, and is 2,088 miles from South America.

In 1444, sailing along the African coast, Dinis Dias traveled as far south as Pointe des Almadies, the westernmost point in Africa and reached the mouth of the Senegal River. Two years later Portuguese explorers discovered the Cape Verde Islands and the Gambia River.

Portuguese mariners made their way down the African coast reaching Sierra Leone in 1460 and Cape Palmas ten years later. It wasn't until 1488 that the Portuguese explorer Bartolomeu Dias rounded the southernmost tip of Africa. Ten years later in

1498 Vasco da Gama became the first navigator to follow this route and reach India.

"In wisdom gathered over time I have found that every experience is a form of exploration."
Ansel Adams, an American photographer and environmentalist

Spain enters the Race to Asia

In 1469, the regions of Aragon (*Aragón*) and Castile (*Castilla*) were united by the marriage of Ferdinand II and Queen Isabella I, thus creating *España* or Spain. The treasury of this fledgling nation had been depleted by the many battles they had waged against the Moors. The Spanish monarchs, seeing Portugal's economic success, sought to establish their own trade routes to the Far East. Queen Isabella embraced this concept from the religious standpoint of going out into "all the world" and converting the pagan people of Asia to Christianity.

At the same time, a tall, young, middle-class man, said to have come from Genoa, Italy, who held that his father was a fabric weaver and cheese merchant, sought to become a navigator. As such, Columbus sailed to Portugal where pirates allegedly attacked the ship he was on. Fortunately, he managed to swim ashore and joined his brother Bartholomew as a cartographer in Lisbon. Apparently to him, becoming a mapmaker must have seemed boring when there was a world to explore. Returning to the sea, he sailed to places as far away as Iceland to the north, and ventured south as far as Guinea on the West-African coast. It is reasonable to assume that he had heard or perhaps even read the stories about the Vikings that took place almost five hundred years prior to Columbus' arriving there.

Christopher Columbus, being a navigator, knew that the Earth was round, as did most educated people of the time, and he understood that reaching the Far East was theoretically possible by going west. In 1479, Columbus married Felipa Perestrello Moniz, an impoverished Portuguese noblewoman, who had been relegated to the convent of the church on the island of Santo, in the middle of the Atlantic Ocean. She was the daughter of the Governor of this Atlantic island. Porto Santo is not much more than one long beach with a tiny bit of an island attached to it and lies 30 wet miles northeast of Madeira. Many scholars question how this marriage could have happened, had not Columbus been born of nobility. Since Felipa was a novitiate at a convent, she had to be released from her vows to marry him. Perhaps he was actually the illegitimate son of a Spanish nobleman, instead of being a middle class Italian. After much speculation, there still is no definitive answer....

The following year they had a son whom they named Diego. Much later Diego became the Spanish Governor of the West Indies. Living on an island and being able to look out to the horizon in all directions, gave Columbus the understanding and opportunity to formulate his theories. It also did not escape Columbus that having a wife with the right political connections could open doors that could make his dreams come true. Four years later in 1484, he presented his plans to King John II of Portugal, who, disappointingly, rejected them. It was during this same year that unfortunately his wife died. Apparently without fanfare, she was entombed in her family crypt in Lisbon.

The next year Columbus moved 368 miles to Andalusia, Spain, where he met Beatriz Enríquez de Arana who became his mistress, and in 1488 Columbus had his second son, who was born of this union.

In 1492, Ferdinand and Isabella's troops captured Granada, which was the last remaining Moorish city in Spain, thus ending Islamic rule on the Iberian Peninsula. The Catholic Church quickly took moral control of Spain, in effect placing it under the auspices of the Pope. The Spanish Monarchy agreed to the Spanish Inquisition, which was intended to strengthen the Christian beliefs imposed upon the remaining Jews and Arabs, who were forced to change their ideology from Judaism and Islam to Catholicism. This compulsory imposition of the faith was further strengthened by royal decrees issued later in 1492 and 1501. "The Tribunal of the Holy Office of the Inquisition," shortened to read "The Spanish Inquisition," was enthusiastically approved of by Pope Innocent VIII. Although many of the converts to Christianity were forced into compliance, some still continued to practice their original religion in secret.

With this viewed as a great victory, the royal couple looked forward to competing with Portugal in expanding Spain's overseas interests. When Bartolomeu Dias rounded the Cape of Good Hope, it opened a sea route to Asia for Portugal. Trading with the countries in Asia presented financial opportunities that Spain wanted to get a part of. The income that could be expected from trading with the Far East would go a long way in stabilizing their beleaguered treasury. When the ambitious young man named Christopher Columbus approached them with his concept of a shorter, faster route to Asia, they listened with interest and agreed to give him the financial backing he needed.

Since they approved the grant during difficult times, the funding was considered the same as stimulus money, and it was understood to be used only to discover a new route to the East Indies.

Christopher Columbus, although still considered Italian by birth, received a "Commission of Status" by Queen Isabella of Spain. His commission was to explore the uncharted sea-lanes leading west and ultimately to the Far East. There is a good possibility that although he knew that the Earth was round, that he had mistakenly miscalculated its size. If he thought that the Earth was smaller than it really was, it would have led him to believe that he was closer to the East Indies than was actually the case.

It could also have been a conniving deception on the part of Columbus that led him to that conclusion. He knew that Queen Isabella was paying him to discover a trade route to the Far East, when in fact he did not accomplish that goal. What he had discovered was another continent, which could well have been part of what the Vikings had discovered some 500 years before. There was no doubt, but that his purpose was to find and establish trade routes, as well as to develop colonies in the East Indies, but this obviously was not what had happened! Queen Isabella had been generous in all that she had granted Columbus, so was this the reason why his paycheck was withheld until the end of his fourth voyage?

It would be naive to believe that the new lands lying west beyond the horizon of his home in Porto Santo, were not known to Columbus. The Vikings had sailed far afield from their homes in the 8th and 9th centuries. They were a fearsome lot, as they sailed their open *knarr* boats, both west to Greenland and North America, as well as south in the direction of the Mediterranean and Africa. There was very little that was not known about the Atlantic Ocean, only the details had to be filled in.

Even though most of the news of the day concerned itself with the Inquisitions and the Crusades, Columbus must have heard the adventurous stories of how Leif Ericson discovered Baffin Island, Labrador and Newfoundland, as part of a vast new land to the west.

"Ancient metaphysics underwent many changes at the hands of medieval thinkers who brought it in line with the dominant religious and theological movements of their day." Wilhelm Dilthey, German historian and philosopher

The Vikings

Columbus discovered Cuba and the West Indies for the Spanish Crown, while at the same time professing that he had discovered a new route to Asia. With this, the question of who really discovered America becomes legitimate! Although the Viking Bjarni Herjolfsson apparently reached North America in 985, he never set foot there, leaving the actual credit of the discovery of America to Leif Erikson.

Erik Thorvaldsson known as "Erik the Red," and his father Thorvald Ásvaldsson, must have been a roughhewn lot, since Thorvald and his son Erik were banished from Norway in about 960, on charges of manslaughter, after having had a serious quarrel and fight at a town meeting. Exiled, they left Norway, sailed west to Iceland, and settled on the Hornstrandir peninsula, where Thorvald died sometime before 980.

Erik the Red, relocated to a valley by the name of Haukadal, east of Reykjavík, where he married Thjodhild and started a farm. Living the life of a farmer, he had two sons, Leif Erikson and Thorstein, as well as a daughter named Freydis. All went well until Thornstein and his father lost their cool and got into a fight, resulting in them being banished from Iceland for three years.

In 982, Gunnbjorn Ulfsson reported that he had journeyed to another land having fertile green fields, about 200 miles to the west. Out of duress, Eric the Red now 32 years old, decided to uproot his family and move there. Eric and his family sailed the treacherous distance between the two landmasses safely and named the new location Greenland.

Three years later when he could return to Iceland, he told astounding stories about where he and his family had settled. His stories must have sounded inviting since he encouraged many other settlers to join them there, especially considering that a famine had devastated Iceland. Not knowing any better, they had severely overworked the cold soil in Iceland, putting their very existence into jeopardy. Knowing that they could not survive another winter, 980 people on 25 boats left for Greenland. It must have been a cold, rough crossing because only 14 boats succeeded in making it to Greenland. However, Eric later learned that some more of the boats had survived and had managed to return safely to Iceland. In time, there were about 5,000 settlers in Greenland. The official records indicate that two sizable Norse settlements had been founded in fjords on the southwestern coast of the island. Other smaller ones were located on the same coast as far north as present day Nuuk. Most of the settlements which were founded in about the year 1,000, remained inhabited until well into "The Little Ice Age," which started in 1350 and lasted for approximately 500 years. In the beginning when the weather was considerably warmer, about 400 farms were started by the Viking farmers. However later, the extreme cold and glacial ice made farming nearly impossible in these frigid northern latitudes. Recently, archaeologists discovered a Viking village that was radiocarbon dated back to circa 1430.

In the year 985, having been blown off course, Bjarni Herjolfsson became the first Viking to see the coast of North America. However, he missed his chance for fame.... Being more interested in getting home, he never set foot on the "New Continent." Instead, he set his course back to Greenland, leaving the discovery of America to others.

With the shifting winds and foggy conditions, navigation in these cold waters was difficult, causing the Viking navigators to frequently lose their way. The Viking term *hafvilla* refers to a state of confusion that frequently happened to them when they were blown off course or were engulfed by fog. There were also icebergs that were carried south by the cold currents flowing south through the Labrador Straits. What was in their favor, however, was that the distances across the open waters of the Atlantic Ocean were relatively short on their voyages to the east coast of America.

In 1960, a Norwegian explorer Helge Marcus Ingstad and his wife Anne Stine, an archaeologist, found remnants of a Viking settlement in L'Anse aux Meadows or "Jellyfish Cove," on the northernmost tip of Newfoundland, Canada. They were the first to prove conclusively that the Vikings had found a way to cross the Atlantic Ocean to North America, roughly 500 years before Christopher Columbus. There are separate accounts of a Norse settlement in North America dating back to 1009, and of Leif's older brother Thorvald, being killed by Indians in Newfoundland. The mysterious disappearance of a Viking settlement in Greenland, during the late 14th century, might also be explained if the settlers sailed west, migrating to North America.

A Norwegian coin of the Viking era was once found in Maine; however, no indication of a settlement was found that could be used to verify the exact location of any landings. Perhaps it just became too cold and the growing season too short for them to linger on in this cold region.

What is relatively certain, is that it was not uncommon for the Vikings to sail their *knarrs* west from Greenland to present-day Labrador. Markland was the name given to one of three locations on Canada's Atlantic coast explored by Leif Eriksson. For all the good it does, Viking records indicate that it was located south of Helluland and north of Vineland.

The Vikings hunted, cut lumber and traded with the Skroelings, which is what they called the indigenous Inuit people. During the summer months, the warmer currents carried them north along the western coast of Greenland to what is now known as the Davis Strait, and from there they most likely headed due west for about two hundred miles over open water to Baffin Island. The Labrador Current could then have taken them as far south as the coasts of Newfoundland, Prince Edward Island, Nova Scotia and possibly Maine and Cape Cod.

Although Leif Ericson is credited with being the first European to set foot in America, much of the history of the 10th and 11th centuries was lost by not being documented until much later. The Sagas of the Icelanders were written two hundred years after the fact, in the 13th and 14th centuries. There are still conflicting stories as to the actual locations of Helluland, Markland and Vineland, all of which Leif Ericson and his brothers discovered. Although there has always been an abundance of speculation, these named places have never been decisively located.

Helluland may have been near Baffin Island, with Markland and Vineland farther south. During the longer and warmer days of summer it is quite likely that the Vikings may have come as far south as New England. They learned that by sailing just a little farther offshore they would encounter the Gulf Stream, which could then make their return to Greenland, or even Iceland and Europe, relatively simple. The point being is that it was documented and understood by historians, as well as the navigators of that time, that the Vikings had discovered new lands to the west of the Atlantic Ocean, and at no time were any of them eaten by sea monsters, nor did they fall off the edge of the World.

"Be not a braggart, for if any work done be praise worthy, others will sing your praises for you." Old Viking Quote

Others Who Claimed to have Discovered America

In December of 2007 human bones including skulls, which have been radiocarbon dated back to between 1304 and 1424, were found in a museum in Concepción, Chile. These skulls were originally discovered on Isla Mocha, which is located 25 miles off the south-central coast of Chile. Since some of them have definite telltale signs of being Polynesian, the strong suggestion is that there was a pre-Columbian interaction between the local Mapuche people and the Polynesian seafarers. This contact is further supported by forensic evidence found near the Chilean site of "El Arenal," which is a sandy dune approximately 3 miles inland from the coast.

Pottery found in Ecuador, predating the arrival of Columbus in America, have markings similar to pottery found on the southernmost island of Kyushu, Japan. Radiocarbon dating has determined the date of organics in the clay that survived the firing, or from food or liquids stored in the pottery, to be 4500 years old with a possible variance of 200 to 500 years, thus predating Columbus by a wide margin. There is no reason to doubt these findings, which indicate that Asians and Polynesians sailed to all parts of the Pacific Ocean, including the vast continents of North and South America that border it on its far eastern side.

There are two major currents that flow along the coast of Japan. They are the northern Oyashio Current, which becomes the California Current, and the Kurshio Current, better known as the Japanese Current. It is possible that either one of these currents could have carried fishermen, who had been blown off course, to an unexpected destination in the Americas. However, many so-called experts have indicated that to be on an open boat of about 20 feet, without adequate food for that length of time, would be too long a stretch for anyone to survive. Fishermen are a hardy and resourceful lot, and this sort of reasoning underestimates the ability of human beings to survive such a crossing.

Between 9,000 and 17,000 years ago, during the last part of the Pleistocene ice age, the Paleo-Indians walked across the Bering land bridge, or perhaps paddled the 51 miles of the Bering Straits in small boats. The two Diomede Islands in the middle of the Straits are 2.4 miles apart, and have the "International Date Line" running between them. Big Diomede Island or *Ratmanov* Island to the west is Russian and in the far eastern reach of Asia. Little Diomede Island or *Ignaluk*, belonging to Alaska, is on the eastern side and as far west as you can go before it is 24 hours away and becomes tomorrow. There are approximately 170, mostly Native Americans, living on the American island. During winter, an ice bridge usually spans the

2.4 miles between these two islands, therefore there are times when it is possible to walk between the United States and Russia. This little stroll is not advised; however, you can definitely see Russia from America.

Existing evidence indicates that the Polynesians were the next to discover America. There is no doubt but that the Polynesians sailing around the Pacific Ocean in their Hokulea, *"Hōkūle'a,"* twin-hulled, balsa built canoes, were the first known people to discover and populate the Pacific Islands.

There is also evidence to support claims that 962 years prior to Columbus setting foot in the Bahamas, Saint Brendan, an Irish monastic priest known as "Saint Brendan the Navigator," looked for the "Isle of the Blessed." What island he found has been lost to history and is still unknown; however, legend names it "Saint Brendan's Island." Many believe that in his journeys across the Atlantic Ocean he actually landed in America in 1150, or 342 years prior to Columbus' discovery.

In 1981, archaeologist Robert L. Pyle discovered some stone carvings in West Virginia and Kentucky. These "Petroglyph Sites" have carvings done in "Ogham," an ancient alphabet found in Ireland, Scotland, England and Wales. These carvings were verified as to their authenticity and may be the most important physical evidence available to support the Legend of Saint Brendan.

In 1170, Prince Madoc, the son of Owain Gwynedd, King of Gwynedd and the first Prince of Wales, was also believed to have sailed to America, over 300 years before Columbus' time. He is said to have arrived at Mobile Bay on a Saxon ship, similar in construction to the ones used by the Vikings. Legend has it that he actually made two crossings, during which some of them went inland to what is today called DeSoto Falls and Fort

Mountain, Georgia. The members of this Welsh landing party are said to have been integrated with the Mandan Indian tribe, now known as the "White Indians."

The Vikings purportedly respected the Irish for having traveled farther across the Atlantic Ocean than they had. There is actually some circumstantial evidence of this, such as the construction of Irish boats being comparable to the boats of the Mandan Indians, who had then lived along the banks of the Missouri River and some of its tributaries.

The Chinese also have a very strong claim, regarding their discovery of America. Zheng He, formerly known as Ma He, was born in 1371. He was captured by the Muslim army of Lan Yu and Fu Youde and was summarily castrated, with the intention of making him a court eunuch. After being released from the court, he became a loyal soldier and sent to the northern frontier to fight in military campaigns against the Mongols. In 1421 during the Ming Dynasty, winning the favors of the Prince of Yan, he was promoted to the rank of a naval admiral. Given a fleet of 317 ships and 28,000 men, Zheng He was commissioned to sail to the ends of the world. In 1424, Zheng became recognized as one of China's greatest explorers. In all, he made seven extensive voyages of discovery. Zheng himself wrote that he had traveled the equivalent of more than 100,000 miles across the seas and had seen ocean waves as high as mountains rising in the sky.

Although his log entries do not speak of America per se, a chart created by Admiral Zheng was used to make a detailed map of the world. A copy of this map, drawn in 1763, was found in a second-hand bookshop and was offered as evidence that Zheng's fleet was the first to discover America. At the age of 61, Admiral Zheng died aboard ship and befittingly was buried at sea.

The Chinese sailed on very large ships, some of which were 450 feet long and 180 feet wide, in fact larger than any other of that time. They were certainly large enough to circumnavigate the world. Typical donut-shaped stone anchors of the type used by the Chinese have been found off the coast of California, as well as the west coast of South America, substantiating their claims.

Zheng's journal states that it took 270 days to sail from China to California on his voyage across the Pacific. On another expedition, he described rounding the bottom of Africa and sailing into the Atlantic, to what could well have been South America and the Caribbean.

Navigating the oceans has been done since the beginning of time, and there is ample evidence to substantiate that people have continuously migrated around the world. There are Roman charts that were used during those years that show the shorelines of Florida, Brazil, the Gulf of Mexico, and Peru.

There is ample reason to believe that people arrived on the shores of both North and South America prior to Columbus. However, as it pertains to this book, it was Columbus and his men that stayed, and were instrumental in the colonization of the new World.

"Man cannot discover new oceans unless he has the courage to lose sight of the shore." André Paul Guillaume Gide, a French author and winner of the Nobel Prize in Literature, 1947

The Earth is Round!

In the 8th Century, the Greek philosopher Homer thought that the Earth was flat. Many of the less educated people in the 15th Century still held on to that concept when Columbus set sail, following the setting sun west. The less informed warned Columbus and his crew of the danger of sailing right off the edge of the Earth. However, navigators and mathematicians knew better, since Greek philosophers in the 5th Century such as Parmenides, Empedocles and Pythagoras had already proved, by using various scientific methods, that the Earth was round. In about 200 BC Eratosthenes, who lived along the Nile near Alexandria, Egypt, calculated the circumference of the Earth to within a very close tolerance. Later in Prussia, Copernicus presented his concept that the Sun was the center of the Solar system and theorized that the planets revolved around it.

It was not coincidental that Copernicus did this shortly after Columbus discovered the new continent. Although the ancients did not have radio and television, they could communicate by various means, and definitely knew what was going on. However there were those who remained superstitious, believing that there were monstrous sea creatures near the edge of the Earth. But Columbus and other relatively educated people knew better!

Since the historians of the day knew about the Vikings and that the earth was round, they were also aware of the land beyond the horizon. Columbus and the Spanish Royal Court theorized that he could possibly reach the Far East by going west, and that became his primary mission. The unknowns however, were still daunting! Without charts, they had no idea of what to expect ahead. Chronometers, modern quartz crystal or atomic clocks, had not yet been invented, so mariners didn't have an accurate timepiece with which to determine longitude. Therefore, ascertaining a position was extremely difficult....

Columbus Sails West to find the East....

Columbus' best guess was to calculate the distance his ship covered daily, by estimating its speed through the water. He did this with some degree of accuracy, by throwing a block of wood off the bow and then pacing it back to the stern. Projecting the distance traveled over a twenty-four hour period would give him the estimated longitude. This method of navigation, crude as it was, would give him some idea of how far west of the Spanish coast he was. Every day that the sun shone, he could confirm his north-south location by noting the height of the sun above the horizon at high noon in degrees, and compare it to what it should be at any given latitude. Between the two, he could adjust his dead reckoning position, to prevent becoming what the Vikings called *hafvilla*, or perhaps the Spaniards would say *desorientado*. Nevertheless, as could be expected, in the end his guess was off... and instead of arriving in Asia he arrived on the Atlantic side of the Bahamas and the sunny islands of the eastern Caribbean.

"I may not have gone where I intended to go, but I think I have ended up where I needed to be." Douglas Adams, author of The Hitchhiker's Guide to the Galaxy

Land Ho!

Columbus was given the title "Admiral of the Ocean Sea" by the Royal Crown of Spain in April of 1492, and as such he planned and organized the flotilla needed to accomplish his mission. If the rule of thumb is that a "boat" can be lifted onto a ship, Columbus' small fleet of what would now be thought of as boats, sailed out of the Spanish port of *Castilian Palos de la Frontera* on the evening of August 3, 1492.

La Pinta and *La Niña* were classified as caravels and were built for the Mediterranean Sea, but certainly not the forceful Atlantic Ocean. *La Santa María* was known to her sailors as *La Marigalante*, Spanish for "The Gallant Maria." Being larger and constructed more sturdily, she was a carrack, and designed to withstand the heavier seas. The *Niña* started out as the *Santa Clara*, however her name was changed, since her owner's name was Juan Niño de Moguer. She carried 24 men and was captained by Vicente Yáñez Pinzón, who later went on to discover the Amazon River. His older brother, Martín Alonso Pinzón, served Columbus as the captain of the *Pinta*. All told, Columbus had between 86 to 89 men on this first voyage.

The Portuguese originally developed the design of the smaller caravel, which could hardly be considered a ship, even by 15th century standards. Caravels were relatively light, maneuverable, cargo vessels, only 40 to 60 feet in length with a displacement of no more than 60 to 75 tons. Having a lesser draft, the caravel could sail in shallow coastal waters and cross sand bars into rivers and sheltered harbors. By using triangular lateen sails, held in place by a spar and secured to the mast, they had the ability to tack almost into the wind. Lateen sails were a holdover from the early Roman era and are still being used on Arabic Dhows in and around the Indian Ocean.

La Santa María, the flagship for the mission, was a mid-sized carrack and had a displacement of 108 tons. Her keel was 41 feet long and her length was 62 feet overall. The ship is long gone, but her anchor is still on display at the *Musée du Panthéon National Haïtien* in Port-au-Prince, Haiti.

Columbus' crew was comprised primarily of seasoned seamen or "Old Salts," recruited at Palos. Frequently in cases like this, convicts were solicited to sign on as seamen for lengthy tours, in lieu of having to serve their prison sentence. This time, although the Spanish monarchs offered a pardon to convicts who would sign up for the voyage, only four men accepted. Of them, one was a murderer who had killed a man while involved in an altercation, and the other three were buddies, who helped him to escape from prison.

On August 6, 1492, the rudder of the *Pinta* failed. Only three days into Columbus' epic voyage the ship's rudder broke, requiring the small convoy to put into Las Palmas in the Canary Islands, which at that time was a possession of Castile. The three vessels anchored and were replenished with stores and water. When the required repairs and maintenance were completed, the vessels departed from the islands in September of 1492.

Being the end of summer, the "Trade Winds" out of the east were strong as they filled the sails of Columbus' ships. On this voyage into the unknown, the Admiral apparently did not feel that he had to tell the crew the truth. Knowing that they would be out of sight of land for an extended time, he deliberately told them a ruse about the probable time and distance it would take before they saw land again. By October 10th, having seen only water, the crew's anxiety had almost developed into a mutiny. It had been five weeks since they had left the Canaries and Columbus only avoided a certain rebellion by promising them that if they did not sight land within two days, he would turn the ships around and return to Spain.

Although this may have been just another lie, his luck held out and two days later in the early hours of October 12, 1492, Juan Rodríguez Bermeo, the lookout on the *Pinta*, spotted a light and alerted the other ships by firing the signal cannon. Captain-General Juan de la Cosa, the owner of the *Santa Maria*, woke

Columbus to notify him of this sighting. Rubbing his eyes, Columbus stated that he had seen the light a few hours earlier, thereby claiming in a rather unethical way, a lifetime pension for being the first man to sight land. When they went ashore later that day, Columbus named the island San Salvador. He mistakenly thought that he had arrived in the "Indies," an early name for Asia, and thus named the indigenous natives "Indians." Anthropologists believe that the first natives Columbus encountered on the island were Lucayan-Arawak Indians. In Columbus' logbook, he noted that they had little knowledge of fighting and that they did not wear clothes. Apparently, they were exceptionally clean and washed themselves frequently. Although leery of Columbus and the scruffy newcomers with him, they were very polite and perhaps somewhat fearful of them. It was noted that the women stayed in the background and did most of the work around the village, whereas the men did the fishing. In contrast to these polite people, the members of Columbus' crew were a rough and crass lot.

Columbus' translator was Luis de Torres, who was Jewish by birth, but who had converted to Christianity. Torres spoke Spanish, Hebrew and Arabic, which Columbus thought would be useful in Asia, but Torres certainly did not understand the Taíno Indian language. Columbus soon realized that he needed another approach in how he would communicate with the natives. What he decided to do, was to kidnap a number of the brighter young Taíno boys of the Lucayan tribe. One boy, named Guaikan, was taught Spanish and became the new interpreter. In fact, Columbus took Guaikan along on subsequent voyages and treated him as if he was his adopted son. To become more acceptable to the crew, Guaikan took on the Spanish name Diego Colón (not to be confused with the name of Columbus' first son). Six of these boys were eventually brought to Spain to be baptized at the royal court, with King Ferdinand and Queen Isabella becoming their godparents. Understandably, in time they became homesick and wanted to return to their island. Eventually they were returned to their tribe in San Salvador except for one who, liking his new life, remained behind, becoming a part of the Spanish royal court. Unfortunately, he became sick and died just two years later, because he lacked the natural immunity against the diseases of Europe.

Christopher Columbus' expedition most likely landed on Watling Island, which was another name for San Salvador. From here Columbus passed Rum Cay, sailing on to Long Cay, once known as Fortune Island. There are four islands forming a shallow lagoon known as the Bight of Acklins. Columbus explored these islands as he sailed down their leeward side, before going through the narrow Crooked Island Passage and heading west to what would become known as Cuba.

Columbus was most likely the first to sight the Cuban coast, near present-day Baracoa. There is some controversy as to whether he landed near the Bay of Gibara or the Bay of Bariay. However, there is now a park commemorating his discovery, on a point of land east of the Bay of Bariay, directly across the inlet from Playa Blanca. Columbus is credited with saying that, "It was the most beautiful land that human eyes ever saw."

Although there is some dispute, the Indians Columbus encountered in Cuba, are generally thought to have been Taínos. Furthermore, it is believed that the Taínos originated as part of the Arawak people from the Amazon River basin and in time migrated up through the Caribbean island chain to Puerto Rico, Hispaniola and Cuba. They were without a doubt, the most populous and advanced group of Indians on the island. Anthropologists have divided them into three classifications:

the Classic, Eastern and Western sets, of which the most is known about the Classic Taínos. They were further divided into districts, and each village within the district had a governing chief who could have been of either gender. These districts were in turn ruled by one of these chiefs. Socially, the Taínos were divided by their wealth, and either they were members of the upper strata, or members of the much larger lower class. They grew cassava, sweet potatoes, peanuts, peppers and corn for carbohydrates and fiber. Hunting and fishing provided them with protein. The Eastern Taínos seemed less advanced than the rest and tended to be more aggressive, violent and hostile.

The Caribs, who were linguistically related to the Arawaks, were less organized and more violent than the Taínos, and frequently attacked the Taínos. They were known to take the women as sex slaves and castrate the male children. Although the term cannibal was derived from them, the act of cannibalism was never substantiated. Nonetheless, the Caribs were greatly feared by the Taínos.

The third group of Indians were the Guanahatabey or in Spanish, *Guanajatabey* Indians. Located on the western end of the island they spoke a different language and kept to themselves. Although Columbus' translators could not speak the Guanahatabey language, they could however decipher that the word *"Guanajatabey"* was the name that they called themselves. They lived, hunted and fished as peaceful hunters, gatherers and farmers, as did their neighbors the Western Taínos. They sustained themselves primarily by eating meat, fish, lobsters, crabs, roots and berries. It is believed that at times they lived in the caves that are still there. A rough estimate is that about 100,000 Guanahatabey Indians originally inhabited Cuba and that they had most likely come from

Florida, whereas the Taínos had come to Cuba via a difficult migration up the Antilles from South America, and were originally part of the Arawak people. The name "Cuba" was derived from the Taíno word *Cubanacan*, meaning "this is where the fertile land is abundant." They also named the Guanahatabey Indians "*Ciboney*," meaning Cave Dwellers.

Pinar del Río Province on the extreme western end of the island has 17 charted caves, including the largest cave in Cuba. Presently, for a modest price you can visit them, but there are still many more caves that haven't yet been explored. These caves provided shelter first for the Guanahatabey Indians and later for escaped slaves. "Che" Guevara and his comrades stayed in these same limestone caves, during the 1962 Cuban Missile Crisis. Painted over the top of one of these caves is a garish mural commissioned by Fidel Castro, depicting a family of cave dwellers. The nearby *Cueva de Los Portales* bungalows used by tourists were damaged by hurricanes Gustav and Ike in 2008, but by May of 2009 the accommodations had been re-built. These cabins have been upgraded and now have air-conditioning.

With his newly trained interpreter, Columbus was able to communicate with the Taínos. He knew that what he most wanted was to find the source of gold, and to get the golden jewelry worn by some of the Indians. The Taínos named gold "*Guanine*," and the Spanish word for it is "*Oro*." The Indians made their jewelry from an alloy they prepared, which was an amalgamation of gold, silver and copper. Not understanding the value of their jewelry, the Indians sometimes traded cheap trinkets for their precious gold!

"Thanks be to God, the air is as soft as April in Seville, and it is a pleasure to be in its fragrance." Christopher Columbus, from his Journal of the First Voyage

Hitting the Rocks

Unfortunately, on Christmas morning 1492 the *Santa María* ran aground on the northern coast of what is now Haiti. Not having any way to refloat her, the crew off-loaded the provisions and equipment from the ship before she broke up. For protection they then built a flimsy fortification on the beach, calling it "*La Navidad.*" With the consent of the local Indian Chief, Columbus left behind 39 men with orders to establish a settlement, and appointed Diego de Arana, a cousin of his mistress Beatriz, as the Governor.

On January 16, 1493, Columbus left Navidad and sailed for Portugal and Spain on the *Niña*. Everything went well until the two remaining ships, the *Niña* and the *Pinta*, became separated from each other. Columbus was convinced that the captain of the faster *Pinta* would get back to Spain first, thereby garnering all the glory by telling lies about him and his discoveries. On March 4th, a violent storm off the Azores forced him to take refuge in Lisbon. Both ships, amazingly enough, arrived there safely. A week later, Columbus continued on to Palos, Spain, on the Gulf of Cádiz, from whence he had started. Finally, on March 15th, he arrived in Barcelona. It seems that all's well that ends well, because he was hailed a hero and news of his discovery of new lands spread throughout Europe like wildfire.

In 1888, the 197-foot tall *Monument a Colom* was erected at the foot of *Las Ramblas*, Barcelona's famous pedestrian walkway, commemorating Columbus' first voyage to the Americas.

After this voyage of discovery, Columbus was appointed "Viceroy of the West Indies" a title bestowed upon him in addition to his being the "Admiral of the Ocean Sea." He was recognized as a hero, a perception that somehow has lasted until present days. In the 14th and 15th century, the Catholic Church exercised great power and to his credit Columbus always had a passionate interest in the Bible. In his mind, as well as Queen Isabella's, a major part of his mission was to spread Christianity.

"The Great Spirit is in all things, he is in the air we breathe. The Great Spirit is our Father, but the Earth is our Mother. She nourishes us, that which we put into the ground she returns to us." Big Thunder Bedagi Wabanaki Algonquin

The Second Voyage

On September 24, 1493, Columbus sailed from Cádiz, Spain, and again headed for the Canary Islands, this time with a larger fleet of 17 ships. From the Canary Islands Columbus headed west across the Atlantic to Dominica and the Island of Guadeloupe, before sailing along the southern coast of Puerto Rico and returning to Hispaniola.

Most of the Spaniards in power paid little mind to the feelings and welfare of the Indians, treating them worse than chattel. Even their friends admitted that Columbus and his brothers had committed barbaric acts of violence. Michele de Cuneo, a childhood friend of Columbus, sailed with him as a scribe and was one of the crewmembers who had survived the sinking of the *Santa Maria* on that Christmas morning in 1492. Being a close friend didn't stop him from writing a letter to the crown that implicated both him and the admiral. Columbus had figured a way to earn some extra money for both himself and his crew. As a reward for helping Columbus and his brothers capture 16,000 Taíno Indians, he rewarded the sex-starved seamen by allowing them to keep some of the most beautiful young girls to serve as their personal toys.

Cuneo wrote that he had captured a very beautiful Carib woman, who Columbus, the Lord Admiral, then gave to him. Overjoyed, he took her to his cabin. She was naked as was the custom and he was filled with a desire to take his pleasure with her. Attempting to satisfy his lust, he made his advances, which not surprisingly were rejected. His continuing attempts to force himself on her were met by her slashing him with her nails. Cuneo wrote that he wished he had never started his attempts to rape this Indian maiden, but having started, he took a rope and whipped her soundly. She screamed loudly as he beat her until she relented, at which time he stated that they came to terms. "I assure you," he wrote, "that you would have thought that she was brought up in a school for whores." In 1493, Columbus wrote to the Queen that he had captured many "cannibals." We don't know what Columbus was thinking since the Queen was against slavery. The term "cannibal" that he used for the Indians did not fit, but his justification was that although they were living beings, their value was "as good as gold." Being an attractive people, many of these Indians were rounded up and traded in Europe as sex slaves. His part in the slave trade and the illegal trafficking of people eventually led, in part, to his arrest followed by his return to Spain.

Cuneo's letter provided evidence to the crown that Columbus and his brothers took part in these unpardonable atrocities and that they knowingly took part in the mistreatment of the Indians.

Juan Ponce de León

It was on this same voyage that Juan Ponce de León accompanied Columbus along with 1,200 soldiers, sailors, and colonists. In 1502, destroying most of the native Taínos, Ponce de León was commissioned to become the first Provincial Governor of Puerto Rico.

According to legend, on April 2, 1513, while searching for the Fountain of Youth, Ponce de León discovered Florida. In actual fact, it was more likely that he was out seeking the gold that the Indians were always talking about. The Indians did this in the hope of keeping the conquistadors away from them and continuing to pursue their greedy ambitions in other directions. Returning to Spain in 1514, Ponce de León was recognized for his service to the crown and was knighted. Given his own coat of arms, he became the first conquistador to be honored in this way.

Although Ponce de León did bring back a substantial amount of gold, much of it had been stolen from Indians that he had enslaved. In 1521 Ponce de León set out from Puerto Rico to colonize Florida. He had two ships containing about 200 men. In this case his exploratory party was peaceful and included farmers, priests and craftsmen. However he was attacked by Calusa braves, a tribe of Indians who lived on the coast and along the rivers and inner waterways of Florida's southwestern coast.

In the skirmish, Ponce de León was wounded when an arrow, believed to have been dipped into the sap of the "Manchineel Tree," also called Poison Guava, pierced his thigh. After fending off this attack, he and the colonists retreated to Havana, where in July of 1521, he succumbed to his wound and died. In 1559 his body was moved from Cuba and taken to San Juan, Puerto Rico, where he was interred in the crypt of San José Church. In 1836, his remains were exhumed and transferred to the Cathedral of San Juan Bautista in San Juan where they have remained until this day.

"Among my services I have discovered at my own cost and expense, the Island La Florida, and others in its district, that have not been mentioned as they are small and inconsequential." Juan Ponce de León, Spanish explorer and conquistador

A Miserable Return to La Navidad

On November 27, 1493, when Columbus returned to Navidad, he found that the 39 crew members that he had left behind had been murdered, and instead of finding a peaceful settlement, he found their corpses bleaching on the beach. The local Taíno Indians had killed them all, because of the ignorant and cruel treatment they had received from the Spaniards. Little wonder that, from that time on, Columbus had problems with the Taínos. Columbus wisely decided to abandon Navidad and established La Isabela as the first capital of Hispaniola. La Isabela's location was across a sand bar on a shallow river along the coast of what is now the Dominican Republic.

On March 10, 1496, Columbus departed from La Isabela and sailed across the Windward Passage to Cuba. This time he decided to explore the southern coast of Cuba and sailed west as far as the Isle of Pines, which he named *La Evangelista*, the Evangelist. Sailing northwest, he reached "Pinar del Río," where he decided to turn around and head east again. Had he gone another 197 miles, Columbus would have reached the far western end of the island, and would have known that Cuba was actually an island, instead of a peninsula off the coast of mainland Asia. Instead, based on information that he received from the Indians in the area, he set his course due south from Cabo Cruz and discovered Jamaica on May 5, 1494.

It became apparent to the surviving settlers that Columbus had left behind, that there was very little gold discovered in the mountains of Hispaniola. When Columbus returned from Cuba again, he found the settlers close to revolting, and at war with the local Indians. The colonists resented the Carib Indians, thinking them insolent and arrogant. They justified attacking and taking them prisoners, saying that they were aggressive towards the more docile Taínos. Columbus, in turn, sent a letter to Queen Isabella requesting permission to take the Indians as slaves. His request was denied, but Columbus deliberately disobeyed the Queen and took many Indians as slaves anyway. These Indians were primarily from the Arawak tribes. The Caribs resisted and fought back, creating an unstable situation which was hard to control. It didn't take long for the settlers, who considered it beneath them to work the land themselves, to become hungry, sick and diseased. Many of them left La Isabela and crossed the island to the southern coast where they established a new capital they named Santo Domingo.

"No Man Is an Island entire of itself; every man is a piece of the continent, a part of the main." John Donne, English poet, satirist, lawyer and a cleric in the Church of England

The Third Voyage

In May of 1498, on his third voyage, Columbus left Sanlúcar, Spain for the Canary Islands with six ships. Sailing from La Gomera on the island of Tenerife, three of the ships traveled independently directly across the Atlantic to Hispaniola. In hopes of finding a direct passage to Asia, Columbus took the remaining ships on a more southerly course to the Cape Verde Islands before crossing the Ocean. From the natives of Guinea, the Portuguese had heard of land to the southwest of the Cape Verde Islands. The natives had apparently paddled that enormous distance in canoes. Of course, this was based on legend, but similar feats were accomplished by the Polynesians in the Pacific. This time Columbus' crossing the Atlantic took him to the island of Trinidad, where he arrived on the last day of July 1498. His journals indicate that he spent some time fantasizing that he had discovered the Garden of Eden, as he sailed south of Trinidad and through the Gulf of Paria. Once out into the open waters of the Caribbean, Columbus sailed west to Isla de Margarita, which became known for its pearls. Over the years, the harvest of pearls and gold from this island accounted for a third of all the wealth Spain accumulated in the New World. Heading in a northerly direction, six days later he arrived at the new, bustling capital of Santo Domingo, Hispaniola.

Although Columbus was only 49 years old at the time, arthritis had set in and was starting to affect his health. When he arrived in Santo Domingo, Columbus attempted to resume his role as Viscount and Governor. He was surprised that many of the settlers that had survived, hated him and opposed his administration. They didn't find any of the gold they had expected and Columbus kept almost anything of value that was found. The enraged colonists accused him and his brothers of

"We are more gullible and superstitious today than we were in the Middle Ages, and an example of modern credulity is the widespread belief that the Earth is round. The average man can advance not a single reason for thinking that the earth is round. He merely swallows this theory because there is something about it that appeals to the twentieth century mentality."
George Bernard Shaw, Playwright and Author

Sex, Swine and Syphilis

The poor Indians that Columbus encountered lacked any natural immunity to European diseases and they quickly found themselves infected by some of the most devastating illnesses of the time. These diseases, which were brought to the islands by the Spaniards, included the dreaded smallpox. Most of the Indians who survived were assimilated and/or forced into slavery, along with the black slaves that were later brought in from Haiti and Africa. DNA sampling indicates that interracial breeding forced upon them by the Spaniards, considerably diluted the original Indian stock.

In time, the Europeans brought in pigs and horses, both of which were allowed to run wild and multiply. Pigs in the wild soon became aggressive feral boars with tusks, eating everything in sight. Corn, which the Indians depended upon, was attacked and uprooted by the pigs before maturing, thus leaving the Indians without an important source of nourishment. Although pigs provided a necessary source of protein, they were also known to host worms and parasites, and spread bacterial and viral diseases. If undercooked, the meat could cause trichinosis infections that, depending upon the severity, could result in death in four to six weeks.

The sailors returning to Europe brought with them tobacco and syphilis, both of which could be fatal. Syphilis is the gift that keeps on giving and soon spread throughout Europe and England. Unknown prior to the discovery of America, it became another blight on the European continent.

"Perhaps more than any other disease before or since, syphilis in early modern Europe provoked the kind of widespread moral panic that AIDS revived when it struck America in the 1980's."   Peter Lewis Allen, Scholar, Author and Educator

Columbus Reads his Bible

Apparently, Columbus' reading of the Bible did not alter the cruel way he treated the Indians. Believing that not having been baptized, the Indians had no inherent rights as human beings, thus it was all right for him to treat them as animals. In 1500, when members of the clergy complained about the atrocities the notorious brothers committed, Christopher and his brothers were *"Esta situacion ha salido a la luz"* or brought into the limelight.

The newly appointed governor was Francisco de Bobadilla. In August of 1500 he had arrived in Santo Domingo with 500 men and a handful of native slaves that were being returned to the island. Columbus had brought them to Spain on a previous voyage and they were now being released by Royal Decree. The new governor found the situation as bad, if not worse, than he had expected. There was little love left for Columbus among the settlers. Bobadilla arrested Columbus and his brothers and placed them all in chains. They were held in a dungeon until October of 1500, when the three Columbus brothers were sent back to Spain in shackles.

Having been returned to Spain, Columbus and his brothers still had to cool their heels for an additional six weeks of imprisonment while awaiting trial. They were charged with multiple improprieties, starting with the cruel and inhumane treatment of their subjects. Although the charges were factual, upon hearing their whining pleas, King Ferdinand relented and returned the brothers back to wealth and status. However, Columbus never became governor again.

It was brash on the part of the Admiral, whose health had taken a downward turn, however he knew the royal couple and stood his ground, emphasizing his views to them. Perhaps it was that Queen Isabella was experiencing ill health and personal tragedies herself, that she felt compassion for Columbus. It still took some convincing on his part, but the Spanish Crown finally agreed to sponsor a fourth, and what was to be the last, voyage for Columbus.

"Riches don't make a man wealthy, they only make him busier." Christopher Columbus, First Viscount of the Indies

A Fleet of Thirty Ships

The infamous Fray Nicolás de Ovando y Cáceres, who had sniveled around the Royal Court wanting to become a favorite of the pious Queen Isabella, was appointed Governor of the Indies, replacing Francisco de Bobadilla, the man who had been responsible for sending Columbus from Hispaniola, back to Spain in irons. Prior to his appointment Fray Nicolás de Ovando had been a Spanish soldier, coming from a noble family, and was a Knight of the Order of Alcántara. On February 13, 1502, Fray Nicolás sailed from Spain with a record breaking fleet of thirty ships.

Since Columbus' discovery of the islands in the Caribbean, the number of Spanish ships that ventured west across the Atlantic had consistently increased. For reasons of safety in numbers, the ships usually made the transit in convoys, carrying nobility, public servants and conquistadors on the larger galleons that had a crew of 180 to 200. On these ships a total of 40 to 50 passengers had their own cabins midship. These ships carried paintings, finished furniture, fabric and, of course, gold on the return trip. The smaller vessels including the popular caravels had a crew of only 30, but carried as many people as they could fit in the cargo holds. Normally they would carry about 100 lesser public servants, soldiers, and settlers, along with farm animals and equipment, seeds, plant cuttings and diverse manufactured goods. For those that went before, European goods reminded them of home and were in great demand. Normally the ships would sail south along the sandy coast of the Sahara until they reached the Canary Islands, where they would stop for potable water and provisions before heading west with the trade winds. Even on a good voyage, they could count on burying a third of these adventurous at sea. Life was harsh and six to eight weeks out of sight of land, always took its toll!

In all it is estimated that 30,500 colonists made that treacherous voyage over time. Most of them had been intentionally selected to promote Spanish interests and culture in the New World. Queen Isabella wanted to introduce Christianity into the West Indies, improve the islands economically and proliferate the Spanish and Christian influences in the region.

Another of the passengers was Francisco Pizarro, who was the illegitimate son of a renowned Spanish infantry colonel. Not having gone to school, he was illiterate and lacked the advantages of a formal education. However, he did not view this disadvantage as a hindrance. Being a distant cousin of the flamboyant Hernán Cortés de Monroy y Pizarro, a famous conquistador and explorer, he hobnobbed with the elite and took advantage of his access to many prominent people. Seeking to enrich himself, he listened carefully to the stories of the vast treasures to be had in the New World and greedily wanted a part of them.

After arriving safely, Pizarro joined Martín Fernández de Enciso, a navigator and geographer from Seville, and Alonso de Ojeda, a navigator and conquistador, and sailed from Santo Domingo to Cartagena, and the still wild Isthmus of Panama. Their goal was to explore what is now Venezuela and Colombia, of course primarily seeking gold. Once at sea, they found Vasco Núñez de Balboa as a stowaway, hiding inside a barrel with his dog Leoncico. Annoyed, they wanted to abandon Balboa and his dog on an uninhabited island, but finding him useful as a guide, they brought him along. On September 1, 1513, with 190 Spanish soldiers, a few Indian guides, and some dogs, Balboa started his journey across the Isthmus of Panama. They encountered resistance along the way and had to fight their way through difficult terrain, combating hostile Indians. However, on September 25th, standing on an elevation, Balboa saw the Pacific Ocean, known as the "South Sea." Recognizing the importance of this discovery, the officers marked the location with their swords.

Pedrarias Dávila y Ortiz de Cota had been sent to Panama as the appointed administrator, representing the Crown. One of his first acts was to write Balboa a letter asking for a meeting with him to take place as soon as possible. Balboa honored the request, but on his way encountered a company of soldiers commanded by none other than Francisco Pizarro, who instantly arrested him and his party in the name of the Governor and accused him of opposing Pedrarias' authority. Bewildered, Balboa denied this and insisted that he be allowed to defend himself at a fair and legal trial in Spain.

Pedrarias, in cahoots with Martin Enciso, ordered that the trial take place in Panama and without delay. Balboa pleaded that he had always been loyal to the King, but Pedrarias was not to be dissuaded, and after a short, mock trial, he ordered Balboa's execution. The executioner must have been an amateur, since he made a mess of it. It took three swings of his axe before he managed to behead Balboa, but then with greater dexterity he more deftly beheaded four of Balboa's companions, while Pedrarias stealthily watched from the shadows. When the gruesome act was over, their heads were unceremoniously stuck on poles and remained to be seen for several days, as a warning to the people. Shortly thereafter, in mid-January 1519, Balboa's corpse was clandestinely disposed of and as a result, his gravesite remains unknown to this day.

Pizarro was later rewarded for his role in the arrest and killing of Balboa. He became the mayor and magistrate of Panama City, a position he held from 1519 to 1523. After his term as mayor, Francisco Pizarro went back to his exploration of the Pacific coast of South America. He undertook two expeditions, one in 1524 and another in 1526, both times failing to conquer the Inca Empire. He continued his quest and eventually reached northern Peru, where he finally got access to Inca gold. This discovery gave Pizarro the motivation to plan a third expedition to overrun and totally crush Peru. He returned to Panama to reorganize, but then ran into problems with the autocratic governor. These circumstances encouraged him to return to Spain, where he resolved these problems. Returning to Panama with his wife and supporting friends, Pizarro intended to pick up from where he left off. Persistent in his quest for gold he returned to Peru and fiercely battled the hapless Indians for their wealth. Not everyone agreed with what he was doing, which led to a quarrel with Diego Almagro, a former friend. Feeling all-powerful, he had his friend executed. When Diego's son heard of his father's murder, he sought revenge and on June 26, 1541, he assassinated Pizarro. Francisco Pizarro was laid to rest in the Basilica Cathedral of Lima without any of his ill-gotten treasures.

The conquistadors being soldiers, explorers, and adventurers were a fearsome, ruthless group. They committed atrocities in the name of the Royal Crown of Spain that cast a shadow on their own legacy, that of the King and Queen, and that of the Vatican. Columbus and his brothers were part of this barbarism that was considered the norm of that era. At the same time however, ordinary people flocked to the Caribbean and settlements flourished. Many of these grew, becoming cities that rivaled those they had left behind in Europe....

"One day an intrepid sole will climb this mountain on its east side, reaching the summit and the passage that exist between the main peak and secondary peaks, by which he can descend to the west side of the mountain. It is at this site near Lake Brunner, between the main peak and an adjacent stone pyramid, in a "hidden cave" that has been sealed by earthquakes common in the region... where lust for Inca gold must end for some... but for that intrepid sole... it shall be just the beginning!" Steven J. Charbonneau, author of INCA GOLD: History, Conquest & Legend and LUST FOR INCA GOLD, second edition

Columbus on his Fourth and Last Voyage

On May 11, 1502, Christopher Columbus left Cádiz, on his fourth and final voyage to the West. Now as an ailing 51-year-old man, he set sail for the Indies. With four aging ships, Columbus was accompanied by his stepbrother Bartolomeo, as well as Diego Mendez, and his 13-year-old son Fernando. With a crew of 140 men, they first sailed to *Asilah*, on the northwest tip of Morocco. *Arzila*, as it is known in Portuguese, is a fortified town situated along the Atlantic coast, about 20 miles west of Tangier. His first mission was to rescue a group of Portuguese soldiers that were being attacked by hostile Moors. However on this voyage his idealistic concern was to find a way to Asia. Columbus thought that he could find the Straits of Malacca off the coast of Malaysia, which at the time he thought to be near Cuba.

Having gained a better knowledge of the "Trade Winds" and weather patterns, this final voyage only took 21 days to cover the 3,500 miles of open Atlantic Ocean. He arrived during the heat of summer at Le Carbet, a commune on the island of Martinique. After a short stop to replenish his fresh water supply, he continued northwest through the Lesser Antilles, making his way around Puerto Rico and across the Mona Passage to the island of Hispaniola.

The new Governor, Nicolás de Ovando y Cáceres, had replaced Francisco de Bobadilla, the former governor, only weeks before. Out of spite, he enjoyed refusing Columbus entry into Santo Domingo since Queen Isabella held Columbus to a strict written agenda, which prohibited him free trade in the Caribbean or access to Santo Domingo. So it was that Ovando was simply holding Columbus to that royal edict.

Columbus was aware of dangerous weather indicators that were frequently a threat in the Caribbean during the summer months. Although the barometer had not yet been invented, there were definitely other telltale signs of an approaching hurricane.

Had the governor listened to Columbus' advice and given him some leeway, he could have saved the convoy that was being readied for a return trans-Atlantic crossing. Instead, the new inexperienced governor ordered the fleet of over 30 caravels, laden, heavy with gold, to set sail for Spain without delay. As a result, it is estimated that 20 of these ships were sunk by this violent storm, nine ran aground and only the *Aguja*, which coincidently carried Columbus' gold, survived and made it back to Spain safely. The ferocity of the storm claimed the lives of five hundred souls, including that of the former governor Francisco de Bobadilla.

Many of the caravels that sank during this hurricane were ships that were part of the same convoy that Ovando had traveled with from Spain to the West Indies. However he felt about this tragedy, which could have been prevented, he continued as the third Governor of the Indies until 1509, and became known for his brutal treatment of the Taíno Indians.

Columbus' ships fared somewhat better in that terrible storm, and survived with only minor damage. Heaving in their anchors, Columbus' small fleet of ships left Hispaniola to explore the western side of the Caribbean.

After stopping for more fresh water in Jamaica, Columbus took his exploration to the Bay Islands off the coast of Central America. On August 14, 1502, he landed on the continental mainland near Puerto Castilla, Honduras. He then continued south along the east coast of Nicaragua, and Costa Rica, before arriving in Almirante Bay, Panama, on October 16, 1502. Here the Indians told him of a vast Ocean just west, across a mountain range from where they were anchored. By now Columbus, feeling the effects of crippling arthritis, wanted to return to Spain. However in January of 1503, he heard of the existence of a gold mine upstream in the dense jungle. Reluctantly he established a small garrison at the mouth of the Belén River in Panama.

On April 6th one of his ships ran aground on a sandbar and became stuck in the river. Seeing that Columbus was vulnerable, the Quibían Indians attacked the garrison and severely damaged his other ships. Having sailed in tropical waters for almost a year didn't help. Barnacles and shipworms, that are marine mollusks with long, soft, naked bodies, had burrowed into the wooden hull, causing damage by weakening the planks. His ships had definitely seen better days when he left Panama and set his heading North, hoping to make it back to at least Santo Domingo.

Columbus could feel his age, because of the achy feeling in his bones. He knew that it was time to head back. It took him three weeks after leaving the Belén River before sighting the Cayman Islands, which he named "Las Tortugas" because of the many sea turtles found there. From the Caymans, he proceeded east along the coast of Cuba, where his dilapidated ships ran into yet another hurricane. The heavy seas violently tossed his small vessels around, opening seams, thus making it impossible to control the intake of seawater. This storm blew his ships south towards Jamaica, where his only recourse was to beach them in St. Ann's Bay on June 25, 1503.

Instead of alienating the local Indians who already felt that these Spaniards were aggressively intrusive, Columbus schmoozed them with stories. Cannibalizing what was left of the ships, the crew built shelters and settled in for the long wait they could expect before being rescued. With few options left, he sent one of his captains, Diego Méndez, and some natives to paddle a canoe against the wind all the way to Hispaniola. Seeking help from the governor Nicolás de Ovando was futile, and instead of helping Mendez, he immediately had him imprisoned and held him for the next seven months. Ovando also refused to allow any vessel to save the stranded men in Jamaica. Upon his release, Méndez did however find a small ship returning to Spain that came and rescued them.

In the meantime Columbus, in a last ditch effort to stay on the good side of the Indian chiefs, predicted a lunar eclipse on the leap-year day of February 29, 1504. Impressing them with this astronomical magic, they continued supplying the marooned men with food. For one year and four days, Columbus and his men remained stranded on the beach in Jamaica. Help finally arrived on June 29, 1504, taking the motley crew on the long voyage back to Sanlúcar, Spain. He arrived in Castile on November 7, 1504.

In all, Columbus had made four voyages between 1492 and 1504. He never realized that Cuba was an island and, instead, he continued to believe it to be a peninsula. It wasn't until 1508, two years after Columbus' death, that Sebastián de Ocampo, a Spanish navigator, sailed west along the northern coast of Cuba. After rounding Cape San Antonio he conclusively proved that Cuba was an island. Ocampo's voyage took a long eight months before returning to Hispaniola, since he tacked against the prevailing winds and bucked the swift Gulf Stream.

I have come to believe that this is a mighty continent which was hitherto unknown. I am greatly supported in this view because of this great river, and by this sea, which is fresh. Christopher Columbus, Admiral of the Ocean Sea

The Treaty of Tordesillas

After Columbus returned from his first voyage in 1492, the Pope deemed it advisable to divide the sectors of exploration and colonization between Spain and Portugal, which were the only two countries actively exploring the world at that time, and which conveniently were also Catholic. Between Columbus' second and third voyages, Pope Alexander VI issued a Papal bull authorizing the Treaty of Tordesillas on June 7, 1494. The treaty gave everything located beyond 370 leagues or exceeding 1,110 nautical miles west of Cape Verde to Spain for exploration, and everything east of this meridian went to Portugal.

The traditional trade route leading to Asia was overland, traveling east from the countries of Europe. Marco Polo established this trade route in the 13th century, but it required ships to carry the heavy loads of silks and spices. Henry the Navigator charted the course from Portugal to the Cape of Good Hope on the southern tip of Africa. Five years after Columbus discovered the West Indies, Vasco da Gama rounded the southern point of Africa and discovered a sea route to India.

Because the lines of demarcation that were specified in the Treaty of Tordesillas did not encircle the Earth, the treaty was basically worthless. Concerned about a developing conflict between Portugal and Spain over the Maluku Islands or the Moluccas, formerly known as the Spice Islands, another treaty called the Treaty of Zaragoza was drafted. King John III of Portugal and Emperor Charles V of Spain signed the treaty on April 22, 1529. This gave control of discovery of most of Asia to Portugal, and the islands of the Pacific Ocean to Spain.

"I am not afraid of the darkness. Real death is preferable to a life without living." Vasco da Gama, Portuguese Navigator and Explorer

Columbus' Final Years and Legacy

Columbus had visited Cuba on three of his four voyages. Because of his success, the Spanish Monarchs authorized twelve new expeditions to the West Indies including Columbus' fourth and final voyage. Upon his return to Spain, after his fourth voyage, Columbus was exhausted and in ill health. He had hardly returned when, two and a half weeks later, Queen Isabella died at the relatively young age of 53 years. Columbus knew that with her passing, any chance of another voyage was gone.

He was now wealthy beyond his wildest dreams and wanted for nothing, so Columbus retired to Valladolid, which at one time was considered the capital of Castile and Leon, a historic region of northwestern Spain. On October 19, 1469, Queen Isabella and King Ferdinand had been married at the *Palacio de los Vivero*, in the city of Valladolid, giving it great significance for Columbus. It was only a year and a half after retiring, on May 20, 1506, that Christopher Columbus quietly died. Dr. Antonio Rodriguez Cuartero, a professor of Internal Medicine at the University of Granada, stated that the Admiral died of a heart attack caused by Reiter's Syndrome, also known as reactive arthritis. He was only 54 years of age; however, he had been suffering from arthritis for quite some time prior to his death.

His son Diego, who had now become the Governor of Hispaniola, had his father's body moved from Valladolid to Seville, Spain, three years later. Sometime between 1536 and 1541, his remains were again transported across the Atlantic to

Hispaniola, where they were buried under the right side of the altar of the Cathedral of Santo Domingo. They rested in the Cathedral for over two hundred years. Then in 1795, after the French captured the Island of Hispaniola, Columbus' body was moved, first to Haiti and then to Havana, where it remained until after the Spanish-American War. There has been some confusion regarding all of this, since the remains could also have been those of Diego Columbus, who was buried near his father under the other side of the altar. The right side of the altar could have been the left side if viewed from the other side. In this case, heaven only knows what happened! After Cuba's War of Independence in 1898, the relics of Columbus, being considered a Spanish national treasure, were returned to Spain, and now rest in a crypt outside the Cathedral of Seville.

To this day, there are still questions regarding the human relics in the small coffer that incidentally also contained a bullet. Found under a wall of the Cathedral of Santo Domingo, it is inscribed with the name "Columbus." It seems likely that Columbus' remains are in two places, or that these bones are those of his son, or perhaps even his brother. The mystery lingers on since DNA testing has been refused by the Dominican Republic. However being related, the remains of all the family members would have very similar DNA characteristics.

Columbus proved on a practical level that the earth was round, however he modified his concept of a perfectly round earth when his calculations indicated that there was a slight bulge at the equator, which has since been confirmed by modern science. His findings suggested that the earth was pear shaped, with a comparatively slight rise, which he described, "As like a woman's breast, upon which rested the Terrestrial Paradise or Garden of Eden, past which no man could sail without the permission of God." It seems that Columbus was still fantasizing about the "Garden of Eden."

The oldest known map that shows America is the "*Mappa Mundi*," drawn in 1500 by Juan de la Cosa, who was the former owner and captain of the *Santa Maria*. It shows the outline of Cuba as an island, which, until his death, Columbus continued to believe was a peninsula and part of Asia. In 1513 Piri Reis, an Ottoman Admiral, drew a world map that included Cuba and Florida. For this, he used about twenty existing maps as his reference, including one drawn by Columbus himself....

Christopher Columbus and his brothers were no different from many of the Spanish adventurers of the time. They were a roughhewn lot, who wrote the rules by which they lived. As with their fellow conquistadors, they had a code of honor that sadly did not include the Indians. Since most of the Indians were never baptized, killing or enslaving them was not considered sinful. Human life was cheap to them, as they lived and died by the sword. The same was not true of the gentry or the clergy, many of whom saw that their responsibility was to administer "the Great Commission" as mentioned in the Bible, which was to convert the heathens to Christianity. However, many of the Spanish Adventurers never got outside of their own bubble and had no idea what the World was really all about. It is interesting that Columbus Day is celebrated, when in fact he was not the first to discover. America, nor was he really an honorable person, as we understand the word "honorable" now. It can only be said that things were different. Things were the way they were!

"By prevailing over all obstacles and distractions, one may unfailingly arrive at his chosen goal or

destination." Christopher Columbus, Great Admiral of the Ocean Sea

Controversies Surrounding Christopher Columbus

Recently much of what has been accepted as gospel, regarding Christopher Columbus, has been brought into question. There is no doubting his heroic feats of discovery, so most of the new queries concern themselves with his religion, the place of his birth, and whether the remains in the Cathedral of Seville in Spain and the Cathedral of Santo Domingo in the Dominican Republic, are actually his. To think of Columbus as anything other than Italian would almost be sacrilegious; however this is one part of the puzzle that is being questioned.

On Monday, June 2, 2003, DNA testing was allowed on Columbus' remains in Spain. His vestiges were exhumed in the presence of two of his descendants, hoping to solve some of the questions that have plagued historians through the years. Marcial Castro, the lead researcher, was one of two high school teachers respected for their genetic research and forensic anthropology. Another recognized researcher was Jose Antonio Lorente, a forensic geneticist and the director of the genetics laboratory at the University of Granada. The team undertook the project, expecting that their testing would reveal the truth regarding the "Great Admiral of the Ocean Sea."

Unfortunately, upon examining the remnants of Columbus contained within a small coffer, they discovered that the contents had degraded and had been contaminated through the years. Very little of what remained was in a satisfactory enough condition to undergo testing. They also exhumed the remains of his son Ferdinand Columbus, also known as Hernando, who was born of an extramarital affair. His remains are certain, since he has never been moved following his burial in 1539. The team also exhumed a third container, which held the bones of his eldest son Diego.

The researchers have found that 80% of Columbus' remains were unsuitable for research and that the 20% left rendered uncertain deductions. There was however an absolute match between the remains of Christopher Columbus and his brother Diego. The Y-chromosomes from Christopher Columbus are exceedingly scarce, as they were expected to be, so those of Hernando were used in lieu of Christopher Columbus', in order to carry out the study. In conclusion, the researchers felt confident that the remains taken from the Cathedral in Seville are in fact those of the navigator, but there are still some doubts regarding the bones alleged to be his in the Cathedral of Santo Domingo in the Dominican Republic. Until DNA testing is permitted there, no definitive answer can be expected.

Dominican authorities refuse to accept the DNA testing completed on the bone fragments from Spain, and at the same time refuse to allow DNA testing to be done on the bones allegedly his in the Cathedral of Santo Domingo. The reason is most likely that the Dominican Government dreads the repercussions of a negative outcome; however many still believe that Columbus's remains are in both places. When they were originally taken to Cuba in 1795, they had already been reduced to a powdery residue containing only some small bone fragments that could easily have been divided, leaving half behind.

The team has also attempted to resolve whether Columbus was Italian or Catalonian. Most of the evidence regarding this indicates that he may well have been the latter, since there is no evidence that he had ever written anything in Italian. Reinforcing this are authenticated letters that he wrote in

Spanish, with words and phrases reflecting a Catalonian influence. Based on this, many experts believe that he was Spanish, born of nobility and originally came from the Kingdom of Aragon. His birth was never recorded, so he could well have been the illegitimate child of a Spanish nobleman. However, Columbus claimed that he was born in Genoa, Italy. Columbus is a common Italian surname, but he could also have been born in Majorca, which is one of the Spanish Balearic Islands.

There is nothing of substance to indicate that Christopher Columbus was Jewish. However, in the later part of the 15th century, many Jews fearing the inquisition, claimed to be Catholics. The DNA matches from his brother and son do not bear any traces that could imply a Jewish heritage. However, Estelle Irizarry, a linguistics professor at Georgetown University, has pointed out that some of the punctuations used by Columbus, were of a style used by Ladino-speaking scribes, and that Spanish could well have been his second language. She added that this could indicate that he had a Jewish heritage.

As if there's not enough confusion concerning Columbus' background, there is also some speculation that he may have adopted his name from a pirate named Vincenzo Columbus, with whom he may well have sailed. Frequently when asked where he came from, he would reply with *"Vine de nada,"* "I came from nothing...."

"I am a most noteworthy sinner, but I have cried out to the Lord for grace and mercy, and they have covered me completely. I have found the sweetest consolation since I made it my whole purpose to enjoy his marvelous Presence." Christopher Columbus, "Admiral of the Ocean Sea"

Pictures – The Early Years

Leif Ericson discovering North America

Columbus' First Voyage

Queen Isabella of Spain

Ferdinand II of Aragón

Christopher Columbus

Columbus before Queen Isabella

La Santa María, La Niña and La Pinta

Replica of *La Santa María*

Replica of *La Pinta*

Replica of *La Niña*

Christopher Columbus arrives in America

Diego Velázquez de Cuéllar

Chief Hatuey

"A Painting is silent poetry, and poetry is a painting that speaks." Plutarch, a Greek historian, biographer, and essayist

A Vintage Cuban Travel Poster

The Exciting Story of Cuba.... Part 2

The Colonial Era

Early Spanish Colonization

The dusty facts are that: Ferdinand II, the Regent of Castile, was 63 years old when he died on January 23, 1516; his wife Queen Isabella was 53 years old when she died on November 26, 1504; and Columbus had passed away almost 10 years prior on May 20, 1506. The earlier death of Isabella and the death of her children changed the normal succession of heirs, forcing Ferdinand to yield the government of Castile to Philip of Habsburg, the husband of his second daughter Joanna. The son of Joanna and her husband Philip I of Castile was Charles I, who would inherit Spain from his maternal grandparents as well as the Habsburg and Burgundian Empires of his paternal family. Thus, the grandson of Ferdinand and Isabella became the most powerful ruler in Europe and by 1516 King Charles I of Spain also ruled the Netherlands. In 1519 as Charles V, he became the ruler of the Holy Roman Empire, King of Germany, as well as the King of Italy.

During the early part of the 16th century, Portuguese and Spanish exploration spread to the four corners of the world. Once the age of discovery had started, other countries such as England, Holland, Italy and France joined in, seeking their piece of the newfound wealth. Ships from all of these maritime nations sailed around the southern part of Africa and crossed the Indian Ocean to trade with Asia. In the Caribbean and South America, Spanish conquistadors continued their quest for gold.

Diego Velázquez de Cuéllar

Diego Velázquez de Cuéllar, following the orders of Columbus' son Diego, took a group of 800 men to the island of Cuba, or *Caobana*, looking for gold. Many settlers seeking new beginnings followed, and although not much gold was discovered on the island, land was available for the taking and the soil was fertile. As they settled in, the Spaniards continued to be overbearing in their relationship with the Indians, causing the situation to remain hostile between them.

Chief Hatuey was the *Cacique* or Chief of 400 Taíno Indians that had fled from the Spaniards in Hispaniola for Cuba. Hatuey resented the ruthless Spaniards and encouraged the Arawakan-speaking people to rise up against them. Seeing the malice of these new intruders, they had no other option but to engage them in guerrilla warfare. Hatuey rallied the local Taínos, telling them that the Spaniards were merciless and that their god was gold. A number of the local Indians actually joined him in the fight. When the Chief was ultimately captured, the Spaniards tortured him, and when he refused to tell them the location of the gold, they burnt him at the stake. A bust on top of a monument honoring Chief Hatuey is located in the town of Baracoa, Cuba. It reads *"Primer Rebelde De America Immolado En Yara De Baracoa"*, "First rebel of America, Sacrificed in the town of Yara in Baracoa." He is considered by many to be the first hero of Cuba. His last words were that he did not want to go to Heaven, if that is where Christians go when they die.

With their chief gone, the Indians gave up their attempt to continue fighting. When things became quiet again, Velázquez established a number of coastal villages with the territorial administration in Baracoa, which was very near Columbus' first sighting of Cuba.

Shortly after officially becoming governor of Cuba, Velázquez established an advisory committee of settlers, so that Cuba could answer directly to Spain as an independent colony, thereby bypassing Diego Columbus' unwanted authority. In 1514, the colonial seat of government was moved to Santiago de Cuba, in the southeastern quadrant of the island. Later that year the first settlement of Havana was established on the banks of the Mayabeque River, near the present town of Surgidero de Batabanó on the Caribbean coast. To promote expansion, the fledgling community was relocated due north, adjacent to a natural harbor on the Gulf Coast. On August 25, 1515, the future city of Havana was founded 472 miles to the west of Santiago, with the thought of it becoming the territorial capital.

In 1525, Diego Columbus officially delegated Diego Velázquez with the authority to conquer, occupy and govern the island for Spain; thus Velázquez became the first Spanish governor of Cuba. Although it was the primary objective from the very beginning, the Spaniards refused to believe that gold was not abundant having seen the Indians' jewelry. However, not many gold deposits were found on the island. Three hundred black slaves were brought in to work the existing Jaguar mine, where very small amounts of the precious metal had been found. More crucial than the miniscule amount of gold that was mined, was that the land lent itself to farming, thereby allowing agriculture to flourish. The number of Indians that originally worked the land had been greatly reduced because of the brutal treatment bestowed upon them by the conquistadors, and from an economic point of view, they needed to be replaced. Two years after assuming office and with special permission of the Spanish monarchy, Velázquez legally permitted the first African slaves into Cuba from Haiti, for the express purpose of replacing the Indians working in the fields. By 1533, only six years later, Cuba experienced its first slave rebellion in these same gold mines. The Spaniards, however, viciously squashed the strike.

Hernando de Soto

While under the Spanish flag, the Crown rigorously controlled the number of slaves allowed into Cuba and charged the settlers a 20% royalty for each slave they imported. In 1537, Havana was invaded and briefly occupied by the French. On April 6, 1538, Hernando de Soto with about 950 men and horses on ten ships sailed from Sanlúcar de Barrameda, Spain to Santiago de Cuba where he took over as the Governor of Cuba. From Santiago, he sailed around Cuba to Havana with a nine-ship convoy and set up a base which was administered by his wife and used as a stepping-stone to Florida. Anticipating this expedition, he sent Juan de Añasco with two ships to find a suitable landing site along the west coast of Florida. Añasco, who was Hernando de Soto's scout, returned with four Indians who told fabricated stories about gold in Florida, which De Soto accepted as true. After some months preparing for the expedition, De Soto left Cuba and arrived at Shaw's Point near present-day Bradenton, Florida, where he started his long trek in search of gold and silver.

"If you don't do anything stupid when you're young, you won't remember something funny when you're old..." Old Spanish Proverb

Pirates Plunder Cuba

During the following years, French pirates and marauding, escaped slaves plundered Santiago and burned Havana to the ground. Even the Dutch, led by Piet Heyn in 1628, sacked the Spanish fleet lying at anchor in Havana harbor. When the English fleet captured Santiago de Cuba in 1662, they opened the city up for trade with Jamaica. Now, under British rule, even more slaves were imported to work in the cotton fields, but Britain agreed to leave Cuba when Spain recognized England's ownership and governance over Jamaica.

Plagues were nothing new to Europe.... They were recorded as far back as 1347, and continued on until 1750. In 1649, a terrible epidemic was brought into Cuba by one of the ships that had arrived from Europe. Most likely it was the Bubonic Plague, which, at the time, killed roughly a third of Cuba's population. As bad as it was, and in spite of this setback, by the end of the 1600's, Havana had become the third largest city in the Americas.

The municipality of Havana was constructed in accordance with a specific building code. The whitewashed houses had red tiled roofs, much the same as in Spain. The streets, churches and squares were laid out according to approved plans, with the primary plaza located in the center of the city. Trade was restrictively controlled and had to be exclusively with Spain, using only Spanish ships as a means of transportation. Over half of the 20,000 people in Cuba lived within the walled city, which officially became the capital of Cuba in 1607. Pirates, many of whom came from Port Royal, at the mouth of Kingston Harbor in Jamaica, continuously plundered the island. Under constant siege, Cuba failed to develop in comparison to the French and English possessions. The excessive Spanish taxes and regulations also served as a hindrance to development. In 1728 the University of Havana was founded by King Philip V of Spain, in the Villa San Cristóbal in old Havana, under the authority of Pope Innocent XIII. Much later, in 1902, it was moved to its present location in the newer Vedado section of the city.

A hundred years after the English invasion of Santiago de Cuba, the British returned again, this time in force. On July 30, 1762, British troops captured and occupied Havana, as part of the Seven Years' War. A year prior, the Spanish Admiral Gutierre de Hevia y Valdés arrived in Havana with a flotilla of seven ships of the line and 1,000 troops reinforcing the number of defenders of Havana. When the Spanish garrison became weakened by yellow fever, they were overrun by the British, who in turn also suffered great losses from the same disease.

The British Invasion

When the British attacked Havana, Admiral de Hevia failed to scuttle the ships under his command. Thus, his ships fell into the hands of the British. The Admiral was returned to Spain where he was court-martialed, stripped of his titles and sentenced to house arrest for 10 years. Fortunately, he was pardoned three years later, on September 17, 1765. Reinstated he returned to active duty as the commander of the Marine Corps in Cadiz. He died seven years later on December 2, 1772, at Isla de León, Spain.

Havana being under the rule of the British governor Sir George Keppel, the 3rd Earl of Albemarle, the British opened trade with their North American and Caribbean colonies, causing a dramatic transformation in the culture of Cuba, as well as bringing an increase to the population. Thousands of additional slaves were brought to the island under British rule, ostensibly to work on the new sugar plantations.

The British occupation, however, didn't last long, since the Seven Years' War ended less than a year after the British arrived, and with the signing of the Peace of Paris Treaty the English agreed to surrender Cuba in exchange for Florida. In Britain, many people believed they could have done better, had they included Mexico and some of the colonies in South America, as part of the deal. The Florida Keys, not being directly connected to the Florida mainland, also remained in dispute, but it was not contested as long as free trade was permitted. After the deal was made with the British, Spain retained control of Cuba until after the secessionist movements were ended with the Treaty of Paris, signed on December 10, 1898. The United States Senate ratified the treaty on February 6, 1899.

In 1793, many more slaves were imported into Cuba when French slave owners fled from Haiti during the Slave Rebellion, also known as the Haitian Revolution. This brought 30,000 white refugees and their slaves into Cuba. With their knowledge of coffee and sugar processing, they founded many new plantations. This period of the English occupation and French influx, although chronologically short, was when the floodgates of slavery were opened wide. It was at this time that the largest numbers of black slaves ever, were imported into the country.

Now I confess myself as belonging to that class in the country who contemplate slavery as a moral, social and political evil... President Abraham Lincoln, October 7, 1858, Debate at Galesburg, Illinois

There's Gold In Them Thar Hills!

Cuba has a history of mining that dates back to 1520, when the Spaniards opened the previously mentioned Jaguar gold mine. In 1533, the Jobabo mine was the site of a four-slave uprising which lead to their deaths. To intimidate the slaves and calm the colonists' fears, the bodies of the strikers were decapitated and put on display in Bayamo. Although the number of strikers was small, the ramifications of this strike were lasting. For the remainder of the 16th Century, a number of confrontations continued between slave owners and their indentured servants consisting of Indians and African field workers. In most cases, their slaves just simply ran away. In 1550, needing replacement workers, Spain granted a group of merchants the right to import additional African slaves into Cuba.

Working conditions under Spanish rule were generally unregulated. For the mineworkers conditions were deplorable and continued to be unsafe and unacceptable for another 400 years.

What Happened to the Receipt?

The following story is a little different from the usual stories concerning gold.... In 1599, Don Francisco Manzo de Contreras was sent to Cuba as King Phillip II's Chief Justice, with a directive to stop the smuggling of gold and other valuables. He settled in the town of Remedios in Villa Clara Province, near the northern coast seaport town of Caibarién, and over time, he became very wealthy doing exactly what he had been sent to stop! He filled his chests with gold bullion, but the heavy, bulky gold is not something that can easily be taken with you!

In 1776, his heirs were three Catholic nuns, who had stashed six chests of gold into the walls of the Santa Clara Convent. Being afraid of pirates, they commissioned their nephew Joseph Manzo de Contreras to take the gold across the Atlantic to be deposited in the Bank of England in London. Being an obedient nephew, according to him, he took the gold to England and followed his aunts' instructions to the letter.

Many years later, the half-forgotten fortune was handed down to Angel Contreras, who claimed that his great grandfather, Joseph Manzo, once had a receipt for it. The receipt was handed down through the family and when his uncle took possession of this valuable paper, he hid it, attempting to protect the family treasure. Ultimately, he was murdered when he refused to tell the thieves where it was.

Unfortunately, the receipt is now lost, and although the family has searched high and low for it, it has never been found. Angel lived in Majagua, Cuba, where his family worked at a candy factory. He claimed they looked everywhere for it, but the receipt was definitely gone! With almost six decades of communistic control, the family decided to lay low and do nothing more to find it. They feared that the State would take whatever inheritance was rightfully theirs, and they probably would be right.

Some of the Manzo family have since left Cuba and now live in Florida. They staged protests at the British Consulate in Miami, accusing the Queen of having reached a deal with the Cuban government. They stated that what should have been their money, was sent to Fidel Castro. During these demonstrations, nine members of the family were arrested for causing disturbances but not much else came of their claim. The Bank of England stated that the story of lost gold is just a myth, and that they have no record of it. Although this is the sad ending to the story for now, the family is continuing with their claim. However without a receipt, it seems unlikely that they have much of a case!

"They put him in a madhouse," Angel said, "and then they killed him. All for greed... they wanted the money." Angel Contreras, referring to what had happened to his uncle....

The Exciting Story of Cuba.... Part 3

Struggle for Freedom

Early Attempts at Liberation

Ever since the United States was founded in 1776, and even prior to that as a colony, the United States has had an economic interest in Cuba. At the time of the American Revolution, Havana was the third largest city in the Americas, with a larger population than New York City.

Most of the original settlers in Cuba were poor whites from Spain, seeking a better life. In 1795, Nicolás Morales, a free black man, led both white and black Cubans in a revolt to wrest the island from Spanish control and establish equality between the races. The uprisings started in Bayamo and quickly spread throughout the eastern part of the island. For the most part, the rebellions were about political independence and the abolition of sales taxes. The rebels were no match for the Spanish army that easily overpowered them. However, this was just the beginning of a protracted struggle for the freedom of the Cuban people.

In 1812, José Antonio Aponte, a free black carpenter who held the rank of Captain in Cuba's black militia, led an uprising with similar objectives. He organized one of the most notable slave conspiracies in Cuba, which at the time became known as the Aponte Conspiracy of 1812. His objective was simply to free the slaves from Spanish oppression. During an uprising in February, eight of his followers were caught and imprisoned. He was also eventually caught and on April 9, 1812, was put to death. After being hanged at the gallows, Antonio and some of his followers were decapitated. His head was encased in an open iron cage and hung in front of the house he had lived in. To further accent this gruesome example set by the Spanish régime, following their execution, the heads of Aponte's cohorts were also openly displayed around Havana.

Early Cuban liberation movements, like the one headed by Narciso López, continued to plague the Spanish government. Narciso López was born in Caracas, Venezuela, on November 2, 1797. As a young man, he was conscripted, or drafted, to serve in the Spanish army. During his service to Spain, he fought against the freedom fighters of Simón Bolívar, the liberator of South America, in the city of Valencia, Venezuela. Withdrawing in defeat after the Battle of Lake Maracaibo, the Spanish army left for sanctuary in Cuba. Narciso López was only twenty-one years of age when he was promoted to the rank of Colonel. After the war, he was discharged in Spain and worked for the city administration of Seville. He lost his position when the government experienced a drastic change in 1843. Disillusioned, Narciso López returned to Cuba where he joined the existing anti-Spanish movement.

The Spanish representative government in Cuba cracked down on the revolutionary partisans, forcing Narciso López to flee to the United States. In 1848, López tried to launch a return to the island with the intent of freeing Cuba. He was thwarted in this ambitious endeavor when he failed to win the cooperation of important people such as Jefferson Davis and Robert E. Lee.

In 1850, with 600 volunteers, López landed in Cuba and held the city of Cárdenas for a few hours before being driven out by Spanish troops. He escaped to the United States to regroup.

Eventually in 1851, after previous attempts, López managed to return to Cuba with several hundred men, many of whom were indeed Americans. Once again, Spanish forces stopped him. However, this time the Spanish administration didn't treat him kindly. On September 1, 1851, he was executed in Havana, along with many of his followers.

Unrest in Cuba continued. In 1868, plantation owners in the eastern Oriente Province formed small bands of rebels and rose up against the occupying Spanish troops. Carlos Manuel de Céspedes del Castillo, a respected planter and the owner of an estate and sugar mill known as *La Demajagua*, sought and spearheaded Cuba's fight for freedom from Spain. On the third day of fierce combat, he freed his slaves, most of whom then volunteered to join his band of rebels, now totaling 147 men in the fight for freedom.

At the time, the conflict was between the creoles born in Cuba, and the recent immigrants from Spain, known as *peninsulares*. The Spanish forces and the peninsulares were backed by rich Spanish merchants and assumed a defensive position. However as tensions grew, an all-out war of independence from Spain became inevitable. On October 10, 1868, Céspedes del Castillo declared his country's independence from Spain, thus igniting what came to be known as the Ten Years' War.

The number of rebels grew to an army of 12,000 men within a month, at which time he attacked and captured both Bayamo and Holguín.

Céspedes del Castillo was hailed as a hero of Cuban Independence and is best known for unfurling and proudly raising one of the numerous flags, used to denote the rebellious attitude of the people at that time against Spain. This flag became known as the Céspedes flag. In the midst of the war, on February 27, 1874, Céspedes was killed by a marauding Spanish patrol. This became the first war for Cuban independence and caused approximately 200,000 casualties!

Ongoing battles for Cuban freedom from Spain continued until the end of the 19th century. In 1895, a Cuban force of 3,000 volunteers defeated the Spanish army during the battle of La Reforma, thereby keeping the remaining Spanish forces on the defensive. The Battle of La Reforma ended on December 2, 1895. During this time, the United States offered to buy the island nation from Spain. Even with the many problems they had with the inhabitants of Cuba, Spain turned down all of the numerous offers made.

José Martí

José Martí is recognized as the George Washington of Cuba or perhaps better yet, as the Simon Bolivar, the liberator of South America. He was born in Havana on January 28, 1853, to Spanish parents. His mother, Leonor Pérez Cabrera, was a native of the Canary Islands and his father, Mariano Martí Navarro, came from Valencia. Families were big then, and it was not long before José had seven sisters. While still very young his parents took him to Spain, but it was just two years later that they returned to Santa Clara where his father worked as a prison guard. His parents enrolled José at a local public school. In September of 1867, Martí signed up at the *Escuela Profesional de Pintura y Escultura de La Habana*, an art school for painting and sculpture in Havana.

Instead of pursuing art as a career, Martí felt that his real talents were as a writer and poet. By the early age of 16, he had already contributed poems and articles to the local newspapers. In 1865 after hearing the news of Abraham Lincoln's assassination, he was inspired to seek freedom for the slaves in his country, and to achieve Cuban independence from Spain. In 1868, Cuban landowners started fighting in what came to be known as the Ten Years' War. Even at this early age, Martí had definite opinions regarding political affairs, and wrote papers and editorials in support of the rebels. His good intentions backfired and he was convicted of treason. After confessing, he was sentenced to serve six years at hard labor. His parents did what they could to have their son freed but failed, even though at the age of sixteen he was still considered a minor. In prison, Martí's legs were tightly shackled causing him to become sick with severe lacerations on his ankles. Two years later at the age of eighteen, he was released and sent to Spain where he continued his studies. Because of complications stemming from his time in prison, he had to undergo two surgical operations to correct the damage done to his legs by the shackles.

Martí still had to consider himself lucky, since in 1871 eight medical students had been executed for the alleged desecration of a gravesite in Havana. Those executed were selected from the student body by lottery, and they may not have even been involved in the desecration. In fact, some of them were not even in Havana at the time, but it quickly became obvious to everyone that the Spanish government was not fooling around!

Some years later Martí studied law at the Central University of Madrid (University of Zaragoza). As a student he started sending letters directly to the Spanish Prime Minister insisting on Cuban autonomy, and he continued to write what the Spanish government considered inflammatory newspaper editorials. In 1874, he graduated with a degree in philosophy and law. The following year Martí traveled to Madrid, Paris and Mexico City where he met the daughter of a Cuban exile, Carmen Zayas-Bazán, whom he later married. In 1877 Martí paid a short visit to Cuba, but being constantly on the move he went on to Guatemala where he found work teaching philosophy and literature. In 1878 he published his first book, *Guatemala*, describing the beauty of that country. The daughter of the President of Guatemala had a crush on Martí, which did not go unnoticed by him. María was known as "La Niña de Guatemala," the child of Guatemala. She waited for Martí when he left for Cuba, but when he returned he was married to Carmen Zayas-Bazán. María died shortly thereafter on May 10, 1878, of a respiratory disease, although many say that she died of a broken heart. On November 22, 1878, Martí and Carmen had a son whom they named José Francisco. Doing the math, it becomes obvious as to what had happened.... It was after her death that he wrote the poem "La Niña de Guatemala."

The Cuban struggle for independence started with the Ten Years' War in 1868 lasting until 1878. At that time, the Peace of Zanjón was signed, giving Cuba little more than empty promises that Spain completely ignored. An uneasy peace followed, with several minor skirmishes, until the Cuban War of Independence flared up in 1895.

In December of 1878, thinking that conditions had changed and that things would return to normal, Martí returned to Cuba. However, still being cautious he returned using a pseudonym, which may have been a mistake since now his name did not match those in the official records. Using a pseudonym made it impossible for him to find employment as an attorney.

Once again, after his revolutionary activities were discovered, Martí was deported to Spain. Arriving in Spain and feeling persecuted, he fled to France and continued on to New York City. Then, using New York as a hub, he traveled and wrote, gaining a reputation as an editorialist on Latin American issues.

Returning to the United States from his travels, he visited with his family in New York City for the last time. Putting his work for the revolution first, he sent his family back to Havana. Then from New York he traveled to Florida, where he gave inspiring speeches to Cuban tobacco workers and cigar makers in Ybor City, Tampa. He also went to Key West to inspire Cuban nationals in exile. In 1884, while Martí was in the United States, slavery was finally abolished in Cuba. In 1891 Martí approved the formation of the Cuban Revolutionary Party.

Returning to New York City, Martí held a number of diplomatic positions for various Latin American countries and again wrote editorials for Spanish-language newspapers. Many considered Martí to be the greatest Latin American intellectual of the time. He published his newspaper *Patria* as the voice of Cuban Independence. While in the United States, he wrote several acclaimed volumes of poetry and along with other friends in exile, he spent time planning his return to Cuba. During the following year in 1892, he traveled throughout Central America, the Caribbean and the United States raising funds at various Cuban clubs. His first attempt to launch the revolution, with a few followers, was drastically underfunded and failed. However, the following year with more men and additional backing, he tried again. Although he admired and visited America in the interim, he feared that the United States would annex Cuba before his revolution could liberate the country from Spain.

With small skirmishes, the Cuban War of Independence started on February 24, 1895. Marti's plan for a second attempt at freeing Cuba included convincing Major General Máximo

Gómez y Báez and Major General Antonio de la Caridad Maceo y Grajales, as well as several other revolutionary heroes of the Ten Years' War, to join him. Together they launched a three-pronged invasion in April of 1895. With bands of exiles, they landed separately, using small boats. The main assault was on the south coast of Oriente Province, where their objective was to take and hold the higher ground. During this maneuver Martí was directed by the commanding officer General Máximo Gómez to remain with the rearguard, since he would be much more useful to the revolution alive than dead. However Martí, exercising his usual exuberance, took the lead and was instantly killed during one of the first skirmishes. Thus, he met his death on May 19, 1895, fighting regular Spanish troops at the Battle of Dos Ríos just north of Santiago de Cuba, at the relatively young age of 42.

Punta Brava and the nearby town of Guatao, on the northwestern side of Cuba, just 12.8 miles southwest of Havana, was the scene of a battle during the war in which the Spaniards caught the Cubans by surprise. General Antonio Maceo y Grajales, the second-in-command of the Cuban Army of Independence, was killed there on December 7, 1896. He was 51 years of age at the time of his death.

*"It is a sin not to do what one is capable of doing."
José Martí, Cuban Statesman, Soldier, Poet and Journalist*

Captain Joseph Fry

One of the nicest parks in present day downtown Tampa, Florida, is the Cotanchobee Fort Brooke Park. The 5-acre park, which lies between the Tampa Bay Times Forum (Amalie Arena) and the mouth of the Hillsborough River at the

Garrison Channel, is used for many weddings and special events such as the dragon boat races and the duck race. Few people give thought to the historic significance of the location, or to Captain Joseph Fry, considered Tampa's first native son, who was born there on June 14, 1826.

Going to sea was a tradition in the Fry family, starting with his paternal great-grandfather Samuel Fry from East Greenwich, Rhode Island, who was the master of the sloop *Humbird*. As a young man, Joseph attended the United States Naval Academy and graduated with the second class in 1847. Starting as an Ensign, he served as a commissioned officer in the U.S. Navy until the Civil War, at which time he resigned and took a commission as a Lieutenant in the Confederate Navy.

The Ten Years' War, also known as "the Great War," which started in 1868 became the first of three wars of Cuban Independence. In October 1873, following the defeat of the Confederacy and five years into the Cuban revolution, Fry became Captain of a side-wheeler, the S/S *Virginius*. His mission was to take guns and ammunition, as well as approximately 300 Cuban rebels to Cuba, with the intent of fighting the Spanish army for Cuban Independence. Unfortunately, the mission failed when the ship was intercepted by the Spanish warship *Tornado*.

Captain Fry and his crew were taken to Santiago de Cuba and given a hasty trial and before a British warship Commander, hearing of the incident, could intervene, they were sentenced to death. After thanking the members of his crew for their service, Captain Fry and fifty-three members of his crew were put to death by firing squad, and were then decapitated and trampled upon by the Spanish soldiers. However, the British Commander

Sir Lambton Lorraine of HMS *Niobe* did manage to save the lives of a few of the remaining crewmembers and rebels.

This act of violence was published in American newspapers with the intent of inciting the public. For several weeks, it seemed that the United States would declare war on Spain. However, the U.S. Attorney General ruled that since Captain Fry and his ship were not on official business, this horrific act would not be seen as an act of war. William Randolph Hearst's newspaper, the *New York Journal*, and Joseph Pulitzer's *New York World*, as well as most other American newspapers, stoked the fires of war with what came to be known as "yellow journalism." On December 17, 1873, Spain turned the S/S *Virginius* over to the U.S. Navy and nine days later in heavy seas, the hapless side-wheeler sank off Cape Hatteras. Although a conflict was averted for a time, the pot was boiling and the United States was ready for a war.

USS *Maine*

The continuing unrest and a threat to the U.S. Embassy in Havana by Spanish officers, in the days following the declaration of Cuban autonomy, were described in newspapers in a provocative way. Again, it was typical of "yellow journalism" and the inflammatory way newspapers covered their stories. Because of this aggressive journalism and in anticipation of problems, to insure the safety of Americans and their interests, President McKinley decided to deploy the battleship USS *Maine* to Havana. As a backup, more naval ships were deployed to Key West and other potential hot spots involving Spain.

The USS *Maine*, designated ACR-1, was built by the New York Naval Shipyard in Brooklyn, New York, and was commissioned in 1895, as the first battleship to be named after the state of Maine. She was originally built because of an increase in naval forces in Brazil and other Latin American countries. Although technically the ship was modern when she was designed, her protracted construction antiquated her by the time she was launched. The *Maine* was one of the first naval vessels to be built without masts and sails, due to the anticipated dependability of her steam engines.

Most American citizens identified with the people of Cuba, and compared their struggle to the American Revolutionary War. The arrival of the USS *Maine* in Havana harbor, with only 18 hours advance warning, was contrary to diplomatic protocol. However, by that time it was no longer an important consideration.

At 9:40 p.m. on February 15, 1898, a massive explosion rocked the Port of Havana and sank the battleship while she was at anchor, taking with her the lives of 266 American sailors. Although the cause of the explosion was never proven to be sabotage, the U.S. press and government did attribute the explosion to being caused by a bomb, placed by Spanish operatives. In actual fact, it was most likely caused by an unnoticed smoldering coal fire in one of the ship's bunkers. "Remember the Maine, To Hell with Spain!" became the American battle cry.

Spanish-American War

On April 11, 1898, President McKinley asked Congress for the authority to use military intervention in Cuba, reasoning that it would bring an end to their civil war. As anticipated, yellow journalism fired up the American public to the extent that Joint Resolutions supporting the Cuban revolution were authorized by a vote of 311 to 6 in the U.S. House of Representatives, and 42 to 35 in the Senate. On April 20th, it was signed by the President and by the next day, the United States Navy blockaded all of Cuba's major ports. On April 23rd, Spain reacted by declaring war against the United States, and then on April 25th, Washington followed with a "Declaration of War" against Spain. Later Congress declared that a state of war actually existed from April 21st, when the U.S. Navy had started the blockade.

"A Splendid Little War" is what John Hay, Secretary of State, called the Spanish-American War

Theodore Roosevelt

Theodore Roosevelt, the Assistant Secretary of the Navy and an advocate of the Monroe Doctrine, proposed military intervention in Cuba, using U.S. Army troops and Marines. He and Leonard Wood, a career medical officer, formed the 1st Volunteer Cavalry, naming them the Rough Riders. On May 29, 1898, 1,060 men and 1,258 horses under the command of Colonel Wood, who was acting in the capacity of a field officer rather than a medical officer, traveled by rail to Tampa, Florida. They got off to a bad start, with a quarter of the Rough Riders having already died of malaria or yellow fever during training. Due to hasty planning and carelessness, there was a lack of provisions and a shortage of transportation, which was desperately needed to take the remaining men and horses to Cuba. Because of this haste, General William R. Shafter, known as "Pecos Bill," a Medal of Honor recipient and the Commander of the Army's V Corps gave the order to leave before they were prepared. In the confusion, only eight out of the available 12 Companies actually left Tampa for Cuba, leaving most of their horses and all of their mules behind. When they landed on the southern coast of

Cuba, near Daiquiri and Siboney just east of Santiago de Cuba, the troops that went without their horses complained that they had become nothing more than ground pounders, meaning infantry. The Calvary always felt that they were superior to the Infantry. Feeling dejected they became disgruntled and lost the little spirit they had left for the fight ahead. It took Colonel Roosevelt's charisma and consistently upbeat attitude to rally the troops when they were called upon to fight the Battle of San Juan Hill.

Guantánamo Bay

In 1898, the U.S. Marines took Guantánamo Bay with the help of naval support and, due to the provisions in the Platt Amendment of 1903, the U.S. Naval Base built there remains in the hands of the United States to this day. In 1934, the lease for the Naval Base was carried forward, becoming an important proviso in the Treaty of Relations. After Fidel Castro took over the Cuban government in January of 1959, some sleight of hand and deception on the part of the United States made this document no less effective.

When at noon on December 31, 1999, the United States turned control of the Panama Canal over to Panama, Chinese interests quickly moved in.... How can the United States believe that the Russians or the Chinese will not move in, when the U.S. Navy moves out of its strategic naval base at Guantánamo Bay?

The Spanish Fleet

Spanish Admiral Pascual Cervera y Topete's fleet had been blockaded in Santiago harbor for two months. The naval battles that ensued, starting with the first shot being fired by the USS *Oregon*, caused the annihilation of the Spanish Caribbean

Squadron. The United States Navy effectively destroyed one ship at a time, as they sailed out of the harbor.

On land the U.S. Army fought the difficult battles of Las Guasimas, El Caney and the well-known Battle of San Juan Hill. U.S. troops also fought the entrenched Spaniards in Santiago de Cuba. Using obsolete Civil War weapons and outdated military tactics such as open frontal assaults, led to 200 American deaths and about 1,200 wounded. However, the rapid firing Gatling guns they used, eventually tipped the balance in favor of the Americans. The Spanish forces however managed to defend Fort Canosa, thus preventing the Americans from entering the city of Santiago. Both Cubans and Americans, working together, fought the bloody siege of Santiago de Cuba, keeping the Spaniards on the defensive.

At night, on the eastern side of the city, the Cubans dug trenches and parapets ever closer towards the Spanish lines, which were then occupied by American troops on the following day. This continued until the Spanish positions were substantially weakened and then overrun. At the same time, the Cubans fought their way in from the western side of the city, causing the Spanish forces to be caught in the middle of this pincer movement, where they were then overpowered.

With devastating defeats in Cuba and the Philippines, and with the Spanish fleets annihilated, Spain sued for peace. On August 12, 1898, hostilities were halted. Representatives from the United States and Spain met in Paris on October 1, 1898, producing a treaty that would bring an end to the war after six months of hostilities. However, the Americans found themselves negotiating in a hostile atmosphere because Europe, with the exception of England, considered the United States as an upstart and therefore favored Spain. The following year on March 19th, the Queen Regent of Spain, María Christina, signed the Treaty of Paris, breaking a deadlock that occurred in the Spanish courts because of these tensions, thus ending what John Hay in a letter from London to Theodore Roosevelt, called "A Splendid Little War." With some conditions, most of Spain's contested possessions were ceded to the United States.

Rum and Coca-Cola

"*Cuba Libre*" became the battle cry for Cuban Independence by the Cuban Liberation Army. When Coca-Cola was introduced to Cuba in 1900, the Cuba Libre became a popular drink made with rum and Coca-Cola. It became Cuba's favorite national drink....

"I don't need to know how they make Coca-Cola. I think it tastes just fine not knowing what the ingredients are. I think there are some things that should be kept secret." Colin Hanks, American actor

Cuban Casualties

The Spanish-American War lasted less than four months for the United States, however for Cuba this was only a small part of their War of Independence from Spain, which went through many phases starting with the Ten Years' War and lasting almost 20 years. The U.S. government originally was neutral, but became involved when the Spanish Governor forced thousands of Cubans into concentration camps. Americans joined the Cubans in their fight against the Spaniards after the *Maine* exploded and sank in Havana harbor. During these years, 5,180 Cuban insurgents died in battle and over 40,000 died from various diseases such as Yellow Fever. Colon Cemetery in Havana is one of the great historical cemeteries of the world and was built just in time to receive the victims of the Cuban Wars of Independence.

José Martí was killed on May 19, 1895, and buried in a mass grave near where he fell. Four days later, his body was exhumed and ultimately brought to the cemetery of *de Cuba Santa Ifigenia* in Santiago. On June 29, 1951, his cremains were interred in a magnificent mausoleum named *Retablo de los Héroes*, the Monument of Heroes. This cemetery is also the final resting place of many other heroes of the Revolutionary Wars.

American Casualties on the USS *Maine*

As noted previously, approximately 266 American sailors were killed prior to the declaration of war, when the USS *Maine* exploded and sank in Havana harbor after a massive explosion of undetermined origin. The first Board of Inquiry regarding the incident stated that a mine placed on or near the hull had sunk the ship. Later studies determined that it was more likely heat from smoldering coal in the ship's bunker that set off the explosion in an adjoining ammunition locker.

In February 1898, the recovered bodies of the American sailors who died on the battleship were interred in the Colon Cemetery, in Havana. Nearly two years later they were exhumed and now 163 of the crew that were killed in 1898 are buried at Arlington National Cemetery, near the USS *Maine* Memorial.

Total American Casualties

The war was fought by regular U.S. Army troops and State Volunteers that are now known as the "National Guard." About 250,000 enlisted men and 11,000 officers served in this war.

Most of the volunteers came from New York, Pennsylvania, Illinois and Ohio. Even though the Spanish-American War was short, still 3,289 troops died before the peace treaty with Spain was signed in Paris. During the Spanish-American war, relatively few Americans were killed or wounded, when compared to the Civil War that had been fought just four decades prior. The Spanish-American war instilled an optimism that left many Americans believing in a national exceptionalism that continues to this day. It reinstated the United States into a singular union again and caused Europe to recognize America as a powerful player on the world stage.

Other American military personnel who were killed in the Spanish-American War are buried near the Spanish-American War Memorial in Arlington National Cemetery in Virginia.

Heroes

On November 2, 1899, eight members of the United States Navy were awarded the Congressional Medal of Honor for extraordinary heroism and service beyond the call of duty. On the night of June 2, 1898, they had volunteered to scuttle the collier USS *Merrimac*, with the intention of blocking the entry channel to Santiago de Cuba. On orders of Rear Admiral William T. Sampson, who was in command, their intention was to trap Spanish Admiral Cervera's fleet in the harbor.

Getting the USS *Merrimac* underway, the eight men navigated the ship towards a predetermined location where sinking her would seal the port. Their course knowingly took them within the range of the Spanish ships and the shore batteries. The sailors were well aware of the danger this put them into, however they put their mission first. Once the Spanish gunners saw what was happening, they realized what the Americans were up to and started firing their heavy artillery from an extremely close range. The channel leading into Santiago is narrow, preventing the ship from taking any evasive action. The American sailors were like fish in a barrel and the Spanish gunners were relentless. In short order, the heavy shelling from the Spanish shore batteries disabled the rudder of the *Merrimac* and caused the ship to sink prematurely. The USS *Merrimac* went down without achieving its objective of obstructing navigation and sealing the port.

Taken prisoner by the Spaniards, the eight courageous men listed below were later returned to the United States Navy as part of a prisoner exchange.

<u>Lieutenant George Charrette, USN</u> was born in Lowell, Massachusetts, on June 6, 1867. He enlisted in the United States Navy on September 24, 1884, and served as a Gunner's Mate Third Class. Charrette retired from the Navy in 1925 and died on February 7, 1938, in Lowell, Massachusetts. He is buried in Arlington National Cemetery.

<u>Claus Kristian Randolph Clausen</u> was born on December 9, 1869, in Denmark. He enlisted in the Navy from the State of New York and served on the USS *New York* as a Coxswain. In the failed attempt to block the entry channel to Santiago, he was rescued by the Spanish and became a prisoner-of-war. Clausen died on December 23, 1958, at the U.S. Naval Hospital located in St. Albans, New York. Clausen's cremains are interred in the U.S. Columbarium in Middle Village, New York.

<u>Warrant Officer Osborn Warren Deignan, USN</u> was born in Iowa on February 24, 1873, enlisted in the U.S. Navy in 1894 and was later promoted to the rank of Warrant Officer. As an officer, Deignan served in various posts and on various ships throughout the Navy until retiring in 1906. He died in Colorado

on April 16, 1916, at 43 years of age and is buried at Forest Lawn Memorial Park cemetery in Glendale, California.

Rear Admiral Richard P. Hobson, USN was born on August 17, 1870. He served as a Navy Lieutenant during the Spanish-American War and was later promoted to the rank of Rear Admiral and served as a Congressman from Alabama from 1907 until 1915. After leaving Congress, Hobson became involved in promoting the prohibition of alcohol and became known as the "The Father of American Prohibition." Admiral Hobson died on March 16, 1937, in New York City, at the age of 66.

Francis Kelly was born in Massachusetts on July 5, 1860, and was a "Watertender" aboard the USS *Merrimac*. Kelly remained in the Navy after the Spanish-American War and ultimately became a Chief Machinist's Mate. He died in Glasgow, Scotland on May 19, 1938, and is buried there at the Sandymount Cemetery.

Daniel Montague was born on October 22, 1866, in Wicklow, Ireland. He enlisted in the U.S. Navy during the mid-1890's and served on the USS *New York* as the Chief Master-at-Arms during the Spanish-American War. Montague was promoted to the rank of Warrant Officer on June 15, 1898. After many tours of duty he retired. Montague died at 45 years of age and is buried at the U.S. Naval Academy Cemetery in Annapolis, Maryland.

John E. Murphy was born on May 3, 1869. He enlisted in the U.S. Navy and served as a Coxswain on the battleship USS *Iowa* (BB-4) during the Spanish-American War. On June 15, 1898, while in Spanish custody, Murphy was promoted to the rank of Warrant Officer. After serving on numerous ships as a Boatswain, he retired on August 1, 1905. Chief Boatswain Murphy died on April 9, 1941, at 71 years of age and is buried in Fort Rosecrans National Cemetery, San Diego, California.

<u>George Fredrick Phillips</u> was born on March 8, 1862, in Saint John, New Brunswick, Canada. He joined the United States Navy in March 1898 in Galveston, Texas. Phillips became a Machinist First Class and displayed extraordinary heroism throughout the Spanish bombardment during their operation. Phillips was discharged from the Navy in August 1903, and died a year later at the age of 42 in Cambridge, Massachusetts. His body was returned to Canada where he was interred at the Fernhill Cemetery in his hometown of Saint John, New Brunswick.

The Destruction of the Spanish Fleet

On February 17, 1898, Captain William T. Sampson, USN was the President of the Board of Inquiry, investigating the explosion that sank the USS *Maine*. On March 26, 1898, he was given command of the Navy's North Atlantic Squadron, with the temporary rank of Rear Admiral. Aboard the flagship USS *New York*, he sailed to Havana from Key West where he bombarded the city for several days, resulting in minor damage to the city. As part of his duties, he sealed Havana harbor and supervised the blockade of the island.

Attempting to find the Spanish fleet commanded by Admiral Pascual Cervera y Topete, Admiral Sampson sailed to San Juan with U.S. Army General William R. Shafter, where they captured the city. At the same time, unknown to Sampson, the Spanish fleet had sailed from the Cape Verde Islands to Santiago de Cuba. On May 29th, the whereabouts of the Spanish fleet was discovered and using the blockade, they trapped the ships in the harbor.

Early on the morning of July 3, 1898, Cervera's fleet started to come out of the harbor. At the time, Sampson was ashore with General Shafter, strategizing an attack on Santiago.

Commodore Winfield Scott Schley, who had been on station with his "Flying Squadron" at Cienfuegos, Cuba, left his position to refuel in Key West, without Admiral Sampson's knowledge. When he received orders to investigate the situation at Santiago, he waited for three days before returning to Cuba. On July 1, 1898, arriving on the USS *Brooklyn* he positioned his squadron offshore from Santiago de Cuba, forming a bulwark which controlled the narrow entrance to the harbor. On July 3rd, some of the most modern American warships engaged the older Spanish ships as they appeared. In a fierce battle lasting five hours, every Spanish vessel was sunk or destroyed. The following morning Admiral Sampson sent his well-known message... "The Fleet under my command offers the nation, as a Fourth of July present, the whole of Cervera's Fleet." His message never mentioned the involvement of anyone other than himself, even though he was never involved in any of the fighting. At the request of Admiral Schley, this led to a Naval Board of Inquiry hearing regarding the part he played in the battle.

Rear Admiral Sampson was awarded the honor of being a companion of the Military Order of the Loyal Legion of the United States and received the Military Order of Foreign Wars. In October 1901, he was also awarded an honorary doctorate by Yale University. On May 6, 1902, at 62 years of age Admiral Samson died in Washington, D.C. and was buried at Arlington National Cemetery. His legacy includes four destroyers, three schools, a New York State Park and Sampson Hall at the Naval Academy, all named in his honor.

Sampson didn't praise Schley's role in the battle because of professional jealousy. On April 14, 1899, Schley was promoted to the rank of Rear Admiral, however on September 12, 1901, a court of inquiry was opened. Schley was charged with many counts of negligence and that he failed to proceed to Santiago promptly. One officer actually accused Schley of cowardice. However the respected Admiral George Dewey praised Schley on several counts, and gave him the credit for destroying the Spanish fleet.

No action was taken, and the outcome vindicated Schley. However the Secretary of the Navy John Davis Long supported Sampson on the grounds of his rank and seniority. In 1902, Schley appealed the verdict to President Theodore Roosevelt, who backed Secretary Long's decision. Rear Admiral Winfield Scott Schley died on October 2, 1911, and was buried with all military honors at Arlington National Cemetery.

Spanish Prisoners of War

The USS *Saint Louis* and the USS *Harvard* arrived in Portsmouth, New Hampshire on July 10, 1898, carrying a total of 1,562 Spanish prisoners. Approximately 1,700 Spanish prisoners of war were eventually divided between POW camps in Annapolis, Maryland, and the Navy Yard near Portsmouth, New Hampshire, which is actually in Kittery, Maine. To guard them U.S. Marines were brought in from the Boston Navy Yard.

The internment camp was known as Camp Long, which was named for Secretary of the Navy John Long. From July 11, 1898, to September 12, 1898, the stockade held 1,612 Spanish prisoners, including Admiral Pascual Cervera. After a time these prisoners were granted parole and allowed fifteen days of liberty, permitting them open access to Seavey's Island in

Kittery, Maine, as well as the Navy Yard, and the town of Portsmouth, New Hampshire. Despite the best efforts by both U.S. Navy and Spanish physicians, thirty-one prisoners died during their incarceration. On September 12, 1898, the prisoners were released and returned to Spain on the S/S *City of Rome*.

On April 12, 1916, the Spanish transport ship *Almirante Lobo* came to take the bodies of the Spanish prisoners that had died during their internment. U.S. Marines from the Portsmouth Naval Shipyard and U.S. Navy personnel from the cruiser USS *Washington*, the USS *Sacramento* and the USS *Southery* served as honor guards as the coffins were brought to the pier. The caskets were then carried on board with pomp and dignity for their final voyage to Spain, as a bugler from the USS *Washington* sounded taps.

There are still three Spanish sailors buried in the Captain Theodore H. Conaway Memorial Naval Cemetery near the Naval Medical Center in Portsmouth, Virginia. On April 17, 2012, Spanish Navy personnel, assigned to the frigate SPS *Blas de Lezo*, came to pay their respects and laid wreaths on the graves. The Spanish sailors were not forgotten....

"Everyone is a prisoner of his own experiences. No one can eliminate prejudices - just recognize them." Edward R. Murrow, an American broadcast journalist and my late neighbor in Pawling, NY

The Panama Canal

The Panama Canal Zone was the only Latin American territory not acquired as a result of the war with Spain; however it was governed as if it had been. As president, Theodore Roosevelt understood the importance of a canal connecting the Atlantic to the Pacific Ocean. It would allow the United States to move its fleet from one coast to the other in a relatively short time, which had been a major problem during the war with Spain. To facilitate this he received authorization from Congress to purchase the assets of the failed French attempt to build a canal. The primary obstacle was in acquiring the necessary land to build a canal across the Isthmus of the Americas, which prior to 1903 was part of Colombia. When the United States showed an interest in building the canal, the Colombian government immediately demanded a larger percentage of the tolls than had been previously agreed upon with the French. Negotiations dragged on through 1902 and into 1903. Early in 1903, the United States signed a treaty with the Colombian government, giving the United States a strip of land 6 miles wide, from the Caribbean to the Pacific Ocean. On August 12, 1903, the irate Colombian Senate unanimously voted down the agreement and refused to give the United States the land. Panamanian insurgents with the backing of the United States perpetrated a revolt against the Colombian government, causing Colombia to lose the coveted parcel of land north of its present border. The fledgling nation of Panama was protected from Colombia by a dense jungle and the might of the United States.

On November 3, 1903, after 57 years of policing Bogotá's interests, the United States, looking out for its own best interests, sided with Panama against Colombia. A treaty was quickly drafted between the two new allies, giving Panama $10,000,000 of investment money, plus $250,000 per year in perpetuity. It also allowed the United States to purchase the remaining French assets that had been left behind. On November 18th, with the signing of the Hay-Bunau-Varilla Treaty, the Panama Canal Zone was formed.

The Panamanian government turned the land known as the Canal Zone over to the United States. The American flag was raised over the Zone on May 4, 1904, demonstrating that the United States had sovereign ownership of the Panama Canal Zone.

Let's Spend our Next Vacation in Cuba...

Disfrute en Cuba, Poster
"Enoy Yourself in Cuba"

The Exciting Story of Cuba.... Part 4

Entering the 20th Century

The Platt Amendment

The Platt Amendment was designed to prevent foreign intervention into Cuban affairs, but as a safeguard it allowed such intervention by the United States. Although it was initially rejected by the Cuban assembly, pressure was applied onto the smaller nation by the powerful democracy to its north. Eventually under duress, Cuba accepted the terms of the Platt Amendment in 1902, and dutifully integrated it into their Constitution.

In 1899, Theodore Roosevelt was quoted as saying... "The guns that thundered off Manila and Santiago left us echoes of glory, but they also left us a legacy of duty. If we drove out a medieval tyranny only to make room for savage anarchy we had better not have begun the task at all. It is worse than idle to say that we have no duty to perform, and can leave to their fates the islands we have conquered. Such a course would be the course of infamy. It would be followed at once by utter chaos in the wretched islands themselves. Some stronger manlier power would have to step in and do the work, and we would have shown ourselves weaklings, unable to carry to successful completion the labors that great and high-spirited nations are eager to undertake."

"Far better is it to dare mighty things, to win glorious triumphs, even though checkered by failure... than to rank with those poor spirits who neither enjoy nor suffer much, because they live in a gray twilight that knows not victory nor defeat." Theodore Roosevelt, the 26th President of the United States

Cuban Independence

On May 20, 1902, Cuba declared its independence and José Martí became a legend. He is still considered a hero by all Cubans, and his birthday, January 28th, is celebrated every year as a national holiday. José Martí is remembered for his writings, his devotion to Cuban freedom and for the abolishment of slavery. Some of his writings are found in the front part of this book.

American Appointed Governors

After the war, the United States appointed military governors for Puerto Rico, the Philippines and Cuba, as well as the Panama Canal Zone, which had been wrested away from Colombia.

Leonard Wood was a physician who served as a line officer when he commanded the Rough Riders during the Battle of San Juan Hill, for which he was awarded the Congressional Medal of Honor. In 1898, he was appointed the Military Governor of Santiago de Cuba.

From January 1, 1899, until December 23, 1899, John R. Brooke served as the first military governor of Cuba, after having been the Governor of Puerto Rico. Previously, in June of 1864 during the American Civil War, he was critically wounded during the battle of Cold Harbor in Virginia. In 1890, Brooke served on the western U.S. frontier where, on orders of General Nelson Miles, he rushed the 7th U.S. Cavalry to Wounded Knee, South Dakota. It was the 7th Cavalry that was responsible for killing more than 300 Indian men, women and children who were being relocated to the Sioux reservation at Pine Ridge, South Dakota. In 1897 during the Spanish-American War, he became a major general and was assigned to command the First Army Corps. General Brooke retired July 21, 1902, and lived in Philadelphia until his death in 1926. He is buried at Arlington National Cemetery.

Major General Leonard Wood followed Brooke, becoming the second military governor of Cuba on December 23, 1899, through May 20, 1902. As governor and being a physician, he was instrumental in making improvements to the medical and sanitary conditions in Cuba. Prior to the Spanish-American War, Wood was stationed at Fort Huachuca, Arizona, where he participated in the campaign against Geronimo in 1886. He distinguished himself for carrying dispatches 100 miles through hostile territory and for assuming command of an infantry detachment that had lost its officers in hand-to-hand combat against the Apaches. For his bravery, he was awarded the Medal of Honor. In 1910, Wood was named Army Chief of Staff by President Taft. In 1920, Wood attempted to make a bid for the U.S. Presidency on the Republican ticket. When this failed, as a civilian he was appointed Governor General of the Philippines, a post he held until 1927. Wood died of a brain tumor on August 7, 1927, in Boston, Massachusetts, and is buried at Arlington National Cemetery.

Major General George Winfield Davis served as a military Governor of Puerto Rico before becoming the first Military Governor of the Panama Canal Zone. The Panama Canal

Company operated the Canal Zone, along with the U.S. Military, until October 1, 1979, when the Panama Canal Commission took over its governance. On December 31, 1999, the Panama Canal Zone reverted back to Panama. Davis joined the 11th Connecticut Infantry Regiment and served as a sergeant in the Quartermaster Corps during the American Civil War. In 1862, he saw action fighting in the battle of Antietam near Sharpsburg, Maryland. By the end of the American Civil War, he had attained the rank of Major. At the beginning of the Spanish-American War, Davis was promoted to Lieutenant Colonel and held the temporary rank of Brigadier General of Volunteers. In 1902, he was promoted to the rank of Major General. After retiring, Davis became chairman of the American Red Cross from 1907 to 1915. General Davis died in Washington, D.C., on July 12, 1918, at the age of 78.

Cuba's First President

Tomás Estrada Palma was a Cuban-born American citizen, who was a moderate and had worked with José Martí in New York. He became the leader of the Cuban Revolutionary Party after Marti's death. On December 31, 1901, Tomás Estrada Palma was duly elected to become the first President of Cuba. Estrada Palma and the Cuban Congress assumed governance on May 20, 1902, which then became the official birthdate of the Cuban Republic.

In 1906, Estrada Palma appealed to the United States to intervene in the revolt that threatened his second term. As Secretary of War during the Roosevelt administration, William Howard Taft was sent to Cuba, after having been the first civilian Governor-General of the Philippines. For the short period of time from September 29, 1906, until October 13, 1906, Taft was the Provisional Governor of Cuba. During this time,

5,600 U.S. Army troops were sent to Cuba to reassert American authority, giving Taft the muscle to set up another provisional government. Later, on March 4, 1909, Taft was elected the 27th President of the United States.

The Last American Governor

American lawyer, judge and diplomat Charles Magoon, having been governor of the Panama Canal Zone, was sent to be the civilian American Provisional Governor of Cuba, with absolute authority and the backing of the U.S. military. His term as governor lasted from October 13, 1906, until January 28, 1909. During this time, he supervised the construction of 125 miles of highway. He also saw to the reorganization of the Cuban army. Having suppressed the Liberal Party riots, he was well regarded by Republicans in the United States. However, he remained unpopular amongst Cubans and was viewed as corrupt and interfering. The newspapers accused him of returning Cuba to the corrupt practices of colonial times. In 1920 after his retirement, Magoon died in Washington, D.C., following surgery for acute appendicitis.

Labor Conditions

Working conditions under Spanish rule were largely unregulated. For the workers in the mines, conditions were deplorable and unsafe for almost 400 years. It wasn't until after the Spanish-American War that the Cuban workers could expect their conditions to improve. Being very slow to improve, it took until World War II before modern and safer mining techniques were adopted.

When the Cuban flag first flew over the capitol, the people placed great expectations on the government. For one, they expected sweeping improvements in labor laws. However on May 26, 1902, reality set in when the newly formed Cuban Congress called for a conservative economy and demanded public tranquility. Other than that, very little was accomplished by the representatives. During those first few years, the fragile republic suffered from increasingly radical politics and social problems. On November 24, 1902, a general strike was declared in protest. The workers united and, expecting progressive changes to be made, were so furious that guards had to be hired to assist the police in maintaining order, bringing the chances of progress in the workplace to a halt.

Palma's Administration

In spite of a shaky start to the Republic, Estrada Palma's administration built over 200 miles of roads, resulting in property prices on the island to increase seven times over. Taking a progressive approach during his administration resulted in an increase to Cuba's inflation. He also gave government employees lavish salary raises and increased the pensions received by the remaining veterans of the Army of Liberation.

In 1906, Estrada Palma was re-elected, even though this outcome was claimed to be fraudulent by the Liberal Party. The revolt that occurred in July of 1906, threatened the young Republic. Estrada Palma's appeal to the United States to intervene in Cuban affairs, effectively ended his Presidency when the United States established another provisional government, which lasted until 1909 under the unpopular rule of Charles Magoon.

José Miguel Gómez

José Miguel Gómez was born on July 6, 1858, in picturesque Sancti Spíritus, centrally located in the former Las Villas Province. He was a general during the War of Independence and was elected to the presidency on November 4, 1908. With peace restored, he assumed the office on January 28, 1909, thereby returning Cuba to democratic rule. President Gómez became the second elected president of the Republic, following two American-appointed military governors. His vice president was Alfredo de Zayas, who later became a formidable political adversary. At the beginning of his term, Gómez was well liked and considered to be a thoughtful and generous man who cared for the Cuban people, but this was soon to change.

Under his leadership, the government began subsidizing newspapers, with the intention of slanting the political editorials in his favor. Following this, it did not take long for outright corruption to creep into his administration, causing several major scandals and a complete reversal of the favorable public opinion he had enjoyed. Before long, people talked behind his back and he was given the descriptive nickname *El Tiburón*, "The Shark."

In February of 1909, favoring the military, Gómez went to the Cuban Congress for an increase in funding for the army. The Cuban army grew to a high of about 5,000 men, and his national budget went far beyond that of any previous administration. Although Cuba had won its independence from Spain, within the government there were still sympathizers supporting the former Spanish rule. The National Council of Veterans denounced their opponents and called them "Traitors and Guerillas." Although unrest continued to ferment, public sentiment remained with the veterans and against the pro-Spanish faction still festering among the civil servants.

On January 28, 1911, having lost heart, Gómez stated, "I wish to have the honor of being the first to oppose my own re-election." On April 25, 1912, he penned an open letter to General Machado stating that he would not run for a second term. However his problems were far from over.... Aside from the increasing political unrest among the general population, groups of hard working black laborers were starting to complain about their living and working conditions. This discontentment led to an unrelenting undercurrent as they started to organize. As this was happening, the administration issued a ban limiting immigration by any additional black Haitians and Jamaicans.

The conflict continued among the black workers and finally the Independent Party of Color, "*Partido Nacional de Color*," planned a mass demonstration. Throughout Cuba, newspapers portrayed the demonstration as a race war, creating an inordinate fear among white Cubans. The public was also reminded of the quarantine placed on ports in southeastern Cuba thirteen years before, because of malaria and yellow fever, which they blamed on the black immigrants.

The United States Ambassador, representing American interests, warned that there would be a use of military force if American lives and property could not be protected by the Cuban administration. On May 31, 1912, U.S. Marines from the United States gunboat, USS *Paducah*, landed at the seaside town of Daiquiri. Known for its iron mines, Daiquiri is located about 14 miles east of Santiago de Cuba in the Oriente Province.

On June 3, 1912, President Gómez, hoping to squash the ongoing protest, asked the Cuban Congress for the right to impose martial law. Finally, on July 18, 1912, a full-blown race war erupted. Throughout Cuba, black workers were hassled, arrested and even killed. By August, thousands of Afro-Cubans had lost their lives, including their leaders. After the race riots were quelled, many of Gómez' supporters, being fed up, shifted their allegiance to Vice President Zayas.

Gómez withdrew from the election of 1912, having lost popular support due to the intense violence in the streets, and on May 20, 1913, Gómez' term ended with Cuba in a total state of turmoil.

José Miguel Gómez remained active in Cuban politics; however, he never regained any of his former status. He died in New York City on June 13, 1921, at 62 years of age, and his remains were brought back to Havana for burial in the Colon Cemetery.

Mario García Menocal

Mario García Menocal was born on December 17, 1866, in the town of Jagüey, located southeast of Havana in the Matanzas Province of Cuba. His parents sent him to a prestigious preparatory school in New York State. Following high school he studied at the Maryland Agricultural College. He then attended, and later graduated from, the School of Engineering at Cornell University, where he was a fraternity member of Delta Kappa Epsilon. As a young man, he was a partisan in Cuba's fight for independence and he later became a prominent conservative politician.

On May 26, 1900, American interests held sway over education in the rural parts of Cuba. In part, this grew out of the funding that went to Harvard University in an attempt to Americanize Cuban education. Over 1,000 Cuban educators were sent to the United States during their summer vacation for the purpose of attending advanced programs in "Teacher Education." The hope was that these teachers would return to Cuba bestowing praises upon their "Big Brother" to the north. Between 1906 and 1909, two important laws regarding education were passed, in the hope of raising the country's educational standards and insuring acceptable certification of teachers. On May 16, 1915, in an attempt to "Cubanize" the schools again and wanting to improve the educational system, many teachers pushed for the construction of seven boarding schools for women. These Normal Schools, *"Escuela de Instruccion,"* were primarily expected to instruct teachers from the rural areas of the country. Of these, one was constructed in each of the provincial capitals and two were built in Havana. They were semi-military in nature and administered by the army. Strange as it seems, although the army is meant to protect the country from invaders, it is frequently called upon to serve in other capacities. In Cuba, they were called upon to provide for the education of schoolchildren in the rural districts, and they did a relatively good job of it. Of course, possibly the ulterior motive was to provide a way to brainwash and control people.

Menocal was elected to the presidency of Cuba in 1912 and assumed the office in 1913. During his administration, he strongly supported business and corporations as he had promised in his platform. While in office, Cuba also established its own currency, but the United States dollar continued to be the only paper money in circulation on the island until 1934.

In 1916, Cuban politics continued to be in turmoil. The Conservative Party used violence and other underhanded methods during Menocal's campaign for a second term. The Liberal Party in turn contested the results of the elections. However, when the dust settled, Menocal won the presidency for a second term.

It was on April 7, 1917, that Cuba sided with the United States against Germany and entered into World War I. During the war, a prosperous economic time was enjoyed in Cuba, primarily due to the escalating prices of sugar. However once the war ended, the sugar market plunged and the country slid into a recession.

In 1920, President Menocal hosted the Delta Kappa Epsilon Convention. It was the first time that the fraternity held its annual meeting outside of the United States and Menocal personally made certain that it became a successful social event. Then, on April 11, 1921, with new underwater cables having been laid, a direct telephone link between the United States and Cuba was completed. President Harding talked with President Menocal and renewed assurances of friendship and good will to the president of the island nation.

Although his presidency ended on May 20, 1921, Menocal remained in politics, running against Gerardo Machado for the Cuban presidency in 1924. In 1931, he attempted an unsuccessful revolution, following which he was forced into exile in the United States. Not giving up, he returned to Cuba and again unsuccessfully ran for the presidency for a final time in 1936. He died in Santiago de Cuba on September 7, 1941.

Alfredo Zayas

On February 21, 1861, Alfredo de Zayas was born in Havana into an aristocratic family that owned sugar plantations. As a young man he changed his name to Alfredo Zayas to better identify with the people. He became a respected leader of the last insurrection of liberation against Spain in 1895.

Later Zayas became known for his successful legal practice in Havana. He was active in Cuban literary circles and was the co-editor of the journal *"Cuba Literaria."* Zayas became involved in politics and served variously as prosecutor, judge and mayor of Havana. He rose to the position of President of the Senate in

1906, after which he became Cuba's vice-president during José Miguel Gómez' 1909 term as president and served as such until 1913. After Menocal's term expired in 1921, Zayas ran for the presidency as the candidate of the Cuban Popular Party, which had split away from Gómez' Liberal Party.

During this election, Zayas had the popular backing of the people to oppose Gómez and win. He wooed the women's vote by standing for their rights and promoted equal pay for equal work. Gómez complained that the election was rigged and although cheating certainly happened, Zayas beat Gómez for the presidency in the 1920 election.

Gómez went to the United States to meet with President Warren Harding, hoping to get the United States to intervene, but it was no surprise to anyone that the conservative American President took little interest in Cuban political rivalry. Some historians believe that Gómez would most likely have won, had the elections been fair and honest.

Alfredo Zayas opposed the United States' interference in Cuba and was against the Platt Amendment. Opponents constantly smeared his administration with accusations of corruption; however, these charges were never proven. Zayas enjoyed his presidency and seldom showed any signs of stress or apprehension. He was laid-back in his decisions and never arrested any of his critics. He always allowed full freedom of expression and never censored the press.

Using diplomacy, Zayas settled a long time dispute with the United States when he negotiated the return to Cuba of the Isle of Pines, which had been confiscated by U.S. troops during the Spanish-American War. On October 10, 1922, the first Cuban radio station, PWX, was inaugurated, and although Cuba was bankrupt after World War I, Zayas managed to obtain a fifty million dollar loan from the American philanthropist J.P. Morgan to initiate many social improvements, particularly in education.

After his term as president ended in May of 1925, Zayas never ran for a political office again. Instead, he spent his last years working on his literary and historical interests. He published the 2-volume *Lexicografia Antillana*, which still sells for $575.00 on Amazon. Alfredo Zayas died in Havana on April 11, 1934, when he was 73 years old.

Gerardo Machado

In 1925, Gerardo Machado defeated the conservative Mario García Menocal by an overwhelming majority, becoming Cuba's 5th president. A colleague of Alfredo Zayas, he was also a popular Liberal Party member, and a General during the Cuban War of Independence. General Machado was best known for rustling cattle from the Spanish Imperial Army livestock herd, with the good intention of feeding the poor during the revolution. This brazen act of kindness won him a great deal of support among the people. As President, he undertook many popular public projects, including the construction of a highway running the entire length of Cuba. During the beginning of his career as president, he had the National Capitol, as well as other government buildings, constructed in Havana. At first, he did much to modernize and industrialize the mostly agrarian nation.

Benito Mussolini and his march on Rome impressed Machado. He admired Mussolini for demanding that liberal King Victor Emmanuel III of Italy elevate the Fascists to power, instead of the Socialists. Although Mussolini originally started his political career as a Socialist, with power and wealth he became a staunch anti-communist. When he was elected as the 27th Prime Minister, he turned Italy into a Totalitarian State.

Machado's ambitions and admiration of Mussolini caused him to emulate the dictator and to misread the importance of his own office. Becoming a "legend in his own mind," he overreached and started down a slope that led to his administration's failure and earned him the hatred of the Cuban people. From the very beginning, he fought with the labor leaders and anarchists for control of the labor unions, which represented the workers in the sugar industry. This brought him into a serious conflict with the plantation owners who were mostly wealthy Cuban families and Americans. Keeping the cost of labor down became a priority for the Sugar Barons, and Machado used patriotism as a tool to keep the workers in line. His dictatorial, arrogant ways created unrest within the labor force, as well as with the politically active university students.

Anarchists Create Problems

The anarchist movement in Cuba was considered politically dangerous to the Cuban government. From the very beginning, they completely rejected any form of infringement on what they considered to be their rights. They even rejected the Cuban flag and reviled at the idea that schoolchildren had to pay allegiance to it. Their philosophy was the rejection of the state regardless of what form it took, so it came as no surprise that they would be willing to throw bombs or shoot people to get their way.

In its ultimate form, anarchists seek freedom not only from government but also from any infringement of their ideologies, such as religion and capitalism. They believe that they should be able to do whatever they want to, as long as it does not interfere with others, although bomb throwing and shooting people in the streets certainly seemed acceptable to them. At the Anarchist Congress of 1920 in Havana, they openly sided with the Bolshevik governments in the Russia of Lenin and Trotsky. The Cuban anarchists started to gain strength as early as 1921, when they handed out pamphlets and periodicals on the streets. They started organizing the workers during the unconcerned presidency of Alfredo Zayas. Their leader in 1923 was Alfredo López, who saw an opportunity to influence students by helping Julio Antonio Mella establish the Communist Party at the University of Havana.

By 1925, anarchists had become such a thorn in President Machado's side that he was compelled to persuade Congress to pass laws and physically restrict their aggressive activities. Shootings and bombings continued as they challenged the government at every turn, however eventually the police subdued them.

"Every anarchist is a baffled dictator." Benito *Mussolini Italian, journalist, and Fascist leader of Italy from 1922 until his demise in 1945*

Machado Tightens his Grip

Machado tried to retain a generous and honest public image, but the rot had already set in as politicians, including Senators, staked out their claim for the rights to the distribution of the national lottery tickets. Machado's son-in-law got his foot in the door and reaped the profits from Havana's *Compañia Cubana de Electricidad*, which controlled the utilities in the capital city. His close friends also did well, as they got most of the country's lucrative construction contracts. With a booming economy, 1925 was a great year for sugar production, and by keeping the cost of labor down Machado kept sugar profits up. During these prosperous times, the tyrannical president was responsible for the murder of over 147 people involved in the labor movement and as a result, the American Federation of Labor soundly censured him.

In October of 1925 after a series of bombings in Havana, the police arrested Alfredo López. Julio Mella, the Communist leader, saw the handwriting on the wall and fled the country. The next year, López was released from prison and was offered a cushy position with the Machado administration. Refusing the offer may have been a costly mistake. Continuing his violent anarchist activities, on July 20, 1926, after a series of bombings in Havana, he was abducted by the police. Although his followers searched for him, his remains were not found until after Machado was forced out of office in 1933.

With Alfredo López gone from the scene and Julio Antonio Mella out of the country, Machado had a new law enacted requiring half of the nation's labor force to be comprised of Cubans. Not being able to find employment, many of the anarchists who were Spaniards were forced to leave the country.

On August 13, 1926, in the midst of Machado's reign and without fanfare, Fidel Castro was born at his father's farm near Birán, in Oriente Province. At the time, Cuba only had six provinces, and Birán has since become part of the Holguín Province.

The Good Times that Didn't Last

Machado always had an eye for the ladies and enjoyed partying at the swankiest nightclubs in Havana. For a time he even owned his own club, which was the place for his political hacks to be seen. Machado was frequently there in the company of some of the most enticing ladies in the country.

Through a combination of threats and bribery, he maintained control of the Army. In April of 1928 the Cuban Congress at the behest of Machado passed a law barring any presidential nominations by any party other than the Liberal, Conservative and Popular parties. Interestingly enough Machado declared himself the only legal candidate for those parties, and thus ran for a second term unopposed. Not only had he overspent money from the national treasury, but now he also alienated the Cuban public, who denounced him as an authoritarian nationalist and tyrant. Students, labor unions and intellectuals branded him an outright dictator. It was during this time that Marxist thinking was gaining strength throughout the world. The Communist philosophy was also becoming ever more popular among intellectuals, professors and students at the *Universidad de La Havana*. Realizing that he was now in danger of losing control, Machado made a power grab and declared Martial Law in Cuba. Intent on holding on to power, he became even more despotic than ever, creating a secret police known to the people as *La Porra*, meaning a big stick! Machado became openly vindictive and did not hesitate to torture or even assassinate his foes in order to maintain tight sway over the Cuban population.

With the Great Depression of 1928, things only got worse. The economy, which was single-sided, was extremely dependent upon sugar. Poverty was widespread, and even necessities all but disappeared, leaving the Cuban people destitute and in misery.

"The happiness of society is the end of government."
John Adams, a political philosopher and the second
president of the United States. He also said: "People
and nations are forged in the fires of adversity."

The Downfall of Machado

It became ever more difficult for President Gerardo Machado to
hang on to power. The Communist Party that Julio Antonio
Mella had founded some years before was now bombing hotels
and theaters in Havana. Labor leaders organized a general
strike that slowed down the country's economy and helped end
Machado's régime. There was chaos in the streets, causing the
death of many innocent people. The conservative veterans of
the Cuban War of Independence turned on Machado and,
wearing the green shirts of the anti-Machado groups, they
nipped at his flanks. For every attack on the Machado régime
there was retaliation in kind. On December 28, 1930, the police
even shut down the Havana Yacht Club, based on a tip that
anti-Machado activists were using boats to flee the island.

Finally, early in May of 1933, President Franklin Delano
Roosevelt could no longer ignore what was happening in
neighboring Cuba, and sent Ambassador Sumner Welles,
whom he had appointed Assistant Secretary of Latin American
Affairs, to Havana as his special envoy.

Roosevelt gave Welles instruction to renegotiate the Platt
Amendment in such a way as to preclude the United States
from having to intervene in Cuba's domestic problems. Further,
he was to convince Cuban President Machado to step down
and make room for democratic reform.

Arriving May 8, 1933, Sumner Welles sought to convince Machado to reinstate the constitutional guarantees that had been taken from the people in June of 1931, and to resign and support an orderly transfer of power. Welles made President Machado a final offer of safe passage out of Cuba, providing he leave office.

Many of Machado's followers, including Cuban War of Independence Veterans, Civic Leaders, and Army Officers, reinforced this decision, but Machado was not yet in the mood to listen. With contempt, he denounced the American intervention and told Welles, in no uncertain arrogant terms, that, "The re-establishment of the guarantees is a prerogative of the President of Cuba, and will be done when the President considers it necessary."

Frustrated, Welles turned to the leaders of the Cuban army, and with the support of General Herrera and his staff, he negotiated an end to Machado's presidency. Finally on August 12, 1933, realizing that he had run out of options, Machado fled Cuba for the Bahamas, leaving his country in a terrible state of confusion. In a hailstorm of bullets, he departed from Cuba in an American-built twin-engine, 8-seat amphibious aircraft called "The Explorer's Air Yacht." More specifically, it was a Sikorsky S-38 amphibian aircraft originally owned by Pan American, but which at the time was owned by *Cubana*, which in turn was owned by Pan American. Although confusing, this story is true.

Gerardo Machado spent several years in exile, first in the Bahamas and then in Europe and Montreal, before being granted an entry visa to the United States.

From the very beginning of his exile, Machado stayed in contact with his supporters, many of whom also lived in exile, hoping to return to Cuba. The "Plan Miami," as it was called, was drafted on October 21, 1934, and called for the recognition of an interim government that would oversee changes in Cuba's Constitutional law as well as guaranteeing Machado's return to the presidency. The plan contained the reorganization of the Cuban military and the settling of the financial obligations of Machado's former government with the United States. It was all a pipe dream, as Machado, aged 67, died in Miami Beach on March 29, 1939, without ever returning to Cuba.

Machado had been very popular when he was first elected in 1925, but he allowed the power of his office to go to his head. His presidency could have made a significant difference in Cuba, but in the final analysis, he was just another dictator during an era when many countries came under the heels of fascist rule!

"Cuba ought to be free and independent, and the government should be turned over to the Cuban people." William McKinley, 25th President of the United States

The Exciting Story of Cuba.... Part 5

Communism

The Development of Communism in Cuba

At the turn of the nineteenth century, the Cuban population was comprised primarily of white Caucasians, who were Spanish-born colonists called peninsulars or *peninsulares*. Their descendants of mixed races, *mestizos*, and Spanish Nationals who came in from the Canary Islands were known as creoles or *criollos*.

By the middle of the century, the largest portion of the population was comprised of blacks, who had been brought in to work as slaves. There was also a sizable population of Chinese who came to work as cheap laborers. With the mixing of the races, the growing *mestizo* group increased in its relative size during the 1960's, particularly when many of the white Cubans left the island for the United States.

Initially, after the advent of the Cuban Republic, at about the turn of the twentieth century, little was made of the social and racial differences between people. Segregation was relatively unknown until it was introduced from the southern tier of the United States. After that time, a feeling of superiority developed among many of the more affluent white people, and unfortunately a new caste system of social stratification found its way into the fabric of Cuba.

The philosophy of Communism was first presented when Karl Marx and Friedrich Engels co-published *The Communist Manifesto* on February 21, 1848. During that year Marx was the editor of the *Neue Rheinische Zeitung*, a controversial newspaper in which he published pro-communistic articles. In 1848, a series of revolts led by revolutionary socialists caused Marx to be routinely harassed by the police in Germany, Belgium and France. The only country that offered him freedom from persecution was England, so Marx and his family moved to London in August of 1849.

Once settled in London, Marx started writing newspaper articles promoting his socialistic philosophy. Both Marx and Engels began writing editorials, which were distributed worldwide in foreign newspapers. Marx became a European correspondent for the *New-York Daily Tribune* that had been established by Horace Greeley in 1841. To a great extent, up until that time the world had not heard of Communism, but that was soon to change.

In Russia, Vladimir Lenin was the leader of a group of revolutionaries who followed a Marxist philosophy. He introduced his form of Bolshevik Communism into Russia in 1912. It was with the "October Revolution" of 1917 that Bolshevism took root in Russia. Lenin became the Chairman of the Council of People's Commissars of the Russian Soviet Federative Socialist Republic, a position he held from November 8, 1917, until December 30, 1922, when he became the Chairman of the Council of People's Commissars of the Soviet Union, better known as the Premier of the Soviet Union. (*The Russians have a thing for lengthy titles.*) He held this office until March of 1923, when at 53 years of age he died in Gorki, Russia.

Lenin had a medical history of strokes; however, it was his third stroke that caused his demise. Controversy surrounds his actual death, but most historians agree with the Communist Party's version, that after lingering for almost a year, with difficulty writing and speaking, Lenin finally succumbed to his third and last stroke on January 21, 1924.

There is also the theory that he died of arteriosclerosis or syphilis. An autopsy confirmed that for some years he had suffered from both of these illnesses, however they were seemingly not the cause of his death. There is also the more sinister speculation that Stalin may have poisoned him, after Lenin aligned himself with Leon Trotsky. Since both his body and brain have been preserved, there is still a chance that the truth of his death may be determined. After Lenin's death, his deputy Alexei Rykov took over the reins of government and became the Chairman of the Soviet Union.

As the leader of the Revolutionary Party in Russia, Vladimir Lenin promised to liberate the working class in his country. In Italy, Benito Mussolini founded Fascism, which has been defined by some as Socialism with a Capitalistic veneer. The rules were simple, if you did not agree with the government; you were wrong and deserved to die.

The Axis Alliance of World War II grew out of the Anti-Comintern Pact, an anti-communist treaty that was directed against a Communist organization called the "Third International." It had its start when it was signed by Germany and Japan in 1936, with Italy joining the following year. Eventually fourteen countries, many of which had fascist governments, signed this treaty. The war ended in 1945 with the defeat of the Axis powers and an end to their alliance.

Hitler's rise to power in Germany followed the Fascist protocol, as did Francisco Franco in Spain, who ruled between 1936 until his death in 1975.

Both Communist and Fascist régimes tended to become dictatorships even when they had their start with democratic elections. People everywhere were disappointed and sought freedom from government oppression and, where they could, they experimented with their options. Their choices included a Liberal Democracy, Conservative Capitalism, Fascism, Socialism, Marxism or perhaps even a Benevolent Dictatorship, which sometimes included Royalty.

Cuba was no exception. With the end of the Ten Years' War, and later the Spanish-American War, their experimentation began. A free country, where the people matter, is seldom a gift and usually a struggle, however the stakes were high. Once free of Spanish domination, Cuba became such a Country!

"I spent a great deal of time with "Che" Guevara while I was in Havana. I believe he was far less a mercenary than he was a freedom fighter." Maureen O'Hara, Singer and Movie Actress

Pablo Lafargue

On January 15, 1842, Pablo (Paul) Lafargue was born in Santiago de Cuba. Although his mother had him registered as a French citizen at the French Consulate, historians credit him as being the first known Cuban communist, although he spent more time in France than he ever did in Cuba. His father, Francisco Lafargue, was a wealthy French landowner of coffee plantations in the Oriente Province of Cuba, and his mother was Ana Virginia Armaignac, a Creole woman from Kingston,

Jamaica. They came to Cuba at the time of the Haitian Revolution at the turn of the nineteenth century. Lafargue's early schooling was in Santiago de Cuba, until his family moved back to his father's hometown of Bordeaux, France, where he continued his secondary school studies.

As a young man, Lafargue went to the University of Paris and although his interests were primarily political, he majored in medicine. As a disciple of Karl Marx and Auguste Blanqui, he became involved with the controversial International Students' Congress in Liège, France. Their clandestine meetings in October of 1865 did not go unnoticed by the university administration. As a consequence, two law students and five medical students were reprimanded for atheistic and socialistic activities. Lafargue was punished by being banned from all French universities. Wanting to continue his education, he moved to England where he enrolled at Saint Bartholomew Hospital School in London. (The school is now a part of the University of London.) It was here that Lafargue met Karl Marx and Marx's second daughter Laura, whom he married in London in 1868. In time, they had three sons, all of whom unfortunately died as infants.

At his first opportunity, Lafargue moved back to France, where he gave up practicing medicine to become a political journalist. Following the Franco-Prussian War, the Paris Commune, a revolutionary, socialist government, ruled Paris from March 18 until May 28, 1871. Fearing for their lives, Lafargue and his wife Laura fled to Spain. The week of May 21, 1871, became known as the "bloody week" in France, as about 20,000 insurrectionists, known as Communards, were killed on the streets of Paris by government troops. Once safely in Spain, the young couple settled down in the Spanish capital of Madrid, where Lafargue contacted revolutionaries who were predominately anarchists.

Single-mindedly, Lafargue led the anarchists towards Marxist principles and helped them organize their leadership. In 1872 he represented this Spanish group of activists at The Hague's "Congress of the International Workingmen's Association." After writing an inflammatory article against Madrid's new Federal Council, called *The Federation of Madrid*," he was expelled from Spain and moved back to London.

Living in 1880's London, which was basically the England that Charles Dickens portrayed in *Oliver Twist, David Copperfield* and *A Tale of Two Cities*, Lafargue became editor of the French language newspaper *L'Egalite*, published in London. As a political activist and journalist, he wrote leftist articles and editorials, attempting to reorganize the French Workers' movement. Pablo Lafargue is best known for writing an anti-work book, *The Right to Be Lazy*. He claimed that combining not working with human creativity, is the essence of human progress. In 1882, he returned to France where he directed the newly organized "French Workers' Party." In 1891 while in police custody, interestingly enough he was elected to the French Parliament, becoming the first Socialist to ever hold a parliamentary position.

In 1908, Lafargue moved to the picturesque French village of Draveil, a community in the southern suburbs, a mere 12 miles from the center of Paris. Here he unified the various socialist parties into one single party to fight the opposition Social Democrat Reformist Party. Unbeknownst to others, he had long before decided to end his life before reaching the age of 70. In his last letter, he wrote that he did not want old age to strip him of his physical and mental powers, and wanted to end his life while still healthy in body and mind. To accomplish this he injected his wife and himself with a hypodermic of cyanide acid. The last sentences of his final letter read: "The cause to which I have been devoted for forty-five years will triumph. Long live Communism! Long live the "Second International!"

Although Pablo Lafargue spent most of his life in Europe, he is recognized as the first Communist of Cuba. Lafargue's status has also been elevated and he is now considered a national hero by the current Cuban government!

"There are many who lust for the simple answers of doctrine or decree. They are on the left and right. They are not confined to a single part of the society. They are terrorists of the mind." A. Bartlett Giamatti, Late President of Yale University

Communism Takes Hold

It is amazing how the pieces of history sometimes come together to form an interesting, historical vignette. In this case artists, intellectuals and politicians interacted, creating a murder mystery that is worthy of being a Hollywood movie script. The roaring twenties were an exciting intellectual era throughout most of the world, and Havana was no exception. People spent time in coffee houses and cafés discussing the events of the time, as well as expressing a renewed interest in Fredrich Engels' *"Condition of the Working Class in England,"* Georg Hegel's *Theory of the Unity of Opposites* and Karl Marx's views in the *Communist Manifesto*. In Russia, Lenin followed by Stalin, had firmly installed their economic concept of socialism, blended with a dictatorship, to rule the masses. Leftist leaning students, authors and poets in Cuba viewed the possibility of a communistic government as their grand experiment. Some of the students at the University of Havana, such as Blas Roca, Aníbal Escalante, Julio Antonio Mella and Fabio Grobart, were the original founders of the Cuban Communist Party. Grobart, who was Jewish and born in Poland, was considered the party's historian. It is controversial, but he also purportedly claimed to have recruited Fidel Castro into the Communist fold in 1948. Following the 1959 revolution that brought Fidel Castro to power, Grobart was considered a top planner in guiding Cuba's revolution ideologically and served on the party's Central Committee as a Member of Parliament. In his later years, he again became the party's historian. Fabio Grobart died in Havana on October 21, 1994, at 89 years of age.

A popular Cuban writer at that time was Mariblanca Sabas Aloma, who championed the feminist movement and published her thoughts in *El Cubano Libre*. She was also a full-time, left-leaning columnist for the weekly magazine *Carteles*.

The conditions under which workers lived during the 1920's were dreadful, and their wages were miniscule when compared to the long hours of work required of them. The life style of the working class was miserable and beyond comparison with how the elite lived. Dockworkers and workers in the sugar industry were attempting to improve their income by unionizing. Their battle cry being *¡Trabajadores del mundo uníos!* or "Workers of the World Unite!" was the same as in the rest of the world. With their economic conditions so deplorable, there was a groundswell of people ready to take Cuba into the uncharted waters of Communism.

"Communism doesn't work because people like to own stuff." Frank Zappa, American jazz musician

The Exciting Story of Cuba.... Part 6

A Tale of Intrigue, Mystery and Murder

Julio Antonio Mella

The principal character of this story, which is set in Cuba and Mexico, is "Julio Antonio Mella" who, at birth, was named Nicanor McPartland by his mother. In 1898, at seventeen years of age, his Irish mother Cecilia McPartland came to New York on the *S/S Campania*. Soon after arriving, she moved to the flamboyant city of New Orleans, where she met Julio's father Nicanor Mella, a dapper, much older and married Dominican man, who was the son of a war hero of the Dominican Revolution. He was a haberdasher and tailor by trade, and owned an upscale tailor shop in the quaint section of Old Havana. Doing what was very common in Cuba, and virtually accepted by the community with a "wink, wink," he set up the oh-so-willing, young Cecilia in a nearby house. With this arrangement, it did not take long before she had two sons by him, young Nicanor McPartland who was born on March 25, 1903, and Cecilio McPartland, born in 1906. In their household discussions, politics was always a lively topic during the early years of the new Cuban Republic.

Havana has always been a hot, damp city with frequent rain that nourishes the ugly black mold that is marbled all over the sides of the city's old buildings. Partially because of this, many of the residents living in the city suffer with respiratory ailments causing them to become chronically ill. Julio's mother Cecilia was compelled to return to New Orleans in order to seek medical attention for a persistent cough, brought on by a respiratory ailment most likely caused by this vile fungus. Not having enough funds to keep her children with her, she sent her boys back to stay with their father in Havana. It was during this time that young Nicanor's name was changed to "Julio Antonio Mella" by Nicanor's wife, Mercedes. When Mercedes died the following year, the boys, retaining their new names, were returned to their natural mother who enrolled them in the New Orleans' public school system.

Leaving high school, Mella was still underage when he enlisted in the U.S. Army. On hearing this, his father, objecting to his serving in the United States military, presented Julio's birth certificate at the U.S. Consulate in Havana, whereby he was released from the service and returned to Havana. When Julio returned to Cuba, his father first sent him to Academia Newton and then to the prestigious Catholic private preparatory school, *Escolapios of Guanabacoa*. Being a gifted young man but certainly unconventional and extremely outspoken, Julio was expelled from the prep school and was sent to a public high school in Havana, from which he successfully graduated. Then in 1921, in preparation for college he attended the Institute of Secondary Education of Pinar del Río, situated on the far western end of the island.

Upon completion of his education at the Institute in Pinar del Río, Julio was accepted by the University of Havana. The university had the reputation of being a hotbed of extremism, which suited him just fine. Having a gregarious personality Julio soon became respected as a leader, although this positive quality was not always applied to his studies.

The Communist Party of Cuba really had its start during the 1920's, but not wanting to appear all too radical, the founders dropped the word "communist" and softened its name to the "Popular Socialist Party." The more radical faction of the party eventually won out and again changed the name of their party to the more militant "Communist Revolutionary Union." One of the primary founders and leaders of this Communist movement was our young man in Havana, "Julio Antonio Mella." He never accepted things at face value and challenged authority whenever he felt that they were becoming abusive or self-serving. There was no doubting that he always stood out from the crowd. Not only was his influence felt among the students and faculty but he also had a reputation as an audacious ladies' man. Being handsome, well-built, with a head of wavy brown hair and sensuous lips, he was known to have bedded many of his female followers. Some of these women said that he resembled a Grecian God. Athletically inclined, he worked out and also became a valued member of the university rowing team.

Prior to graduation and under his leadership, Julio and his peers effectively took over and occupied the University of Havana. He made headlines, as news of his actions went well beyond the university campus and became a well-known event. Feeling his oats, Mella and some of his followers forcibly occupied the university's administrative offices. They exercised their position of power by making demands for changes that included free education, the revision of textbooks, and that he be permitted to run the university for a day. The leadership of the university silently agreed with his demand that the school be made autonomous and free of politics and legislative rule.

Of course he had to be officially reprimanded, however part of his amnesty agreement, amazingly enough, was that he, in fact, be able to administer the university for a day. It was no surprise to any that knew him, that he would be completely competent and up to the task!

He may have taken things a bit too far when he spoke out against and verbally insulted Alfredo Zayas, the duly elected president. Although Zayas didn't like incarcerating his political enemies, he did however make Mella an exception to the rule. In 1923, President Zayas had him arrested in a pre-dawn raid. Dragged out of bed, Mella was charged with slandering the president.

Rubén Martínez Villena, Esquire, a young attorney in Havana, represented Julio and was able to get him off from this serious charge. Martínez continued to represent Mella and remained loyal to the Communist Party until he died in Havana on June 16, 1934. A postage stamp was issued by the Castro government on December 20, 1999, commemorating Martínez as a revolutionary hero.

Mella's demands regarding a free education and new textbooks for the students eventually all came to pass, but not without difficulties.

Mella's Influence on the University of Havana

The University of Havana remains unique in that for years it has been the middle of intolerable, offensive behavior, which definitely would not be accepted anywhere else in the world. Autonomy may encourage student demonstrations, however it does not sanction violence. This concept may not be in writing, however it is understood. It should also be noted that in general Latin American universities are quite different from their American and European counterparts. They place far greater emphasis on how education can be used to serve Latin

American regions in a more socialistic manner, as well as service to the country where the university is located.

During most of the 1950's students pressured the *Consejo Universitario*, the University Council, to shutter the University of Havana as a protest against Batista. The students insisted that classes not be held, as long as Cuba was ruled by a dictator. It is important to note that the university closure was imposed by a minority of radical students and professors and not by the majority of the students or the Batista régime. Since the university was autonomous and self-governing, it was the University Council, and not the government, that exercised its power to close the university. The closing of the University of Havana affected more than ten thousand students, as this closure lasted until 1959. During this time, the government continued paying the faculty and staff their salaries, although the closure left an educational hole in the skills needed by young professionals coming into the labor market.

Autonomy for Cuba's university system was even granted by the present Communist government. On November 27, 2007, five thousand people signed a petition insisting on autonomy from the state as well as freedom of expression for the universities. The concept of "University Students without Borders" was endorsed by both the students and faculty members, representing universities in the provinces throughout the country. The State of New York University (SUNY) in Albany, now offers their students the opportunity to pursue courses in Cuban history, culture and politics. Most of these courses, as well as intensive Spanish language classes, are taught in Cuba.

¿Julio Settles Down?

Many people believed that it was Mella's oversized ego that motivated him, but others said that he really was sincere and believed that he could bring about significant changes by his demands. There were also a number of female students known for being political radicals, who played an important part in shaping Julio's life at that time. Rosario Guillauma (Charito) and Sarah Pascual were both close friends of Julio, as well as being fellow travelers. The overt communist cell at the university continued to grow dramatically under his leadership and many of the university students became active members of the party.

Just about this time, Julio suddenly got married to his primary girlfriend Olivia Zandiver. Perhaps the fact that she became pregnant by him influenced this decision and soon after the wedding, they had a daughter whom they named Natasha.

Marriage did not stop Julio from having other affairs. With his wife taking care of Natasha, he was still out seeing others. There was Sylvia Masvidal, Edith, Margarita, Lucitta and lastly Tina Modotti. He had what the Cubans like to call *machismo* or, loosely translated, male chauvinistic virility. There was no doubt but that he was interested in the ladies, and they in him. His fellow students of both genders always listened intently, as his compelling voice promoted his communistic philosophy, which, incidentally, constantly challenged the government.

These were turbulent times, with the police routinely shooting down labor leaders. On November 27, 1925, after a speech in which he denounced President Machado, Mella was arrested and charged with planting a bomb at the Payret Theatre in Havana. During his incarceration, Mella started a much publicized eighteen-day hunger strike, which was opposed by the Cuban Communist Party (PCC), but proved effective. As pressure mounted, Rubén Martínez Villena called some influential people to have him released. Julio was released from jail just prior to Christmas in 1925, but understood that being free was not the end of it. Many of President Machado's foes, upon being released from jail, were later found floating in Havana harbor, sleeping with the fish, and the story was always the same... that they had supposedly committed suicide. Mella's low point came when he was ostracized for insubordination and failure to take orders from the duly-elected newbies of the party that he had helped to build.... When Mella was again ordered to appear before a judge, he knew that the jig was up, and that his only hope was to flee Cuba and go into exile. That is, at least until President Machado's régime could be overthrown....

Fortunately for Mella, even though the PCC tribunal had accused him of various counts of opportunism and lack of Party discipline, he still continued to be respected and admired by the majority of university students. With the help of Lucitta, an Italian art student who was conspicuous by her beauty and seldom-seen, blonde hair, they fled from Havana for Cienfuegos, located on the southern coast of Cuba. The very next day, they arrived without incident in the port city of Cienfuegos, known as *La Perla del Sur*, the Pearl of the South. Lucitta had arranged for Mella's escape from Cuba with the former Captain of a German ship, who had sought safe haven in Cuba, when his ship was seized as a prize of war by the United States. In Cienfuegos he operated a charter boat, *Die Heimat*, and was willing to take Mella to Central America for a price. Once the deal was made, there was no turning back.... *Kapitan* Wilhelm's boat could not hold enough fuel for the 650-mile sea voyage, but by stopping in the Cayman Islands and Isla Roatán, it became possible. From all accounts, the voyage was uneventful and the weather remained relatively calm, but lust and politics were another matter. Lucitta knew Russian politics, and discussed how Trotsky was compelled by Stalin's régime to deny many of his beliefs. It seemed that Mella, believing in one's own personal independence, developed an interest in Trotsky's philosophy.

"I love boats. I can be on a boat for days." Olga Kurylenko, a French actress and model

Basically, Trotsky believed that an international revolution should be initiated by the people, and that Communism wouldn't succeed if it were only in one country surrounded by capitalistic states. Stalin countered that Marxism should be concentrated and strengthened under strong leadership in one country, which was the case in Russia. It didn't help Trotsky's cause within the Communist Party, when he contended that Stalinism in reality was "Tyranny disguised as Communism."

"The people who cast the votes don't decide an election, the people who count the votes do." Joseph Stalin, Premier of the USSR

A Geographical Cure

Upon her return to Havana, Lucitta bragged to her friend Sylvia that Mella was very much the romantic. With Machado's *La Porra* after him, Mella's life was far better off on a boat, in the middle of the Caribbean, than it would have been in a damp cell, deep within the "*Fortress de San Carlos de la Cabaña.*" Or worse yet, feeding the many sharks in the Gulf of Mexico....

It took Captain Wilhelm's boat almost a week to reach Nicaragua, on the western coast of the Caribbean. The weather was unusually cool on that late January day in 1926, when they arrived at Tela, Honduras. Mella's reputation had preceded him and the authorities were on the lookout. It is fairly difficult for a stranger with a Cuban accent in his Spanish, to remain unnoticed for long in a foreign country. When he was apprehended by the police in Honduras, they showed him the way to Guatemala, where the police kindly gave him residence in their jail. Luckily, and with the help of some fellow travelers, Mella eventually made it to Mexico.

Settling in with the help of the left wing social society of Mexico City, he joined the Mexican Communist Party (PCM) and the *Liga Anti-Imperialista de las Américas*. Julio with his charisma, soon became a leader of the local International Red Aid. To him the independence of the working class in Cuba was of paramount importance, as was his ambition to free Cuba from the stranglehold of President Machado. Mexico had a liberal policy towards the Communist Party and allowed him freedom of speech.

It was here that he wrote editorials for the Mexican Communist newspaper *El Machete* and started to organize a network of exiled Cubans. His ambitious plan was to train a guerilla army to liberate Cuba and overthrow Machado's régime. It was during this period that Mella became involved in bureaucratic wrangling to become the Latin American Communist Representative to Russia, however on an illegal trip to New York City, he became disillusioned with the excessive meddling of Moscow into the internal affairs of the many national communist parties. He also traveled beyond the borders of Mexico to Montevideo, Uruguay, where he was accused of being too involved in Trotsky's philosophy and did not adhere to the discipline expected by the PCM. His antagonist in this was Ricardo Martínez, a Stalinist organizer originally from Venezuela. There were many others that expressed their differences in how they viewed the PCM's relationship with the Mexican Trade Unions. Most of them were ignored or ostracized and it was only later that assassins came from Russia to thin out the ranks of the dissidents.

Mella's position was that the independence of the working class was important and that they should be free of any national dominance. During the summer months of 1927, he traveled first to Brussels and then to Moscow, representing the Latin American Communist Movement against Colonial Oppression and Imperialism. The following year he returned to Moscow for their Fourth Congress of International Labor Unions, known as the *Profintern*. During the latter part of 1928, the relations between Mella and the party became exceedingly tense. Rafael Carrillo, the General Secretary of the PCM, argued against Trotskyism and believed that those in defense of it would have to be harshly dealt with! Mella declared that it had become impossibly difficult to work with the PCM leadership, and was forthwith expelled from the Mexican Communist Party. After this dramatic blow up, Mella reconsidered his views and decided to modify his ultra-staunch position, conceding that he was wrong in opposing his fellow Communists. He knew that without the backing of the party he wouldn't have a platform for his agenda. The Mexican Communist Party leaders, in turn, realizing that ousting the person who founded the Cuban Communist Party wouldn't look good, relented and reluctantly reinstated Mella.

About a year prior to this, Mella briefly met a beautiful Hollywood movie star at a photographic expedition in Mexico City. It was a meeting he could not forget and when he saw her again, he didn't allow the opportunity to escape him for a second time. From that moment on, the two of them became an item and thus they became the delicious victims of lust and violence.

"The line between love and lust was thin as a whisper."
Julia Karr, author of XVI

Movie Starlet

Tina Modotti is the principal female character in this tale. She was born in Udine, Italy, and at 16 years of age, she legally came to the United States as an immigrant, via Ellis Island in New York. Young Tina continued across the vast American continent to join her father, who owned a photography studio in San Francisco. She was no stranger to the craft and had been introduced to photography by her uncle in Italy, and showed a flair for the art of composing and taking photos. In the early 1900's the beautiful Tina appeared in several operas, plays and silent movies, one of which was *The Tiger's Coat*, a clip of which can still be viewed on "YouTube."

Later in 1918, Tina met the painter and poet Roubaix de l'Abrie Richey, originally from Quebec. She moved in with him and shared his bed as common-law husband and wife. It seemed that Tina's movie career had reached its zenith in *The Tiger's Coat*, since she only did a few more minor roles after that. Tina was usually cast as the femme fatale, and because of her Latin appearance was perfectly typecast as a Mexican, harem or gypsy girl. Concentrating on photography, she and Richey met Edward Henry Weston, a renowned photographer, who later received great acclaim for his work and articles in photo magazines and trade journals. Frequently his photographs won national awards that led to his becoming the first photographer to receive a Guggenheim Fellowship.

Wild Sex in Los Angeles

Weston, having been born in Chicago, was raised with typical, well-grounded, mid-western values. On his 16th birthday, his father gave him a Kodak camera with which he started what would become his lifetime vocation. During the summer of 1908, Weston met Flora May Chandler, a schoolteacher who was seven years older than he was. The following year the couple married and in time they had four sons.

Weston and his family moved to Southern California and opened a portrait studio on Brand Boulevard, in the artsy section of Glendale, California, called Tropico. His artistic skills soon became apparent and he became well known for his portraits of famous people, such as Carl Sandburg and Max Eastman. In the autumn of 1913, hearing of his work, Margrethe Mather, a photographer from Los Angeles, came to his studio, where Weston asked her to be his studio assistant. It didn't take long before the two developed a passionate, intimate relationship. Both Weston and Mather became active in the growing bohemian cultural scene in Los Angeles. She was extremely outgoing and artistic in a most flamboyant way. Her bohemian sexual values were new to Weston's conventional thinking, but Mather excited him and presented him with a new outlook that he found enticing. Mather was beautiful, and being bisexual and having been a high-class prostitute, was delightfully worldly. Mather's uninhibited lifestyle became irresistible to Weston and her photography took him into a new and exciting art form. As Mather worked and overtly played with him, she presented a lifestyle that was in stark contrast to Weston's conventional home life, and he soon came to see his wife Flora as a person with whom he had little in common.

Weston expanded his horizons but tried to keep his affairs with other women a secret. As he immersed himself further into nude photography, it became more difficult to hide his new lifestyle from his wife. Flora became suspicious about this secret life, but apparently suffered in silence. One of the first of many women who agreed to model nude for Weston was Tina Modotti. Although Mather remained with Weston, Tina soon became his primary model and remained so for the next several years. There was an instant attraction between Tina Modotti, Mather and Edward Weston, and although he remained married, Tina became his student, model and lover. Richey soon became aware of the affair, but it didn't seem to bother him, as they all continued to remain good friends. The relationship Tina had with Weston could definitely be considered "cheating," since knowledge of the affair was withheld as much as possible from his wife Flora May.

Perhaps his wife knew and condoned this new promiscuous relationship, since she had also endured the intense liaison with Margrethe Mather. Tina, Mather and Weston continued working together until Tina and Weston suddenly left for Mexico in 1923.

As a group, they were all a part of the cozy, artsy, bohemian society of Los Angeles, which was where they were introduced to the then-fashionable, communistic philosophy.

Communism in America

At that time fascism was undermining all vestiges of democracy in Europe and dictatorships were prevalent in most Latin American countries. Therefore, communism was considered by many as the best alternative for the working masses, and was embraced by many scholars, artists and authors, as a viable alternative form of political thinking. Many people in the Hollywood film industry became members of the "Communist Party of America," or at least they agreed with the communistic views and became what was called "fellow travelers." The Communist Party meetings were where people of like mind could gather and share ideas, as well as help each other with their budding careers. It did not take long for Weston, Mather and Modotti to make friends with other party members, including Ricardo Gómez Robelo. Known as "Robo" to his friends, he had been appointed to head the Fine Arts Department of Mexico's Ministry of Education. He graciously offered fellow Communists access to the Mexico Academy of Fine Arts, as well as the use of an art studio he had in Mexico City. Being more tolerant politically, Mexico attracted many Americans who felt persecuted in the United States. Heading south of the border was a geographic cure that many of them embraced.

In December 1921, Robo went to Mexico City with some of his photographs, and took along some of Edward Weston's work as well, hoping to display them at an art exhibit there. A little later Tina followed, and became shocked to hear that Robo had died of smallpox, just two days prior to her arrival. Devastated by his death, but determined to go on, Tina managed to see Robo's ambitions become reality. In March of 1922 she managed to open a two-week exhibition of photographs by both Robo and Weston, as well as including some of her own photographic work. Later that month tragedy struck again, when she learned that her father had died in San Francisco, necessitating her immediate return to the United States, yet again.

When Tina arrived in California she spoke to Weston about what had transpired in Mexico, and they both recognized the great potential in Mexico for photography, or as he called it, "Art in the eye of a camera." He was interested in folk art and the landscape of the country, whereas Tina was captivated by the people and their culture. Planning to make a life for themselves in Mexico, Weston informed his wife of their plans to move south of the border. Flora may have suspected that there was more to their relationship, but it wasn't until now that their affair was confirmed. At a previous photo shoot Tina had frolicked, and she loved to frivolously pose in the nude for Edward's camera. With such goings on, Flora should have been aware of their affair sooner. Perhaps she was!

On July 30, 1923, when Tina, Edward and his son Chandler, sailed by packet steamer from California to Mexico, Edward's wife Flora saw them off and is said to have called out from the dock, "Tina, take good care of my boys." Apparently, there wasn't much, if any, animosity between them....

"I was a Communist, but being left-wing was fashionable. I was no different from thousands of middle-class kids." Miuccia Prada, Italian Fashion Designer

Lust and Murder

After being reinstated into the PCM, Mella again become entrenched in the Mexican Communist Party and, although he did not completely adhere to strict party lines, he apparently was accepted. Most party members liked him and tended to overlook his foibles. What mattered most was that he fought against capitalism. Julio wrote articles for a number of newspapers, condemning President Machado, who continued to rule Cuba with an iron fist. Mella visualized the day when he could return to Cuba, with an army of liberation to overthrow the tyrannical régime. Unbeknownst to Mella, agents of Machado's *La Porra* had been keeping an eye on him. They had planted moles amongst the exiles in Mexico and watched Mella's every move. Machado made repeated requests of the Mexican government to curb Mella, who was now openly planning a paramilitary attack on Cuba. Mexico however declined the requests and maintained its open door policy for all dissidents.

While this was happening, Tina and Weston opened an upscale portrait studio and became involved in the avant-garde community of San Angel, a fashionable southern suburb in Mexico City, which was at one time a weekend retreat for Spanish nobility. It wasn't until about sixty years ago that this still-quaint district became an integral part of Mexico City.

Tina, as usual, modeled and romped in the nude, this time for Diego Rivera, an internationally acclaimed artist. In 1926, Diego's wife Lupe Marín, accused him of having an affair with Tina and insisted that he not see her again. Not being daunted by his wife's insistence, Diego frequently hung out with Tina and her younger friend Frida Kahlo, who in turn also enjoyed Diego's company. It was all just part of the wild times in San Angel, however it probably led to Diego and Lupe's separation and ultimate divorce.

In 1927, Tina, became more active politically and joined the Mexican Communist Party. Her photographs began appearing in art magazines as well as left-leaning publications, including *El Machete*. Tina's work in photography included taking photos of the artistic murals by José Clemente Orozco and Diego Rivera, which are on permanent display in several public buildings in Mexico, including the *Palacio Nacional de Mexico*. Tina also took many photos of Mexican workers and laborers, which showed a great compassion for the plight of the common people.

Since Mexico accepted communism as a legitimate political party and allowed refugees greater flexibility of thought, it became a haven from persecution. Moreover, living in Mexico was less costly than most countries, the weather was usually sunny and no one objected to the swinging lifestyle that many engaged in. It was for these reasons that Julio Mella, Leon Trotsky and others sought refuge there. It also attracted many actors, authors and artists from the United States, many of whom were Communist or, at the very least, had leftist leanings. Although the stated basic reason for the Communist Party's existence was to improve conditions for the working class, it became a hub for the avant-garde, who felt liberated socially as well as politically. The bohemian enclave of Coyoacán, where Frida Kahlo was born, was located just east of San Angel and was at the time a district of Mexico City. It also became the gathering place for personalities such as the American actor Orson Welles, the beautiful actress Dolores del Río, the famous artist Diego Rivera and his soon-to-be-wife Frida, who became and is still revered as the illustrious matriarch of Mexico.

The Hollywood starlet turned photographer, Tina Modotti was caught up in and loved the carefree life, as well as the many social events that took place in Coyoacán during the flapper era. She not only took photos professionally, but also enjoyed the freedom of modeling in the nude, which demonstrated a very risqué and liberated courage on her part. Tina set the tone, and her audaciousness is still admired by many.

Having met briefly the year before, Tina and Julio Antonio Mella soon renewed and intensified their relationship. The two not only shared common political interests, but also enjoyed a sexual interaction that became very obvious, to the delight of their friends. One of their hiding places was in a storage room in the back of the *El Machete* newspaper office, where they enjoyed their sex on top of piles of newspapers. From all accounts, there was no doubt regarding how *caliente* their affair was.

After dark, on the night of January 10, 1929, Tina and Julio were walking down a quiet street on their way home. They had just come from a Communist Party meeting, when suddenly two shots rang out. Julio collapsed on the cobblestone street as Tina held him, crying out for help. Although an ambulance arrived quickly and took Mella to the hospital, it was too late.... Newspapers identified Tina as the person responsible for Julio's death, and perhaps falsely labeled her, "The fierce and bloody Tina Modotti."

Other suspects were accused as well. However, the most likely suspect was Vittorio Vidali, who was identified as a friend of Diego Rivera, and coincidently was another of Modotti's lovers. In an Italian police file, Vidali was described as a Bolshevik terrorist. Once while in Moscow, he was enlisted into Stalin's secret police, the NKVD. Vidali was "bad news," a Stalinist and a member of the Third International, known as "the *Comintern*" or Third Communist International. It was known by the "in crowd" that he had performed many assassinations on Stalin's behalf.

In the Arsenal was a mural that Diego Rivera painted in 1928 depicting the Mexican Revolution. It was painted on the wall of the National Palace in Mexico City, just prior to Mella's assassination. Encrypted within the mural are people that were known to him, positioned as they related to each other. Vittorio Vidali, the most likely assassin, is shown with his face half-hidden and wearing a black hat. He is seen looking over Tina Modotti's shoulder, as she gazes lovingly at Julio Antonio Mella. What did Diego Rivera know? There is little doubt but that Vidali assassinated Mella, partly because of rivalry between the two men over Tina, and also because the revolver used to murder Mella matched the one he usually carried. A witness stated that Vidali was walking alongside the two. The pieces of the puzzle fit, since Mella's wounds were determined to be from point-blank range. Vittorio Vidali is also the most likely since his assigned mission, from Moscow, was to assassinate Trotskyites.

There are still some who believe that the Cuban President Machado may have been behind the killing, but although there was no love lost between the two men, it seems rather unlikely. A police report puts Vidali at the scene of the shooting, but Modotti covered for him by giving the police a false name, most likely identifying José Magriñat as the murderer, in hopes of throwing the cops off the trail. Although Mella had been shot from a very close range, Tina, standing right next to him, was not hurt and "wisely" stated that she did not see the assailant. Tina and the communist activist José Magriñat were arrested and held for a short while. However due to the lack of substantial evidence, they were eventually released.

It is interesting that later in 1933, Magriñat was also assassinated in Cuba, apparently by rival communist operatives. There is little doubt that Tina's life would have been over, had she said anything to the police regarding Vidali's probable involvement in the shooting. Vidali was known to play for keeps and he always got what he wanted, and at that time he wanted Tina!

In 1930, the year following Mella's death, Tina Modotti was expelled from Mexico, and taken under guard to a ship bound for Rotterdam. Using the pseudonym María, and with the help of communist activists, she traveled from Holland to Switzerland before continuing on to Moscow. In the Soviet Union she was trained to be a Soviet operative and conducted several missions in Europe, ostensibly for the International Workers Relief Fund. In 1936, Modotti was seen in Spain, on the arm of none other than Vittorio Vidali. Following the Spanish Civil War, they both left Spain and returned to Mexico.

"I cannot solve the problem of life by losing myself in the problem of art." Tina Modotti, photographer, model, actress and revolutionary political activist

The Aftermath of Gerardo Machado's Régime

Gerardo Machado's régime, beginning with his second term in office, experienced problems from the start. His opposition claimed that he had become dictatorial and had bullied his way into a second term. An underground secret society that would do anything to unseat Machado was known as the ABC. It had its start in the latter part of 1931 and was primarily a middle-class group in opposition to Machado's autocratic government. However, it wasn't long before the group started to resort to violence, including murder, as their preferred weapon to intimidate and eliminate opponents. By 1932, policemen in the Oriente Province were being shot and killed on a daily basis. In response the constabulary retaliated with equal viciousness, only it was indiscriminately directed against the public in general.

After August 12, 1933, the date Machado fled Cuba, Manuel Capero, a loyalist, warned Arsenio Ortiz, Machado's chief hatchet man, that his life was in danger and that the ABC had targeted him for assassination. Not heeding this pertinent warning, the ABC carried out their threat by cutting Ortiz' throat and slicing off his tongue and ears. They also left a message that read: "The punishment of ABC on all those who see and talk too much." There was no doubt but that the worm had turned and that the Machado supporters were on the run.

On September 29, 1933, a large crowd, organized by the Communist Party, carried Julio Antonio Mella's cremains, which were returned from Mexico, for entombment in a monument built near the University of Havana. It came as no surprise when the government challenged the demonstrators, stating that they were not allowed to display their red flags or conduct a burial anywhere other than at a cemetery.

Anticipating trouble, Communist sharpshooters positioned themselves on the rooftops of nearby houses and fired shots down on the soldiers. At the same time, Julio Mella's friend and attorney, Rubén Martínez Villena, gave a speech that further incited the crowd. Suddenly a gunfight broke out between the radical Communists and the soldiers, killing Captain Hernandez Ruda, the commanding officer of an artillery unit from Camp Columbia. The firing also wounded two other soldiers assigned to support the government's position. The fighting continued throughout the night, during which six people were killed and twenty-seven more were wounded. The monument in the park that was built to be Mella's final resting place was destroyed and Mella's ashes fell into the hands of the military. The army, not wasting any time, prepared to have the cremains interred at the cemetery in Colon.

Eventually the soldiers broke up the demonstrations, but the numerous revolutionary organizations had what was called by the newspapers, a "wild day of uncontrolled shooting." In the end, the government relented and Julio Antonio Mella's ashes were returned to the officials of the Communist Party and are now entombed under another monument, which is located in the small park on San Lazaro Street, just downhill from the imposing front steps of the University of Havana.

Covert Agents

The official position of the present Cuban government is that President Machado had Mella assassinated, but it recognizes that both Vittorio Vidali and the vivacious Tina Modotti were Stalinist operatives. Vidali was well known in Spain as Carlos or *Comandante Contreras*, the Commander of the Communist 5th Régiment of the Republican Militia. He was greatly feared, being a known assassin, and was allegedly responsible for the deaths of many anti-Stalinists within the Communist ranks. Later when he returned to Mexico, Vidali was acknowledged as having been involved in the May 24, 1940, failed attack on Trotsky's life. On August 20, 1940, another Stalinist, Ramón Mercader, an accomplice to Vidali, sank a mountaineering pickaxe deep into Trotsky's skull. Taken to a Mexico City hospital, Trotsky lingered long enough to identify his attacker and died the following day. Mercader was convicted and sentenced to twenty years in a Mexican prison for the murder. During his time in prison, Joseph Stalin as leader of the Soviet Union awarded him the Order of Lenin, in absentia. After his release in 1961, Mercader officially became a Hero of the Soviet Union. On October 18, 1978, at the age of 65, Ramón Mercader died in Havana.

In 1948, after the split between Marshal Tito of Yugoslavia and Premier Stalin of the Soviet Union, Vidali became the head of the Communist Party of the Free Territory of Trieste. He established strong links with the Italian Communists and was influential in removing Marshal Tito from his key position as a member of the Trieste Communist Organizations. In 1954, when Trieste became part of Italy again, Vidali became a representative in the Italian Parliament.

Tina was a captive of Vidali's strong will and threatening demeanor. For her there was only one way out.... Desiring her freedom, she wanted him dead, and told this to Valentin González, the skillful, brave and tough bearded Communist Commander of the Spanish Republican Army. Known as the peasant, *El Campesino*, González was given the assignment to assassinate Vittorio Vidali, and is mentioned in Ernest Hemingway's book *"For Whom the Bell Tolls."* When he didn't carry out his mission, Tina told him, "You should have shot him, I hate him! Now I have to be with him until I die!" This statement gives a vivid insight into the dreadful relationship Tina must have had with Vidali. As for González, he went to the Soviet Union where he was suddenly captured, perhaps on the say-so of Vidali and was imprisoned in the notorious Vorkuta Gulag. In 1978 he escaped and made his way to France. Eventually he returned to Madrid, where he died on October 20, 1983.

Tina Modotti died on January 5, 1942, of what was ostensibly said to have been congestive heart failure. It happened suddenly, during a visit by Hannes Meyer, supposedly a close friend and a Swiss architect, who had taught at the Soviet Academy of Architecture. At the time, Diego Rivera speculated that Vidali murdered Tina for knowing too much. Vittorio Vidali was responsible for the murder of as many as 400 people in Spain alone! His forte was killing people and he knew that an overdose of alcohol or cocaine could bring on heart failure.... Of course, Vidali could have persuaded Hannes Meyer to do the dastardly deed as well!

Vittorio Vidali was 83 years old at the time of his own death in Trieste on November 9, 1983.

I believe that sex is one of the most beautiful, natural, wholesome things that money can buy." Steve Martin, Actor

A Vintage Cuban Travel Poster

The Exciting Story of Cuba.... Part 7

The Concrete Ship

A Cruise to Nowhere...

The First World War was over, but ships that had already been contracted for and were under construction were allowed to be completed, and so it was with the SS *Cuyamaca* and the SS *San Pasqual*. These sister ships were oil tankers, having a length of 434.3 feet and a beam of 54 feet. At the time of the war's end they were in the final stages of completion at the Pacific Marine Construction Company in San Diego, California. What made these two ships unusual was that they were not constructed of traditional materials, but instead were made of ferro-cement.

For years, ferro-cement had been used in marine construction. During the late 19th century, barges were built in Europe out of cement, and when steel was in short supply during the war, even oceangoing ships were constructed this way. The largest cement ships built during World War I were the SS *Selma* and her sister ship the SS *Latham*. Although these ships cost less in materials, their construction was far more labor intensive. Most of them are now gone, or are being used as storage tanks, breakwaters or artificial coral reefs, but the SS *San Pasqual* is unique in that she is still intact and until recently has been in use. You might say that she went on cruises to nowhere.

The SS *San Pasqual* was launched on June 28, 1920, but less than a year later was severely damaged in a heavy storm. In 1924, the "Old Time Molasses Company of Havana," a leading Cuban-American molasses company, bought her to be used in Santiago de Cuba, as a floating storage container for raw molasses. Eventually her superstructure was somewhat dismantled and she was towed to Havana, where she remained until 1933. Later, she was once again towed. This time the SS *San Pasqual* was taken along Cuba's northern coast and purposely run aground off Cayo Santa María.

During World War II, the SS *San Pasqual* was outfitted with machine guns and light cannons. Since the ship was hard aground, she was unable to chase Nazi submarines, but she was far enough off the coast to serve as a submarine lookout post. A footbridge was constructed out to her, providing access from the mainland, but time, tides and hurricanes have washed away all signs of the old bridge.

During the revolution "Che" Guevara and his army fought the decisive battle of Santa Clara, which was only an hour's drive away, making the SS *San Pasqual* an ideal prison ship for his captives. After Castro's victory, the ship was again used, this time as a sportsmen's club and a platform for fishing competitions.

Finally, in the 1990's the interior of the *Pasqual* was furnished with ten hotel rooms, a small reception area and a bar. It was someone's idea, but not a good one, and she became a not-so-luxurious hotel, accessible only by boat. Her tanks still contain the original molasses, which by now must have turned into a well-aged rum. For a time, life was good aboard the Hotel Pasqual, and all were welcome, except for American tourists due to the political embargo. Unfortunately, the ship is no longer a hotel, but it is still there, abandoned but accessible. Who knows what lies in her future...? The only certainty is that being made of concrete she won't rust away.

"Being on a ship is also really nicer than being in a luxury hotel in a foreign country. You have all the comfort and all the fattening food without being nagged by the feeling that somehow you ought to be out broadening your cultural horizons." Jean Kerr, Irish-American Author & Humorist

Cuban Mission Poster
A Vintage Cuban Travel Poster

The Exciting Story of Cuba.... Part 8

The Batista Era

August 12, 1933, the Transfer of Power

On August 12, 1933, Machado fled Cuba with ABC terrorists shooting at his airplane as it prepared to take off from the runway, leaving Cuba without any continuity of leadership. A smooth transfer of authority to the next administration became impossible in Havana.

American envoy, Sumner Welles stepped into the vacuum and encouraged Carlos Manuel de Céspedes y Quesada to accept the office of Provisional President of Cuba. Céspedes was a Cuban writer and politician, born in New York City, son of Carlos Manual de Céspedes del Castillo who was a hero of the Cuban War of Independence. Wearing a spotlessly clean, crisp white suit, Céspedes was installed as the Provisional President of Cuba, on what was his 62nd birthday.

This expedient political move failed to prevent the violence that broke out in the streets. Mobs looted and behaved with viciousness that lasted for six long hours and created a mayhem not witnessed since Cuba's Independence from Spain. Students from the university ransacked the previously pro-Machado newspaper *"Heraldo de Cuba."* The Presidential Palace was stormed and severely damaged, with the culprits leaving a "For Rent" sign hanging on the front gate. The temperament of the mob that rallied against the Machado supporters, including the hated *Porristas* who had been left behind, was ferocious. They wounded over 200 hapless souls and cost 21 people their lives. Five members of the *Porristas* as well as Colonel Antonio Jimenez, the head of Machado's secret police, were summarily shot to death and trampled upon. The rioters then tied the mutilated body of Jimenez to the top of a car and paraded his bullet-riddled carcass through the streets of Havana, showing it off as a trophy. When the howling throng of incensed people finally dumped him in front of the hospital, it was determined that he had been shot 40 times.

Students hammered away at an imposing bronze statue of Machado, until piece by piece it was totally destroyed. Shops owned by the dictator's friends were looted and smashed, as were the homes of Cabinet members living in the affluent suburbs.

Fulgencio Batista y Zaldívar

On January 16, 1901, Batista was born in Banes, Cuba, located in the Oriente Province, to Belisario Batista Palermo and Carmela Zaldívar González, who were veterans of the Cuban War of Independence. Considered a *mestizo*, he was born with a mixture of Spanish, African, Indian and Chinese heritage. His early education was at a public school in Banes, however he soon advanced himself by taking courses at night at an American Quaker school.

When Batista was 20 years old, he joined the Cuban army in Havana, with the entry rank of private. He was taught typing and shorthand and served as a stenographer. In 1923, after his initial military tour was completed, he left the army and briefly was employed as a stenography teacher before joining the

Guardia Rural, which was the national police, originally set up to keep internal peace at the time that American troops occupied the island. Soon after, Batista transferred back into the regular army with a promotion to corporal. His proficiency allowed him to become the secretary to the colonel of his regiment, where he had access to privileged information. In 1932, known in the army as the *mulato lindo*, meaning the pretty mulatto, he had risen to the rank of Sergeant Stenographer.

Revolt of the Sergeants

Less than a month after Céspedes y Quesada's inauguration and with the help of his army compatriots, Sergeant José Padraza and Sergeant Manuel López Migoya, Batista cleverly orchestrated what came to be known as the "Revolt of the Sergeants."

On September 4, 1933, at Camp Columbia, an army base in Havana, Batista with his inner circle of conspirators took over power as he forced a military coup. Labor leaders who had opposed Machado's re-election, along with "The Student Directory" comprised of teachers as well as students, joined the sergeants in assuming control of the government. In this way, Batista turned the revolt within the military into the full-blown "Revolution of 1933."

The name Camp Columbia came from a historic and poetic name for the United States. It was founded in 1898, for the purpose of housing U.S. Army troops during the provisional American protectorate over Cuba. It was also called "the First American occupation of Cuba," established in the aftermath of the Spanish-American War. After the withdrawal of American troops, the military establishment was turned over to the

Cuban government and became the largest Cuban army base on the island.

Colonel Juan Blas Hernández had been a leading figure in the revolt against Machado, and had led numerous successful campaigns against the Machado-controlled regular Cuban forces. Later when Hernández turned on Batista and unsuccessfully tried to outflank him, he made the fatal mistake of attempting to surrender. Hernández was immediately singled out from a group of captives and taken aside by Batista's followers. Without the benefit of a trial, he was shot dead where he stood.

Batista Considers His Options

Sumner Welles, the United States Assistant Secretary of State and Special Envoy to Cuba, was described as extremely gloomy and despondent regarding the state of affairs in Cuba, as was Cordell Hull, the American Secretary of State who instituted the Latin American "Good Neighbor Policy."

After having influenced Carlos Manuel de Céspedes y Quesada to serve as the Provisional President of Cuba, the influential American diplomats entertained misgivings in regards to the future of the island nation. Hull informed President Franklin Delano Roosevelt of the problems in Cuba that had become relatively enormous, causing Roosevelt to order the U.S. Navy to dispatch a battle cruiser to Havana.

Seeing American warships off the coast of Havana, Batista feared the possibility of another American occupation and wanted to know where he stood in the eyes of the United States.

On the morning of September 5th, Batista paid a visit to Sumner Welles, wanting to know what the United States' position was regarding his revolutionary government. Making an officious entry and accompanied by a sergeant, he paid a visit to President Roosevelt's special envoy to Cuba.

Welles had previously expressed his thoughts favoring intervention into Cuba's instability by bringing U.S. Naval ships directly into Havana harbor. During his meeting with Batista, he softened his stance by stating that he did not have a definite opinion regarding the Cuban conflict. He emphasized to Batista that he would make no comment as to his viewpoint and intended to keep his options open. Although he did not commit the United States to any definite position, Welles quietly assured Batista that he would maintain an open door policy, and offered him moral support. However as a precautionary measure, Welles advised all American citizens in Havana to gather at the *Hotel Nacional* for their own safety.

"A man only learns in two ways: one by reading, and the other by association with smarter people." Will Rogers, an American humorist, social commentator and motion picture actor

The Pentarchy

Soon after, the still-President Carlos Manuel de Céspedes y Quesada, who incidentally was a lieutenant colonel at one time, holding the prestigious position of governor of the Province of Santiago de Cuba, obediently cooperated, by resigning, when Batista demanded it of him. The short-term president submissively handed in his resignation to the five-member executive committee, known as *La Pentarquía* or the Pentarchy, that had taken over control of the government.

The former President Céspedes y Quesada was paid for his prudent loyalty and returned to the Foreign Service to become Cuba's Ambassador to Spain. Not bad, since this post was considered a most coveted appointment and put him far away from the ongoing fray in Cuba....

For a fleeting moment, the faculty and students at the University of Havana entertained the thought that it fell to them to fill the country's legislative vacuum. Whereas, they were right in that they were the only surviving institution aside from the army that had the organization to carry this out, they were quickly reminded that their ambitious concept was far beyond their constitutional rights.

On the same day that Batista went to see Sumner Welles, Dr. Ramón Grau San Martin, an anti-Machado activist, became a member of the Pentarchy. Others that were members were Sergio Carbó y Morera, a journalist; Porfirio Franca y Álvarez de la Campa, an attorney, banker and economist; José Miguel Irisarri y Gamio, an attorney; and Guillermo Portela y Möller, a faculty member at the University of Havana's School of Law. A proclamation written by Sergio Carbó, announcing their status as the ruling body in Cuba, was published in every Cuban newspaper the following day. The proclamation stated their existence as the executive branch of government and was signed by eighteen civilians. The only military representative to the Pentarchy, although not a member, was Fulgencio Batista.

Batista closely allied himself with this new short-lived, five-man Presidency of Cuba. Sergio Carbó y Morera, a member of the new Executive Commission of the Pentarchy, became Batista's inside man. On the morning of September 8th, with the country in a precarious state of instability and as the self-appointed head of the Provisional Government of Cuba, Carbó y Morera appointed Batista as "Chief of the Army" and promoted him to the rank of Colonel. This promotion was supposedly "for merits of war and exceptional services to the country." Of course, everyone knew that this appointment was only made because of Batista's demands and it happened without the approval of the other four members of the Pentarchy.

Ascending to the rank of Colonel without the proper approval, Batista took over "Command and Control" of the Cuban army and unbelievably, summarily discharged the entire cadre of Commissioned Officers.

The Pentarchy met at the National Palace and discussed the advantages of reorganizing the Cuban Army. Sergio Carbó set up a meeting of the new Colonel Batista with Colonel Hector de Quesada and Colonel Perdomo who represented the ousted army officers. Carbó, reflecting Batista's wishes, strongly suggested that the command of the army include the now Colonel Batista, along with the two other colonels and two sergeants, who were appointed by Carbó in concert with Batista. Both of these Colonels immediately balked at this, demanding that all the officers be first reinstated to their former ranks, with the exception of those who had committed crimes during the Machado régime.

When Carbó appointed Batista to reorganize the Armed Forces, there could no longer be any doubt as to the former Sergeant's position. Batista was now the Chief of the Cuban Army, making him the most powerful man in the country.

As the U.S. Naval presence increased, the fear of intervention became a greater threat. Although he restrained from setting foot on Cuban soil, the U.S. Secretary of the Navy was within sight of Havana on the USS *Indianapolis*. At the same time, the former senior Cuban army officers had been meeting at the

Hotel Nacional. Apparently they had gathered arms, ammunition, stores and water at that location in preparation for a planned counterrevolution. Most of these officers doubted that the new and fanciest hotel in Cuba would ever be attacked, and many still believed that the United States Navy would intervene on their behalf.

Batista called upon the members of the Pentarchy to convene a council of war. Those who attended were divided as to whether an attack on the hotel was prudent, especially since many Americans had checked in on the advice of Sumner Welles. The fact was that Batista himself was undecided and Dr. Ramón Grau made it a point not to be there, so that he could avoid the issue. Most of the left-leaning students from the university objected to the attack on the hotel, as did many noncommissioned soldiers still serving in the army without leadership. Everyone feared an armed American intervention.

In the early morning hours of October 2, 1933, an armored army vehicle drove up to the front portico of the hotel. The driver was ordered by sentries to stop but he replied by firing his weapon at them. With this, a firestorm commenced from all directions starting a full-blown skirmish. With the light of dawn, light artillery was brought in from Camp Columbia and opened fire on the hotel. Fifteen soldiers were killed in this battle, with many others wounded. One American spectator, who should have kept his head down, became a casualty in the crossfire. When it became obvious that the United States Navy wasn't going to intervene, Batista ordered the Cuban Navy to bombard the building.

In utter disbelief, many of the senior officers now fearing for their lives, barricaded themselves deeply into the new hotel. The fact that there were Americans present and that the National Hotel had become a symbol of Cuba's stability, was not enough to stop Batista from using the warship *Cuba* to fire on it. Those officers that were not killed outright in this callous bombardment of the hotel were jailed, and with Batista elevated to the position of Supreme Chief of the Armed Forces, "Pax Batistiana" began.

Grau became another "Short-Term" President

Dr. Ramón Grau San Martin was a physician and a well-liked Professor of Physiology at the University of Havana. In the 1920's, Grau became involved in the student anti-Machado protest movement, for which he was imprisoned in 1931. Upon his release, he fled to the United States. However shortly after the "Revolt of the Sergeants," knowing that Machado had been forced out of office, he returned to Havana with the intention of practicing medicine again. Being an activist by nature, he could not resist returning to politics and on September 5, 1933, was appointed to the Pentarchy.

Being a cumbersome body and having outlived its usefulness, the members of the Pentarchy were ousted by the Student Directory and on September 10, 1933, Dr. Ramón Grau became the Provisional President. Grau, who was an unapologetic socialist, upheld the anti-imperialistic views valued by many. He viewed the United States as a threat to Cuban independence and defended nationalism. Grau was influential in rescinding the constitution of 1901 and he enacted numerous labor reforms, including the institution of an eight-hour workday. He denounced the Platt Amendment, purged the government of Machado's cronies and put an end to the old political machine.

In retaliation, the United States denied the formal recognition of Grau's administration. Conservative American business interests rationalized that they had justifiable concerns, after all, Grau had declared himself a Socialist and only a Communist could be worse!

Grau only held office for a little over 100 days, and on January 15, 1934, Batista pressured him to resign. The most obvious reason as to why he was ousted, was that he had made many enemies among influential, pro-American interests. On the positive side was that he created a Department of Labor and enacted a rule that 50% of all employees in Cuban business corporations and agricultural enterprises, had to be Cuban nationals. Any importation of cheap labor from outside Cuba became illegal. Of course, this was not what Batista and his American friends wanted to hear....

"The inherent vice of capitalism is the unequal sharing of blessings; the inherent virtue of socialism is the equal sharing of miseries." Winston Churchill, Prime Minister of the United Kingdom

From Colonel to President

The United States, ostensibly looking out for American interests, maintained warships in Cuban waters. Although these ships didn't directly intervene in Cuban affairs, their threat was obvious. Wanting a complete separation from the giant monolith to the north, Grau had his backers, but was quickly marginalized by Cuba's new strongman. Batista strengthened his position by separating the military from the civilian sectors of the government, which conveniently left the management and direction of the army up to him. Thus, he established himself not only as the commander in chief of the Cuban military, but became the de facto leader of Cuba. His threatening position rippled throughout the governmental bureaucracy. In 1934, with his grip becoming ever more powerful, his influence became most apparent when he forced Grau's resignation. Once out of office, Grau founded the Cuban Revolutionary Party, *El Partido Revolucionario Cubano Auténtico* or PRC. The primary purpose of this political party was to fiercely stand in opposition to Batista and everything he stood for....

Ending the sham, Batista severed ties with the leftist leaning student groups, including the influential Revolutionary Directorate. In 1935 labor went out on a general strike, which Batista quickly brought to an end using the military. With this, he moved his position to the political right, solidifying ties with both the wealthy elite and the United States government. By seizing control of Cuba, he became the puppet master in command of a string of Cuban presidents until 1940. These presidents started with Carlos Hevia who had close ties to the United States....

Carlos Hevia y de los Reyes-Gavilan

Carlos Hevia was born on March 21, 1900, in Havana. He graduated from the United States Naval Academy, with the class of 1919 and then went to medical school to become a surgeon. Active in politics, Hevia as a member of the Cuban Revolutionary Party was the Minister of Agriculture when riots erupted in the streets of Havana. When Batista forced Grau to resign the presidency, he next considered Carlos Hevia for the job.

At the time, Hevia was thought to be Batista's best choice to become the new president. He declined at first because of the threatening mobs, however Batista convincingly persuaded him to accept the office, although he knew that he was unpopular with the military. To protect him, Batista ordered 100 army troops from Camp Columbia to the Presidential Palace.

Hoping to receive Carlos Mendieta's endorsement, Hevia met with him in the early morning hours prior to his inauguration on January 15, 1934. Mendieta had served as a colonel during the Cuban War of Independence and was actually the candidate Batista choose to replace Grau. However, not respecting the upstart sergeant who made himself a colonel and seized control of the Cuban army, Mendieta became Batista's archrival. Mendieta refused to cooperate with Batista but because of Carlos Hevia, agreed to a wait-and-see philosophy by remaining neutral.

That day, having been handpicked by Batista, Hevia was sworn in as the President of Cuba by his father-in-law Dr. Juan Federico Edelmann, who also happened to be the chief justice of the Cuban Supreme Court. The extensive gala ceremonies at the Cabaña Fortress finally concluded with the firing of a 21-gun salute.

After these festivities the new president sought to have members of the rebellious labor unions join his cabinet, however the labor representatives refused to take part in the charade and didn't waste any time before voting to go out on a nationwide strike. Not being able to negotiate a stop to this strike, Hevia handed Batista his resignation early on Thursday morning, January 18, 1934, after only 40 hours in office. As he left the Presidential Palace at 2:15 a.m., he was heard to say, "I am going back to my fields to cut some sugar cane."

Once out of office he broke politically with Batista and joined the defiant *Auténtico* Party. In 1948, Hevia returned to public life and served in President Prío's administration as the Foreign Minister of Cuba until 1950. In 1952, he ran for the presidency again, which came to an unexpected sudden end when Batista seized power in a coup d'état.

During the early 1960's, Hevia fled from Castro's Cuba to the United States, and in exile became active in the Miami based anti-Castro movement. Here, just three weeks prior to the "Bay of Pigs Invasion," the CIA structured the Cuban Revolutionary Council (CRC). The Board of Directors of this activist organization included: Antonio de Varona, Justo Carrillo, Carlos Hevia, Antonio Maceo, Manuel Ray, and Manuel Artime. José Miró Cardona, the former Prime Minister of Cuba, served as the chairman of the CRC. In Miami, Hevia also operated a private school named the "Pan American Merchant Marine Academy."

Dr. Carlos Hevia died at 64 years of age of a heart attack in the town of Lantana in Palm Beach County, Florida. He is buried at Miami's Woodlawn Park cemetery on Eighth Street and 32nd Avenue, along with two other former presidents of Cuba, Carlos Prío Socarrás and Gerardo Machado.

Carlos Manuel Agustín Márquez Sterling

On August 28, 1872, Carlos Manuel Agustín Márquez Sterling y Loret de Mola was born in Lima, Peru. During the Ten Years' War his father was a guerrilla fighter and a delegate to Peru, representing the "Cuban Republic-in-Arms." It was because of these circumstances that he was legally a Cuban citizen by birth.

In 1894, he met José Martí and became active in the preparations for the War of Independence. Sterling's first claim to fame was that he was a renowned chess player at the Paris Tournament of 1900.

Becoming a journalist and an attorney, he was appointed General Consul of Cuba in Buenos Aires in 1907. Later he became the Cuban Ambassador to Mexico, although silently he remained in opposition to the Machado dictatorship. In 1921, the National University of Mexico conferred on him the degree Doctor Honoris Causa.

When Carlos Hevia resigned the presidency before having appointed a Vice President, Sterling, being the Secretary of State at the time, assumed the presidency. On January 18, 1934, his time in office lasted for only about 6 hours. His moments of grandeur lasted from six in the morning to noon, after which he transferred the reins of office to Carlos Mendieta.

On May 29, 1934, after returning to the Diplomatic Corps as Cuba's Ambassador to the United States, Márquez signed the Treaty of Commercial Reciprocity between the two countries, thus abolishing the Platt Amendment. After the signing, he was heard to say, "Now I can die in peace."

Only months later on December 9, 1934, Carlos Manuel Agustín Márquez Sterling died in Washington, D.C., at 62 years of age.

Carlos Márquez Sterling, nephew of Carlos Manuel Agustín Márquez Sterling y Loret de Mola, was born in Camagüey, Cuba. He was also a politician in Cuba and his political legacy is frequently mistaken for Hevia's. It was Carlos Márquez Sterling, who as the president of the constitutional assembly, took part in the writing of the new Cuban Constitution of 1940.

Carlos Mendieta y Montefur

Carlos Mendieta was born on November 4, 1873, in San Antonio de las Vueltas, Las Villas, Cuba. Although he wasn't very dynamic, nor was he an outstanding orator, he was considered as reliable and honest as any *político* could be. In August of 1898, at the end of the War of Independence, Mendieta was promoted to the rank of colonel in the Liberation Army. However, professionally he was both a physician and a politician. In 1901, as a member of the Federal Republican Party of Las Villas, Mendieta was elected to the Cuban House of Representatives. Then, during the 1914 elections, he was re-elected to a second term, during which time he created the Liberal Unionist Party. It was under this banner that José Miguel Gómez became president. In 1916, Mendieta teamed up with Alfredo Zayas to oppose the re-election of the conservative President Menocal, who was America's favored candidate. For his loyalty, Zayas picked Mendieta to run as his vice-presidential candidate

In 1917, a liberal coalition led by former President José Miguel Gómez and including Gerardo Machado, Alfredo Zayas, Carlos Mendieta and Cuban General Enrique Loynaz del Castillo, of the Spanish War of Liberation, took up arms against Menocal's conservative administration.

Although their actions were considered radical, it was a protest against the obvious electoral fraud that returned Menocal to office. After several skirmishes, the revolt, called the Chambelona War, was finally won by the conservative side, which had the strong support of the United States. Carlos Mendieta was captured during one of these battles in Caicaje, 15 miles east of Santa Clara, but escaped and went into exile.

After returning from exile, he was re-elected and returned to the House of Representatives, representing Las Villas. In 1924, Alfredo Zayas was considered a traitor to his cause, when he gave up his presidential bid in favor of Gerardo Machado. Because of this, Mendieta also lost his opportunity to become the vice-presidential candidate on the Zayas/Mendieta ticket.

His opposition to President Machado landed him in prison, however he was released on January 9, 1932, as an admired and well-known figure among the anti-Machado liberals.

After the Sergeants' Revolt of 1933, Batista sought a reliable senior officer whose background dated back to the War of Independence. In addition, he wanted someone who was respected by the military, but who could still be controlled by him. The person he chose was Carlos Mendieta, a member of the National Union Party. Mendieta was installed as the Provisional President of Cuba in 1934 by Batista's military junta. During his time in office, he accomplished two important pieces of legislation: Women were finally granted the right to vote and the detested Platt Amendment was repealed. Cuba in 1935 was still unsettled and the pressure of Batista's will, as well as ongoing protests, caused Mendieta to resign.

Still Carlos Mendieta continued to be politically active as Batista's appointed delegate to the "Sugar Stabilization Institute," where he remained until December 15, 1943. During his retirement he was involved in cockfighting, a dreadful but popular sport in Cuba. On September 27, 1960, Carlos Mendieta at 87 years of age, quietly died at home in the Miramar section of Havana.

José Agripino Barnet y Vinagres

José Agripino Barnet was born in Barcelona, Spain on June 23, 14, 1864. Having graduated from the School of Law at the University of Havana, he became the Cuban Consul in Paris. He later served as the Cuban Consul in Liverpool, Rotterdam and Hamburg.

As a member of the National Union Party, Barnet served as President from December 11, 1935, until May 20, 1936.

Returning to Spain after his term as president, he died in Barcelona in 1945, at 81 years of age.

Miguel Mariano Gómez y Arias

Gómez, the son of Cuba's second president, was born on October 6, 1886, in Sancti Spíritus, Cuba. He attended a Jesuit school in Cienfuegos and later studied law.

Gómez was elected to several terms as a member of the House of Representatives and in 1926 he was elected mayor of Havana. Having been a participant in the 1931 revolt against the Machado Régime, he went into exile in New York City. However, after the fall of Machado, he returned to Cuba and was again elected Mayor of Havana.

As a member of the National Union Party, Gómez was elected to the Presidency of Cuba in 1936 and served for seven months, from May 20, 1936, until December 24, 1936, at which time he was impeached at the behest of Batista and his junta, for having vetoed a bill creating a rural school system under military control. As frequently happened, he may have been persuaded by American money to veto the bill, or he may have held the strong conviction that the schools should come under a civilian "Board of Education." Whatever his reason, Batista took umbrage to the veto and exercised his power as the "Puppet Master."

Fleeing Cuba, Gómez sought refuge in the United States but returned to Cuba in 1939. Then in 1940, he ran again for the position of Mayor of Havana, however this time lost to Raúl Menocal.

Retired from public life, on October 26, 1950, Miguel M. Gómez died in Havana at 61 years of age, after a lengthy illness.

Federico Laredo Brú

Federico Laredo Brú was born April 23, 1875, in Remedios, Las Villas. In January of 1936, Brú started his political career as a member of the National Union Party, becoming Cuba's Vice President during Miguel Gómez's administration. After Batista concocted the impeachment of Gómez in 1936, Laredo Brú, being next in line, served as president for the remaining years of Gómez' term. Inadvertently or not, this opened the path to the presidency for Batista.

Laredo granted many amnesties, including one to the all-but-forgotten Geraldo Machado. He also signed many benefit programs and laws regulating working hours, minimum wages, insurance and pension programs that the Congress had passed. Laredo also won favor with the labor unions by regulating shorter working hours.

In 1937, Laredo pushed for the passage of the Sugar Coordination Law, which combined smaller farms into cooperatives. He approved the unionization of agricultural workers, and assured that tenant farmers receive a share of the proceeds from the fields they worked. Laredo also issued a ruling that specified that Cuban citizens head all businesses in Cuba. During Laredo's administration the Communist Party gained greater influence in labor through the Confederation of Cuban Workers. Strikes became illegal, and independent labor unions were banned. In 1938, Batista ordered that a new constitution be drafted and decided to run for the presidency at the end of Laredo's term. In the midst of Laredo's term, on May 27, 1939, the M/S *Saint Louis* arrived in Havana, carrying 937 Jewish refugees from Hamburg, Germany.

After becoming the President of Cuba, Batista appointed Laredo as the Minister of Justice, a position from which he worked with a selected committee to draft a new Cuban Penal Code. In July 1946 at 71 years of age, Federico Laredo Brú died in Havana.

The M/S *Saint Louis*

The M/S *Saint Louis* was a German passenger liner owned by the Hamburg-America Line. She was most notable for her voyage in 1939, in which her Captain Gustav Schröder attempted to find homes for her passengers. On May 13, 1939, just prior to the Second World War, 937 German-Jewish refugees boarded the ship in the hopes of escaping the holocaust that was to follow. Although the passengers had previously purchased legal Visas, they were denied entry into Cuba due to contrived red tape. While the ship was in transit, Cuba changed its laws restricting entry to all but U.S. citizens. Even though the Nazi régime had already started to persecute Jews, the Captain of the *Saint Louis* insisted that the crew treat the passengers with courtesy and respect. Even though the crew followed the captain's orders, the passengers became distressed when it was announced that they would not be allowed to enter Cuba. President Roosevelt and his envoys Cordell Hull, Secretary of State, and Henry Morgenthau, Secretary of the Treasury, as well as the American Jewish Joint Distribution Committee, tried to persuade Cuba to accept the refugees. However, their actions were to no avail. It is believed that the German ambassador, on orders from Berlin, put pressure on Cuba. The passengers were refused permission to land, even though they were refugees fleeing persecution.

With passengers threatening to commit suicide, Cuban officials relented and allowed 22 non-Jewish passengers to disembark. Ultimately, only relatively few refugees were permitted to disembark before the ship was turned away. Even after long negotiations on the part of the Captain, the 915 passengers remaining on the ship were forced to depart from Cuba. With an obvious communications failure, Captain Schröder was not aware that the Dominican Republic had offered to accept 100,000 Jews.

So, when he could no longer negotiate with Cuban officials, Captain Schröder sailed his ship to Florida. When the media learned that the ship was coming to the United States they suggested that the Captain might contemplate running the *Saint Louis* aground. Two Coast Guard Cutters were dispatched to intercept the *Saint Louis* with orders to prevent this. The refugees were not only refused entry but allegedly the ship was even fired upon with a warning shot across its bow, with the intention of keeping them away from shore. Legally, the passengers were prohibited from entering the United States even as tourists, since they did not have a required return address. When the *Saint Louis* was turned away from the United States, clergy and anti-Nazi academics in Canada attempted to persuade their Prime Minister Mackenzie King to offer sanctuary to the hapless *Saint Louis* passengers. Canadian immigration officials and some anti-Semitic cabinet ministers were against any Jewish immigration into Canada, thus preventing this from happening.

Having been denied entry into Cuba, the United States, or Canada, the ship had to return to Europe where they were finally accepted into various countries in Europe. The *Saint Louis* arrived in Antwerp on June 17, 1939. After lengthy negotiations by Captain Schröder, 619 passengers were permitted to disembark in Antwerp, 224 were accepted by France, 214 by Belgium, and 181 by the Netherlands. The United Kingdom opened its doors to 288 people providing they could find their own transportation across the English Channel.

In the aftermath of this debacle, it has been estimated that after their return to Europe, approximately a quarter of them eventually died in Nazi concentration camps. The *Saint Louis* was severely damaged on August 30, 1944, by Allied bombings in Kiel, Germany. However, she was repaired two years later and used as a floating hotel in Hamburg. Then in 1952, the ship was finally scrapped.

Following the war, Captain Schröder assumed a desk job and never went to sea again. He was considered a hero and released from de-Nazification proceedings due to the glowing testimony given by some of the surviving passengers. Later in life, with minimal success, Captain Schröder tried to publish his life's story.

In 1946, the Federal Republic of Germany awarded him the "Order of Merit". Captain Gustav Schröder died in 1959 at the age of 73. In March of 1993, he was posthumously named as one of the "Righteous among the Nations" at the *Yad Vashem* Holocaust Memorial in Israel.

Batista Ascends to the Presidency

The new Constitution that Batista advocated in 1938 came to fruition as the Constitution of 1940. The National Assembly passed it under the leadership of Blas Roca, a young, former shoemaker-turned-activist and legislator. He had helped organize the Revolution of 1933 and now was instrumental in presenting a balanced document that protected the rights of both the wealthy and the working class. Carlos Marquez Sterling exercised his influence as the President of the Convention.

The new Constitution supported full employment and boosted the social security system for the working class. The concept of "equal pay for equal work" was instituted and the large plantations known as *latifundios* became less profitable. The workers and the original Communist Party, which had been started by Julio Antonio Mella, threw their support behind Batista and his new Democratic Socialist Coalition.

In 1940, Grau ran for the presidency, and even though he had a significant following, he lost the election to Batista. Many observers were convinced that Batista won unfairly but strangely enough, independent observers from the United States considered the 1940 elections fair and stated that the elections had been conducted in a just way. The Communist Party, as well as the majority of the working middle class who were members of labor unions, supported Batista. In fact, the Communist Party criticized the anti-Batista opposition, proclaiming that Grau and his followers were "fascists." In reality Batista was a transparent capitalist, who had used the Communists to get the votes necessary to win. Defeating Grau for the presidency, he became the first non-European Cuban to hold the office.

World War II

In spite of his Communist affiliations, Batista was considered a staunch ally of the United States, which tolerated and supported him in return for his loyal backing during World War II. As part of Roosevelt's "New Deal" policy, the Platt Amendment, which had given the United States the right to intervene and set up military bases in the region, was replaced in 1934 with a permanent Cuban-American Treaty of Relations. This new treaty, referred to as the Treaty of Resolutions by the U.S. Senate, gave Cuba the right to exercise its own national defense. It also allowed that the terms of the lease, regarding the U.S. Naval Station in Guantánamo, would continue to remain in effect.

Cuba helped the Allies in their fight against the Axis powers by contributing manganese, nickel and some copper to the war effort. Because of the high demand for these minerals and the money it brought in, working conditions finally improved for the miners.

In 1944, the way the Constitution was written, Batista was prevented from holding the office of President again for eight years. To protect his interests, Batista picked Carlos Saladrigas Zayas, who had served as Senator, Minister of Justice, Foreign Minister and Prime Minister of Cuba, as his replacement. However, unexpectedly, the still-popular Dr. Ramón Grau defeated Zayas. Batista, seeing the handwriting on the wall, thought it best to leave Cuba for the United States.

Living in exile and no longer having to pretend having any affection for his wife Elisa, Batista sought a divorce and married Marta Fernández Miranda, who then took his name and became Marta Fernández Miranda de Batista. They moved to Daytona Beach where Batista set up a shadow government at the opulent mansion he had bought for just this sort of possibility. For the next eight years, he remained behind the scenes spending most of his time between his home in Daytona Beach and the hotel Waldorf-Astoria in New York City, where he deliberated his future.

The Mafia Comes to Havana

In Cuba, the Mafia had its beginnings with Al Capone, during the Machado era in the 1920's. While the United States experimented with the restrictive idealism known as

"Prohibition," the Cosa Nostra had been busy establishing itself on the island nation. With the Constitutional ban on the making, using and transporting of alcohol in the United States, Cuba came into its own as a "party" destination. The island was also convenient as a staging point for rum-running operations into the largely undeveloped and unprotected peninsula to its north. Not only did it help put Miami on the map, Florida made access to the more northerly states relatively easy.

In the early 1930's Salvatore Lucania earned the nickname Charles "Lucky" Luciano by living through a few harrowing mob-related experiences, evading arrest, and being a consistent winner at the crap tables. He became a member of Joe Masseria's crime family. Taking advantage of restrictions brought on by Prohibition in the 1920's, he became involved in bootlegging booze, prostitution and the narcotics racket. During this time, he befriended a Jewish street kid named Meyer Lansky, whose rebelliousness on the streets won him Luciano's friendship and respect.

Luciano and Lansky supplied booze to Manhattan speakeasies. In 1931, Luciano had both Masseria and his rival boss Salvatore Maranzano murdered and by 1934 Luciano had established himself as the "boss of all bosses." Because of Lansky's business acumen and Luciano's brazen strategy, they changed the history of organized crime. Although he was jailed for prostitution and pandering in 1936, Luciano continued to operate his syndicate from his prison cell. In 1946 his sentence was commuted, and he was deported to Italy, where he continued to direct drug traffic and the smuggling of aliens into the United States.

Before 1945 cocaine hardly existed as a problem, but during the next five years "mules" began smuggling it into the United States from Peru. Although both Lansky and Luciano professed to be against any drug trafficking involvement, they recognized the potential income it could provide.

It was not until much later that the Colombian Cartel came into its own, making it the most violent and sophisticated drug trafficking organization in the world. Even with the relatively modest Mafia involvement, what started as a small cocaine smuggling operation grew into an enormous, lucrative, multi-national cocaine empire.

"Wherever there's opportunity, the Mafia will be there." Johnny Kelly, drummer for the band "A Pale Horse Named Death"

The Beginning of "The Wild Years"

In 1934, strongman Fulgencio Batista forced President Grau's resignation. Then in 1940, Grau lost his bid for the Presidency to his adversary Batista. He did however win the election in 1944 and took office for a four-year term on October 10th. After Grau won the election and was the President elect, Batista still in office, blatantly attacked the National Treasury, leaving the cupboards bare by the time Grau actually became the President.

Since Grau and Batista were staunch adversaries, it is highly unlikely that any deal could have been made in 1946 to allow "Lucky" Luciano into Cuba, especially with Luciano having been exiled to Sicily by the United States government that preceding February. Still, Lansky had enough political pull within the Cuban government to prepare for a strong Mafia presence in Havana.

In October of 1946, in an attempt to keep his whereabouts a secret, "Lucky" Luciano covertly boarded a freighter taking him from Naples, Italy, to Caracas, Venezuela. Then Luciano flew south to Rio de Janeiro and returned north to Mexico City. On October 29, 1946, he arranged for a private flight from Mexico City to Camagüey, Cuba, where Meyer Lansky met him. Having the right connections, Luciano passed through Cuban customs unimpeded and was whisked by car to the splendid Grand Hotel.

Luciano, having just arrived in Cuba, was looking forward to setting up operations. Cuba would actually be a better place than the United States for what he had in mind.

Luciano never would have believed that Thomas E. Dewey, the Chief Assistant U.S. Attorney for the Southern District of New York, who later became governor of New York, would have him deported back to Italy, after recommending that his prison sentence be commuted. In Luciano's way of thinking, having helped Naval Intelligence, during the Second World War, should have earned him a full pardon. The truth of this story can be considered fuzzy, but it is generally believed that he garnered classified enemy information and collected military intelligence in Sicily, which was helpful in the Allied Invasion of Italy and thus Europe. With his extended connections, he took credit for preventing labor problems and keeping the Port of New York open throughout the war. Luciano believed that this should have earned him the right to return to the United States as a free man.

Here in Cuba it would be easier to buy off corrupt politicians and run roughshod over the existing laws. He also believed that he would eventually be able to return to New York. To him this island of sunshine would be the best pathway forward.

The following day, accompanied by a bodyguard, the two men continued on to Havana. Luciano still felt bitter, but with the tropical sun shining, the beautiful day helped abate any negative feelings. The pleasant 7-hour drive from Camagüey to Havana gave Lansky and Luciano time to talk and catch up on their plans for the future. As he looked out of the car window, Luciano felt a freedom in Cuba that he assumed was deservedly his....

Things hadn't gone too well for him since 1936, when Dewey and his army of G-men had raided 80 of his brothels in and around New York City. Arresting hundreds of prostitutes along with their "madams," Dewey made a name for himself as he broke up one of the largest prostitution rings in history.

To avoid time in prison some of the girls zeroed in on Luciano, whom they identified as their Mafia "Overlord." Dewey made headlines with his well-publicized conviction of Luciano, who received a sentence of 30 to 50 years in the slammer.

Luciano had grown accustomed to living in a luxurious penthouse suite at the New York Waldorf Astoria Towers, where he was registered as Charles Ross. He had lived the good life but now he knew that it was time to flee. In March of 1936, Luciano departed New York and made his way to Hot Springs, Arkansas, where he was eventually apprehended and returned to face Dewey in New York City. Taking up residency at Dannemora, a New York State Correctional Facility, Luciano could no longer consider himself all that "lucky." He resented Dewey for having put him behind bars and, what seemed worse to him, he resented that he was being put away on 60 counts of compulsory prostitution charges.

At the time, he decided to be a model prisoner and in 1946 his sentence was commuted. He had never become an American citizen, and thus he was deported to Italy. The U.S. government blocked all of his attempts to return to the Americas, and that included Cuba. He knew that unless he took matters into his own hands, he would have to spend the rest of his days in Italy.

Now that he was in Cuba, Luciano was convinced that things would become better. As Luciano and Lansky motored along, they left the past behind and turned their attention to what they expected to be a brighter future. Lansky and Luciano could now make plans and one of the first things would be to set a date for a clandestine meeting of all the Mafia Chiefs.

After a day on the road, the two men finally arrived in Havana. For the first two weeks, Luciano relaxed and unwound at the *Hotel Nacional*, on the eastern end of the Malecón. Luciano liked Havana and, expecting to stay, rented, with an option to buy, an impressive Spanish-style mansion, on an estate owned by a "Sugar Cane Baron," who apparently had huge loses playing cards with sharks like General Genovevo Pérez Dámera, Chief of the Cuban General Staff, and Senator José Suárez Rivas. Conveniently, the estate became available to Luciano for $800 a month, which included maid service.

Luciano's luck, once again, held out when an assassination attempt on his life failed during the evening of December 27, 1946, inside the *Gran Casino Nacional*. Luciano had surrounded himself with local influential friends, one of whom was Dr. Indalecio Pertierra, a member of the House of Representatives from the Province of Las Villas, who had arranged for two guards from the Presidential Palace to provide protection for him. Pertierra, José Suárez Rivas, who was now the Minister of Labor, along with Colonel Manuel Quevedo who had the original idea, started *Aerovías* Q. The new airline operated from Camp Columbia, the Cuban army base near Havana, thereby avoiding Cuba's Immigration and Customs officials, as well avoiding the payment of taxes. This conveniently facilitated the trafficking of drugs for themselves and the Colombian cartel. Luciano prudently brought in a number of his friends from New York, to help protect him and the Mafia's stake in Havana.

The thugs who were responsible for the assassination attempt managed to get out of the casino and sped away in a large black Cadillac. Who had hired them was unclear, but it appeared to be a family feud, concerning an unresolved turf conundrum. After this most recent attack on Luciano's life, he frequently would find other places to spend the night and never announced where he would go next nor would he travel between places the same way twice in a row. The family was a brotherhood, but knowing whom to trust became an art form.

On December 22, 1946, it was during a meeting at the *Hotel Nacional* that Meyer Lansky, Santo Trafficante, Jr. from Tampa, Florida, and other underworld figures planned Havana's future as the new playground for the Americas. Joe Bananas, Vito Genovese and Frank Costello, just to mention a few of the Mafia hierarchy, were present for the largest Mafia forum since the Chicago meeting of 1932.

One of the main topics at the Havana Convention was the narcotics trade. It was a long-standing myth that the Mafia was against narcotics trafficking. Their involvement actually started when Luciano was a kid and running narcotics for the mob in New York City.

The execution of Benjamin "Bugsy" Siegel was the next "hot button" topic. Meyer Lansky had been a lifelong friend of Bugsy Siegel. Their relationship stemmed back to when they were bootlegging whiskey together, as youngsters in New York City. Siegel knew the gaming business from his casino venture in Las Vegas and inspired Lansky to do the same in Havana. Everyone liked Bugsy, but the big mistake he made was to let his girlfriend Virginia Hill become a project overseer during the construction of the Flamingo Casino & Hotel project. It seemed that she was lining her pockets. But worse, Siegel was suspected of skimming and depositing the money into a Swiss account. When the $1.5 million project reached $6 million in overruns, the bosses meeting in Havana decided that something drastic had to be done.

The following year, on June 20, 1947, not suspecting what was about to happen, Bugsy Siegel was sitting on a couch in the living room of Virginia Hill's home at 810 Linden Drive in Beverly Hills. As he was reading a newspaper, an assassin fired a number of shots, from a rifle, through the front window. Siegel was shot twice in the head, with one bullet exiting his skull near the bridge of his nose, causing his left eye to be blown out of its socket. He was also hit twice in the torso. His death was instantaneous and the graphic photos of his bullet-riddled body made headline news. Although there were enough suspects to go around, Eddie Cannizzaro, the "Cat Man," a connected west coast mobster, made a deathbed confession that he was the one who carried out the contract. Although the case isn't closed, it is cold and will most likely remain so, as it rests on the desk of Detective Les Zoeller of the Los Angeles Police Department.

In Havana, Vito Genovese, the patriarch of the Genovese family, met with Luciano in his room at the luxurious *Hotel Nacional*. Genovese informed him that the United States government knew where he was and was applying pressure on the Cuban Government to deport him. It was with this in mind that Genovese proposed that Luciano should turn over his interests to him. Luciano flipped out and rejected Don Vito's suggestion. Consulting with his capos "*caporegimes*," Anthony "Little Augie Pisano" Carfano and Michele "Big Mike" Miranda, who was soon to become his advisor and counselor "*consigliere*," they firmly believed that, here in Cuba, Luciano would be able to survive the onslaught and be able to remain in Havana. He also understood that if he remained in Cuba it would cost him, and buying his way out of this mess would only be the beginning.

Now, just before the Christmas holidays, Frank Sinatra, the idolized crooner known as "The Chairman of the Board," and other top celebrities offered entertainment for the otherwise somber Mafiosos. The media was given a cover story that the conference was nothing more than a gala party for Luciano and friends.

Frank Sinatra had flown to Havana with friends who happened to be Al Capone's cousins, Charlie, Rocco and Joseph Fischetti. One of Sinatra's acquaintances from Chicago, Joseph "Joe Fish" Fischetti, was assigned to be his bodyguard. Charlie and Rocco Fischetti also had a heavy suitcase for Luciano, containing $2 million as his share of the American business interests (rackets) that he still controlled.

Urban Legend had it that Jack Dempsey, the popular American World Heavyweight Boxing Champion from 1919 to 1926, better known as "Kid Blackie" or "The Manassa Mauler," also came to Cuba at Lansky's behest to provide companionship. During the 1920's, Dempsey was second only to Babe Ruth as the favorite American sports icon. During World War II Dempsey first joined the New York State National Guard as a first lieutenant. He resigned this commission to accept a commission as a lieutenant in the U.S. Coast Guard Reserve. Dempsey was honorably discharged from active duty as a full commander in September 1945. Jack Dempsey was a man to be trusted and supposedly Luciano trusted him to be his mule, his reliable courier, transporting large amounts of money from the

United States to Cuba. Of course, another trusted celebrity was purportedly Frank Sinatra.

No one would ever believe that these "All American Icons" were working with members of the mob....

On May 31, 1983, Jack Dempsey was 87, when he died of heart failure in New York City. His wife Deanna was at his side when he spoke his last words, "Don't worry, honey, I'm too mean to die."

It was obvious that Frank Sinatra enjoyed friendly relations with Mafia notables such as Carlo Gambino, "Joe Fish" Fischetti and Sam Giancana. The Federal Bureau of Investigation kept their eye on Sinatra for almost 50 years. Meyer Lansky was said to have been a friend of Sinatra's parents in Hoboken. During this time Sinatra spoke in awe about Bugsy Siegel and was in an AP syndicated photograph, seen in many newspapers, with Tommy 'Fatso' Marson, Don Carlo Gambino 'The Godfather', and Jimmy 'The Weasel, Fratianno.

A memo in FBI files revealed that Sinatra felt that he could be of use to them. However, it is difficult to believe that Sinatra would have become an FBI informer, better known as a "rat."

Sinatra was being treated at Cedars-Sinai Medical Center in Los Angeles, where physicians were attempting to stabilize his medical downhill spiral, when he told his wife Barbara, "I'm losing." Frank Sinatra died on May 14, 1998, at 82 years of age. It is alleged that he was buried with the wedding ring from his ex-wife, Mia Farrow, which she slid unnoticed into his suit pocket during his "viewing."

Aside from his perceived personal and public image, Frank Sinatra's music will shape his enduring legacy for decades to come. His 100th birthday will be celebrated at the Hollywood Bowl on Wednesday, July 22, 2015, and elsewhere for the remainder of the year.

"Lucky" Luciano, having arrived in Cuba using a bogus passport, was at the helm and took charge of the convention. Bosses and their representatives from the Cosa Nostra attended the Havana Conference, coming from New York and New Jersey, as well as New Orleans and Florida. At the same time, there was a somewhat lesser Jewish participation, but primarily the intention was to discuss a joint Cuban-based business venture. In Cuba the Mafia bosses believed that they were beyond the reach of the United States. They already had many local government officials in their pockets and thought that they could work with President Grau's administration. Greed was one of the motivating factors and it seemed that almost everyone was on the "take." Of course, there was always another way to take care of anyone who balked.

Santo Trafficante, Jr., known as "Louie Santos," moved to Havana in 1946 to oversee the interests of the Florida La Cosa Nostra, as well as his own "Sans Souci" nightclub and casino business. He also had a lesser-known, part ownership in several other Cuban gambling casinos. In Tampa, he owned a part of the elegant Columbia Restaurant located in Ybor City, as well as several other restaurants and bars in the greater Tampa Bay area. After Castro's revolution, Trafficante returned to the United States, where he died on March 17, 1987, at the age of 72.

Luiciano is Ousted from Cuba

Although his moves were clandestinely planned, the news media managed to catch up with him. A freelance journalist, Harry Wallace, recognized Luciano and exposed his whereabouts to the world. At about the same time, "Lucky" Luciano met Beverly Paterno, a high society party girl from New York at one of the social events in Havana. As Luciano said, "I'm only human" and so she became his escort for many of the parties and events held in Havana. Although it was not unusual for these affairs to be covered by the press, what had started as a secret plan quickly became fodder for the tabloids, all because of the press and a girlfriend that was far from discrete. Being one that enjoyed the limelight, she apparently notified the press ahead of time about where she and Luciano were going, so they were continually greeted by the press when they went out.

By February of 1947, the newspapers had discovered that Luciano was in Cuba. The well-known American federal drug agent, Harry J. Anslinger, demanded that Cuba immediately deport Luciano to Italy. As the United States put pressure on the Cuban government to expel him, Luciano referred to Anslinger as that "Sun of a bitch, Asslinger," which certainly didn't help Luciano's cause, but most likely it didn't make all that much difference. On February 21, 1947, Anslinger warned the Cuban government that the United States would stop all shipments of narcotic prescription drugs from entering Cuba, for as long as Luciano was in Havana. It only took two days before the Cuban government made its decision and took Luciano into custody. He was unceremoniously placed on a Turkish freighter and within 48 hours, Luciano was on his way back to Italy.

Traditionally, control of cocaine trafficking had been maintained by the Colombian cartel. However, the strategic location of Cuba as a way station for drugs grown in South America made Cuban participation an interesting possibility to the Mafia. The American Mafia has always cultivated the myth that they had nothing to do with narcotics, but next to the Colombian Cartel, they were right up there.

In October of 1947, a meeting between the American and Sicilian mobsters, including our notorious *paesano*, "Lucky" Luciano, plus Joseph Bonanno of the American delegation, occurred at the Grand Hotel in Palermo to discuss how the Sicilian and American Mafia could peacefully divide the handling of drugs. Although this meeting was the beginning of a turf war that lasted until 1984, millions of dollars changed hands, proving that the mob had no problem with the smuggling of drugs as a business.

The pressure was on and the time was right, so relying on the Cuban military and friends in government to assist him, Batista made his move. First, in anticipation of the 1948 elections, he campaigned for a senate seat in absentia. Surprisingly enough, he won, and immediately decided to plan another bid for the presidency in the 1952 election. Having won the interim election, Batista returned to Cuba on November 20, 1948. Carlos Prío Socarrás, of the Authentic Cuban Revolutionary Party, was the sitting president at the time, but this didn't prevent Batista from forming the new United Action Party, "*Partido de Acción Unitaria.*" There was no doubt but that Batista was back!

Planning the Future

Clandestinely, Meyer Lansky acted as a go-between, establishing a cooperative atmosphere between Batista and the Mob. Both Lansky and Batista were outsiders to the Sicilian-run criminal organization, but they both were ambitious and had greed as a common value. This unholy alliance continued as long as Batista's interests coincided with the interests of the

Mafia. During a meeting at the Waldorf Astoria in New York City, Batista offered Meyer Lansky control of the racetracks and casinos in Havana if he would help him return to the Cuban presidency.

Now that the Mafia could clearly see the potential Havana had to offer, they decided to move ahead on the racketeering venture in Cuba. Batista became an important part of the complicated puzzle. Although the former Sergeant/Colonel had lived in exile, he finagled his return to power as a Senator, providing the Mafia with a way of openly buying their way into Cuba.

Meetings between Batista and Meyer Lansky provided them both with a common goal. The planning for a territorial takeover began, with both men maneuvering to improve their advantage. Lansky figured out how to make money and Batista offered him his cooperation and protection in return... depending of course, on his return to the Presidency.

"Ours is a government of checks and balances. The Mafia and crooked businessmen make out checks, and the politicians and other compromised officials improve their bank balances." Steve Allen, a musician, composer, actor, comedian, and writer, as well as an American television personality

Setting up the 1952 Elections

In 1948, Carlos Prío Socarrás replaced Grau as the President of Cuba. He then stayed in power until March 10, 1952. Carlos Prío Socarrás was known as "The Cordial President." He once admitted, while talking to a friend, that, "Yes, they say that I was a bad president, but I'm still the best president that Cuba ever had."

Actions spoke louder than words and everyone could see what was happening. In the background, Batista was maneuvering to make a grab for the presidency and Prío didn't stop him when he could have. With the help of old friends from eight years before and a relatively small cadre of younger, disgruntled officers, Batista moved to seize the Army and the National Police throughout Cuba. At the same time he continuously attempted, and sometimes succeeded, in bribing politicians. With money from his backers, but with limited success, he attempted to influence the management of radio and television stations.

The Shot that was not heard

Eduardo René Chibás Ribas was an esteemed Cuban senator who had a weekly radio show on station CMQ at dinnertime every Sunday. The radio station had just launched CMQ-TV, and was about to become an NBC affiliate. CMQ, being a respected radio station, was on the air throughout Cuba and people listened to Chibás when he voiced his popular, anti-corruption views.

In 1945, Fidel Castro enrolled at the University of Havana as a law student. He admittedly was an activist and had socialistic leanings, but saw Chibás as his mentor and valued him for his highly respected, straitlaced approach to politics. During this era, Castro learned to appreciate the media as a tool to influence the public.

In 1947, Eduardo Chibás, known to his listening public as "Eddie Chibás," formed the *Partido del Pueblo Cubano, Ortodoxo*

Party. A large assembly of Grau's former constituents rethought their previous convictions and joined this non-communist group of political reformers, whose goal it was to clean up politics and expose corruption. Chibás felt that a revolutionary change was necessary in Cuba, but that it should be constitutional instead of violent. He ran for the Cuban presidency in 1948, but still being relatively unknown, came in third place. Having had name recognition and the backing of lobbyists, Carlos Prío won the election, leaving Chibás as the leader of the opposition party. Fidel joined the *Ortodoxo* Party, and years later on August 26, 2007, Castro even wrote an article in the Communist Youth newspaper, the *Juventud Rebelde*, praising Eduardo Chibás for the consistent honesty he had always shown.

On August 5, 1951, Eddie's listening public was waiting for him to expose the national Minister of Education, Aureliano Sánchez Arango, of fraud and embezzlement. In a July broadcast, Eddie Chibás had accused Sánchez of stealing from the children's breakfast funds, as a way to construct his own private housing project in Guatemala. In this previous broadcast, Chibás promised to present evidence that would prove that Arango was nothing more than a thief. Instead of this, during his August 5th radio show, he warned his listeners to beware of Batista and the strong possibility of his carrying out a military coup d'état. For what at the time seemed to be strange, Chibás followed this by repeating his position and ended his commentary with a farewell statement.

The members of the Cuban Congress that were to have presented him with the proof he needed, betrayed him by backing out, leaving Eddie twisting in the wind, without any hard evidence to present to his audience. There were however some that thought the entire incident may have been a ruse to entrap Chibás and undermine his credibility.

Feeling that he had let down his followers and going into a depressed state of mind, Eddie believed that the only way out of this dilemma was to commit suicide. Doing this while on the air, was in some bizarre way his idea of vanquishing himself. After emphasizing the importance of the issues concerning political corruption, he signed off. Pride can be a terrible thing! When Eddie pulled the trigger of his pistol, a shot rang out in the station's studio. However, it was thought that being overwrought, his aim and timing may have been off, or perhaps he intended for the shot to just wound him for the purpose of gaining sympathy. The fact is that the bullet penetrated his abdomen, as the airways carried a lyrical commercial with a Latin beat for "Café Pilon." Instead of the dramatic, reverberating sound of a gunshot, his listeners only heard a commercial for the popular coffee.

Chibás lingered on for eleven days, all the while being under constant intensive care. In spite of the fact that he was originally expected to survive, he did not... and on August 16, 1951, Eddie Chibás died at the hospital in Havana.

His funeral became a national event, as he was ceremoniously buried in the Colon Cemetery. The entire nation mourned his passing and with it, Cuba lost a strong and honest contender for the 1952 presidential election.

Batista Seizes Power

A few weeks after Chibás' suicide, but before the scheduled elections, Castro actually met with the then-Senator Batista. The two men spent several hours discussing political issues at Batista's ranch. What was said is not known exactly, but

Batista entertained ideas that would fulfill Chibás' worst fears, some of which had been expressed prior to his death.

For a second time, Batista made a bid for the presidency of Cuba, this time in a three-way race. The media polls showed that his popularity had waned and that he was a distant third with Roberto Agramonte, of the *Ortodoxo* (Orthodox) Party leading, and Carlos Hevia of the *Autentico* (Authentic) Party holding second place.

Apparently losing in the opinion polls, Batista, with military support and a still loyal labor force backing him, overthrew the legitimate government. On March 10, 1952, Batista forced President Carlos Prío Socarrás out of office, blatantly taking the seat of the presidency for himself and declaring himself the Provisional President. Shortly after the coup, the United States government officially accepted Batista as an ally, and officially recognized his new régime.

Although he made many promises, Batista did not continue the progressive social policies of his first term. Instead, he quickly turned democratic Cuba into a "Police State." According to some perhaps questionable reports, Batista was accused of murdering 20,000 Cubans during the following seven years, thereby destroying individual liberty for the people. The Eisenhower Administration, influenced by "Special Interest Groups," sent aid to his régime. To a great extent, it was American politics that enabled Batista, who had come to power illegally, to get financial support for his "Reign of Terror." Administration spokesmen publicly praised Batista, hailing him as a strong ally and a good friend to America! All this was happening at a time when Batista was responsible for murdering thousands of his people and destroying the last remnants of freedom, while at the same time stealing hundreds of millions of dollars from the Cuban Treasury.

Opposition to Batista Grows

With so many Cubans in opposition to Batista, it was no surprise that groups formed throughout the country to wrest him out of office. One of these was organized by Fidel Castro who had previously met with Batista when he was a Senator. On July 26, 1953, Fidel mounted an attack on the Moncada Army Barracks in the Oriente Province, with an additional attack on the Bayamo barracks. Militarily the raid failed and very little success could be claimed. However, the mere fact that it happened was a political victory for those who sought liberation from the oppressive Batista regime. There was no doubt in anyone's mind but that similar skirmishes would follow. The raid heightened public awareness and Fidel Castro's name became a household word. Because of this, Castro received international recognition, and his following grew, primarily among young people and university students.

In 1955, José Antonio Echeverría, a student leader and Cuban revolutionary, created the *Directorio Revolucionario* ("DR") or Revolutionary Directorate, to fight Batista as an underground paramilitary. Although not all of those involved in the *Directorio Revolucionario* resorted to violence, the ones that did engaged in sabotage, terrorism and assassinations, to overthrow the Batista régime. The "DR" operated as the militant arm of the Federation of University Students FEU and the *Partido Auténticos*, also known as the Authentic Cuban Revolutionary Party or PRC-A.

Murder in the Streets

Some of Batista's followers intimidated, jailed and even killed political opponents. One of the pro-Batista paramilitary thugs was Rolando Arcadio Masferrer Rojas, who was born in Holguín on July 12, 1918. He had been a member of the Abraham

Lincoln Brigade, organized in 1936 by the Communist International during the Spanish Civil War. Returning to Cuba, he became a staunch supporter of Batista, who at that time had the backing of the Communist Party. Masferrer was by no means the average run of the mill thug and, in addition to being a lawyer, he ran for office and won a seat in the Cuban Senate. He was also a guerrilla leader, political activist, a member of the Cuban Communist Party, a newspaper publisher, and responsible for the founding of "Los Tigres de Masferrer," a guerrilla organization he organized to support Batista militarily. He also published two newspapers, *Tiempo* in Havana and *Libertad* in Santiago de Cuba.

Becoming a radical anti-communist, he was ousted from the Cuban Communist Party. Regardless, Masferrer was a dangerous man and people learned to keep their mouths shut and play it low key when he was around. As a pro-Batista political activist, he took credit for supposedly attacking Castro's rebels in the Sierra Maestra Mountains. Actually, in most cases his group of not-so-fierce fighters stayed safely within the city limits of Santiago de Cuba, extorting money from the residents.

In 1959, after Castro's successful entry into Havana, Masferrer fled to the United States where he befriended American union bosses such as Jimmy Hoffa and got to know Mafia leaders such as Santo Trafficante in Tampa, Florida. Masferrer worked with Richard Bissell of the Central Intelligence Agency, planning another assassination attempt on Castro. He was seen at a ranch owned by multi-millionaire Howard Hughes, where he was training paid assassins, and he even met with President Kennedy in Washington.

With money contributed by fellow Cubans living in Florida, he later planned to carry out the assassination of Fidel Castro by attacking him from a distant base in Haiti. It all ended when, on October 31, 1975, Masferrer was killed by a car bomb in Miami. Although his figures may be somewhat exaggerated, Castro claimed that Masferrer was responsible for the death of as many as 2,000 people during the Batista era.

The Man in the White Suit

Esteban Ventura Novo, known as the white-suited assassin, was infamous in Havana's Fifth Precinct, although he later moved to the Ninth Precinct. He was known for his killings, massacres and for the cruel torturing of his adversaries. Ventura started as a police snitch who gained his promotions by means of his cruel, vicious conduct and the efficient way he dispatched the so-called "enemies of the state." Rewarded for his brutal loyalty, Ventura eventually was promoted to the rank of lieutenant colonel.

The Military, Police and Other Cutthroats

Lieutenant Colonel Pilar García, originally in Cuba's Military Aviation branch, became the commander of the Goicuria garrison, the military headquarters in Matanzas Province east of Havana. He heavy-handedly killed anyone in his Precinct that he perceived as being an enemy of Batista. On April 29, 1956, the Goicuria Barracks in Matanzas were attacked by rebel forces. The attackers barely got to the gates when they and their leader, Reynold García, were massacred by the pro-Batista forces, headed by the Colonel. Of the survivors, six were arrested and each sentenced to 6 years in prison.

Pilar García was promoted by Batista to the esteemed position of "National Police Chief," a position he held until fleeing Cuba with Batista.

Batista, also quietly enlisted Lieutenant Colonel Antonio Blanco Rico, as chief of the *Servicio de Inteligencia Militar* (SIM), his secret police, and promoted the ambitious Rafael Salas Cañizares to the rank of Brigadier General in the Cuban National Police, with orders to maintain order and seek out Castro's pesky rebels. On October 29, 1956, Colonel Blanco Rico was killed as a target of random opportunity, at the Montmartre Night Club in Havana. Fidel Castro publicly condemned the assassination and rebuked Echeverría's *Directorio Revolucionario* as well, stating that, "Such acts must not be indiscriminate." Castro added, "From a political revolutionary standpoint, his assassination was not justified. Blanco Rico was not a Fascist executioner." Colonel Marcelo Tabernilla was also targeted, however bullets intended for him struck and severely wounded his wife Marta Poli.

The next day Brigadier General Rafael Salas Cañizares of the National Police received a telephone call that Castro's hitmen, responsible for the killing of Colonel Antonio Blanco Rico, had sought asylum in the Haitian Embassy. Violating International Law, the Chief of the National Police led an assault on the embassy. The rebels were all killed in the ensuing exchange of gunfire. General Salas Cañizares was also wounded in the shootout and died two days later.

There was a standing mandate that all of Batista's goons had to give their leader a kickback on anything they stole or seized from the people. Salas Cañizares was said to have brazenly violated these orders. There are those who believe he may have walked into a bullet because of this.

Innocent people were no longer safe from the violence that permeated Havana. The residents became polarized and were compelled to choose sides. Communities that were once harmonious found themselves engaged in open warfare and hatred. Batista promoted the worst cutthroats to high positions within the police.

Attack on the Presidential Palace

The *Directorio Revolucionario* ("DR") existed during the mid-1950's and it was a Cuban University students' group in opposition to the dictator President Fulgencio Batista. It was one of the most active terrorist organizations in Havana. Although they were given orders not to attack the rank and file police officers, semantics became important, as their targets were no longer "assassinated," but rather were "executed." To them the term sounded more legally acceptable. However, regardless of how it is phrased, murder is murder!

At 3:20 on the afternoon of March 13, 1957, fifty attackers from the "DR", led by Carlos Gutiérrez Menoyo, attacked the Presidential Palace. Menoyo had fought in the Sahara Desert against the German forces under General Rommel during World War II. By demonstrating great courage, Carlos had been decorated and given the rank of second lieutenant in the French army and was uniquely suited for this task. Now, with workers representing labor, and rebellious students from the university, they drove up to the entrance to the Presidential Palace in delivery van #7, marked "Fast Delivery S.A." They also had two additional cars weighted down with bombs, rifles, and automatic weapons.

With guns blazing, they exited their vehicles and attacked the unwary guards at the Presidential Palace. Running, the attackers stormed into the dining room and then on to the offices on the lower level, only to find them empty. Since the elevator was up on the third floor of the building, the attackers were momentarily stymied. Although they had previously studied a floor plan of the palace, they became disoriented, perhaps from the intense fighting that had already claimed about ten of their number. An equal number or more of the president's elite guards also lay dead on the presidential grounds. For a moment those attackers still alive had difficulty in locating the grand marble staircase to the second floor. Once they did, they were repelled by a hail of gunfire from the guardsmen, now fully aware of what was happening. When Carlos Menoyo was fatally hit on the stairs, Menelao Mora Morales took charge of the assault and managed to ascend to the top of the stairs, where he also was shot dead. About nine men made it to the second floor, but without leadership, they didn't know where to go from there.

Trapped on the second floor, they searched for a way out. The hapless, amateur warriors couldn't retreat down the stairs where their leaders lay and where the shooting was still intense. Stuck, they didn't know how to get up to the third floor or back down the staircase and out of the building. Batista was on the upper floor with his family, as the remaining attackers were now being methodically killed. To them the third floor could only be reached by elevator, which was effectively being kept in place at the top of the lift shaft, thus preventing the assault from reaching Batista and his family.

Although some few managed to escape during the next few hours, thirty-five of the attackers were killed in and around the palace. A final count revealed that five of the palace guards were killed along with one tourist, who just happened to be there at the wrong time. Only three of the rebels managed to find a way out and escaped.

Radio Station CMQ

At the same time the attack on the Presidential Palace was taking place, the leader of a second band of rebels, José Antonio Echeverría, the president of the "DR," led an attack on a local radio station. His group, armed with machine guns and handguns, assaulted *Radio Reloj Cuba* CMQ, an international radio station that had been founded on July 1, 1947, and normally broadcast the ticking of a clock, along with news, information and the time of day.

Shooting their way into the radio station, they took control of the broadcasting studio and went on the air. Echeverría attempted to read a three-minute message to the listening audience, affirming that Batista was dead, but due to technical reasons, only the first few words were actually aired. He was unaware that his message failed to get out on the airwaves and, leaving the building, he hurried back to his car. On his way back to the University of Havana, which was located just a few blocks away, he encountered a police patrol. The firefight that ensued only lasted a few minutes, during which Echeverría was killed.

The failed attempt to assassinate Batista brought on brutal retaliations. The very same evening Senator Pelayo Cuervo Navarro, a non-violent member of the Ortodoxo opposition party, was dragged out of his house by the Cuban Bureau of Investigations, taken to a nearby lake and shot dead. In the days that followed, other members of the "DR" were rounded up by the police and were tortured before being killed. The notorious Police Captain Esteban Ventura brought in and arrested many of the surviving students who were forced to turn in others, many of whom were innocent of any participation in these attacks. The fact that people were executed by the police without benefit of representation or a trial, showed the world the brutality of Batista's régime.

Surprisingly, within and outside of the country, Batista was hailed a champion of business interests. Batista considered this support a direct endorsement of his régime. Sugar prices remained high during this period and Cuba enjoyed one of its best years agriculturally. For those at the top of the ladder, the Cuban economy flourished!

At the same time, the numerous funerals in the days following the attacks and the funerals for others slain by the police were attended by large crowds, indicating a strong support for the anti-Batista factions.

The Killings Continue

For a long time, Batista turned a blind eye to the unlawful proceedings. The police continued to take it upon themselves to seek out and kill many other opposition leaders to the régime. People soon realized that what had happened to Senator Pelayo Cuervo Navarro, who had nothing to do with the attack on the Presidential Palace, could happen to them.

Although the rebels failed in their attempt to overthrow Batista, still they reportedly killed soldiers and policemen in the ongoing chaos and, in return, many of their own number were also being killed.

Castro, high in the Sierra Maestra Mountains, heard of this attack on his radio and remarked that it was a brave act although rash... "Foolhardy" was a word that he used. The M-26-7 and the "DR" never did see things eye-to-eye and now more than ever Castro became annoyed with the "DR's" random killings. However, Castro's M-26-7 militia also had a reputation of indiscriminately placing bombs, one of which blew a female employee to pieces in the restroom at the once-grand theater, "Teatro America."

A farmer, who failed to cooperate with Batista's army, was locked into his home with his wife and his daughter, which was then set on fire killing them all. They also allegedly got even for the atrocities committed at the attack on the Moncada Army Barracks by cutting the genitals off their opponents. On September 26, 1957, 18 young males were found dead in the Oriente Province. Among them were two girls that had been sexually molested by the police, murdered, and then left lying in the streets naked. Sometimes these acts were carried out by the police or army and then blamed on the M-26-7.

Although there was a great deal of doubt, at the time the "DR" was said to be killing Pro-Batista students. The M-26-7 had placed signs in movie theaters seeking to avenge the murders they claimed were committed by the police. Police Captain Esteban Ventura Novo of the 9th Police Precinct became more notorious for his increasingly vicious methods. Because of the heavily polarized partisan views, it became evermore difficult to distinguish truth from fiction. Each side told of ever-increasing atrocities by the opposition side. Like in war, the first casualty was the truth...

Cuban Grand Prix

Batista established the Cuban Grand Prix in 1957, as a way of augmenting the national income. On February 23, 1958, during the second annual Cuban Grand Prix, world champion "Formula One" racecar driver Juan Manuel Fangio from Argentina was kidnapped at Havana's Hotel Lincoln by urban rebels, thereby preventing him from competing. He was held for

29 hours at three different locations in Havana, during the time of the Grand Prix. However, since he wasn't involved in politics he was released by his captors. At a later date, he stated that he was treated well and that he remained friends with his captors.

Cuban Grand Prix Poster - 1957

El Presidente

Because of his massive ego, Batista also demanded that the upper strata of Cuban society socially recognize his wife as the "First Lady" and himself as *"El Presidente."* Because of his heritage, they had never really accepted him into their elite social circles. This time his primary goal was to improve his own social status by demanding due deference, by force if necessary, and of course to always increase his personal wealth.

Despite Batista's constitutional abuses and his alliance with the Mafia, the years under his régime were the most prosperous ones in Cuba's history. Cuban workers fared relatively well as their wages rose. At the lower end of the economic ladder, a maid could expect to make $25 to $30 a month, whereas the average high school teacher made about $140. Of course people in business could expect more and some made as much as $750 per month. It has been estimated that at that time this approximated the average income of families in some of the Mediterranean countries of Europe. Without a doubt, it was the best in the Caribbean.

Soon, with Mafia guidance, drugs, prostitution, shows and the casinos flourished. Prostitutes were seen near the casinos, standing in doorways. They also made their availability known as they smiled at sailors and tourists while strolling the streets, or waving from open windows. One estimate stated that approximately 11,500 young ladies worked their trade in Havana.

Meyer Lansky's concept became a reality. His scheme worked and people came! Despite Batista's heavy-handed dictatorship, it was an immediate success! By 1954, Batista had abandoned his socialistic alliances and formed the conservative, pro-capitalistic "Progressive Action Party."

Havana had become an adult playground. This happened even before Las Vegas came into its own. The inexpensive *Cuba Libre* was the drink of choice, with the popular Coca-Cola actually costing more than the rum. Beautiful girls were abundant and readily available at a price. The Montmartre Club became famous for its dance floor featuring Pérez Prado and his mambo beat. Many famous American actors performed at the hotels, and things were swinging. Although Havana became a party town, there were always shadowy figures in the background maintaining tight control. Cuba became a totalitarian police state! It was some time later that Fidel Castro estimated that 20,000 Cubans were murdered during the 7-year Batista régime. Of course, Castro might have exaggerated and the figure may have been as few as 5,000 Cubans, but regardless of the actual number, there is no doubt that many people were killed. Batista turned his back on former allies and became ultra anti-communistic, thus hoping to gain additional support from the United States.

Some of the statistics that Castro used in his speeches were said to have been invented by Miguel Angel Quevedo, the editor of the magazine *"Bohemia."* Later Quevedo broke his ties with Castro and left Cuba. Feeling ashamed of the part he played in this myth, he committed suicide.

Meyer Lansky's brother Jake became the manager of the *Hotel Nacional*, to which they had now built another wing to house the casino. The enormous take from gambling was split nightly and a personal bagman went around collecting 10% of all the profits for Batista's wife. It was not a bad take considering that she didn't even pay income taxes on her share! No one dared to intervene in her financial enhancement activities and a squad of goons protected her interests. It seems that she was not taking any chances when it came to her portion of the take.

Prostitution and the casinos kept the lights burning and the coffers full! In 1960, Senator John F. Kennedy criticized the Republican Party and President Eisenhower for supporting

Batista. It was estimated that hundreds of millions of dollars were stolen from the Cuban people and went into private pockets. According to Kennedy, at the start of 1959, United States companies such as United Fruit and Lykes Brothers owned about 40% of the Cuban sugar lands. They owned almost all the cattle ranches and 90% of the mines and mineral concessions. Eighty percent of the utilities and practically all of the oil industry was American owned, and the United States supplied two-thirds of all Cuba's imports. Although some of the figures used by Kennedy may have been exaggerated, there is no doubt but that he said it.

Lobbyists representing American interests openly bribed and, in turn, controlled Cuban legislators. The chosen few were living high off the hog and "Let the good times roll" was the credo of the rich, while Cuba's poorer people languished. As an example, International Telephone and Telegraph Corporation, "ITT," owned the Cuban Telephone Company, and in appreciation they presented Batista with an ostentatious, gold-plated telephone as a small expression of gratitude.

Kennedy may have exaggerated somewhat when he said, "I believe that there is no country in the world including any and all the countries under colonial domination, where economic colonization, humiliation and exploitation were worse than in Cuba." However, his sentiments were sound. At that time, Kennedy was in agreement with Castro, who proclaimed independence and an end to corruption in Cuba. With such a top-heavy economy, things were bound to change....

The Tide Turns Against Batista

A strategy of terror on the part of the government followed, but this brutal behavior backfired and led to forty-five Cuban organizations signing an open letter supporting the 26th of July Movement. After serving time in prison and returning to Cuba on his boat, the *Granma*, from exile in Mexico, Fidel orchestrated his ultimate revolution. War against the Batista régime started in earnest after 1956, from an encampment high in the Sierra Maestra Mountains near the southeastern end of the island.

Listening to the lobbyists and not wanting to upset the apple cart the United States continued to supply Batista with ships, planes, tanks and equipment. In March of 1958, newspapers and television announced that American-made napalm was being used against Cuban civilians. International newspapers caused an uproar when they published photos of Cuban bodies in the streets, due to these actions.

Actually, napalm was used against Castro in the mountains and the photos showing bodies in the streets were mostly as the result of military and police action. The propaganda ploy worked and the United States, understanding the political consequences, stopped the sales of arms to the Batista government. On December 11, 1958, the U.S. Ambassador Earl T. Smith informed Batista that the United States would no longer support his régime. Later at the United Nations, Cuba leveled charges against the United States when Castro reminded the delegates that Batista had used American-made bombs and napalm on innocent civilians, as well as on his forces.

Just east of Havana, the revolution was raging in Santa Clara and although the newspapers were censored, everyone was receiving firsthand accounts of the progress the rebels were making. "Che" Guevara and Camilo Cienfuegos had the disheartened Cuban Army on the run and it was only a matter of time before they would be entering Havana.

The excesses in Havana were incredible, but it was the cruelty to the Cuban people during Batista's régime, that provoked them. From about 1957 on, the killings in the streets increased, with the newspapers counting victims daily, without actually blaming the government or identifying the killers. To some extent, it was not that the people were supporting Fidel, but rather it was that they had had enough of Batista killing their fellow citizens and at the same time openly lining his pockets, at their expense.

During the end of 1958, people were not in the mood to celebrate the holidays. A heavy feeling of uncertainty hung in the air. Scattered around Havana, few people, other than the remaining tourists that were staying at resort hotels, celebrated. However, some of the wealthiest and most influential people in Havana celebrated at the Riviera Hotel. Although they were bringing in the New Year, for them it was really a doom's day celebration.

Although in 1957 and 1958, commercial aviation between Cuba and the United States increased, it was only because people feared for their lives and were leaving the island. The lasting effect was that many potential tourists were now staying away from Cuba and, in particular, away from Havana. What had started out as a fun town and a lucrative tourist bonanza was becoming a dangerous and depressing battle zone. Americans were beginning to look west to Las Vegas as their gambling and entertainment mecca.

Batista could sense the unrest growing across the country. With the rebels moving in from the east, he knew that his time was extremely limited, so he brazenly raided the Cuban Treasury, which was flush with United States dollars due to increased sugar sales and recent elevated world sugar prices. On December 31, 1958, at a private New Year's Eve party for the

"Chosen Few," Batista told members of his Cabinet and some of his closest followers, that he was departing from the country. Batista was aware that the party was over and that if he remained any longer it would most likely cost him his life!

During the early hours of January 1, 1959, Batista having already set up a Swiss bank account boarded a commercial airliner at Camp Columbia with Brigadier General Pilar García and his sons and their families, as well as the dictator's Chief-of-Staff, General Francisco Tabernilla with his family. As Castro's forces approached Havana, they departed from Cuba.

This time with public opinion opposing the atrocities of his régime, the United States refused Batista entry. His dilemma was that he had also been denied asylum in Mexico.

Aside from his Swiss account, Batista took along an additional 300 million dollars of loose change that he had accumulated through graft and payoffs. He and some of his buddies grabbed an estimated 700 million American dollars in cash, paintings and other objets d'art.

As the first leg of his journey, he and 40 of his ardent supporters as well as their families flew to Ciudad Trujillo in the Dominican Republic. Later on that night, another plane departed from Havana, carrying additional politicians and Cabinet members. Other affluent people left on their own yachts for Florida. In all, there was an estimated 180 people that left Cuba that evening.

Batista remained in the Dominican Republic until Portugal's Prime Minister António de Oliveira Salazar extended him safe exile, providing he would refrain from politics....

The First Day in Cuba without Batista

The next day, with most streets empty, Castro's supporters provided security and began patrolling the streets. Unlike the riots after Machado left Cuba, they secured the city and insured a relatively tranquil takeover. The expected looting was minimal, although the hated parking meters were vandalized and gaming machines were overturned in the casinos. For a week, it almost seemed like "the calm before the storm." Then, on January 8, 1959, Fidel Castro and his army of liberation rolled into Havana....

Batista lived for a time on the island of Madeira before moving to Estoril near Lisbon. He served as the Chairman of a Spanish life insurance company and wrote some books. On August 6, 1973, he died of a heart attack at Guadalmina near Marbella, Spain, just two days prior to a supposed assassination attempt. Following Batista's death, his wife Marta returned to the United States where she died on October 2, 2006, at her West Palm Beach home, a result of Alzheimer's disease.

With Batista gone and no longer the protector and benefactor that the Mafia depended upon, people like Meyer Lansky retreated to a quiet life in South Florida. One of his favorite haunts, where he and friends would meet, was "Wolfie's Rascal House" on Maimi Beach.

It was here that my friend Juan, an informative acquaintance, while having lunch with his grandmother, had the occasion to meet one of the men inconspicuously sitting in the back with his cronies. The man, unimpressive, small in stature and having a quiet demeanor, shook my friend's hand, remarking what a good boy he was. Later Juan expressed his views to his grandmother saying what a fine gentleman he had met. Meyer Lansky, a gentleman in many ways, was a heavy smoker and it caught up with him when he died of lung cancer at 80 years of age in Miami Beach. He was buried in an unassuming plot, at the Mt. Nebo cemetery in West Miami. The death of the "Chairman of Murder Incorporated," as he was called, closed a significant chapter in an era of crime that involved both Cuba and the United States for almost half a century.

"I want to put you all at ease. We will tolerate no guerrillas in the casinos or the swimming pools!" Fulgencio Batista, as Dictator of Cuba

Photographs
Early Cuban Heroes

Narciso López (1797 – 1851)

José Antonio Aponte

Ten Years' War and Beyond

Cuban Patriotic Poster, c 1900

José Martí

Carlos Manuel de Céspedes del Castillo

Generals – Cuban War of Independence

Máximo Gómez

Calixto García

Antonio Maceo Grajales

Spanish–American War

USS *Maine* entering Havana Harbor – 1898

Teddy Roosevelt and the Rough Riders

Admiral Cervera y Topete
Admiral of the Spanish Fleet

Colonel Theodore Roosevelt
Commander of the Rough Riders

The Roaring Twenties

Julio Antonio Mella

Tina Modotti
Temptress, Photograher and Soviet Agent

Edward Weston   Margrethe Mather

Vittorio Vidali   Leon Trotsky

Dolores Del Rio   Frida & Rivera

Birds of a Feather

Diego Rivera, Delores del Rio, Frida Kahlo & Orson Welles

In the Arsenal by Diego Rivera

Tina Modotti and Julio Mella with Vittorio behind them wearing a black hat. Frida Kahlo, Rivera's wife is in the middle.

Interesting Times

The SS *San Pasqual*

The ship that became a hotel off the coast of Cayo Las Brujas, Cuba

Vintage Cubana Airliners

DC-3

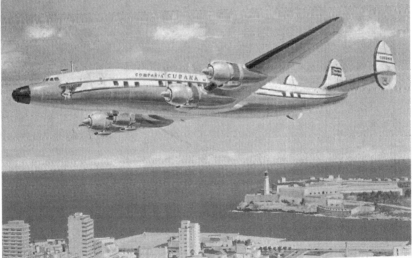

Constellation

Cuban Presidents

Pres. Tomás Estrada Palma
First Elected President

Pres. Jose Miguel Gomez
Second Elected President

Pres. Mario García Menocal
Third Elected President

Pres. Alfreso Zayas
Fourth Elected President

Los Supremos

Pres. Gerardo Machado
Sept.28, 1871 - Mar.29, 1939

Pres. Fulgencio Batista
Jan.16, 1901 - Aug.6, 1973

Also...

Pres. Federico Laredo Brú
*President who denied the Jews
from debarking in Havana*

Captain Gustav Schröder
*Master of the M/S Saint Louis
"Righteous Among the Nations"*

M/S *Saint Louis* – 1939

Lucky Luciano, Lansky & Batista
The Mob in Havana - c 1946

The Moncada Barracks after being attacked

Batista's soldiers execute one of Castro's rebels

Cuban Vessels of War

The Warship *Cuba*
Bombarded the Hotel Nacional *in 1933*

The *Granma*

The Castro Era

Fidel & Raúl Castro   "Che" Guevara

Camilo Cienfuegos & Fidel

January 8, 1959

Fidel, Osvaldo Dorticós and "Che" Guevara

"Che" Guevara and Comrades

Bay of Pigs Invasion, 1961

Air attack during the Bay of Pigs Invasion

Fidel Conducting Operations during the Bay of Pigs
Invasion, near Playa Girón

Surrender of Brigade 2506 "Freedom Fighters"

Women of the Revolution

Vilma Lucila Espin

Celia Sánchez

Vilma, Fidel and comrades in the mountains

Vilma with Fidel

Fidel Castro in New York, 1959

Papa Hemingway

Hemingway's Fish Story!

Ernest Hemingway & Fidel Castro

Spencer Tracy, Ernest & Mary Hemingway
"La Florida," Havana, Cuba - 1955

CIA Operatives

Marita Lorenz

Frank Sturgis

The Cuban Missile Crisis

The Blockade

"Che's" Bolivian Insurgency

Tamara Bunke   President René Barrientos

Aleida March & "Che" Guevara

Felix Rodriguez & "Che" Guevara
Moments prior to "Che's" Execution

Tamara Bunke dressed as a peasant girl

"Che" Guevara's Monument and Mausoleum

Cuba's Future

President Raúl Castro & Vice President Díaz-Canel
The Old Guard Ushers in Cuba's Future

Present-Day Cuban Army

President Raúl Castro & President Vladimir Putin
of Russia reviewing Cuban Troops
© picture-alliance/dpa

Soviet Intelligence Base in Lourdes, Cuba
© Getty Images

"A picture is worth a thousand words." Arthur
Brisbane, editor of The New York Times, discussing
journalism and publicity

The Exciting Story of Cuba.... Part 9

Fidel Castro, the Early Years

A Cuban Dilemma

Many conflicting views regarding Cuba have been published. Deep-seated opinions are firmly rooted in people, regarding this relatively recent part of Cuban history. The story of Fidel Castro's revolution had many twists and turns in it, so to maintain a clearer perspective, the many sides of this historical episode deserve to be viewed in an unbiased way. Neither side had a monopoly on the truth and there are frequently more than just two sides to a story.

Prior to the revolution of 1958, the communists, although very vocal and exceptionally strong in many ways, were not as influential on a national level. This held true, especially among the university students and the members of the labor movement. It was for this reason that they constantly had to make alliances with other groups... especially when they were not hiding from the secret police.

Neither Communism nor Capitalism has always served Cuba well, but on the other hand, neither one has always been totally wrong. Simplistically, it was Capitalism that first established agriculture, commerce and industry; however, it was Communism that allowed the poorer middle-class to take a greater part in the nation's future. At times, the pendulum swung wildly from one extreme to the other and often the nation's leaders were either too weak for the position they held, giving in to corruption, or too strong, forcing their unbending will on the country. In the background were students, labor parties and special interest groups ready to take their petitions to the streets and, if need be, to riot in order for their voices to be heard....

"In a progressive country change is constant; change is inevitable." Benjamin Disraeli, British Conservative politician, writer and aristocrat who twice served as Prime Minister

The Castro Family

Fidel Castro was born on August 13, 1926, on his father's farm in what is now the Holguín Province, located in the Eastern region of the country. It is frequently called *el granero de Cuba* or Cuba's barn. Fidel's father, Ángel María Bautista Castro y Argiz, came to Cuba from Galicia in the northwestern part of Spain. He first came to Cuba, having agreed to take someone else's enlistment in the Spanish Army, for the express purpose of fighting against the Cuban revolutionaries during the War of Independence. During his time conscripted in the Spanish military in Cuba, Ángel could see the possibilities of settling in Cuba. In 1898 after the war, the military shipped Ángel back to Spain to be discharged. However, having ambitious ideas, Ángel returned to Cuba the following year as an immigrant.

Starting as a laborer for the United Fruit Company, he soon founded his own company, which hired temporary farm workers out to United Fruit, as well as to other companies that needed day laborers. As his wealth increased, he eventually bought land in northeastern Cuba and became the wealthy plantation owner of over 27 thousand acres, supplying sugar cane under contract to United Fruit Company for their mills.

Without the benefit of being married to Ángel, Lina Ruz González had seven children by him, three boys and four girls. She was a simple woman who worked for him as a domestic servant. Fidel was her third child.... Lina married Fidel's father in 1943, after his first wife, María Luisa Argota y Reyes, who was sarcastically known as the "Princess," died, leaving her five children behind. From all accounts, it didn't seem as if anyone missed her.

In addition to the five children that Maria had, there was also a farmhand's daughter, Generosa, who bore Ángel at least one son, by the name of Martin.

Fidel was given his mother's name "Ruz" before her marriage to his father, but even after his mother's marriage, when Fidel was a teenager, although he was accepted, he continued to be treated as a bastard child, rather than a son, by his rough-hewn father. Much of Fidel's early life is obscure, but as a teenager, there were times that he acted impulsively, as with most boys.... Once when he was refused the use of the family car, he threatened to set it on fire. At another time, he rode his bicycle as fast as he could into a stonewall on a dare; of course he got scraped up, but fortunately for him, it didn't take long before he made a complete recovery.

Fidel's mother came from Pinar del Río, on the far western end of Cuba. Her family originally came to Cuba from the Spanish Canary Islands.

Fidel's father never did settle down and lived a rough and tumble life in the "wild" Oriente territory. It seemed that his sexual appetite was such that he never wanted to settle down with just one woman. Although his father was rich and could afford to raise all of his children in a more genteel, educated fashion, it just was not in him. Consequently, Fidel and his siblings were raised right alongside the migrant African/Haitian field workers.

When he was six years old, Castro and his elder siblings, Ramón and Angela, were sent to live with a teacher in Santiago de Cuba. His parents did not seem to show much love or interest towards their children. The family was divided and having children was accidental, in those times before birth control. Ramón later became the quartermaster for the rebel fighters during the revolution, and is presently over 90 years old and married. He lives in Havana and has two grown children.

Angela died on February 29, 2012, after a lengthy illness at a clinic in Havana. She was 88 years old, suffering from cancer and Alzheimer's disease.

In 1942 after attending two Jesuit institutions, Fidel entered the *Colegio Belén* preparatory school in Havana. Although he was never much of a scholar, he did have a photographic memory and could memorize entire pages of text at a time. Fidel enjoyed sports, especially baseball, and was always considered a superior athlete.

At fourteen years of age, Fidel wrote a letter to U.S. President Franklin D. Roosevelt conveying his pleasure at Roosevelt's re-election. He continued the letter by asking Roosevelt for a green ten-dollar bill since he had never seen one before. He ended the letter with, "Thank you very much. Good-bye. Your friend, Fidel Castro." Perhaps things in Cuba would be different today had Fidel received a written reply and a green ten-dollar bill from Franklin D....

"The test of our progress is not whether we add more to the abundance of those who have much; it is whether we provide enough for those who have little..." Franklin D. Roosevelt, 32nd President of the United States

Castro's Anti-Imperialistic Activities

During the second semester of 1945, at the University of Havana, Fidel Castro studied law and became involved in student politics. It was during a time when student protesters were exceptionally active. Throughout the régime of Geraldo Machado, university students were suppressed by *La Porra*, and later it was not much better when Batista's forces took over. Things got very physical when student activists and labor leaders were attacked and terrorized by violent, armed, politically motivated gangs. Frequently, even opposing student groups attacked each other. Castro, getting caught up in this gang culture, ran for the position of President of the Federation of University Students (FEU), a group founded by Julio Antonio Mella. Although he was unsuccessful in this endeavor, he did become active in anti-imperialistic movements and campaigned for Puerto Rican Independence and a democratic government for the Dominican Republic. His involvement in these left-leaning groups grew, and although he did not embrace communism, he did protest the political corruption and violence during the Grau administration. In November of 1946, Castro spoke out against President Grau during a student speech, the text of which was printed in several newspapers. As previously noted, in 1947 Castro joined Eduardo Chibás' new *Partido Ortodoxo*, which promoted social justice, political freedom and honest government.

In the summer of 1947, Castro involved himself in a conspiracy to overthrow Rafael Trujillo, the ruthless president of the Dominican Republic. Castro joined an expedition led by Dominican General Juan Rodríguez, to overthrow the Trujillo régime. The attempt failed and many of his co-conspirators were captured or killed, but Fidel managed to escape from the ship where he was being held, by jumping off and swimming to shore.

He objected to the corruption that the Grau and later the Prío administrations accepted as normal, as well as the greed American corporations brought with them to Cuba. When he talked with his fellow university students, Castro called it American Imperialism and condemned the social and economic injustices that were taking place because of it. It seems plausible that as a student the influence of Marxist writings and the teachings of Friedrich Engels and Vladimir Lenin started to become a part of Fidel Castro's thinking.

"North Americans don't understand... that our country is not just Cuba; our country is also humanity." Fidel Castro, retired Cuban politician and revolutionary

The Bogotazo

On January 9, 1948, the city of Bogotá, Colombia, was preparing to host a "Conference of American Nations," with representatives from the United States and Latin America. At the same time, there were also masses of Latin American students coming to a political convention in the city, with plans to protest and become the voices of dissent.

Having become a student activist voice for socialism in Latin America, Fidel Castro had previously carried his liberal message to Venezuela and Panama. In April of 1948, he arrived in Bogotá with a group of students, whose attendance was sponsored by Argentina's President Peron.

Jorge Eliécer Gaitán Ayala was a well-liked, liberal Colombian politician and a leader of a populist movement. He was expected to address the students, but was assassinated while in route to the convention. At 1:20 in the afternoon, the conservative President Luis Mariano Ospina Pérez, being informed of the slaying, called for an immediate meeting of his cabinet. An uproar rapidly developed among the demonstrators as Gaitán's lifeless body was cast onto the pavement of the driveway outside of the presidential palace, known as the *Casa de Nariño*. Rioting students overturned and burned vehicles in the streets of the Colombian capitol. They also ransacked and torched government ministerial buildings and the *El Nuevo Siglo* newspaper offices, as the city burned. As the word spread among the students, similar violent demonstrations took place in many of the other Colombian cities.

Attempting to control the escalating pandemonium, leaders of the Liberal Party appointed Darío Echandía Olaya, the former President of the Senate, to replace Gaitán. He appealed to the crowd to stop the violence, but it was too little too late. As the mobs, now boiling at a fever pitch, attempted to force their way into the palace, they were confronted by the army. Without showing any restraint, the army opened fire, resulting in the death of many of the demonstrators.

At 3:00 o'clock, the uncontrollable mobs broke into the Central Police Headquarters. The officer in charge, Major Benicio Arce Vera, came out with his palms facing the intruders, showing that he was unarmed. He ordered his men not to shoot and pleaded with the crowd to calm down, but to no avail. The rambunctious mob trampled and wounded him. The rioters overran the police station and seized the stored weapons and ammunition. Among this mob was Fidel Castro who was 21 years of age at the time. He and his compatriots became complicit when they stole guns from a police station; however, they were never directly linked to any of the killings. The Colombian Chief of Police claimed that Fidel had been involved in the distribution of Colombian Communist Party leaflets, and suggested that perhaps Castro had been involved in the killing of 32 people. However, the Police Chief never did present enough evidence to warrant an indictment.

Castro was later heard on a local radio station announcing that he represented the Communist Revolution and that the Cuban delegation had supported Gaitán. There are those who believe that Gaitán was actually assassinated by a hit man sent in by the conservatives, but this still remains conjecture on the part of the liberals. The conservatives claimed that they were successful and the winners of the fracas, as well they may have been, but at a tremendous cost.

In December of 1947, Gaitán had been warned by the American Ambassador Willard L. Beaulac, that Communist factions were planning a disruption of the conference and that his Liberal Party would most likely be blamed for it. The riots that ensued, between the Colombian army and the student groups, led to the death of an estimated 3,000 to 5,000 people and became known as *"el Bogotazo."*

Although Fidel is known to have taken part in the 10 hours of continuous rioting, there is much controversy as to how involved he was in the actual fighting. Being only 21 years old, it remains doubtful that he played any real leadership role in the planning of the riots, and it is more likely a coincidence that he and other students had a scheduled meeting with Gaitán, prior to his death.

It seems that even when those around him were being killed, Castro somehow survived without as much as a scratch. On April 18th, the Cuban Embassy in Bogotá arranged to get Castro and his delegation back to Havana on a cargo plane.

"It is a painful fact that the government of Colombia cannot protect its children from the murderous shrapnel of war but stands with trembling knees before the altar of American gold." Jorge Eliécer Gaitán Ayala, politician and leader of the populist movement in Colombia, in 1948

Mirta Díaz-Balart and Family

Fidel is every bit as macho as you would expect a Latino man to be, however he lacked some of the niceties and graces you might expect from a person born to wealth. His life revolved around his revolutionary activities, but when he returned from Bogotá, Colombia, he seemed ready to settle down.

Fidel married Mirta Díaz-Balart, the daughter of Rafael José Díaz-Balart, the former mayor of the town of Banes in Holguin Province, Cuba, and his wife América Gutiérrez. They met on the campus of the University of Havana where she was a philosophy student staying in a dormitory known to the male students as "The Chocolate Box."

Against the wishes of her family, they were married on October 10, 1948, when he was only 22 years of age. Fidel and Mirta spent three months in New York City and Miami on a honeymoon paid for by his father-in-law. When the honeymooners ran out of money in Miami, Fidel pawned his watch to keep their honeymoon going.

Mirta gave birth to their son Fidelito in September 1949, but having a family did not diminish Fidel's political passions. His brother-in-law Rafael Díaz-Balart, who had been Fidel's college friend at the University, became an ardent supporter of Batista. When he became the conservative Cuban Undersecretary of the Interior, he tried to convince Fidel to change his affiliations, but Fidel remained true to his liberal convictions and joined the "September 30 Movement," promoting human rights.

In the Cuban House of Representatives in 1955, Díaz-Balart spoke out against the amnesty granted to Castro by Batista. He went on to become the Majority Leader of the House of Representatives and Minister of the Interior during the Batista administration. Although he was elected to the Cuban Senate in 1958, he was unable to take the seat due to Castro's revolution. Fleeing Cuba, he moved to Spain becoming employed as an insurance company executive, before moving to Miami. In 1959, Díaz-Balart founded the first anti-Castro organization "La Rosa Blanca," "The White Rose." He was the father of former Republican U.S. Congressman Lincoln Díaz-Balart, of the 21st Congressional District in Florida. Lincoln Díaz-Balart and his immediate family were all Democrats, before switching their affiliation to the Republican Party. He was also father of the present Republican U.S. Congressman Mario Díaz-Balart of the new 25th Congressional District in Florida. He had two other sons, José Díaz-Balart, a TV news journalist with Telemundo and MSNBC, and Rafael Díaz-Balart, founder and CEO of Vestec International Corporation, a private banking and investment firm.

Their father, Rafael Díaz-Balart, brother of Mirta, died of leukemia on May 6, 2005, in Key Biscayne, Florida.

"The only poll obviously that matters is the last one, the one that's counted after all the votes are cast." Mario Díaz-Balart, Republican Party Congressman from the 25th district in Florida

Differences of Opinion

In 1948 upon his return to Havana from Bogotá, Castro, as well as others, spoke out against Grau's attempt to raise bus fares, even though they were less than ten cents at the time. Privately operated buses were the primary way students and workers got around. They also spoke out against the violent gangs that roamed the streets. In response, Grau agreed to suppress the gangs, but then found that they were already too powerful for him to handle. In some instances, he elevated gang leaders to high positions in law enforcement to appease the gangs. It was a way of paying them off....

Carlos Prío Socarrás was elected to the Presidency on October 10, 1948, and remained in office until he was deposed by a military coup led by Fulgencio Batista on March 10, 1952.

Castro's political actions were drawing undesired attention to him, forcing him into hiding. He went back to the United States for a short period, but when things cooled down he returned to the university. Since the university was autonomous, neither the police nor the army was allowed on the campus. The University of Havana became a haven for criminals and political radicals. It was at the university that Fidel found a safe haven and managed to remain under the radar until he finished his studies.

About two years later in September of 1950, after having gone back to school, Castro was awarded a Doctor of Law degree.

The Exciting Story of Cuba

Although Fidel worked in a respected law firm named Azpiazu, his heart and soul were not in it. Most of his clients were so poor that he was hard pressed to make a living at it. In later years he recalled how he was constantly in debt and that milk for his son Fidelito was frequently unaffordable. When his electricity was cut off and his credit bottomed out, it became next to impossible for him to find another apartment.

In 1952 when Batista seized power and anointed himself as the President of Cuba for a second time, Castro along with many others, branded him a dictator and started to campaign against him. On June 7, 1952, the Cuban Workers League newspaper *Alerta* carried an article written by Castro directly attacking Batista, but by June 16th the newspaper was shut down by the régime... so much for freedom of the press. Castro initiated legal action against Batista, but realizing that his efforts were ineffective he began to plot other ways to overthrow the Batista administration.

"I joined the people; I seized a rifle in a police station that buckled when it was rushed by a crowd. I observed the spectacle of an absolutely spontaneous revolution... That experience led me to identify myself even more with the cause of the people. My still emerging Marxist ideas had little to do with our conduct; it was a spontaneous reaction on our part, as young people with José Martí's anti-imperialist, anti-colonialist and pro-democratic ideas." Fidel Castro, Revolutionary in Bogotá, 1948

The Exciting Story of Cuba.... Part 10

"The Movement"

Attacking the Moncada Barracks

In May of 1952, about a dozen individuals lead by Fidel Castro formed a group of anti-Batista rebels called "The Movement." Fidel Castro had become a well-known activist and wrote articles intended to fire up the public in an underground newspaper *El Acusador* (The Accuser). In one year, his group grew to about 1,200 people. They began accumulating weapons with the idea that they would openly attack a Batista stronghold as a uniformed militant force. Being careful, Castro kept his intentions secret and only a few people knew that the target would be the Moncada Barracks in Santiago de Cuba.

The attack on the second largest military barracks in Cuba, named after General Guillermón Moncada, a hero of the War of Independence, was worked out in the tiny two-room apartment of Abel Santamaría. Abel and his sister Haydée lived on the corner of 25th and O Streets in El Vedado, Havana. Only Abel, Haydée and seven other people were entrusted with the details of the attack. Tight security was maintained throughout and since the volunteers of the revolution were divided into cells, few of them knew each other.

Coinciding with the mid-summer Saint James festivities, otherwise known as the *"Carnaval de Oriente,"* 132 men and 2 women were being trained to attack the barracks containing 1,000-trained men of Batista's army. At the same time, 28 men prepared to attack the Bayamo barracks. Nine students from the university unexpectedly backed out at the last minute, leaving 153 inexperienced combatants for the fight ahead. Even with the element of surprise, the odds of success were against the rebels.

Castro had spent $20,000 of donated money on this venture, a quarter of which went for the purchase of weapons. Their ammunition was limited and all they had were three U.S. Army rifles, six old Winchester rifles, one ancient machine gun, an assortment of hunting rifles and some revolvers. They paid $80 each for the army rifles. The plan was to capture much-needed additional weapons as they advanced, to supply the volunteers that came unarmed.

On July 26, 1953, at 5:30 a.m., a convoy of 16 cars left Siboney for Santiago, with Castro in the second car and his brother Raúl in the third. About 111 men wore army uniforms, which were mostly obtained by Haydée Santamaría for the rebels, from an army sergeant who later joined the movement. In this way they hoped to give the rebels a military appearance and be able to blend in enough to initially fool the guards they would encounter. However, things started to go wrong right from the beginning.

Arriving at the military complex, two of the cars carrying weapons had lost their way and were missing at the time they were most needed. The men in the first car managed to deceive the guards on duty at the main gate in the pre-dawn hours, and drove through, but the deception did not last very long. The second car, with Fidel in it, lost control and ran over a machine gun emplacement, as well as a group of soldiers standing near the gate. The guards, realizing that they were being attacked, quickly sounded the alarm before the rebels in the second car had a chance to enter the barracks. The rebels, who followed them, jumped out of their cars and took cover behind some parked vehicles, near the steps leading up to the front doors.

A team of 20 men and women, led by Abel Santamaría, planned to take control of the hospital behind the barracks. When discovered, Santamaría and his men got into some of the empty beds, pretending to be patients. This subterfuge failed and most of them were killed or captured. Even some of the actual patients were caught up in this massacre and were stabbed to death in the confusion.

Fidel's brother Raúl was in the third car with Léster Rodríguez. Instead of joining the attack on the Moncada Barracks, they cut across to the other side of the street, where Raúl and ten men easily captured the *Palacio de Justicia*, Palace of Justice.

Gustavo Arcos, a revolutionary who was with Castro in the second car, was shot in his back. The shot severely wounded him and disabled his right leg, thereby causing him a lifetime of pain. A few years later, Arcos went to Mexico with the intention of gathering support as well as money and munitions for the movement. After the revolution, for his loyalty, Gustavo Arcos was appointed the Cuban Ambassador to Belgium. However, as ambassador he became disillusioned with the Soviet form of communism and began to see Castro more as a dictator than a revolutionary leader. When he returned from his duties in Belgium, instead of being able to freely leave Cuba, Arcos was convicted and sentenced to ten years in prison as a counter-revolutionary. In 1981, after his release from prison, he attempted to escape from Cuba, for which he was sent back to prison. After his second release, Arcos decided that he could better serve the people of Cuba by staying and accepting the position of the Executive Secretary of the Cuban Committee for

Human Rights. His committee rapidly grew from occupying a small office in Havana, to being a nationwide organization recognized by the United Nations. Gustavo Arcos died of natural causes on August 8, 2006, at 79 years of age.

Castro and his forces, having lost the advantage of a surprise attack at the barracks, came under heavy fire. Major Morales, the brother of the officer who was among the first killed at the gate, ordered the counterattack. After an hour of intense fighting, Batista's forces had lost three officers, twelve soldiers and three policemen. Another twenty-three soldiers and five policemen were wounded. Castro's revolutionary forces initially lost nine men, four of whom were killed by friendly fire, and eleven others were wounded for the same reason.

Fidel Castro later accused the Batista régime of murdering fifty-six of his rebels after the hostilities supposedly ended. Regardless of who was counting the casualties, there is no question but that the attacks on the Moncada and Bayamo barracks were an appalling military failure, with many members of the 26th of July Movement losing their lives.

The survivors of these battles escaped into the nearby woods. Eighteen of these rebels joined Fidel for the 9-mile trek to the seaside village of Siboney, east of Santiago. Traveling as inconspicuously as possible, they made their way safely back and hid in a shack behind the farmhouse of a supporter. Knowing the danger they were in, Fidel talked to the survivors, telling them that it was his decision to move on and that they were welcome to follow him into the mountains.

The revolt against Batista was intense throughout Cuba, but especially so in Santiago, where, independently from Fidel Castro's group, local rebels led by Frank País were seen as heroes standing up to the dictator. Together they became known as the Revolutionary National Action Group. Although Frank País was a Baptist, the majority of these guerrilla fighters were Roman Catholics and had the popular support of the people as well as the church.

The archbishop of Santiago de Cuba, Monsignor Enrique Pérez Serantes, being very aware of the extensive corruption in government, involved himself in the search for the rebels. He offered to help bring them in and be allowed to personally guarantee their lives and safety, if they peacefully surrendered themselves to the authorities. His participation in the capture of Castro and the surviving rebels was most useful in seeing to it that the guerrilla fighters were treated humanely.

Following the directions provided by some local peasants, Castro and his followers proceeded to move inland, traveling northeast in the direction of the "Cordillera de la Gran Piedra" mountains. However, Batista's army was on to them and during the next few days many of the rebels were captured and summarily slain. On August 1st, Fidel and the rebels with him were intercepted by a patrol led by Lieutenant Pedro Manuel Sarría. It only took two hours for all of Castro's men to be rounded up and arrested.

A total of thirty-eight captives, including the Castro brothers, survived only because Lieutenant Sarría did the honorable thing by handing them over to the civil magistrates, instead of to Batista's henchmen. Because of this, Castro was properly processed into custody. Once he was logged into the prison records, it protected him by preventing Batista's army from being able to execute him and then making his death look as if he had been killed in action.

However, there is no doubt but that many of the soldiers behaved in a cruel and cold-blooded way towards their captives. Batista reacted illogically in regards to the attack and developed a renewed dread of Castro's rebels. He rationalized that if a handful of men could do this to the second largest military barracks in Cuba, what would the revolutionary movement be able to do next? His anger was directed at the Cuban Officer Corps, who knew that this attack was only the beginning. Public opinion also turned against Batista because of the extremely ruthless behavior of his army, which included the violent castration of approximately 30 of Castro's men. At the time, it was incorrectly believed that Fidel and his brother were among these unfortunate men.

Haydée Santamaría, the sister of Abel Santamaría, was romantically involved with Reinaldo Boris Luis Santa Coloma, a man six years younger than Haydée. Boris was a lusty playboy and photographer who soon had an affair with his model Nereida Rodriguez. Of interest is that Nereida was also the thirty-eight year young, legal secretary in Fidel Castro's law office. When Nereida became pregnant, supposedly by Boris, it is believed that Haydée broke off her relationship with him. Therefore, at the time of the attack on the barracks, Haydée was supposedly engaged to Victor Torres, a rebel in Fidel's militia. After the failed attack, the *Guardia*, police, captured Torres alive. Sergeant Montes de Oca, a vindictive member of Batista's forces, cut Torres' testicles off with a machete and carried them in his bare hands to Haydée. Confronting her, he spit out, "Look here bitch, you'd better ask us to f—k you in the future, since your fiancé will never be able do it again." Her other brother Aldo survived, but Abel was captured and severely tortured. His captors gouged his eyes out with a bayonet and threatened to do the same to Haydée if she did not give them the strategically important information they wanted, regarding the whereabouts of Fidel Castro and his men. She may not have known where the Castro brothers were. In any case, she never said anything to help the enemy and, fortunately for her, they didn't carry out their threat. Because of her loyalty, Haydée Santamaría became known as the "Heroine of Moncada."

The attack on the barracks caused a public fury throughout the country. Batista, understanding what this sentiment could escalate into, dreaded what the future could bring. After holding extensive internal hearings, Batista decided to drastically discipline and reorganize his army.

The criminal trial was held at the Palace of Justice on September 21, 1953, where Castro spoke in his own defense. Fifteen days later the trial ended with all of the anti-Batista politicians and some of the rebels being acquitted. However, 55 of the remaining revolutionaries were sentenced to between 7 months and 13 years in prison. In a separate trial, Fidel was sentenced to 15 years, to be served in the hospital wing of the *Presidio Modelo*, Model Prison, on the *Isla de Pinos*, Isle of Pines, 60 miles off Cuba's southwest coast. It was at his sentencing that Fidel Castro delivered his famous *"History Will Absolve Me"* speech.

After Fidel Castro's victory in January of 1959, Haydée married Armando Hart Dávalos. Armando's family originally came from the state of Georgia in the United States, with his grandfather emigrating to Cuba as a child. A follower of Castro, he became an important underground leader in the 26th of July Movement. On April 23, 1958, during the revolution, his brother Enrique Hart was killed in Matanzas while making bombs. Years later Armando Hart and Haydée divorced and on July 26, 1980, she chose to end her life by shooting herself in the mouth with a 45-caliber handgun. Her divorce and death continue to be a mystery, but the fact that her death happened on the anniversary of Castro's attack on the Moncada Barracks certainly seems significant.

> *In February of 1954, less than six months after the well-known trials, as a midshipman in the United States Naval Reserve aboard the T/V State of Maine, I was in Santiago and witnessed first-hand the mood of the country!*
> *Capt. Hank Bracker*

"I would honestly love to revolutionize this country from one end to the other. I am certain that this would bring happiness to the Cuban people." Fidel Castro

Prison and Exile

The *Presidio Modelo* was built under the régime of President Machado between 1926 and 1928, and as a model prison, it was relatively comfortable. About half of the convicted rebels of the Movement, now called the M-26-7, had been sent to the Isle of Pines to serve their sentences at this fairly new facility. Castro was given enough latitude to set up what he called the "Abel Santamaría Ideological Academy." He and other senior members of the M-26-7 taught courses for five hours a day, which included Philosophy, History, English and other languages. They had the use of the prison library, studying Cuban History, Immanuel Kant's Philosophy and Marxist Ideology, as well as English Literature including Shakespeare and Hemingway. Fidel also considered President Franklin D. Roosevelt's "New Deal" as the basis for what should eventually be enacted in Cuba.

Things went well until Batista's visit to the prison, when the inmates heckled him and sang anti-Batista songs. For this, Castro was thrown into solitary confinement and his followers lost their privileges.

During this time, Castro's wife Mirta sided with her brother Rafael Díaz-Balart, now the Under-Secretary of the Ministry of the Interior. Unbeknownst to Fidel, Mirta became employed working for her brother at the Ministry. Discovering that his wife, in effect, was working for the Batista régime, Fidel exploded.

While still in prison, Castro continued corresponding with his wife Mirta. At the same time, he wrote affectionate letters to an attractive Cuban socialite, "Naty" Natalia Revuelta. For whatever reason, his letters became switched with both Mirta and "Naty" receiving the wrong letters. This little mistake, most likely brought about by the Prison Warden, led to both Mirta and Fidel filing for divorce.

On May 15, 1955, Batista made a mistake that would cost him his presidency and change the course of Cuban history. Thinking that Fidel and his rebels were no longer a threat, Batista released Castro and the other political prisoners from jail.

Castro's marriage to Mirta failed primarily because her entire family opposed his political views, however his promiscuous ways certainly did not help. Mirta remained married to Fidel for a total of seven years. In 1955 after he was released from prison for attacking the Moncada Barracks, Fidel fled to Mexico. It was there, while in exile, that his divorce was finalized and Mirta was awarded custody of their son Fidelito.

As soon as she received her divorce from Fidel, Mirta and their son Fidelito moved to Fort Lauderdale. During this difficult time, Mirta had to work two jobs to make ends meet. She taught at a private school and also worked as a hostess at Creighton's Restaurant.

A year later in 1956, she and Fidelito returned to Havana where she met and married Dr. Emilio Núñez Blanco, the son of Emilio Núñez Portuondo. Dr. Núñez Portuondo was the President of the United Nations Security Council during the Soviet invasion of Hungary. Dr. Núñez Blanco's grandfather, General Emilio Núñez was the Vice President of Cuba from 1917-1921, during the second administration of President Mario García Menocal. Immediately after their marriage, they lived in New York City, where Fidelito attended a school in the borough of Queens. For Mirta and Fidelito things were looking up,

Castro's Exile in Mexico

In 1955, violent, open demonstrations, including bombing attacks, caused Batista to crack down on the revolutionaries. Castro's brother Raúl was accused of one such attack and fled from Cuba before he could be apprehended. Fidel was also in danger of arrest or even assassination, so within weeks he followed his brother to Mexico, which offered them safe haven.

In 1956, Fidel Castro, with the help of his sister "Lidia" Angelita, plotted to abduct Fidelito while Mirta was honeymooning with Emilio in Paris. Lidia was trusted to bring Fidelito from Havana to Mexico City for a two-week stay, but as soon as they arrived, Fidel took custody of the boy and held him inside the walled mansion of a confederate, the Cuban singer Orquídea Pino and her husband. A Mexican government investigation determined it to be a family matter, and did not interfere until there was an armed showdown between Fidel's guards and the Mexican police on the streets of Mexico City. Mirta, having come to Mexico to retrieve her son, waited outside the Cuban singer's home. Seeing his mother, Fidelito ran from his Aunt Lidia's car and jumped into his mother's car. With police protection, they sped away without any shots being fired.

Two years later on January 6, 1959, with Fidel taking over control of Cuba, Fidelito was on an airplane flying from New York to Havana with happy, returning exiles. Mirta was at Havana's José Martí Airport to meet him, thinking that the issue of custody was settled, but as soon as the airplane landed Fidel's soldiers appeared and took charge. On January 8, father and son rode on top of a tank making a victorious entry into Havana, while Mirta could only watch the event on television in the company of her family and friends.

Mirta never did regain custody of their son. After Castro overthrew the Cuban government in 1959, Emilio and Mirta moved to Spain where they had two daughters and lived in Madrid until Emilio's death. After his death from advanced Alzheimer's disease in July of 2006, Mirta, who was in Cuba at the time, returned to Madrid. She was uncomfortable with the idea of living in South Florida near her brother and her conservative nephews who were in politics, promoting their anti-Castro views. However, she has been back to Havana a few times to be with Fidelito, and there has been speculation that she may have visited Fidel after he stepped down from the presidency due to ill health.

Being a free agent, Fidel was able to continue his affair with Naty Revuelta, and expanded his relationships to include María Laborde, both of whom claimed that they had a child by him.

"Being divorced is like being hit by a Mack truck. If you live through it, you start looking very carefully to the right and to the left." Jean Kerr, an Irish-American author who wrote Please Don't Eat the Daisies

Returning to Cuba

It was while in Mexico that Raúl befriended an Argentine doctor, Ernesto "Che" Guevara, who believed in overthrowing American Imperialism in Latin America. During their time in exile, the M-26-7 raised money for their revolutionary activities. Castro even went to Florida where he talked to wealthy sympathizers, including former Cuban President Prío, from whom he allegedly received $100,000. Of this money, $15,000 was used to purchase a used 58-foot yacht, named the *Granma*. It was designed to accommodate 12 people. The vessel was built in 1943 and was converted to land 82 trained rebels, armed with 90 rifles, 3 machine guns, 40 pistols and 2 handheld anti-tank weapons (bazookas). Of these, only 20 rebels had taken part in the attack on the Moncada barracks, and 4, including Guevara, were non-Cubans.

During his time in Mexico, Castro, who now commissioned himself with the rank of *Comandante*, remained in contact with the MR–26–7 members who had remained behind in Cuba, and who would now help coordinate his return by staging diversionary actions in Santiago.

Antonio del Conte, known as "The Friend" and said to be an arms dealer, had negotiated the deal to purchase the *Granma*. He also attempted to buy a surplus U.S. Navy Catalina flying boat for Fidel. Unknown to Castro, Batista had his spies in Mexico who continually reported all of Fidel's activities to him.

On the night of November 24, 1956, the *Granma* slipped her moorings with Castro's guerrillas aboard, known as *"los expedicionarios del yate Granma,"* and left from Tuxpan, Veracruz, setting a course across the Yucatán Channel for southeastern Cuba. The 1,200-mile distance between Mexico and their landing point in southeastern Cuba was difficult and included 135 miles of open water and cross currents between Cape Catoche in Mexico and Cape San Antonio in Cuba. They had to stay far enough off the southern coast of Cuba to remain undetected. The overcrowded small vessel leaked, forcing everyone to take turns bailing water out of her, and at one point they lost a man overboard, which further delayed them. In all, the entire five-day trip ultimately lasted seven days. Their destination was a *playa*, beach, near Niquero in the Oriente Province, close to where José Martí landed 61 years prior, during the War of Independence. However, on December 2, 1956, when the *Granma* finally arrived at its destination, it smashed into a mangrove swamp crawling with fiddler crabs, near Los Colorados beach. They were well south of where they were supposed to meet up with 50 supporters. Having lost their element of surprise, they were left exposed and vulnerable.

After the revolution the *Granma* was moved to Havana and is now on display in a protected glass enclosure at the Granma Memorial, near the Museum of the Revolution. Norberto Collado Abreu, the skipper and helmsman on the long voyage from Mexico, was assigned the responsibility of being the custodian of the yacht. During World War II he served in the Cuban Navy and participated in the sinking of the German submarine U-176, northeast of Havana harbor. Norberto died on April 2, 2008. His funeral was held on the same day as his death, at the Pantheon of the Revolutionary Armed Forces in Colon Cemetery in Havana.

Hiding in the Sierra Maestra Mountains

Batista was on the lookout for Fidel and had aircraft patrolling the southern coast. When a Cuban fighter plane spotted the stranded yacht, it radioed its location to a frigate, which moved in and bombarded the hapless men as they fled through the swamp. The rebels' objective now was to head for the Sierra Maestra Mountains. Unbeknownst to Castro, he had been betrayed by a trusted guide. The guerrillas found themselves trapped in a cane field, where they were fired upon by the alerted, regular army troops. Castro was reported dead and most of the facts surrounding this phase of the operation were lost in a sea of confusion. On December 5, 1956, Batista's army attacked the guerrillas, killing many of them. But once again, Fidel and Raúl survived and led the dwindling number of survivors on to the Sierra Maestra Mountains, a rugged mountain range rising abruptly from the sea.

Of the 82 rebels that arrived in Cuba on the *Granma*, only a handful survived. The rest were killed or captured by Batista's army. The few survivors, estimated at between 12 and 20 rebels, included Fidel Castro, "Che" Guevara, Raúl Castro, and Camilo Cienfuegos. Becoming the "Commanders of the Revolution," they managed to reach safety high in the mountains.

Setting up camp, the meager M-26-7 forces began attacking local army posts in what was then the Oriente Province, where they expected to acquire much-needed weapons. Guevara, a qualified doctor, treated casualties on both sides of the conflict for their wounds with compassion. However, the guerillas did execute Chicho Osorio, a despised overseer of the Laviti family estate, a local land company. Chicho Osorio was one of the region's three most notorious plantation supervisors, who had also been accused of killing one of Fidel Castro's rebels several weeks before. This gained the guerrillas favor in the eyes of the local peasants, and helped the rebels to recruit more eager combatants.

Across Cuba, many militant groups had now begun to rise up against Batista. Castro however became the undisputed leader of the revolution when the police shot to death, on the streets of Havana, the independent, charismatic, revolutionary leader José Antonio Echeverria of the *Directorio Revolucionario*, after he launched a direct attack on the presidential palace and the radio station. Another prominent revolutionary leader, Frank País, was fatally shot in the back of his head while in the custody of the Santiago Police Department.

On March 18, 1957, *Time* magazine reported, "Lawyer Fidel Castro's revolt against the régime of President Fulgencio Batista is the sort of affair that appeals more to young zealots than to common sense...." It further stated that some of the sons of naval personnel at the Guantánamo Naval Base went into the nearby mountains to join Castro's militia forces.

"Living in Cuba made me unafraid of whatever could happen to me." Brit Marling, American writer, producer and actress

Fidel's Guerilla Forces

Life in the Sierra Maestra Mountains was difficult. Men that defected due to the hardships and turned themselves over to Batista's army were usually summarily executed. Batista's air force routinely dropped napalm bombs on Fidel's guerillas.

Potable water was scarce and they ate herbs, raw wild corn and crabs. Castro's troops acquired food from local farmers and chewed on sugar cane stalks for energy. In time the fighters became accepted by the local population and could purchase food and supplies in a more conventional way. For two years they lived in the wild, and for two years their contact with the opposite sex was limited. Fidel, knowing that this could cause problems, developed a set of rules:

"Never pass a countryman without a greeting.
Never try to take away his hunting weapons.
Never eat or drink in his home without paying.
Never, but never, trifle with women."
Fidel Castro, Comandante

Mountain Justice

Fidel's justice in the high mountains was harsh and the penalty for violating the last rule was death. Acting as the police, judge and jury when enforcing these rules, Castro would ask the man if he understood the rules of conduct, and then asked the woman bringing the complaint if she understood the consequences. He would then ask the man if he had had sex with the woman. If the answer was "Yes," he would follow up by asking the woman if she allowed the act. If her answer was "No," Fidel, showing rare anger, would turn the offender over to his brother Raúl, who would have him tied to a tree and shot in the face. Fidel never enjoyed executions and typically turned this over to brother Raúl, who carried them out without hesitation. The entire procedure usually took under fifteen minutes. Although curtailing rowdy sex is very un-Cuban like, Castro sentenced nearly 30 of his men to this fate.

In time Fidel had a log cabin built for himself, and was known to have had the company of Celia Sánchez Manduley, who was his longtime clerical aide and lover. She was also his courier and carried messages and money through enemy lines. Fearlessly she carried out her duties like a little bird, and was called "*La Paloma*," the dove.

Castro's Commanders

Aside from "Che" Guevara and Fidel's brother Raúl Castro, among the first *Comandantes* were:

Ciro Redondo, who died on November 29, 1957, in the battle of Mar Verde in the Sierra Maestra Mountains. He was killed in action as a captain of Castro's Army and was posthumously promoted to the rank of *Comandante*.

Camilo Cienfuegos. He became one of the top leaders of the revolutionary forces and received the rank of *Comandante* in 1958. He fought the Battle of Santa Clara with "Che" Guevara. Cienfuegos disappeared on October 28, 1959, during a flight between Camagüey and Havana.

Juan Almeida Bosque was born on February 17, 1927, and died September 11, 2009. He was an original *Comandante* of the Cuban Revolution. After the 1959 revolution he became a politician and one of the most prominent figures in the Communist Party of Cuba. At the time of his death in 2009, he was a Vice-President of the Cuban Council of State.

Major General Calixto García Martinez was born on December 27, 1931, and died in Havana on September 1, 2010. He was buried in the Pantheon of the Revolutionary Armed Forces at the Colon Cemetery in Havana. Martinez participated in the attack on the Garrison in Bayamo on July 26, 1953. Later he went to Costa Rica, where he met Ernesto "Che" Guevara. García Martinez joined Fidel Castro in Mexico and traveled to Cuba as part of the *Granma* Yacht expedition in 1956. He was a member of the Rebel Army in the Sierra Maestra Mountain range and in 1958 he was promoted to the rank of *Comandante* of the Revolutionary Army.

Ramiro Valdés Menéndez is a Cuban revolutionary and politician. A veteran of the Cuban Revolution, Valdés fought with Fidel Castro at the attack on the Moncada barracks in 1953. He was a founding member of the 26th of July Movement and has been a member of the Politburo of the Communist Party of Cuba since October 1965. He also served as the Interior Minister and Vice-Prime Minister. On August 31, 2006, he was appointed Minister of Informatics and Communications.

William Alexander Morgan was born on April 19, 1928, as a United States citizen. Although he didn't become a *Comandante* until later, it is interesting to note that he was a United States citizen when he joined Castro's forces. He fought for the Cuban Revolution with a guerilla force led by Eloy **Gutiérrez** Menoyo, as part of the Second National Front of the Escambray Mountains, a mountain range in the central region of Cuba. Later in the battle of Santa Clara, Morgan was one of about two dozen Americans who had joined the Revolutionary army. He once stated that he did not believe that Castro was a Communist during the revolution, and only accepted the Communist ideology later. Morgan was promoted to the rank of *Comandante* on January 1, 1959. The next year, in October of 1960 he was arrested for treason. On March 11, 1961, when he was 32 years old, just before his death, Morgan said, "the most important thing for free men to do is to protect the freedom of others." He was executed by a firing squad, standing against a stonewall in the moat surrounding *La Cabaña* in Havana. His wife was sentenced to 30 years in a Cuban prison, but was released after 12 years. In April of 2007, Morgan's remains were returned to the United States after having been in Cuba for nearly 50 years. His United States citizenship was restored posthumously in April 2007, after having lost it for serving in a foreign country's military.

Huber Matos Benítez was born on November 26, 1918. He was an activist who, at first, assisted the leaders of the revolution in successfully overthrowing Fulgencio Batista. Considering Batista's power grab in 1952 unconstitutional, he sided with Castro's movement. Matos became a member of the *Partido Ortodoxo* party and moved to Costa Rica, where in 1953 he befriended the Social Democratic president, José María Hipólito Figueres Ferrer, who helped get Matos arms and ammunition for Castro. Following the successful revolution in Cuba, Matos was appointed *Comandante* and Commander of the Revolutionary Army for the province of Camagüey.

As Castro moved further to the left, Matos became increasingly disenchanted with the movement. He allegedly worked with Tony Varona, Carlos Prío and Manuel Artime, with the plans presented by Frank Sturgis and the CIA, for a counter-revolution that evolved into the Bay of Pigs Invasion.

Attempting to resign, Castro refused him saying, "Your resignation is not acceptable at this point. We still have too much work to do. I admit that Raúl and "Che" are flirting with Marxism... but you have the situation under control... Forget about resigning." With Matos insisting on his right to leave the movement, Castro sent Camilo Cienfuegos to arrest him.

Matos warned the popular Camilo that Castro would eliminate any competition. Shortly thereafter Camilo disappeared on a flight back to Havana from Camagüey, exactly as Matos had predicted. Matos was arrested and convicted of "treason and sedition." He was sentenced to 20 years at the Isle of Pines prison, sixteen of which were spent in solitary confinement, before being released in 1979.

After gaining his freedom, Matos joined his family in Costa Rica and then moved to the United States where he spoke out against the Cuban government. Huber Matos Benítez died in Miami, Florida, on February 27, 2014, at the age of 95.

<u>Efigenio Ameijeiras Delgado</u> was born in 1931 in Puerto Padre, Las Tunas Province and was an ardent supporter of Fidel Castro. In 1955, Ameijeiras using the alias "Jomeguia," was briefly jailed on moral charges. He was one of the guerrillas on board the yacht *Granma*, when Castro returned from Mexico in 1956. After the revolution, he served as the Head of the National Revolutionary Police. On April 19, 1961, during the Bay of Pigs Invasion, he commanded a battalion of about 200 police and militia. He later served in the Cuban Army with the rank of Brigadier General and then Major General.

In 1966 Ameijeiras was expelled from the Communist Party of Cuba, again charged with moral offenses.

Operation Verano

As the M–26–7 forces increased their attacks, the Cuban army was forced to withdraw into the larger towns for safety. This caused ever-increasing pressure on Batista. The United States government stopped supplying the Batista régime with weapons and ammunition. In 1958, in spite of an all-out attack and heavy aerial bombings upon Castro's guerrilla forces, known as "Operation Verano," the rebels continued advancing.

At that time Batista's Army had 10,000 soldiers surrounding the Sierra Maestra Mountains and Castro had 300 men under his command, many of them former Batista soldiers who joined the rebels after being appalled by the abuses that they were ordered to carry out. By closing off the major roads and rail lines, Castro put Batista's forces at a severe disadvantage. On January 1, 1959, with his pockets stuffed with money and an airplane full of art, *Presidente* Fulgencio Batista flew the coop. Flying to the Dominican Republic before continuing to Portugal some months later, he left Anselmo Alliegro Mila to serve as Acting President. The next day he was relieved and Carlos Manuel Piedra, who had served as the senior member of the Supreme Court, was appointed Provisional President for a day. It was in accordance with the 1940 Cuban constitution, but his appointment was opposed by the new leader, Fidel Castro. Piedra was 92 years old when he died in 1988.

"Which of us has not felt that the character we are reading about, in the printed page, is more real than the person standing beside us?" Cornelia Funke, German author of children's fiction

A Vintage Cuban Travel Poster

The Exciting Story of Cuba.... Part 11

Ernest Hemingway

The Old Man and the Sea

Having been married twice before, he enjoyed the conveniences and trappings of having a wife, but resented the responsibilities, not to mention the constraints, of raising children. He loved his six-toed, polydactyl cats that required far less care, and frequently were left to fend for themselves at his home in Key West, Florida. Writing was his life and having been a reporter and journalist for the *Kansas City Star* and the *Toronto Star Weekly* gave him the experience and knowledge needed to write the gritty accounts of the Spanish Civil War and World War II. His work took Papa Hemingway to the far reaches of the globe, however he enjoyed life in Key West where he had fishing friends and drinking buddies. He always enjoyed the company of the people he was with, and Sloppy Joe's was his favorite haunt. It was here that he spent hours imbibing and sharing stories with fishermen, beach bums and tourists.

In March of 1937, Hemingway arrived in Spain representing the North American newspaper *Alliance*. At about that time, a friend José Robles Pazos, was arrested and executed by the Communist faction. This left author John Roderigo Dos Passos, another friend, with contempt for the Communists.

Hemingway's friendship with Dos Passos ended when Hemingway accused Dos Passos of cowardice, saying that he had fled Spain to return and hide in America. In the following years, Dos Passos' political position changed drastically when, in the 1950's, he campaigned for Barry Goldwater and Richard Nixon.

Although Hemingway never actively participated as a partisan in the Spanish Civil War, he did sympathize with the left-leaning government in power, opposing Franco's right-wing fascists, and associated with people such as the German writer Ludwig Renn, who served as an officer in the XI International Brigade. During this time, he wrote *The Torrents of Spring*, as he traveled to and from the Spanish Civil War as a journalist.

During his lifetime, Ernest Hemingway had a total of four wives. However, being a ladies' man he always enjoyed having girlfriends on the side. Although he was still married to Pauline Pfeiffer, during Christmas time in 1936, his attention became focused on a guest at his home in Key West, the journalist and writer Martha Gellhorn. Apparently, sparks flew immediately! As a writer for *Vogue* magazine in Paris, it was relatively easy for her to meet up with Ernest in Madrid in 1937. At the time he was writing a play, *The Fifth Column*, as the city was being bombarded. So wasn't it fortunate that Martha happened to be there for him?

It was during 1937 that Hemingway wrote the novel "*To Have and Have Not*" about Harry Morgan, a fishing boat captain who ran contraband between Havana and Key West. Things didn't go well for Morgan when he sank ever deeper into debt and started running his boat between Cuba and the United States, carrying revolutionaries to Cuba and smuggling Chinese immigrants and rum into Florida. The depression during the early 1930's and the hunger experienced by the "Conchs" of Key West is held to be Morgan's motive for ferrying the illegal cargo between the two countries.

When he returned to Florida in the early part of 1939, Hemingway took his boat the *Pilar* across the Straits of Florida to Havana, where he checked into the Hotel Ambos Mundos. Shortly thereafter, Martha joined him in Cuba and they first rented, and later in 1940, purchased their home for $12,500. Located 10 miles to the east of Havana, in the small town of San Francisco de Paula, they settled into what they called *Finca Vigía*, the Lookout Farm. After a difficult divorce from Pauline, Ernest and Martha got married on November 20, 1940. Even though Cuba had become their home, they still took assignments overseas, including one in China that Martha had for *Collier's* magazine. Returning to Cuba just prior to the outbreak of World War II, he convinced the Cuban government to outfit his boat with armaments, with which he intended to ambush German submarines. As the war progressed, Hemingway went to London as a war correspondent, where he met Mary Welsh. His infatuation prompted him to propose to her, which of course did not sit well with Martha.

Hemingway was present at the liberation of Paris and attended a party hosted by Sylvia Beach. He, incidentally, also renewed a friendship with Gertrude Stein. Becoming a famous war correspondence he covered the Battle of the Bulge, however he then spent the rest of the war on the sidelines hospitalized with pneumonia. Even so, Ernest was awarded the Bronze Star for bravery. Once again, Hemingway fell in lust, this time with a 19-year-old girl, Adriana Ivancich. This so-called platonic, wink, wink, love affair was the essence of his novel *Across the River and Into the Trees*, which he wrote in Cuba.

His book *For Whom the Bell Tolls* was an instant success in the summer of 1940, and afforded him the means to live in style at his villa outside of Havana with his new wife Mary Welsh, whom he married in 1946. It was during this period that he started getting headaches and gaining weight, frequently becoming depressed. Being able to shake off his problems, he wrote a series of books on the Land, Air and Sea, and later wrote *The Old Man and the Sea* for which he won the Pulitzer Prize in May 1954. During the same year, he went to Africa for a second time and barely survived two successive airplane crashes. Pain was his excuse to drink even more than ever. Some months later, among much controversy he received the Nobel Prize in Literature. From the end of 1955 and into 1956 Hemingway was bedridden suffering from hypertension, arteriosclerosis and cirrhosis of the liver. Some of his energy returned when a trunk arrived filled with manuscripts he had written while in Paris, during the pre-war years. Returning to Cuba, Ernest worked reshaping the recovered work and wrote his memoir, *A Moveable Feast*. He also finished *True at First Light* and *The Garden of Eden*. Being security conscious, he stored his works in a safe deposit box at a bank in Havana.

"... any man's death diminishes me, because I am involved in Mankinde; And therefore never send to know for whom the bell tolls; It tolls for thee..." John Donne, a Metaphysical English poet

His home *Finca Vigía* had become a hub for friends and even visiting tourists. Hemingway was in Cuba in 1959, and although he was delighted that Batista was overthrown and was on good terms with Fidel Castro, he decided to leave Cuba after hearing that Fidel wanted to nationalize the properties owned by Americans and other foreign nationals. In the summer of 1960, while working on a 10,000-word manuscript for *Life* magazine, Hemingway became disorganized and confused. His eyesight had been failing and he became despondent and depressed. On July 25, 1960, he and his wife Mary left Cuba for the last time.

He never retrieved his books or the manuscripts that he left in the bank vault. Following the Bay of Pigs Invasion, the Cuban government took ownership of his home and the works he left behind, including an estimated 5,000 books from his personal library. After years of neglect, his home, which was designed by the Spanish architect Miguel Pascual y Baguer in 1886, is now being restored as the Hemingway Museum. The museum, overlooking San Francisco de Paula, as well as the Straits of Florida in the distance, houses much of his work as well as his boat.

Eventually Hemingway managed to complete some of his work, including the *Life* magazine article, with the help of a friend. He again traveled to Spain by himself for a last visit, and was photographed for the front cover of an issue of *Life* magazine, which included an article about his adventures. In October of 1960, he left Spain for New York. Hemingway was convinced that the FBI was monitoring him and later it was proven that his paranoia was not unfounded. On July 2, 1961, Ernest Hemingway died of a self-inflicted shotgun blast. At the time it was called an accident, when in fact he had committed suicide at his home in Sun Valley, Idaho.

Hemingway had been invited to the presidential inauguration of John F. Kennedy, but at the time was too ill to attend. In 1965, four years following his suicide, Mary Hemingway established the Hemingway Foundation. In 1970, after corresponding with Jacqueline Kennedy, she donated Hemingway's papers to the John F. Kennedy Library in Boston,

Massachusetts, to which she added some of her own personal papers.

The home that Hemingway left in 1960, now falls under the auspices of the Cuban Council of National Heritage. Democratic Congressman James McGovern from the Second District of Massachusetts has been instrumental in the founding and work of the U.S. non-profit Finca Vigía Foundation, which has been working with their Cuban colleagues to preserve and digitize the papers of Hemingway that were left behind in Cuba. Under agreement, these irreplaceable Hemingway documents are being conserved and shared between the two countries.

On May 6, 2013, the Canadian Broadcasting Company announced that thousands more of Ernest Hemingway's personal papers, from the collection in Cuba, were to be added to the special archive at the John F. Kennedy Library.

Students and scholars can arrange with the research desk at the Kennedy Library to view these manuscripts.

"Always do sober what you said you'd do drunk. That will teach you to keep your mouth shut." Ernest Hemingway, Author & Adventurer

The Exciting Story of Cuba.... Part 12

Cloak & Dagger

What really happened on New Year's Eve, 1958?

The last two years of Batista's régime brought on a feeling of foreboding among the Cuban people. Batista's heavy-handed dictatorship galled people and those that opposed him were frequently jailed or found dead in the streets. However, in some respects, things were better than they had ever been. Prior to Fidel's take over, Cuba fared very well compared to most other Latin American countries. After the worldwide depression in the late 1920's and the 1930's, Cuba's economy grew steadily and by 1958 there were 160 sugar mills. The annual crop produced over five million five hundred thousand long tons of sugar. The cattle industry prospered, as beef consumption grew to an all-time high. Farming and transportation had become mechanized and labor benefited from it. In urban areas, construction work was also up and jobs were abundant.

The major failing was that during the last years of the Batista régime, Cuba became extremely corrupt. Havana became America's adult playground and tourists were bringing in the "Yankee Dollar." Construction companies with the right connections were busy building new gambling casinos and hotels. Girly shows, prostitution and gaming became widespread and people in the service industry made a good income. Those people that were involved in politics or supported Batista's rise in wealth were raking in money beyond their wildest imagination.

While the good times rolled, in the Sierra Maestra Mountains things were fermenting and the revolutionaries were gaining strength. Young people throughout the island were becoming actively involved. Older people, tired of the corruption and decadence, silently supported Fidel Castro. They may not have known what was in store for them, but they did know that Batista and his followers had hijacked their country, and they were willing to back the fresh wind blowing down from the mountains. As the revolution heated up, the *Policía Nacional* and Batista's spy network headed by the Military Intelligence Service, *Servicio de Inteligencia Militar*, resorted to torture and executions. The newspapers always cited that the bodies found alongside remote roads, railroad tracks or ditches, were shot by unknown persons. The bombs that were heard exploding at night reminded people that these were not normal times.

Political enemies of the régime were rounded up and taken to police detention centers located around Havana. Special tribunals, *Tribunales de Urgencia*, were set up to deal with these prisoners. Since these jails were under the control of the local police, there was little or no accountability. Notorious police precincts such as the ones commanded by Captains Ventura and Carratalá prided themselves on the torturous pain they could inflict, using extremely imaginative methods. Most Cubans feared the police and it seemed that everyone knew of someone who had fallen into their clutches, many of whom were later found dead.

Those that were apprehended by the military or the secret police sometimes fared better. The *Castillo del Príncipe*, an old Spanish castle built between 1767 and 1779, facing the Gulf of

Mexico, had special cells that were set aside for political prisoners.

Once incarcerated, their presence was documented and some degree of care had to be provided before they were given a mock trial. However, frequently these prisoners were dispatched before they even got there or they were released and then shot dead in the streets. The story was always the same... "They attempted to escape!"

The castle in Havana is now used by the army for special military ceremonies.

Cars with Florida license plates, originally thought to belong to tourists, were in fact driven by Batista's secret police. A thinly veiled ploy was revealed when you saw that the cars were filled with ominous looking men brandishing automatic weapons. Sometimes the secret police disguised themselves as street vendors. Their informers or stoolpigeons were known as *chivatos*. Batista also maintained a paramilitary force that was made up of street gangs that acted more like professional political thugs.

By October of 1958, most roads leading to the Oriente Province had become impassable. Bridges were cut and dropped by the rebels, making travel to the eastern part of Cuba extremely difficult. The elections in November were seen as an obvious sham and everyone knew that the only way to survive was to keep quiet and wait for changes to take place. Most of Batista's supporters were still in denial and carried out their atrocities with abandon. Tension among the people in Havana had grown and as Christmas approached, it became obvious that this year things would be different. People that had been harassed, or worse, were in no mood to celebrate the holidays. With the country engaged in a civil war that affected everyone,

Christmas was not being celebrated as usual during that winter of 1958.

The week between Christmas and New Year's was filled with uncertainty and the usual joyous season was suspended by many. Visitations among family and friends were few, as people held their breath waiting to see what would happen. It was obvious that the rebel forces were moving ever closer to Havana and on December 31, 1958, when Santa Clara came under the control of "Che" Guevara and Camilo Cienfuegos, the people knew that Havana would be next. What they didn't know was that their President was preparing to leave, taking with him a large part of the national treasury. Aside from the tourists celebrating at the casinos and some private parties held by the naïve elite, very few celebrated New Year's Eve.

A select few left Cuba with Batista, but the majority didn't find out that they were without a President until the morning of the following day.... January 1, 1959, became a day of hasty departure for many of the Batista supporters that had been left behind. Those with boats or airplanes left the island nation for Florida or the Dominican Republic, and the rest sought refuge in foreign embassies. The highflying era of Batista and his chosen few came to a sudden end. Gone were the police that had made such an overwhelming presence while Batista was in power, and in their place were young people wearing black and red "26th of July" armbands. Not wanting a repeat of when Machado fled Cuba, they went around securing government buildings and the homes of the wealthy. Many of these same buildings had been looted and burned after the revolt of 1933.

It was expected that Fidel Castro's rise to power was to be organized and orderly. Although the casinos were raided and gambling tables overturned and sometimes burned in the streets, there was no widespread looting with the exception of the hated parking meters that became symbolic of the corruption in Batista's government. Castro called for a general "walk-out" and when the country ground to a halt, it gave the movement time to establish a new government. The entire transition took about a week, while his tanks and army trucks rolled into Havana. The revolutionaries sought out Batista's henchmen and government ministers and arrested them until their status could be established. A few of Batista's loyalists attempted to shoot it out and were killed. Others were tried and executed, but many were simply jailed, awaiting trial at a later time.

"Che" Guevara seizes *La Cabaña*

"Che" Guevara with about two thousand guerrilla fighters entered Havana on January 2nd. Their entry was relatively quiet as they headed for the old Spanish fortress, overlooking the entrance of Havana harbor. At 3:00 a.m. the next morning, they took over the imposing *La Cabaña* fortress. In anticipation of Guevara's arrival the three thousand soldiers, assigned to the fort, stood in formation as their officers greeted Guevara. Addressing the troops, "Che" light-heartedly told them that they could teach his men how to march, but that his rebels could teach them how to fight.

When they were dismissed, he had them turn in their rifles but allowed the officers to retain their pistols. He granted them all a month's furlough; however, upon their return they discovered that they had all been permanently discharged.

One of "Che's" first official acts was to release the political prisoners, incarcerated there by Batista's régime. The newly emptied cells were then quickly repopulated with enemies of the revolution.

Guevara and his men admittedly didn't know much about administering a prison. As he and Aleida, his second wife, moved into the former *Comandante's* house, one of the more interesting problems was told by Aleida. Apparently a knotty problem occurred that had to be hastily dealt with. Many of "Che's" men had become "horny" and had developed an overpowering sex drive after months in combat without women. Havana still had its cabarets and prostitutes.... In or out of the business, the city had an abundance of willing women, eager to accommodate this band of lusty rebels. It was not unusual for the men to slip out of the fort and meet up with these young ladies, just outside of the Iron Gate. As soon as the sun set, you couldn't help but hear the sounds of girlish laughter, emanating from the bushes growing under an imposing watchful statue of Christ.

Guevara, understanding the possible consequences of these activities, organized a mass wedding. Presided over by himself, a judge and a priest, the men became legally married, even though they may have had girlfriends waiting for them back home.

Castro enters Havana

On January 8, 1959, Fidel made his grand entrance into Havana. With his son Fidelito at his side, he rode on top of a Sherman tank to Camp Columbia, where he gave the first of his long, rambling, difficult-to-endure speeches. It was broadcast on radio and television for the entire world to witness. For the Cubans it was what they had waited for! During the speech, smiling Castro asked Camilo Cienfuegos, "How am I doing?" and the catch phrase *"Voy bien, Camilo"* was born.

The following Christmas the celebrations were exceptional and made up for the drab Christmas of 1958. There were great expectations on the part of the Cuban people, but most of these expectations would be shattered in the years to come. In the United States, people saw things differently. "Kangaroo trials" of Batista's followers, ending with their executions, infuriated Americans who couldn't believe what was happening on what they considered a happy island. Members of the U.S. Congress held formal hearings, interviewing exiled Cubans known as *Batistianos*. The result was that in the United States, people began to rally against Castro and in Cuba, people saw the United States as presumptuous and overbearing. Eisenhower treated Fidel with contempt and Nixon did not hide the fact that he disliked the Cuban leader. It was this combination of events that led Cuban-American relations into a diplomatic downhill spiral, from which the two countries have just now started to emerge. Without American backing, Cuba turned to Communism and looked to the Soviet Union for support. The results that followed should have been expected and were the consequences of American arrogance and Cuban misplaced pride.

"This may have been the only revolution in which the main war criminals were tried and brought to justice, the only revolution that didn't rob or steal, didn't drag people through the streets, didn't take revenge, didn't take justice into its own hands. No one was ever lynched here. Not that some people wouldn't have liked to. Because the crimes committed by Batista's thugs and henchmen, those people who thought they could get away with anything, had been horrible. And if there were no lynchings, no bloodbaths it was because of our insistence and our promise: 'War criminals will

be brought to justice and punished, as examples.'"
Fidel Castro, 1960, as written in Soldier of the Cuban
Revolution *by Luis Alfonso Zayas*

Fidel Becomes a Sex Symbol

Having triumphantly entered Havana on January 8, 1959, Castro became a heroic figure of the Cuban people. He proceeded to set up his command post in the penthouse of the Havana Hilton Hotel, where he met with journalists, foreign visitors and politicians. The exception being politicians, such as his brother-in-law Rafael Díaz-Balart, that had been elected during the Batista régime and who were now banned from holding any political office.

Vilma Lucila Espin Guillois, a graduate of M.I.T. (Massachusetts Institute of Technology) and the daughter of the lawyer for the Bacardi Rum distillery, married Raúl Castro after their victorious entry into Havana. She had been the poster girl of the revolution and served with the M-26-7 in the Sierra Maestra Mountains. Vilma Espin served as the provincial coordinator of the 26th of July Movement in the Oriente Province.

As the conquering hero, women threw themselves at the normally quiet Fidel. Much to his own surprise, he became a sex symbol and was tempted by the many bikini-clad young ladies at the hotel pool. Errol Flynn, the movie star, met Castro and had a number of Hollywood beauties with him, expecting to make a movie in Havana. For the most part Fidel was preoccupied with the affairs of government, but he always made time for the chosen few.

There was a news correspondent by the name of Beverly Gary, who was described as a cool honey-blonde, and an Italian actress Sylvana Pampanini, who announced that she would star in a movie about the revolution, as well as Lia-Aurelia Vasquez, a petite fashion model. Maritza Rosales, a TV actress, even accompanied Fidel to a baseball game. Always in the background was the dapper military aide-de-camp, Jesús Yañez Pelletier. The Captain's responsibility was to make certain that all of Fidel's wants and needs were met, and that Fidel always had the company of intelligent, beautiful women.

Captain Jesús Yañez Pelletier

Captain Yañez Pelletier had been an orderly/guard at the *Presidio Modelo* prison while Fidel and his militiamen were being held captive there in the mid-1950's. As such, his superiors had directed him to mix poison into Castro's food. However, when he openly refused to do this, he instantly became an enemy of the State, but a hero in the eyes of the rebels as "The man who saved Castro's life."

After Fidel Castro successfully ousted Batista, Yañez Pelletier was appointed the new Cuban leader's attaché and bodyguard. Promoted to the rank of Captain, Pelletier accompanied Castro on a visit to Harvard University. In March of 1959, he also accompanied Fidel to Washington, D.C., when he was invited by the American Society of Newspaper Editors to speak at their annual convention. At the time, Fidel did not have an official position with the Cuban government and for this reason did not receive an official invitation from the United States Government. However, when Fidel went to meet with then-Vice President Richard M. Nixon, Captain Jesús Yañez Pelletier was the perfect attaché in his crisp khaki uniform. However, when Pelletier bought fifteen pairs of beautifully made shoes in the United States, he drew a little too much attention to himself.

Fidel was becoming tired of being upstaged by the man who had saved his life. Captain Jesús Yañez Pelletier also knew all the dirty little secrets involving the new "Head of State," and looked too sharp for his own good. It did not take long for paranoia on Castro's part, to dump Pelletier.

Raúl Castro, as the head of the military, insured that the ensuing court-martial earned Captain Yañez Pelletier a 30-year sentence for pro-American activities. Becoming disillusioned with Castro's government, Mr. Yañez Pelletier later helped found the Cuban Pro Human Rights Committee and served as its vice president. On September 18, 2002, at 83, he died in Havana of a heart attack.

Marita Lorenz

Marita Lorenz, born on August 18, 1939, in Bremen, Germany, was best known for her undercover work with the CIA. She was the daughter of Captain Heinrich Lorenz, master of the S/S *Bremen IV*, a German passenger ship, and her mother, an American actress, was related to Ambassador Henry Cabot Lodge, Jr.

Arriving in Havana on her father's ship in 1959, she met Fidel who talked about improving the Cuban tourist business. It was obvious that he was taken by the beautiful 19-year-old brunette, and upon hearing that she was fluent in multiple languages, asked if she would translate some letters for him. She happily agreed and although continuing on to New York, she was persuaded to return to Havana to do the translations. Still in Fidel's good graces, Captain Jesús Yañez Pelletier met her at the airport and escorted her to the Havana Hilton Hotel. When Castro arrived in her room, he revealed his true motives, which for a moment repelled her. The next day Castro reappeared and being more insistent, had sex with Marita. After finishing the act, he simply got dressed and arrogantly walked out. Later he thought better of it and sent flowers plus a gift, which Marita wisely accepted. Although the accounts regarding their relationship differ greatly, she did accompany Castro's entourage to New York and later returned with him to Havana. During this time she told Fidel that she believed that she was pregnant. Castro gave her the option of marrying the ever-faithful Captain Yañez Pelletier, or getting an abortion. She chose not to be married and returned to New York amidst many rumors, and speculations, as to what had happened during the time she was with Castro. Captain Jesús Yañez Pelletier on the other hand didn't fare quite as well, but instead of doing 30 years in prison as his sentence required, he got off serving only a little over a decade behind bars.

The CIA

In January of 1960 Marita, described as a "curvy, black-haired... American Mata Hari" by *New York Daily News* reporter Paul Mcskil, returned to Havana. There she took part in a failed assassination attempt orchestrated by the Mafia and the CIA, to poison Castro. Marita later said that Sturgis was involved, but that his close associate Alex Rorke was responsible for carrying out the operation. Marita brought along poison pills in her cold cream jar, which of course melted in the tropical heat. Besides, she later said that she did not have the stomach for killing her former lover. Apparently, Castro was aware of why she returned to Cuba. He handed her his pistol, with a dare for her to use it. Even after knowing the truth regarding her visit, he allowed her to safely leave Cuba. Sturgis was extremely angry when she returned to Miami and rebuked her for putting the pills into the cold cream, calling her stupid, over and over again.

For a few years after leaving the island, Marita was looked after and protected by a mobster named Ed Levi. It was his job to protect her from, what was considered, a likely attempt on her life by "Cuban Intelligence Operatives."

In 1961, Marita met Marcos Pérez Jiménez, the former President of Venezuela, in Miami. Marcos told her that he was anxious to meet her because he knew she was "Fidel's girl." He successfully pursued Marita, and when she gave in, they had an affair that resulted in the birth of a daughter.

Although she later lived in a luxury apartment, Marita collected welfare from the State of New York. The former Venezuelan President, a recipient of the U.S. Legion of Merit, was arrested on a sundry of charges and imprisoned in Caracas for five years, awaiting trial. Marcos was convicted of the charges, however having already spent more time in jail, his sentence was commuted. He was later exiled to Spain, where he died on September 20, 2001, in Alcobendas, a city located in greater Madrid, Spain, at the age of 87.

In 1970, Lorenz married the manager of her apartment building, located in the close proximity of the United Nations. Since some of the apartments were rented to delegates of the Soviet Union, the FBI recruited her husband as a paid informant. Marita joined in, by going through the trash nightly in search of useful information.

Marita eventually divorced her husband and started dating an unsavory enforcer for the mob, who put her up in an Upper East Side apartment for a while.

Years later, on the Geraldo TV show, Marita claimed that her affair with Marcos Pérez Jiménez was because of an assignment from the CIA. Operation Mongoose was a plot developed on November 30, 1961, early in John F. Kennedy's presidency, to overthrow the Castro régime. The CIA based in Miami enlisted the help of Johnny Roselli, an influential mobster from Chicago, for the expressed intention of assassinating Fidel Castro. The operation was also designed to include sabotage against Cuba's infrastructure and hopefully create open rebellion on the streets of Havana.

Frank Sturgis maintained a close relationship with Marita Lorenz. Perhaps it was because of her former connection to Castro and that she could be of use to him again, or perhaps it was that he found her exciting and attractive. Once again Sturgis enlisted her to work for the Central Intelligence Agency-sponsored, undercover "Operation 40," a small band of guerrillas that was originally started by the CIA in 1960, in anticipation of the Bay of Pigs Invasion. Becoming an assassination organization, it consisted of about 30 anti-Castro Cubans and their American advisors. Marita was retained by Sturgis to possibly seduce and kill Fidel prior to the CIA taking over the Cuban government.

After the failed Bay of Pigs Invasion, circumstances eventually led to the events of the Cuban Missile Crisis of 1962. The U.S. Senate's "Church Committee of 1975" confirmed at least eight separate attempts on Castro's life. The media and the foreign diplomatic corps were also openly asking many awkward questions, some of which would only be answered much later.

Now, a more mature Marita Lorenz was called before the House Select Committee on Assassinations (HSCA), where she testified that Frank Sturgis was one of the gunmen in the Kennedy assassination in Dallas. There are photographs in existence that show three men dubbed the "Three Tramps" that the Dallas police arrested right after the assassination. Although two of the men appear to be Frank Sturgis and Howard Hunt, the Dallas police identified the three men as Gus Abrams, Harold Doyle and John Gedney. They were all said to be derelicts and released, due to lack of evidence linking them to the shooting. Much was made of the photos on the Dick Gregory television show and the details were repeatedly reported in *Newsweek* and the *Rolling Stone* magazine. Since the 1960's this mystery has continued, with links to Jack Ruby and Charles Harrelson. Regardless, the FBI photo lab somehow concluded that the men in the photos were not Frank Sturgis or Howard Hunt. Marita Lorenz's testimony was also dismissed for lack of substantiating evidence. Marita managed to survive over the years by being an ongoing paid informant for local and Federal police agencies, including the FBI, U.S. Customs and the DEA. For Marita Lorenz, life was lived on the edge.

Living on the edge, Marita returned to Havana in 1981, for what would be her final visit with Fidel. "Hello, my little assassin," was supposedly Fidel's greeting to Marita at that time. According to last accounts, she is living in New York City.

"Let's remember, the CIA's job is to go out and create wars." Jesse Ventura, professional wrestler who served as the 38th Governor of Minnesota

Frank Sturgis

In retrospect, Frank Sturgis, formerly Frank Fiorini, had a fascinating career that started when he quit high school during his senior year, to join the United States Marine Corps as an enlisted man. He served in the Pacific Theater of Operations with Edson's Raiders of the First Marine Raiders Battalion under Colonel "Red Mike." In 1945 at the end of World War II, he received an honorable discharge and the following year joined the Norfolk, Virginia Police Department. Getting involved in an altercation with his sergeant, he resigned and found employment as the manager of the local Havana-Madrid Tavern, known to have had a clientele consisting primarily of Cuban seamen. In 1947 while still working at the tavern, he joined the U.S. Navy's Flight Program. A year later, he received an honorable discharge and joined the U.S. Army as an Intelligence Officer. Again, in 1949, he received an honorable discharge, this time from the U.S. Army. Then in 1957, he moved to Miami where he met former Cuban President Carlos Prio, following which he joined a Cuban group opposing the Cuban dictator Batista. After this, Frank Sturgis went to Cuba and set up a training camp in the Sierra Maestra Mountains, teaching guerrilla warfare to Castro's forces. He was appointed a Captain in the M-26-7 Brigade, and as such, he made use of some CIA connections that he apparently had, to supply Castro with weapons and ammunition. After they entered Havana as victors of the revolution, Sturgis was appointed to a high security, intelligence position within the reorganized Cuban air force.

Frank Sturgis returned to the United States, and mysteriously turned up as one of the Watergate burglars who were caught installing listening devices in the National Democratic Campaign offices. In 1973 Frank A. Sturgis, E. Howard Hunt,

Eugenio R. Martínez, G. Gordon Liddy, Virgilio R. "Villo" González, Bernard L. Barker and James W. McCord, Jr. were convicted of conspiracy. While in prison, Sturgis feared for his life, if anything regarding his associations and contacts became public knowledge. In 1975, Sturgis admitted to being a spy, stating that he was involved in assassinations and plots to overthrow undisclosed foreign governments. At the Rockefeller Commission hearings, their concluding report in 1975 stated that he was never a part of the CIA.... Go figure!

In 1979, Sturgis surfaced in Angola where he trained and helped the rebels fight the Cuban-supported communists. Following this, he went to Honduras to train the Contras in their fight against the communist-supported Sandinista government. He also met with Yasser Arafat in Tunis, following which he was debriefed by the CIA. Furthermore, it is documented that he met and talked to the Venezuelan terrorist Ilich Ramírez Sánchez, or Carlos the Jackal, who is now serving a life sentence for murdering two French counter intelligence agents. On December 4, 1993, Sturgis suddenly died of lung cancer at the Veterans Hospital in Miami, Florida. He was buried in an unmarked grave south of Miami.... Or was he? In this murky underworld, anything is possible.

"But I think the real tension lies in the relationship between what you might call the pursuer and his quarry, whether it's the writer or the spy." John le Carré, British Intelligence Services MI5 and MI6, Author

The Exciting Story of Cuba.... Part 13

Cuba Turns Hard Left

Manuel Urrutia Lleó

Fidel Castro held the reins of government and ruled by decree. Without concern for existing laws or protocol, he nominated Manuel Urrutia Lleó, born in Yaguajay, Las Villas, Cuba, to be the first President and leader of the provisional government.

While still in the mountains, he saw Urrutia as the best candidate for the position of president and after his victory, he announced that Urrutia held the office by the popular demand of the people and at the same time proclaimed himself as being "the Representative of the Rebel Armed Forces to the Presidency."

Manuel Urrutia was the liberal Cuban attorney, judge and politician that had supported the rebels in the 1957 anti-government trials, by declaring that the defendants acted within their rights. He was a staunch Batista adversary and became the accepted popular candidate for the presidency following the revolution. Urrutia was an astute liberal politician and judge. As an activist he had been to the United States, where he successfully lobbied for an end to the shipments of weapons to Batista.

The Exciting Story of Cuba

On January 1, 1959, with Fidel Castro's sanction, Urrutia flew into Havana from exile in Venezuela and, without the benefit of an election, assumed the presidency and took up residence in the Presidential Palace. Urrutia's newly established government consisted largely of known Cuban political veterans and pro-business liberals. At the same time, José Miró Cardona became Urrutia's Prime Minister.

Acting decisively, Urrutia cut the pay of all public officials, including his own salary from $100,000 a year to $40,000. Being the new broom, Urrutia swept the prevailing Cuban government clean, bringing an end to the national lottery, the casinos as well as the popular brothels. This caused an instant reduction in Cuba's economy and a national outcry. In doing this, he also reduced the flow of money brought in by tourists, thereby starting the downhill financial spiral in the country. He also was aware that Cuba was embracing socialism and attempted to steer the new government away from this obvious turn towards Communism.

On February 16, 1959, following the resignation of José Miró Cardona, Castro assumed the position of Prime Minister. It didn't take long before the differences of opinion between President Urrutia and the new Prime Minister Castro became an issue. Fidel, being more popular, used his bully pulpit to attempt to force Urrutia into becoming his puppet president, thereby lacking any real authority. The restoring of free elections proposed by Urrutia was soundly rejected by Castro, who claimed that it would return Cuba to the corrupt system of elections that prevailed under Batista. Although Urrutia continued to say that there were no discernable differences between himself and Castro, their many differences became ever more obvious, especially regarding financial issues and the direction, to the left, that Cuban politics was taking.

These basic differences between them festered, with Castro becoming ever more aggravated with what he saw as Urrutia's affluent lifestyle. For the good of the country, both men attempted to contain their concerns and refrained from attacking each other publicly until Castro exploded at a press conference, arranged to be given with a select audience on the evening of July 17, 1959.

Some witnesses to this press conference saw Fidel as being openly disrespectful of his appointed President, since his words went directly to the people. In his speech, Castro pointed out that Urrutia's salary of $40,000 per year was still extravagant and much too high, even though he had given himself a cut in pay. He pointed out that Urrutia's sense of timing was off and out of step with the times when he bought a lavishly expensive villa. Fidel claimed that the extravagant purchase was contrary to the principles of the revolution. Hearing Castro's remarks the Cuban press turned it into an inflammatory topic that Urrutia could not defend himself against.

Instantly things soured between Castro and Urrutia. Still popular, Fidel however was seen as humiliating the President by publicly embarrassing him. At one point, Castro praised Urrutia's honesty but in the next breath added that he lacked common sense. On previous occasions, when Urrutia voiced his opposition to the Communist Party and offered to resign, he was urged to stay on. However this time no one stepped forward on his behalf and, instead, the public, having become disenchanted, shouted for him to resign. It soon became clear to all, that members of the Communist Party were being placed in key positions. Urrutia fired back and made his anti-communist position clear to the *Avance* newspaper, and accused Fidel of being pro-communism. To this, Castro replied definitively, "I am not a communist!" With the United States and the Soviet

Union engaged in the cold war, Urrutia attempted to stabilize his position by making this topic an important talking point. It was however a failed attempt on his part to discredit the still popular Castro.

Fidel made a long speech that lasted until almost midnight. He openly accused Urrutia of everything including treason, and demanded the President's resignation. The air was charged by his words, and so listeners were surprised to hear Fidel resign his position as Prime Minister.

There was little that Urrutia could do. Discrediting Castro would have been impossible, given the popularity that Fidel enjoyed, and his attempt to rally any sizable number of people against the ongoing Communist takeover would be sure to fail.

Castro calculated correctly. The people, not believing what they heard, responded with an overwhelming groundswell of support. Over 500,000 organized Castro supporters came out and surrounded the Presidential Palace. Being coached, they demanded Urrutia's resignation. When asked if he would accept the presidency, Castro answered in the negative with just one word... "No!"

The following day, after only six months in office, Urrutia resigned the presidency, to which people in attendance started to applaud. He simply took off his suit coat and changed into a guayabera. Then leaving through a back door, he made his way to the Venezuelan Embassy where he sought asylum. Shortly thereafter, he emigrated from Cuba to the United States where he became bitter and depressed.

In 1964 the former President Urrutia wrote a book named "*Fidel Castro & Company, Inc.: Communist Tyranny in Cuba*," condemning the Castro régime. Urrutia charged that he had been ousted from the presidency because Castro sought to stop what he called the "neutralization of his own (Castro's) march toward Communism."

On July 5, 1981, Manuel Urrutia Lleó died at St. John's Hospital in Queens, New York. He was 79 years old at the time of his death.

Castro, now without any official title, continued to rule Cuba as the de facto Prime Minister, along with the existing Cabinet.

On July 23, 1959, Fidel officially resumed his Premiership, after having installed Marxist Osvaldo Dorticós as the next President of Cuba. Dorticós had strongly opposed Batista and participated in the Civil Resistance Movement.

Osvaldo Dorticós Torrado

Dorticós was born to a very wealthy family in Cienfuegos, Las Villas Province, on April 17, 1919. He was a teacher before studying philosophy and law at the University of Havana where he became involved with the Communist Party. He graduated from the University in 1941, with a degree in law.

Sometime later, Dorticós became active in the communist controlled "Popular Socialist Party" and thus became a strong opponent of Batista. In 1958, Dorticós was elected Dean of the Cuban Bar Association. Shortly thereafter, he was arrested by the Batista régime and forced briefly into exile in Mexico.

On July 17, 1959, Osvaldo Dorticós Torrado accepted the position of President of Cuba, offered to him by the Council of Ministers. After being ratified, he took office the following day and remained in that position until December 2, 1976. He had also served as a member of the Secretariat of the Central

Committee of the Communist Party of Cuba and continued to serve in this position until after the new Cuban Constitution was adopted.

The Cuban Press becomes Nationalized

The Cuban newspapers were pressured by the Printers' Union to include a clarification of any articles criticizing the government, thus coercing the media to remain loyal to the regíme. The left-leaning union workers at the newspapers continued to be at odds with the writers and editors, who in the past had obeyed Batista's demands. Now under the popular rule of Fidel and his leftist administration, the writers felt marginalized. As a consequence, the Printers' Union, feeling that criticizing the Revolution was tantamount to treason, pressured the management. It followed that the foreign press located in Cuba was also coerced not to forward any news via UPI and Reuters that the unions had not pre-approved.

The newspapers that had traditionally been conservative such as the *Diario La Mañana* were primarily written for the wealthier Cubans. Their criticism of the government was always met by a "note of clarification." This way the government always got in the last word. The *Diario La Mañana*, owned by the Rivero family, and the *Prensa Libre*, which was owned by Sergio Carbó y Morera, a former member of the Pentarchy, were rebuked and eventually shut down by the unions.

Remaining were *El Mundo* and the *Informacion*, as well as the government newspapers: *Revolución*, *Hoy* and *Verde Olivo*. The other independent tabloids were very careful not to offend the communist doctrine. *La Bohemia* became known as the voice of courage and liberalism and from the start, it promoted Fidel and the revolution.

In one deft swoop, all the newspapers were taken over by the government and incorporated into the new official newspapers: *Granma*, named after the boat and published by the Communist Party, the *Juventud Rebelde*, published by the Union of Young Communists and the *Trabajadores*, published by the Centre of Cuban Workers. For the greatest part, the editors and writers of the now defunct newspapers went into exile in the Miami area. Taking up "the pen," some became involved with dissenting publications, in opposition to the Castro régime.

Cuba also created "*Prensa Latina*," the official state news service, countering UPI and Reuters. It was originally founded shortly after the Revolution by Jorge Ricardo Masetti, a friend from Argentina of "Che" Guevara.

As Castro moved closer to the philosophy of the Soviet Union, Cuba became a one-party, socialist state. In 1961, President Dorticós represented Cuba at the Summit of Non-Aligned Nations in Belgrade, Yugoslavia, and in 1962 at the Summit of the Organization of American States in Uruguay. The same year, during the Cuban Missile Crisis, at the United Nations Dorticós announced that Cuba was in possession of nuclear weapons. To the United States, his comment escalated the threat of war.

Stepping down on December 2, 1976, Dorticós Torrado accepted the position of President of the National Bank and a member of the Council of State. He held these positions until after his wife died. He became despondent, presumably over the loss of his wife, and on June 23, 1983, he committed suicide by a self-inflicted gunshot wound.

"My parents were founders of the Cuban Communist Party, and I grew up extremely poor." Guillermo Cabrera Infante, Cuban Novelist

Fidel Castro Agrees to Communism

One of Castro's first acts as Cuba's Prime Minister was to go on a diplomatic tour that started on April 15, 1959. His first stop was the United States, where he met with Vice President Nixon, after having been snubbed by President Eisenhower, who thought it more important to go golfing than to encourage friendly relations with a neighboring country. It seemed that the U.S. Administration did not take the new Cuban Prime Minister seriously after he showed up dressed in revolutionary garb. Delegating his Vice President to meet the new Cuban leader was an obvious rebuff. However, what was worse was that an instant dislike developed between the two men, when Fidel Castro met Vice President Richard Milhous Nixon. This dislike was amplified when Nixon openly badgered Castro with anti-communistic rhetoric. Once again, Castro explained that he was not a Communist and that he was with the West in the Cold War. However, during this period following the McCarthy era, Nixon was not listening.

During Castro's tour to the United States, Canada and Latin America, everyone in Cuba listened intently to what he was saying. Fidel's speeches, that were shown on Cuban television, were troubling to Raúl and he feared that his brother was deviating from Cuba's path towards communism. Becoming concerned by Fidel's candid remarks, Raúl conferred with his close friend "Che" Guevara, and finally called Fidel about how he was being perceived in Cuba. Following this conversation, Raúl flew to Texas where he met with his brother Fidel in Houston. Raúl informed him that the Cuban press saw his diplomacy as a concession to the United States. The two brothers argued openly at the airport and again later at the posh Houston Shamrock Hotel, where they stayed.

During a heated discussion that was overheard by a number of other guests at the hotel, Fidel told Raúl that it was all a misunderstanding and that there wasn't anything for him to worry about. He emphatically emphasized that Raúl's and "Che's" thoughts about him were unfounded and that he continued to agree with them on their basic political philosophy. Those who heard the intense argument on the 18th floor of the hotel said that although they could not make out exactly what was being said, it concerned itself with the direction the Castro brothers wanted to take Cuba. Apparently, their differences were resolved that night and Fidel, being the more charismatic of the two, continued his diplomatic tour. However, it was Raúl who kept Fidel's feet to the fire and got things done.

After his 11-day stay in the United States, Fidel continued on to Canada and South America without wavering from his pro-western position. He returned to Cuba on May 7, 1959, and although he had a friendly meeting at the airport with the American Ambassador Philip Bonsal, things had definitely changed. Property was being expropriated and compensated for with useless twenty-year bonds. By government decree, the sugar industry was prohibited from running plantations after the harvest of 1960. The National Institute of Agrarian Reform (INRA) became the agency with the authority to enforce the rules decreed by Castro's régime after the Agrarian Reform Bill was enacted into law during July of 1959. The INRA was charged with road building, health, education and housing, but more importantly it was responsible for the expropriation and redistribution of land. A complicated agreement between the

Revolutionaries and the Communists would take Cuba in a very new direction. Ambassador Bonsal opposed the American position regarding any future economic sanctions against Cuba, and believed that they would drive Castro further into the Soviet orbit. With "Che" Guevara and his brother Raúl being Marxists and the Cuban Communist Party stronger than ever, Fidel, although he hesitated for a time, knew that he would have to fall in line with the changes, if only for the sake of harmony. On July 26, 1959, Castro gave a marathon four-hour speech, complete with interruptions for dancing and singing. With the crowds shouting "Viva Fidel," Castro proclaimed that Cuba was free from United States influence. From that time on, socialistic programs, primarily advocated by "Che" Guevara and Raúl, were the ones to be instituted and objections would be suppressed, even with the threat of imprisonment and the possibility of execution. Cuba turned a social and political corner, with the hard core of the revolutionaries now being infiltrated with staunch Socialists or, more accurately, Communists.

The suppression of the Cuban people, which started during the end of 1959, became more obvious in 1960. From 1959 through 1993, about 10% of the population left Cuba for Florida. Approximately 1,200,000 people came across the Straits of Florida to the United States. Although some came by airplane, many used small boats or any sort of raft they could find. Many others, less fortunate, were lost at sea.

Earl T. Smith, a former American Ambassador to Cuba, told the Senate at a hearing in 1960, that there was a communist threat to the United States throughout the Caribbean. Until Castro, the United States was such an overwhelming influence that the American ambassador was the second most important man in Cuba. He added that in the past there were times when the U.S.

Ambassador was even more important than the Cuban President. Prior to the Revolution, this could also have been said of the Mafia boss Lucky Luciano.

Using commercial radio and the new media of television, Fidel maintained a close relationship with the people and grew in popularity among most of his constituents. Public housing was constructed. Over 800 houses were constructed every month, in those early years of Castro's government, in an attempt to reduce homelessness. Water supplies and sewer lines were improved. Three hundred million U.S. dollars were spent on water supply and sanitation projects. However in parts of Cuba the water supply is intermittent, and throughout Cuba the quality is marginal, frequently lacking sufficient chlorination or filtration. During the first six months of Castro's administration, 600 miles of road were built in Cuba. Day-care centers and nurseries were built for children, to help working parents, while at the same time other centers opened for the disabled and elderly

Vietnam War

The United States became engaged in hostilities with North Vietnam on November 1, 1955, when President Eisenhower deployed the Military Assistance Advisory Group as advisors to train the army of South Vietnam, better known as the Army of the Republic of Vietnam. Things escalated in 1960, which was about the same time that Cuba established diplomatic relations with Vietnam, the communist country at war with the United States. In May of 1961 President Kennedy sent 400 United States Army Special Forces personnel to South Vietnam for the purpose of training South Vietnamese troops. By November of 1963 when he was killed, President Kennedy had increased the number of military personnel from the original 400 to 900 troops for training purposes. Direct U.S. intervention started with the Gulf of Tonkin Resolution in August of 1964. As things heated up, the number of American troops started including combat units and escalated to 16,000 troops, just before Kennedy's death. During the early hours of April 30, 1975, the fighting ended abruptly, as South Vietnamese President Duong Van Minh delivered an unconditional surrender to the Communists.

Between 195,000 to 430,000 South Vietnamese civilians died in the war and 50,000 to 65,000 North Vietnamese civilians died. The Army of the Republic of Vietnam lost somewhere between 171,331 and 220,357 men during the war. The Communist military forces lost approximately 444,000 men. It is estimated that between 200,000 and 300,000 Cambodians died and another 60,000 Laotians died during this war. In all 58,220 U.S. service members were killed. The last two American servicemen to die in Vietnam were killed during the evacuation of Saigon, when their helicopter crashed.

After the United States pulled out of South Vietnam, the two sections of the country came together under Communist rule. Vietnam has since become Cuba's largest trading partner next to China, and the United States has also returned to a normalized trade relationship with Vietnam.

Castro's First Big Challenge

Castro's first big challenge concerning the United States came when he said that he suspected that the staff at the U.S. Embassy was full of spies. He ordered that the number of staffers be reduced, to match that of the much smaller Cuban Embassy in Washington, D.C. Knowing that this was a ploy, the United States responded by completely closing the

American Embassy in Havana and at the same time increased U.S. aid to the Cuban dissidents in South Florida. Castro accused the United States of economic aggression and turned to the Soviet Union and other Eastern Bloc countries for support. At the same time, he expropriated the sugar mills, the Cuban Telephone Company, and the Cuban Electric Company, much of which was American-owned. In the summer of 1960, Castro, needing fuel oil went hat in hand to the Soviet Union. When pressured by the United States, Shell Oil, Esso and Standard Oil refused to refine the Soviet Union's Urals-blend of crude oil, using the excuse that it was relatively high in sulfur. In answer to this, Castro confiscated the refineries.

The Cuban Communist Party continued to promote the Marxist direction in which Cuba was heading. Castro, fearing the possibility of a military insurrection against his revolution, went to the people and created a "People's Militia." Arming loyalists, he established the "Committees for the Defense of the Revolution." Their primary purpose was to implement neighborhood spy networks with the expressed responsibility of ferreting out counter-revolutionary activities. The commanders of these loyalists acquired progressively more administrative duties, such as distributing food, processing exit visas and administrating abandoned or nationalized houses and businesses. If need be, they could also act as a national military reserve to reinforce the regular army. In effect, they became the face of the government and the people's point of contact to get local things done.

In September of 1960, returning to New York City, Castro spoke at the United Nations. After his speech at the General Assembly, many of his closest followers, including his brother, renewed their assessment that Fidel was becoming politically soft, and felt that they had stronger communistic convictions than he did. Leaders of the socialist and communist Bloc countries, including Nikita Khrushchev of the Soviet Union, Gamal Abdel Nasser of Egypt, and India's Jawaharlal Nehru, knew that Castro was wavering and encouraged Fidel to stand up for his principles and embrace a more socialistic stance.

Kennedy, who was running for the presidency, accused Eisenhower of creating in Cuba "Communism's first Caribbean base." On October 13, 1960, Eisenhower announced a partial economic embargo on Cuba that excluded food and medicine. The following year on September 4th, the *Foreign Assistance Act* was passed in the U.S. Congress. It prohibited aid to Cuba and authorized the President to create a "total embargo." Cuba quickly felt the effects of the embargo as buses and farming tractors broke down and couldn't be repaired for lack of replacement parts.

In 1960, the United States and the Soviet Union were locked into an idealistically-driven Cold War, pitting the Capitalistic West against the Communistic East. Cuba, unable to be self-sufficient, had to pick a side. With the United States putting economic pressure onto the relatively small country, Castro did the only thing his pride would allow. Voicing disdain for his neighbor to the north, Castro proclaimed that his ideological views paralleled those of the USSR. Meeting with the Soviet Premier Anastas Mikoyan, Castro agreed to provide the USSR with food and sugar, in return for a monetary infusion amounting to a $100 million loan, as well as industrial goods, crude oil and fertilizers. Castro's first public admission that his revolution was socialistic was during his speech honoring the people killed in the air strikes of April 15, 1961, during the Bay of Pigs operation. The Cuban government then took over all the banks, except two Canadian ones.

The iron curtain fell between the United States and Cuba as the *Instituto Nacional de Reforma Agraria*, namely the National Institute for Agrarian Reform or INRA, an agency of the Cuban Government, expropriated stores, textile mills, rice mills, cinemas and the remaining sugar plantations. Eisenhower then, covertly, ordered the CIA to prepare for the invasion of Cuba by militant Cuban factions in South Florida. The largest of these groups was an organization called the "Democratic Revolutionary Front."

By 1962, President Kennedy tightened the stranglehold on the island by reinforcing Eisenhower's embargo, making it even more difficult for other countries, including close allies of the United States, to carry on trade with Cuba.

By February 8, 1963, the U.S. Congress passed additional laws, preventing American citizens from traveling to the island to visit friends and family. Tightening the embargo, it became illegal to conduct any kind of commercial transactions with Cuba. To many it seemed strange that the United States could trade with the Soviet Union but not with Cuba. However, the explanation was that the Soviet Union was a permanent government, whereas the Cuban government was not. Many of the laws passed restricted American citizens as much, if not more than, it did Cubans.

"I don't want anything from Cuba. I want them to be free and enjoy the things I enjoy." Gloria Estefan, a Cuban-born American singer-songwriter, actress

Swan Island

By now, the Castro régime had solidified its base and was providing an education with a definite Communistic bias to the young children attending public school. When school was out of session, parents were encouraged to send their children to state run summer camps in the mountains. Many parents remembered how at the end of the civil war in Spain, 5,000 children were sent to the Soviet Union to save them from the Fascists and to expose them to Communistic brainwashing, which was called "social education." Now they feared that their children would suffer a similar fate under Castro.

Gibraltar Steamship Corporation never did any trading, and never owned or operated any ships, however it did operate a 50,000-watt, pirate radio station. Its president was Thomas Dudley Cabot, who in reality was the U.S. Department of State's Director of the Office of International Security Affairs. In actual fact, the radio station, called Radio Swan, was a Central Intelligence Agency covert, black operation, known in intelligence circles as "Black Ops." Pretending to be a normal radio station, it had commercial accounts including R. J. Reynolds, Philip Morris Tobacco, and Kleenex. It broadcast religiously-oriented programs, such as "The Radio Bible Class," "The World Tomorrow" and a Christian program from the Dominican Republic, as well as others. Their news broadcasts were sponsored by the Cuban Freedom Committee, a part of Christianform, an anti-communist foundation. In May of 1960, the pirate radio station started transmitting Spanish language broadcasts to Cuba from Swan Island, or *Islas del Cisne*. In 1961, Radio Swan became Radio America, with its headquarters in Miami.

Swan Island was part of an archipelago consisting of three islands located in the northwestern Caribbean Sea. These islands were claimed by both the United States and Honduras. The private ownership of the island has always been in question, however the Sumner Smith family has maintained a claim of part ownership and seemingly do have some rights to this, according to the U.S. Federal Courts. Being situated approximately 95 miles off the coastline of Honduras, the United States finally dropped its claim to the islands in 1972, yielding all sovereign rights to Honduras. Apparently, this also put the private ownership into jeopardy.

The primary purpose of the Radio America radio station was to undermine the Castro régime by spreading rumors, one of which was that Castro was planning to send school-aged Cuban children to military academies in Moscow. Using old, surplus, transmitting equipment, the station defined itself as "Assisting those who are fighting Castro within Cuba." At first, the radio station was exclusively Spanish speaking. However, later it also had a few English language radio shows, including the religious prerecorded *"The World Tomorrow,"* produced under the direction of Pastor Herbert W. Armstrong. This show was originally a half-hour program, supposedly inspired by the word of God. It was later reduced to fifteen minutes, when translated to Spanish. Radio America was dedicated to spreading previously recorded anti-Castro messages, which included propaganda and editorials from exiled Cuban leaders, interspersed with selective news.

The following year, during the Bay of Pigs Invasion, it became clear that the purpose of the station was to assist in the operations of the invasion. Following the failed military operation, Radio Swan altered its programing. Although, its mission remained anti-Castro, it no longer promoted the overthrow of the Cuban régime, which they then referred to as the Cuban government. The programs on Radio America even started using Fidel Castro's official title, instead of referring to him as a dictator.

Eventually the Radio America station was sold to the Vanguard Service Corporation and remained on the air until May of 1968, when it closed down permanently. Its AM transmitters were crated, removed from the island, and sent to Southeast Asia to assist in the Vietnam Conflict.

Private schools throughout Cuba were pressured by the government to use government-sanctioned textbooks and follow approved curriculums. As the schools started to follow these teaching guides and use approved textbooks, some parents became fearful and decided to homeschool their children rather than send them to private or public schools. In the end, it really didn't matter since even the private schools were taken over or closed by the régime anyway. Believing that Castro's government was just temporary, many of the parents decided to remain in Cuba, although they knew that any effort to overthrow Castro's revolution would certainly be met with ferocity.

Operation Peter Pan

It was like a raging wildfire that the Radio Swan story spread throughout Cuba! Many affluent Cubans, convinced that their children would actually be sent to Moscow for political indoctrination, panicked and sent their children to Florida. In all, as many as 14,000 Cuban children were airlifted to Miami, under a program named "Operation Peter Pan." During the next two years, British Airways, under charter, flew many of the children to the United States by way of Kingston, Jamaica.

The unaccompanied children started arriving in Miami in October of 1960. They arrived in waves, with the children of the more affluent families coming first. Their parents trusted their friends and family in the United States to take care of their children. Most of them still believed that Castro was just a passing phenomenon until a counter-revolution would depose him. As the Castro régime started running into economic trouble, very few people thought that it would last as long as it did.

Unfortunately, the Cuban immigrants that had only just recently arrived in Florida, struggled to maintain their own welfare and had no way of taking on any additional burdens. In their mind, their only solution was to turn to their faith, the Catholic Church. There were also additional groups that lent assistance to "Operation Peter Pan" such as "The International Rescue Committee" and other alliances sponsored by various Protestant Churches.

Father Bryan O. Walsh, who was the Executive Director of the Catholic Welfare Bureau in Miami, took in Pedro, the first of the children that arrived in South Florida, and named "Operation Peter Pan" after him. Families that took in these children also sought help from Dade County's Welfare Planning Council and the Florida State Department of Public Welfare. An estimated 200 children arrived in the first wave alone.... Knowing that many more would follow, the State of Florida established a Children's Service Bureau.

James Baker, the headmaster of Ruston Academy, an American school in Havana, became the liaison for this operation in Cuba. In addition to looking after the large number of children that came to him from concerned parents, he was influential in opening a boarding school in Miami, to receive some of the children that had no other place to go. Other dormitories for these children were located in Florida in Kendall, Opa-locka, Florida City and on Matecumbe Key.

The Exciting Story of Cuba

In August 1961, in Cuba the Boy Scouts became the "Young Communist Pioneers." In the same year, the U.S. Government commissioned a documentary called *The Lost Apple*, which was part of the United States government's anti-communism campaign. The movie dwells extensively on the pain of separation and how the Peter Pan children gained their freedom in the United States.

Presently an effort is underway to identify the children that came to the United States during "Operation Peter Pan." Musician Willy Chirino, born on April 5, 1947, in Consolación del Sur, Pinar del Rio, Cuba, is an entertainer and singer in the salsa style and credited with the "Miami Sound." His wife singer/songwriter Lissette Álvarez, as well as the former U.S. Senator from Florida and Secretary of the Interior during the George Bush administration, Melquíades Rafael Martínez Ruiz, better known as Mel Martinez, were just some of the children who arrived in Miami during those difficult years.

"Operation Pedro Pan Group, Inc." is an organization consisting of Cuban refugee children that arrived in the United States during the early 1960's. The program, which was started by Father Bryan O. Walsh, became the largest exodus of unaccompanied minors in America. Approximately 14,048 Cuban children were sent to the United States in less than two years. The operation lasted from December 1960 to October 1962.

The exodus of children ended with the onset of hostilities brought on by the Cold War and the Cuban Missile Crisis. It is estimated that another 80,000 children were left behind, when all flights between Cuba and the United States came to an end.

"While every refugee's story is different and their anguish personal, they all share a common thread of

uncommon courage: the courage not only to survive, but to persevere and rebuild their shattered lives." António Manuel de Oliveira Guterres, the United Nations High Commissioner for Refugees

The Year of "Alphabetization"

For a time, every year became significant, one-way or another, and was named accordingly. Cuba had suffered a mass exodus of their business class and the more educated people, leaving behind the less informed and lower sectors of society. To counter this brain drain and to improve the quality of life among these people, Castro focused on raising the educational and social levels of those that remained behind. It was at "Che" Guevara's insistence that in consecutive years the emphasis was shifted from agrarian reform to health-care reform, as well as to educational reform. The year 1959 was the "Year of Liberation," and 1960 became the "Year of Agrarian Reform."

The period of time beginning on January 1, 1961, and extending through December 22, 1961, was designated the "Year of Cuban Literacy" or the *"Campaña Nacional de Alfabetización en Cuba,"* meaning the "Year of Alphabetization in Cuba."

The illiteracy rate had increased throughout Cuba after the revolution, and was highest in the countryside where it escalated to almost 42% of the people, compared to 11% of city dwellers. In a speech delivered by Fidel Castro in 1961, he told prospective literacy teachers, "You will teach, and you will learn," meaning that this educational program would become a two-way street. Both public and private schools were closed for the summer in April, two months earlier than usual, so that both teachers and students could voluntarily participate in this ambitious endeavor.

A uniformed army of young teachers stood ready to head out into the countryside, to help educate those in need of literacy education. It was the first time that a sexually commingled group would spend the summer together, raising the anxiety of many that had only known a more Victorian lifestyle. For the first time boys and girls, just coming of age, would be sharing living conditions together. This tended to make young people more self-sufficient and gave them a better understanding of the Revolution, from Fidel Castro's point of view.

It is estimated that a million Cubans took part in this educational program. Aside from the primary purpose of decreasing illiteracy, it gave the young people from urban areas an opportunity to see firsthand what conditions were like in the country. Since it was the government that provided books and supplies, as well as blankets, hammocks and uniforms, it is no surprise that the educational curriculum included the history of the Cuban Revolution. It provided the foundation needed to instill a feeling of socialistic solidarity in the minds of the young students.

The effort to improve literacy in Cuba was not without a counter-revolutionary movement. In some cases, innocent teachers were harassed, assaulted and even lynched. There were stabbings and shootings by terrorists attempting to undermine Castro's régime and his alphabetization program. Accusations regarding the terrorist activities were directed at the United States, which, in fact, was conducting "Operation Mongoose" at that time.

"Operation Mongoose" was a CIA project intended to remove Castro from power and it included undermining the efforts of Cuban teachers. There were times during this early period of internal "Nation Building" that the raw hostile feelings between the factions surfaced. When the anti-Castro terrorists confronted the revolutionaries, who were feeling pride in their accomplishments, blood was shed. In the five years following January 1960, over 680 acts of terrorism, attributed to "Operation Mongoose," were reported.

From the very beginning, the young, motivated teachers were singled out and violently attacked. The most well-known of these incidents happened when 18-year-old Conrado Benítez García was sent to teach peasants and children, in the town of Trinidad in the Pitajones mountains. Unarmed, he was just six days into his assignment when he was murdered by a marauding band of anti-government terrorists led by Osvaldo Ramirez, a defector from Castro's revolution. Afterwards the patriotic teachers were organized into what were called "Conrado Benítez Brigades."

An example of how the literary classes were also used to instill the Communist doctrine is seen in the following translated lyrics...

Anthem of the Brigade of Conrado Benítez – Cuba 1961

We who are in the Brigade of Conrado Benítez,
We are the vanguard of the revolution,
Upon our books, we swore to uphold our goal,
Cuba will excel in literacy.

Our brigade travels to the plains and mountains
Carrying the message of light and truth,
Fighting for our country,
Fighting for peace.

Down with Imperialism and up with Freedom!
Carrying the message of light and truth.

Cuba! Cuba!
We will work and learn how to shoot,
Our Pencils and Textbooks give us Knowledge!
We will Win!

By: Raúl Ferrer, Cuban Communist Old Guard

In spite of setbacks, the literacy campaign was a success and by 1962, the country's literacy rate had escalated to 96%, making Cuba one of the most literate countries in the world.

Many individual youth groups, such as Boy Scout and Girl Scout troops and Catholic Youth groups, remained in existence during this era. However, the Young Pioneers and the Young Communist League, *Unión de Jóvenes Comunistas* or *UJC*, rapidly replaced them.

There is now a museum commemorating the *"Campaña Nacional de Alfabetización en Cuba"* in *La Ciudad Libertad* or the "City of Liberty." This museum is situated in Fulgencio Batista's former office, in the western suburbs of Havana. The museum contains many thank-you letters that were sent to Fidel Castro with gratitude. These letters were also used by UNESCO to gauge the success of the 1961 literacy campaign. Many of these letters are now on display and can be seen along with photographs, taken around the island during that year. Additional materials including the records of all 100,000 volunteers are also proudly kept on file here.

Cuban schoolteachers went beyond their borders to teach literacy in fifteen other countries, and volunteered to serve in third world countries such as Haiti, Nicaragua and Mozambique, for which they received the "King Sejong Literacy Prize" from UNESCO.

"Education is the most powerful weapon which you can use to change the world." Nelson Mandela, President of South Africa, 1994 to 1999

Troubles between Fidel and "Che" Guevara

In November of 1960, when the Democrat John F. Kennedy became President-Elect of the United States, Castro thought that it would be an improvement over the Republican President Eisenhower who had preceded him. In January 1961 Castro said, "For our part we will begin anew." It was beyond his understanding that a liberal American is considered a Progressive, which is far removed from Socialism and a world apart from Communism. Although Republicans try to associate "the left of center" Democrats with Socialism, the fact is that both of the major parties in the United States support a Capitalistic way of life.

All had not been smooth between the Soviet Union and Cuba, however Cuba out of necessity, continued to allow their technicians to come in, even though Castro was a reluctant participant in this Soviet alliance. He was also having a difficult time managing the huge Sugar Plantations, where even relatively minor decisions had to be made by the ever-growing bureaucracy in Havana. Mistakes made by people not having the proper background and training were costly, when they bought too many tractors or built highways that were underrated for the expected flow of traffic. In one instance, a virus infected and killed thousands of chickens, when they were crowded too close to each other and there were not enough qualified veterinarians available to stop the outbreak.

Cuba entered into a five year development plan, but industrial problems such as the repair of existing equipment proved challenging. In January 1961, Castro showed off the Soviet made T-34 tanks, mobile anti-aircraft guns and surface-to-air missiles during the parade commemorating the victory over Batista. There was no longer any doubt but that Cuba had taken a hard left turn towards Communism. Many of the upper and middle class had already left Cuba.

On a daily basis, Cubans came to the United States. Although some came by air, many came in small boats and rubber rafts that made their way across the 90 miles of extremely dangerous water. The Cubans that came successfully by boat were welcomed to the United States, and their boats wound up on a heap of similar vessels at the Key West Naval Base in Florida.

Canada filled Cuba's economic gap to some extent by supplying the spare parts for cars, tractors and other essential equipment, but without a balanced budget, financial difficulties were beginning to produce great stress upon the Cuban government. Eastern Bloc countries welcomed the chance to supply Cuba with their equipment, which however was frequently archaic or of inferior quality. Much of what was used in Cuba was a holdover from Pre-Castro days. Equipment was held together with baling wire, fabricated or adapted parts and modified designs. Cubans, out of necessity, became reconstructive engineers, employing common sense and adaptive skills.

In May of 1961 "Che" Guevara, who had been appointed Minister of Industry, informed Castro that he had signed a large contract with an Eastern Bloc nation to build over a hundred factories. With Cuba lacking the necessary electrical power, greater problems suddenly presented themselves. Being a "medical doctor turned warrior" did not make him a competent businessman. It was because of obvious gaffes like this, that the friendship between Fidel Castro and "Che" Guevara became strained and their differences widened.

Guevara was granted Cuban citizenship by a set of contrived legal conditions that applied only to him and he was given positions of power that only happened because of his friendship with Raúl and Fidel. Although he remained a zealot regarding Communism, he fell short when it came to administering the posts he held. He was in over his head regarding the tasks that he had to perform.

It frustrated his friend Fidel when "Che" mandated arbitrary rulings, such as "Supervisors and Directors were not to have sex with their secretaries." It wasn't that "Che" was completely innocent, when it came to a boss cavorting with an underling.

When Guevara's wife Hilda came to Cuba to join him in 1959, Guevara told her that there was a new woman in his life. He had met Aleida March, one of his military subordinates, during the Battle of Santa Clara. Subsequently, Hilda agreed to divorce "Che," after which he married Aleida. For their honeymoon they went as far as Tarará, a seaside resort town about 12 miles from downtown Havana. Over the next few years they had four children: Aleida, Camilo, Celia, and Ernesto.

It also bothered Fidel that "Che" was more an admirer of Mao Tse-tung and the Chinese brand of Communism, over that of the Soviet Union. The two countries had similar values until the 1950's, when an ideological rift developed. The Soviet Union tried to coexist with the Capitalistic world, whereas China continued to pursue a policy of aggression towards Imperialism. At the same time this huge Asian country, started in earnest to lift its struggling masses from poverty. By 1953, Mao felt confident enough to start his Five Year Plan towards industrialization.

In 1956, Khrushchev made a speech denouncing the former Stalin régime. The Chinese remained in favor of Stalin's leadership style and continued to follow his methods regarding their foreign policy. It is also important to note that, to a great extent, the Chinese form of government was built around Chairman Mao's dynamic personality, which intrigued "Che." "Che's" political stance made Cuba's relationship with the Soviet Union difficult and definitely awkward.

A Vintage Cuban Travel Poster

The Exciting Story of Cuba.... Part 14

In the Soviet Sphere

The Bay of Pigs Invasion

Castro's Cuba continued on the path towards Communism, undermining Capitalism by expropriating the remaining corporations on the island. In early March of 1960, American investors and Cuban expatriates grew more anxious when they became aware of the closer relationship Cuba was developing with the Soviet Union. Castro's incendiary anti-American rhetoric and his attacks on U.S. interests motivated the United States government to take direct action.

On March 17, 1960, the CIA presented their plan for the overthrow of Castro's régime to President Eisenhower and the U.S. National Security Council. The next day, Eisenhower approved a budget of $13 million for a military strategy named "Operation Pluto."

On January 28, 1961, the newly-elected President Kennedy was briefed on "Operation Pluto," which would include an invasion of Cuba by approximately 1,300 trained men. The plan called for a shipborne invasion near Trinidad, Cuba, about 170 miles southeast of Havana, on the Caribbean coast. President Kennedy later moved the operation over 110 miles westward to the "Bay of Pigs" or "*Bahía de Cochinos*" and called it "Operation Zapata." This new location was preferred because it was closer to Havana but farther from populated centers, and had an airfield that could handle bomber operations.

In April of 1960, the Central Intelligence Agency began recruiting anti-Castro Cubans living in South Florida. Beginning in July, a training program was started on Useppa Island near Marco Island on the Gulf of Mexico. Other training facilities were on the island of Vieques in Puerto Rico and at Homestead Air Force Base in Florida, south of Miami, where the CIA carried out a guerrilla warfare program. Later, in October of 1962, Homestead AFB became a major staging area for the contemplated invasion of Cuba. Other activities preparing the recruits took place at Fort Gulick and Fort Clayton in Panama. As the number of recruits increased, another CIA-run base, code-named JMTrax, was opened for infantry training near Retalhuleu in the Sierra Madre mountains, on the Pacific coast of Guatemala. The newly formed paramilitary group became *Brigada de Asalto 2506*, or Brigade 2506, and was commanded by José Alfredo "Pepe" Pérez San Román, known simply as "Pepe San Román." Their political officer was Manuel Francisco Artime Buesa, a medical doctor and a former member of Fidel Castro's rebels.

On November 18, 1977, Manuel Artime died of cancer and on September 10, 1989, "Pepe" San Román committed suicide in Miami. Artime was a close friend to E. Howard Hunt and was even the godfather of his youngest son David. Some consider the circumstances of their deaths suspicious, but this can also be said of what happened to many other operatives involved in Cuban operations. Speculative conspiracy theories abound and continue to circulate in this shadowy netherworld.

On April 15, 1961, eight B-26B Invader Bombers with Cuban markings flew in from Puerto Cabezas, Nicaragua, crossing the Caribbean, and then bombing three Cuban airfields. Two of the airfields, San Antonio de los Baños and *Ciudad Libertad*, formerly *Campo Columbia*, were near Havana, and the third was Antonio Maceo International Airport located in Santiago de Cuba.

The attackers destroyed about seven Cuban aircraft on the ground. However, one of the attacking bombers was damaged by anti-aircraft fire and was forced down about 30 miles north of the island, with a total loss of the crew. Another of these aircraft, which was also damaged but still air worthy, continued north and landed at Boca Chica Key Naval Air Station near Key West, Florida. The following day the crew was quickly returned to Nicaragua.

The United States government announced that the downed aircraft belonged to the Cuban air force and was manned by Cuban dissidents. In reply to this, Castro appeared on Cuban State television and denounced these claims. He put his military on high alert and directed defensive operations from the Cuban Military Headquarters, which had just been bombed by two of the masquerading airplanes. Fidel issued orders to detain anyone who was suspected of conspiracy or treason. Lists of these people had previously been prepared and were used to round up suspected dissenters. Within days, his overzealous police force and army incarcerated about 20,000 Cuban citizens, using whatever means were available, including a sports stadium. In a speech to the people, Fidel finally admitted to the public that his Movement was Socialistic.

The Cuban Foreign Minister Raúl Roa García, successfully presented evidence at the United Nations, proving that the attacks were foreign in origin. Adlai Stevenson, the U.S. Ambassador to the United Nations, replied that the United States had not participated in any action against Cuba. Ambassador Stevenson, knowing better, insisted that the aircraft that had landed in Miami had Cuban markings and therefore must have been of Cuban origin. Stevenson's comments sounded contrived since the aircraft had Plexiglas noses, normally used as the bombardier's station, whereas the actual Cuban B-26's had solid noses with armament. It was obvious to the General Assembly that the United States Ambassador had been perpetrating an outright lie or, in diplomatic double talk, an untruth! It was an embarrassing moment that left the United States' veracity open to ridicule.

In the early hours of April 17, 1961, the invasion's main force landed along an inlet, 20 miles across a vast swamp from Central Australia, Cuba. When it happened, the resistance to the invaders was light and the Cuban defenders were easily forced back by heavy gunfire from the supporting vessels anchored offshore. To their detriment, the insurgents made mistakes from the very beginning. During the initial invasion, some of their landing craft were destroyed when they ran aground onto an uncharted coral reef.

Castro was first informed of the invasion that was taking place at the Bay of Pigs at 3:15 a.m. on the morning of the invasion. With this, he lost no time and flew to the invasion site, where he could oversee the counter offensive. Major Flavio Bravo, an officer who had been a communist prior to the revolution, and a contemporary of Fidel Castro at the University of Havana, was the first officer on the scene at the time of the invasion. On Castro's orders, Major José Fernández, who was the director of the Military Training Academy at Managua, near Havana, replaced Major Bravo, and mounted the counter offensive.

Major Fernández, known as "El Gallego" to his friends, was a career officer who had served as a lieutenant during the Batista era. Fernández and some other officers were jailed by the secret police (SIM) and charged with conspiracy against Batista. After serving nearly three years in prison, they were released a few days before Castro arrived in Havana. Castro made an exception to his guideline of not accepting Batista's officers into his rebel army, by offering commissions to Fernández and some few others.

On their way to the battle zone, Major Fernández and his students came under fire from paratroopers of Brigade 2506. Although they suffered heavy casualties, he held his own and then turned the battle around in his favor. For his valor, Fernández was promoted to *Comandante* and years later rose to the rank of Major General.

Once alerted, the remainder of the Cuban air force began attacking the invaders with a vengeance. During the battle that followed, Cuba lost a B-26 in the firefight. However, the ensuing confusion also proved costly to the invaders. The Brigade 2506 mistakenly fired upon some of their own paratroopers that had jumped in. Much of their equipment became mired down and ultimately lost in the extensive mangrove swamp. Cuban airplanes zeroed in and destroyed the ship that carried the ammunition and fuel. Another landing craft beached itself in the wrong location. It soon became obvious, as the collateral damage began taking a heavy toll, that the invaders had not done their homework. This faux pas presented Castro's forces with a definite advantage.

Assuming the direct control of operations, Castro ordered in heavy reinforcements, including light tanks. The invaders expected an infusion of support from the U.S. Navy and became discouraged and angry when President Kennedy withheld American military intervention. On April 20, the invading force found themselves wallowing in the bug-infested swamp and were forced to surrender to Castro's defending army. It was Castro's glorious moment as he capitalized on his success and had the captives publicly interrogated on television for the entire world to see. Eventually, all but a few of the invaders were repatriated back to the United States in return for a ransom in food and medicine, totaling approximately $53 million in donations from U.S. corporations and private individuals, according to the BBC. The Cuban victory was seen, by the world, as a resounding defeat for the United States, and sent a powerful message to Castro's supporters in Latin America of Cuban strength and tenacity, as well as the failings of the inept CIA. It also solidified Fidel's position with the Cuban people.

Those that had been incarcerated realized that their safety was tenuous, as long as the Castro régime was in power. The best course of action for the remaining dissident Cubans was to make their way across the Straits of Florida to the United States and seek political asylum. Those that had thought they could wait out the régime came to realize that their fence-sitting days were over and that they had to make a choice. Leave or join became their only alternative. At the same time, opposition to Castro's régime was also strengthened by solidifying the many Cubans that had been detained by Castro's police force.

Cubans were becoming weary of the downhill slide that their economy was taking. After the Bay of Pigs Invasion, thousands of Cubans fled for better opportunities in the United States, many without a penny in their pocket. When they arrived in the United States, a lot of them joined the conservative Miami Cubans as part of the continuing opposition to Castro. As they became American citizens, they could politically support the Cuban embargo. Those who departed from Cuba following the Bay of Pigs Invasion were mostly middle class professionals and business people. With the hemorrhaging of these people as well as the loss of the children that left during "Operation Peter Pan," Cuba was beginning to become a crestfallen third world country. It had lost its luster, along with dreams of a brighter future.

Realizing Cuba's dilemma, Castro attempted to solidify his hold on the government in the aftermath of the Bay of Pigs. People were leaving in droves, as the citizens now realized that it would be Castro's way or the highway. The results were that the dynamics of Cuba were degrading. With many of Cuba's skilled population moving north to the United States, it left a relatively loyal but far less educated population behind. The many black Cubans, having fewer resources, couldn't leave and remained on the island, thereby changing the country's demographics. Adding in the other minority groups, the white Cubans that were left behind, only held a slim majority of the total population.

Castro knew that he would have to improve and increase the education of those Cubans remaining, to counter the effects of the sizable exodus. He reasoned that Cuba's future depended on the education of those who remained in Cuba. Although life on the island is still difficult, the Cuban people are now among the most literate in the Caribbean. Cuba excels in science and medicine and exports these skills to other countries. Among other things, they have become the pharmacy of Latin America.

"I am fond of pigs. Dogs look up to us. Cats look down on us. Pigs treat us as equals." Winston Churchill, Prime Minister of the United Kingdom, May 10, 1940, until July 26, 1945

The President Gets His Cigars

Castro tried to sit on the political fence up until the Bay of Pigs Invasion, but after that, he had no choice but to embrace Soviet Communism. He proclaimed himself a "Marxist-Leninist" during a televised speech on December 2, 1961, and sent his son Fidelito to school in Moscow.

What had started as a number of militant revolutionary groups came together and organized as the *ORI* or Integrated Revolutionary Organizations. Following Castro's takeover the various factions combined and on March 26, 1962, became the United Party of the Cuban Socialist Revolution. The Communist Party became the sole legal political party and Cuba was declared a Marxist-Leninist State. For this, the OAS (Organization of American States) expelled Cuba, although many of its members, including Brazil, Argentina, Mexico and Chile, abstained from voting. Moscow increased their economic and military aid to Cuba, cautiously mindful of the basic political differences between them. They were aware that Cuba was developing ideological ties with China. The USSR was also aware of the possibility that other Latin American leaders would now assert additional pressure to contain or restrict their own domestic Communist Parties.

As he infused Cuba with Russian technicians, Nikita Khrushchev compared the economic state of Cuba with that of the Soviet Union after their own revolution. He also fumed over the fact that the United States had nuclear warheads pointed at Moscow and clandestinely tried to even this up by bringing missiles into Cuba. This move was agreed upon in a deal made by Raúl during a conference in Moscow, which was designed to increase Cuba's military strength. At the same time, Kennedy was being reproached for the failed Bay of Pigs Invasion and for allowing Cuba to fall under the control of the Soviet Union.

Cuban dissidents in Miami wanted Kennedy's strong support in reorganizing their forces. To them and the public in general, Kennedy only expressed the tepid view that he hoped Cuba would soon be free again.

On February 7, 1962, President Kennedy announced to his staff that he needed some help finding as many of the prestigious Cuban Petit Upmann cigars as possible. He let it be known that he would like to have 1,000 of these cigars by the next morning. Being the President of the United States, his wish was granted when, on the morning of February 8th, his Press Secretary Pierre Salinger came in and deposited 1,200 cigars on Kennedy's desk. Smiling, Kennedy opened his desk, took out a document and signed it, banning importation of all Cuban-made products into the United States. Some years later when asked about that moment, Salinger said that there were actually 1,201 cigars.

Cuban H. Upmann Cigars – Founded in 1844

The Russians Come to Cuba

It was during the cold month of February in 1950 that the 32nd Guards Air Fighter Regiment, known as the 32nd GIAP, was transferred to *Кубинка,* Kubinka Air Base near Moscow. Being close to the Russian capital, the Regiment was afforded the very best in equipment and aircraft. During the 1950's they received Mikoyan jet fighters, the MiG-15's and the improved version, the MiG-17's, which were the most modern Soviet jet fighters developed during the early part of the Cold War. The MiG-19's, developed in the 1960's, became the Soviet Air Force's most popular fighter and was quite capable of challenging the latest American aircraft over North Vietnam.

In Russia, the 32nd GIAP flew these aircraft during Victory Day flight demonstrations over Moscow and it was two months later in July of 1962 that the regiment displayed the new MiG-21 during an aviation parade over the capital. The decorated Colonel Nikolay Shibanov was in command of the regiment and Lieutenant Colonel Nikolay Shcherbina was his deputy and political officer.

During the summer of 1962, the East German built ship, the S/S *Nikolayevsk,* operated by the Baltic State Shipping Company, sailed to Cuba with an advance party from the regiment. The small cargo-passenger ship could take 350 passengers, which included military personnel as well as civilian employees of the Army and the Air Force. Receiving their orders early in September of 1962, some of the pilots of the 32nd GIAP boarded the S/S *Nikolayevsk* for what would be its second voyage to Cuba. The entire mission was cloaked in secrecy with everyone being ordered not to speak to anyone about what they were doing or where they were going. Regardless of rank, everyone was ordered to wear civilian clothes, which only heightened the suspense. Even to the pilots, the reason why they were going to Cuba was a mystery. It is always sinister when soldiers are ordered to blend in with the civilian population.

Aircraft and repair equipment were loaded onto the S/S *Volgoles*. Normally used as a lumber ship, it was now docked in Baltiysk, Russia, which is located on the northern part of the Vistula Spit and opens into the Baltic Sea. The ship was 407 feet long and almost 55 feet wide. Loading operations went around the clock, with the last 16 MiG fighters crated and placed on top of the hatch covers. Additional aircraft and equipment were loaded onto the S/S *Divnogorsky*, a dry-cargo ship, that also took the remaining pilots and technicians.

A story was told of two pilots that almost missed the ship, because they were overdoing the festivities on their last night ashore. When they did arrive at the bottom of the gangway, they were still happy and singing. The thought of reprimanding one of the more assiduous men, the congenial Lieutenant Beloborodov, faded when he declared that he was a proud Soviet Citizen and would be glad to redeem the offence with his blood. Unfortunately, the other officer, Lieutenant Olkhovik, did not fare as well. Being returned to Kubinka Air Base, he was drummed out of the service without so much as a pension.

On August 17, 1962, the ships sailed out of the port. Being foggy and with the water grey and cold, the ships crept along at a greatly reduced speed. It took two days before they left the Baltic and North seas. Passing through the English Channel the weather improved enough that the pilots could see the lighthouses along the coasts of both England and France. A week later as they approached the American Continent, U.S. Navy P-2 Neptunes suddenly flew overhead. These patrol aircraft continued to observe them, sometimes flying extremely low, just above the ship's masts. The women aboard were ordered up on deck, for the expressed purpose of waving to the pilots. No one on the open deck was to wear any part of a uniform, but it remains doubtful that the vessel was considered just another passenger ship. From Baltiysk, it took two weeks to cross the Atlantic Ocean and arrive in Cuba.

Another ship, the S/S *Nikolayevsk*, mistakenly arrived at the wrong port. So after raising the anchor again, it took another 15 hours before she finally arrived at the bay of La Isabela. Because it was carrying explosives, the ship was anchored a distance from the docks. Looking to the shore, everything seemed dilapidated and some of the older buildings, left over from colonial times, could be clearly seen from the upper decks of the ship. The next day the *Divnogorsky* also arrived and the discharging of the cargo onto barges began in earnest, even though the floating crane being used was an antique. Its steam engine huffed and puffed laboriously, as the old hemp lines were tested to their maximum. Considering the danger, the ship's duty officer, ordered that the ammunition and explosives stowed in a forward hold be off-loaded by hand, which may have been a very wise decision.

The personnel assigned to Headquarters at the Santa Clara Air Base, were quartered in military field tents. Without air-conditioning, these accommodations soon became extremely trying. To make matters worse, on August 5th, they learned that one of their comrades had been killed and three others were wounded in an unforeseen accident. The typical tropical rainstorms with accompanying lightning strikes and the thunderous booms were bad enough, but being in leaking tents and getting flooded out made life unbearable. Some of the tents collapsed from the sudden wind gusts, leaving the airmen totally wet, exposed to the elements and miserable. Following the rain, the sun increased the temperature and raised the humidity. It was also responsible for bringing out the mosquitos and a thousand other insects at night. What the Russians thought would be a tour of duty in a tropical paradise, turned into a purgatory. The aviators who were unaccustomed to the Cuban weather discovered that Cuba did not always live up to the travel books they had read and many of them became homesick, longing to return to Mother Russia and home.

Also moving the crates containing the MiG's from the port to the base was not an easy task. On one occasion, pretending that the huge cases contained tractors, the driver of the oversized truck and trailer struck some overhead electric wires. The local people became upset and indignant that this foreigner tried to drive his long tractor-trailer through their village, but with some careful maneuvering, what could have been a worse calamity was averted. When the huge containers finally arrived at the air base, they were pried open and it was only then that the Cubans learned the truth. Imagine their surprise seeing the sleek fighter-jet, when the first crate was opened and the MiG-21 was wheeled out. "What kind of tractor is this?" one of the workers was heard to ask. Reaffixing the wings and assembling the aircraft in humid temperatures well above 100 degrees Fahrenheit, was another nightmare, but eventually with the aircraft assembled, the actual training could begin.

Life in Santa Clara remained difficult. Communications with the Soviet Union were nearly nonexistent for the airmen. When a young second lieutenant, worried about his sick mother and his young bride, inquired how he might learn of their welfare, he received a curt retort insinuating that he was more interested in his bride's skirt than his military service.

While flying a patrol mission two MiG fighters without any identifying markings, suddenly encountered some American

F-101B Voodoo fighters, but there was never a threat or a shot fired. When the MiG's aligned themselves alongside the intruders, they could see the Americans smiling and waving. Being in Cuban airspace was illegal, but the Americans were thought of as friendly fellow aviators. Following this encounter, they peeled off and headed for the open ocean. It was customary for two MiG's to fly in formation and since the island is relatively small, the patrols were usually only an hour long. Things remained extremely fluid and at the end of October, the Regiment was moved from Santa Clara to San Antonio de los Baños Air Base, about 30 miles southwest of Havana.

On October 22, 1962, the day that the American public learned that there were Soviet missiles in Cuba, the rumor was circulated among the Soviet pilots that the U.S. Navy was given orders to bombard Cuban cities and attack the Cuban Air Bases. Strangely, no one panicked. In fact, it was thought that this was all a big joke and that somehow the political leaders were just kidding. It was not until the order was given to arm the aircraft and keep them on standby that the full impact of the situation sank in. For the next few days, things became very tense with no one knowing what the future held, or understanding how things would play out. No one could sleep knowing that things were escalating. Besides, the pilots had to be ready to respond at a moment's notice and lay on their beds with their handguns and gas masks.

On October 27th, an air-defense battery shot down a U.S. Air Force Lockheed U-2 intelligence, reconnaissance aircraft. Fidel Castro made a big show of congratulating the Cuban soldiers that supposedly brought the airplane down, thus winning an important victory over the American imperialists. It all sounded grand, but in reality it was the Soviet crew of the 1st battalion of the 507th Air Defense regiment that was responsible for this questionable victory. Bringing this spy plane down brought the situation between the United States and Cuba (as well as Russia) to the boiling point. It was almost certain that the world was about to embark on a nuclear war, the likes of which had never been seen. The Soviet Union and the United States were only a hair's breath away from World War III.

Major Rudolf Anderson, Jr., the father of three children and the pilot of the U-2, was lost and presumed dead. The American public following the happenings via the media were ready to attack Cuba. With the distinct possibility of a thermonuclear holocaust, only calmer and clearer heads could save the planet. Nikita Khrushchev told Kennedy, "You want a nuclear war? You will get it!" American F-100 and F-101 fighter aircraft were seen in the sky above Cuba daily but fortunately, the Russians were ordered not to engage them and definitely not to fire at them. There were tense moments when some of the Soviet pilots would push the envelope and stalk the American fighters. However, each time the Americans would use smoke and evasive maneuvers to shake of the Russians and then quickly head out to International Waters.

Since the Soviet MiG's were unmarked, Voice of America broadcast that an unknown pirate airplane had attacked a U.S. Air Force aircraft over Cuba. Knowing the possible consequences of this, all the Soviet aircraft had Cuban markings painted on them overnight. The intense tropical sun was also causing problems with the MiG's. The ultra-violet light from the sun caused the canopies housing the pilots to become cloudy and less transparent. Since they were impossible to clean, new ones were eventually sent from Russia.

On October 26th, Nikita Khrushchev contacted Kennedy and offered to remove the missiles from Cuba in exchange for a promise that the United States would not invade Cuba. A day later on October 27th, Khrushchev sent a letter proposing that the Soviet Union would dismantle their missiles in Cuba, if the Americans reciprocated by removing their missile installations in Turkey. In 1963, although the cold war was far from over, both sides knowing how close they came from an all-out conflict, had a "hot line" installed between Washington and Moscow, hoping to prevent any similar situations in the future. The hot line is sometimes called the red telephone, even though it wasn't even a telephone, nor was it red. The first connection was a teletype machine, after which a fax machine was used. In 1986, the hotline became a computer link and messages are now sent by email.

After the Cuban missile crisis, Major Anderson's body was returned to the United States and on November 6, 1962, was interred at the Woodlawn Memorial Park in Greenville, South Carolina. On January 8, 1964, he was posthumously awarded the first ever Air Force Cross. It is the second highest military award for "Extraordinary heroism while engaged in an action against an enemy of the United States." Anderson was also awarded the Air Force Distinguished Service Medal, the Purple Heart, and the Cheney Award.

Although Major Anderson was the only combat death of the Cuban crisis, there were other Americans that died as a direct result of the hostilities. Between September and November of 1962, three Boeing RB-47 Stratojets of the 55th Strategic Reconnaissance Wing crashed, killing a total of 11 crew members. On October 23, 1962, an additional seven aviators died when a Boeing C-135B Stratolifter carrying ammunition, stalled and crashed on the final approach to Guantánamo Bay Naval Base.

On August 10, 1963, the 32nd GIAP received orders to turn over all the airplanes and equipment to Cuba. This was done at a ceremony on August 25th, witnessed by Raúl Castro, who was the commander of the military at the time. On September 14, 1963, the pilots and service personnel of the 32nd GIAP assembled to depart from the San Antonio Air Base by buses to Havana. Most of the technicians returned to Russia on the S/S *Yuri Gagarin*, whereas most of the pilots returned on Soviet Aeroflot airliners. A few others that had to close down the facility, returned somewhat later on other ships. The entire operation was kept a secret for 26 years and it wasn't until December 28, 1988, that the Soviet public became aware of Russia's Cuban involvement. Most of the participants of the Cuban affair received the military decoration "Soldier Internationalist," for military valor shown while executing an international mission.

It was because of information compiled by the son of Major Victor Sharkov, who headed a group of aircraft technicians during the 1962-1963 Soviet Operation in Cuba and who became a recipient of the decoration "Soldier Internationalist," that these happenings became known. Major Victor Sharkov retired from the Soviet Air Force in 1978 and moved to Kubinka on the Setun River, a town best known for its Tank Museum and Air Base.

The saga of this Soviet Regiment overlaps the following section, which details the Cuban Missile Crisis from a historical perspective.

"I belong to a group of men who fly alone. There is only one seat in the cockpit of a fighter airplane. There is no space allotted for another pilot to tune the radios in the weather or make the calls to air traffic control centers or to help with the emergency procedures or to call off the airspeed down final approach. There is

no one else to break the solitude of a long cross-country flight. There is no one else to make decisions. I do everything myself, from engine start to engine shutdown. In a war, I will face alone the missiles and the flak and the small-arms fire over the front lines. If I die, I will die alone." Richard Bach an American writer, from his book Stranger to the Ground, *1963*

The Cuban Missile Crisis

On the ninth anniversary celebration of the Moncada Barracks Attack, Castro gave a speech in Santiago stating that the only thing Cuba had to fear was a direct attack by the United States. At the same time, the Russians were off-loading men and equipment from ships at the small, hardly-noticed port of Mariel. They transported their equipment, mostly at night, into a thickly wooded area in the mountains near San Cristóbal, which was 26 miles away from the port and approximately 50 miles from Havana. The CIA received a report that a twenty-six foot missile had been seen being transported on Cuban Highway A-1.

This was twice the size of a SAM missile and the CIA deemed it highly unlikely that the Soviet Union would send offensive weapons of this size to Cuba. However, with the cold war in high gear, Khrushchev thought that he could change the balance of power between the United States and the Soviet Union by placing missiles on Cuban soil. This operation was conducted in strict secrecy, with Castro reluctantly agreeing to it. Castro still felt that Cuba's alliance with the Soviet's was risky and that this was a negative compromise undermining Cuban autonomy. Their secret however became confirmed by an Air Force U-2 surveillance aircraft, sent on a reconnaissance mission, dispatched over the western part of the island.

Hurricane Daisy delayed the continuing surveillance, however when they could resume flying on October 14th, the crystal-clear photos indicated that launch sites were being prepared for both mobile medium-sized missiles, and more extensive sites for the larger-sized ballistic missiles. Although the actual missiles were not yet in place, the CIA understood the enormity of the threat. Missiles that could reach 2,000 miles into the United States could not be ignored!

With Cuba only 90 miles to the south of Key West, it posed an extreme threat to national security. On October 22, 1962, the discovery of these missiles was finally announced to the public, and a naval quarantine was implemented around Cuba. President Kennedy was careful not to call it a "blockade," since use of the word would be considered an act of war! Regardless, U.S. warships were deployed that would intercept and board any ship heading to the island. Castro announced that Cuba had the right to defend itself from American aggression. He added that the decision to deploy missiles was a joint action on the part of both Cuba and the Soviet Union. Kennedy discounted Castro's bluster but not the threat. The final decision to remove the missiles from Cuban soil would be between Khrushchev and Kennedy, without any Cuban involvement. Allowing Khrushchev to save face, Kennedy agreed to remove American missiles aimed at the Soviet Union from Italy and Turkey. It also included a commitment that the United States would not invade Cuba.

When Castro learned of the deal made without him, he was furious and felt betrayed by what he considered his ally. Castro, acting on his own, demanded that the United States stop the blockade of the island, and end its support for the militant

Cuban dissidents in exile. He also insisted that the United States return Guantánamo Naval Base to Cuba and stop violating Cuban airspace, as well as its territorial waters. The United States totally ignored him and his demands, dealing instead directly with the Soviet Union. Castro feeling slighted did the only thing left for him, and refused to allow the United Nations access to inspect the missile sites for compliance with the withdrawal agreement.

Although costly, the Soviet Union thought of this entire "missile exercise" as a display of Communist power in the Americas. This was a total disregard of the Monroe Doctrine regarding foreign influences in the Americas. Although ultimately it was a futile attempt, the Soviet Union hoped that it would inspire other Latin countries to follow the move towards Communism. During the next two decades, many attempts were made by Cuba to influence other Latin American countries to accept Communism. This influence was exercised primarily by inserting sympathetic leftist leaning movements into their political structure. However most of these attempts failed with the exception of Nicaragua. In 1967 "Che" Guevara attempted such a blatant movement in Bolivia. In time however many of these Latin countries such as Venezuela, took a shift to the left through their constitutional electoral process and embraced socialistic forms of government on their own.

"Humility must always be the portion of any man who receives acclaim earned in the blood of his followers and the sacrifices of his friends."
Dwight D. Eisenhower, 34th President of the United States

"Che" Guevara moves on

Fidel Castro had learned to depend on "Che" Guevara and used him as a person he could trust. However, "Che" was a medical doctor and not an executive or an economist. He didn't like being an administrator and came up short, especially when he became the Chairman of the Cuban National Bank. With the American embargo, Cuba had to look elsewhere for goods and had to be prepared to provide a balanced economic reciprocity. This became next to impossible for the small, beleaguered nation and although he put in long hours and worked hard, Guevara was not much help. Moving from one position of power to the next, he signed the Agrarian Reform Law, which nationalized the holdings of American agricultural interests in Cuba. "Che" finally realized that he was no longer happy or an asset to the movement. During this time Guevara began to have problems with many of the other Cuban leaders. On March 31, 1965, he handed in his resignation. "Che" wrote a letter of resignation to Fidel Castro and in his much-publicized statement, he announced that he had other ambitions in the furtherance of his beliefs. Castro announced to the public that Guevara had left Cuba and that he had formally resigned his positions of leadership in the Cuban Communist Party, his post as minister, his rank of commander, and his Cuban citizenship. "Che" also wrote that he was not sorry that he failed to leave anything material to his wife and children saying, "I am happy it is that way." Perhaps it was stress but it was the first of many strange things that Guevara did.

Guevara left Cuba that year to incite revolutions overseas. In 1966 when he was unsuccessfully in the Belgian Congo, he shaved his head and changed his appearance before secretly returning to Cuba. After visiting with Castro, he traveled to

Bolivia, leading a small band of rebels against the government of René Barrientos Ortuño in Bolivia.

Historians still debate about how much of Washington's bumbling affected the ideological direction Cuba took in the years after the revolution. Perhaps with a more sensitive diplomatic approach, and a less arrogant stand towards Cuba, a better outcome could have been expected.

"Always remember, others may hate you. But those who hate you don't win unless you hate them. And then you destroy yourself." Richard M. Nixon, Farewell Speech, August 1974

The Solidification of Socialism

To smooth over Castro's ruffled feathers Khrushchev eventually wrote him a personal letter explaining his reasons for reaching an agreement with the United States. In it, he also extended Castro an invitation to come and visit him in Moscow. The Cuban leader, feeling that this enhanced his international standing, set aside his resentments and swallowed his pride, knowing that his country would have to depend on the USSR for its many needs. He also understood that the ideology that brought his country to where it was, had also created many divisions among its people. The United States, whom Cuba had depended on for so many years, was no longer an ally they could trade with, and the new friendship with a distant country created many of its own problems. Many of Cuba's professional class had fled the country for the United States, when the companies they worked for became nationalized. The brain drain the country experienced was hard to replace, and most of those that had stayed, were not prepared to fill the more technical positions. The shelves were bare and people were becoming intolerant of the many domestic problems they were required to face.

In April of 1963, Castro went to the Soviet Union again, this time visiting fourteen cities. On May Day, he watched the military parade from the Kremlin wall and embraced many of the socialistic concepts that he would later introduce in Cuba. He was awarded an honorary doctorate from the Moscow State University and was the first foreigner to receive the Order of Lenin.

In April of 1964, Castro returned to Moscow where he signed a five-year Soviet-Cuban sugar agreement. His influence on domestic affairs strengthened a continuing shift to the left, as he closed down the remaining privately-owned businesses. At the same time, Castro expanded Cuban influence internationally. Against Soviet wishes, he pushed for armed revolutions in capitalistic countries around the world, and even backed the Black Panthers in the United States.

Upon his return to Cuba, he instituted many changes based on what he had seen. He consolidated the media, including the combining of the two prominent newspapers sanctioned by the government into one new newspaper named for the renowned yacht *Granma*.

Castro also instituted new agrarian reforms and in 1970 started compulsive military service to bolster the country's defense system. Central Intelligence Agency records indicate that young Cubans of both sexes between 17 and 28 years of age are subject to two years of military service.

"I saw courage both in the Vietnam War and in the struggle to stop it. I learned that patriotism includes protest, not just military service." John F. Kerry, American war hero, politician and statesman, Speech at George Washington University, September 2, 2003

The Cuban Adjustment Act of 1966

After the political takeover by Fidel Castro in January of 1959, many Cubans fled the island for safe haven in the United States. Although their reasons to leave Cuba varied, all of them did have one thing in common, which was that the United States was within reach. Although there were democracies in other parts of the world, including in Latin America, they were not accessible to the average refugee who was fleeing from the island.

Beginning on that New Year's evening when Batista took his midnight departure, life became difficult, as well as dangerous, for those that did not share Castro's political views. In 1960 Swan Radio went on the air and broadcast its political messages to the Cuban people, starting the unprecedented exodus of children from the island. This was followed in 1961 by professional people leaving due to the nationalizing of hospitals and private sector businesses. In 1965 there was a smaller exodus of boats known as the "Camarioca Boatlift." From 1965 until 1973, people left via the "Freedom Flights" that departed twice a day from Havana. Between April 15 and October 31, 1980, the Cuban government allowed 125,000 Cubans to illegally depart for the United States in what came to be known as the "Mariel Boatlift." Those Cubans, who bravely took to the sea in rafts, became recognized as *Balseros* or rafters. In all, nearly 2 million people left the island nation.

In the year 2000, two young boys, aged 15 and 16, thinking they were heading to Miami, died crammed into the wheel well of a flight from Havana to London. It was estimated that they died early into the flight from a lack of oxygen and exposure to the extremely cold temperatures at high altitudes. Two years later, a Cuban national flew from Havana to Montreal in the wheel well of a DC-10. Being luckier, he was kept alive by a broken tube that emitted warm air. It also gave him something to hang on to when the landing gear was deployed, three 1/2 hours later.

Cubans could legally immigrate to the United States via an immigrant Visa program, or the Special Cuban Migration Program (SCMP), otherwise known by many as the Cuban lottery. In 1966, the Cuban-Americans in the United States were so annoyed with the Cuban government that they exercised their political influence in bringing about the Cuban Adjustment Act. On November 2, 1966, Public Law 89-732 was enacted by the 89th United States Congress and signed into law by President Lyndon Johnson. The law applies to any native or citizen of Cuba and their accompanying spouses and children, who have been inspected and admitted or paroled into the United States after January 1, 1959, and have been physically present in the country for at least one year. They may, at the discretion of the U.S. Attorney General, obtain a green card and receive permanent residence.

As a result of this law, the "wet foot, dry foot" practice toward Cuban immigrants developed. This meant that prospective Cuban immigrants that managed to land on American soil could stay and start the process leading to citizenship. Failing to land on American soil would result in their being returned to Cuba, unless they could show that doing so would be perilous to them due to political reprisals. In time, both Cuba and the

United States agreed that no retaliation would come to those who were returned.

Sports in Cuba...

Fidel Castro, who always enjoyed sports, promoted programs that helped Cuba become a front-runner in Latin America. The island nation fields outstanding baseball, soccer, basketball and volleyball teams. It also excels in amateur boxing. Believing that sports should be available for everyone, not just the privileged few, the phrase "Sports for all" is a motto frequently used. When Castro took power, he abolished all professional sports. Only amateur baseball has been played in Cuba since 1961.

An unexpected consequence of this initiative was that many players discovered that they could get much better deals if they left Cuba. As an attempt to prevent this, Fidel forbade players from playing abroad and if they did leave the island, he would prevent their families from joining them.

Originally, many Cuban baseball players played for teams in the American Negro league. This ended when Jackie Robinson was allowed to play with the Brooklyn Dodgers during the late 1940's. Afterwards, all Cuban baseball players played for the regular leagues regardless of their race. The Negro National League ceased after the 1948 season, and the last All-Star game was held in 1962. The Indianapolis Clowns were the last remaining Negro/Latin league team and played until 1966.

Cuban players with greater skill joined the Major League Baseball (MLB) teams. If they defected to the United States directly, they had to enter the MLB Draft. However, if they first defected to another country they could become free agents. Knowing this, many came to the United States via Mexico.

In all, about 84 players have defected from Cuba since the Revolution. The largest contract ever given to a defector from Cuba was to Rusney Castillo. In 2014, the outfielder negotiated a seven-year contract with the Boston Red Sox for $72.5 million.

Starting in 1999, about 21 Cuban soccer players have defected to the United States. The Cuban government considers these defectors as disloyal and treats their families with disrespect, even banning them from taking part in national sports.

"Baseball was, is and always will be to me the best game in the world." Babe Ruth - the Bambino, an American baseball player whose Major League career spanned 22 seasons, from 1914 through 1935

Cuban Travel Poster

The Exciting Story of Cuba.... Part 15

Events Beyond Cuba's Borders

Assassination of John F. Kennedy

Towards the end of October, 1963, Ben Bradlee, a journalist with *Newsweek*, who later became the executive editor of *The Washington Post*, arranged for Jean Daniel, a left-of-center, French humanist, to meet President John F. Kennedy for an interview. On October 24, 1963, at 5:30 in the afternoon, Daniel waited in the outer office at the White House. Fortunately, that day the president was only running fifteen minutes late and came out to meet Daniel, who wrote for *L'Express*, a weekly French news magazine, and for the *New Republic*, a liberal American magazine, primarily covering art and politics. Much of the following is based on Jean Daniel's articles, "*When Castro Heard the News*" and "*Unofficial Envoy*," as well as the John Simkin book "*Assassination of John F. Kennedy Encyclopedia*."

Once comfortably seated on a semi-circular sofa in the Oval Office, facing the president who sat in his rocking chair, Kennedy asked how things were with General de Gaulle. It was somewhat strange, since Kennedy and de Gaulle did not really understand each other and Kennedy had once said that he had decided that it was a waste of time pursuing Franco-American relations. He did however mention that France had a strange way of expressing its independence. This patter was most likely the president's way of easing into what he hoped would be a subtle conversation about Castro, which of course was his real interest as well as a national concern.

The principal reason for having this interview was that Kennedy had heard that Daniel was flying to Havana the following month for an interview with Fidel Castro, and this would give Kennedy a non-official way of conveying his views to Castro. Since the time that diplomacy failed between the two countries, the United States used the Swiss Embassy in Havana, to convey confidential messages. This conduit was cumbersome and accessible to others, usually allowing the official correspondence to become public knowledge. Candidly, Kennedy suggested that he believed that the United States created the Castro movement without even realizing it. Of course he was referring to his predecessor President Eisenhower, but more so, to his Vice President Richard Nixon. He added that, "Now we shall have to pay for those sins." Kennedy wanted to convey the message that he was aware that the United States had done wrong in the past, but that the United States could do much good in Latin America, providing that communism did not take over.

Before parting, Daniel mentioned that he had never been to Cuba but that he knew that the Cuban people were suffering due to their economic dilemma. He asked Kennedy what America expected to gain from the blockade, and was the economic isolation of Cuba a punishment or a political maneuver? It was obvious that Kennedy had his doubts and was looking for a way out.

When Daniel arrived in Havana, he found that the hotels still had American travel brochures available for tourists, with the thought that things would normalize soon. He spent three weeks interviewing various people representing different segments of the Cuban population. Although he continued to request an interview with the Prime Minister, it began to look as though he would never get an interview, when suddenly, to his surprise, Fidel showed up at his hotel.

It was already late in the evening when Castro and Daniel started their discussion in Daniel's room. It was immediately apparent that Fidel was interested in what Kennedy had to say. He listened intently, as he pulled on his beard, when Daniel told him that the American President believed that Castro was almost the cause of "a war fatal to all humanity."

Castro remained silent for a long pause. "I believe that Kennedy is sincere," Castro said. He added, "I also believe that today the expression of sincerity could have political significance." Castro mentioned that he thought that Kennedy had inherited a difficult task. Speculating that the President of the United States is never really free, Castro voiced that he believed that Kennedy knew that he had been misled, regarding the Bay of Pigs Invasion. Furthermore, he felt that he could work with Kennedy and reach an understanding with him.

Daniel and Castro continued their dialog for the following two days, discussing the Bay of Pigs disaster and the part that the CIA played in orchestrating the invasion. He spoke of the reasons as to why Soviet missiles were installed in Cuba and why it was important to convince the United States that any attack on Cuba would be the same as an attack on the Soviet Union. Castro made the point that the Russians didn't want war. He added, "How could we Cubans have refused to share the risks taken to save us?" He felt that although Cuba was Socialist and the United States was a Capitalist nation, that the two could coexist. Before leaving, Castro made it clear that he did not want anything from Kennedy, but that he wanted Daniel to be an emissary for peace.

At 1:30 on the afternoon of November 22, 1963 Jean Daniel was having lunch with Fidel Castro, at his modest summer residence on the beautiful Varadero Beach, located about 75 miles east of Havana. Their interview was suddenly interrupted by a telephone call from the Cuban President Osvaldo Dorticós Torrado, informing Castro that President Kennedy had been shot in Dallas, Texas. The Cuban Prime Minister appeared distressed as he repeated, "this is bad news," "*Es una mala noticia*," three times. For a time Castro hoped that Kennedy would live, but listening to the clear NBC broadcast from Miami, the news of his death soon became a reality. Castro stood up and said, "President Kennedy is dead, everything has changed." He continued by saying, "Kennedy was an enemy with whom he had become familiar. This is a serious matter, an extremely serious matter."

Castro realized there was nothing that could be done. He reminded Daniel that he could no longer refer to what Kennedy had said, since there would now be a new administration and policy in the United States. The news broadcast later reiterated that John Fitzgerald Kennedy, the 35th President of the United States, had been assassinated at 12:30 p.m. Central Standard Time, in Dealey Plaza, Dallas, Texas, thus ending any opportunity to stabilize relations between the two countries at that time. Castro wondered aloud about Lyndon Johnson. He voiced that his critics would find a way to blame him, and he wondered about the position the CIA would take.

In later years, Pierre Salinger still maintained that the two men would have found a way to lift the embargo and normalize relations. However, due to horrendous circumstances this did not happen..... It would take another five decades before anything would ensue to ease the relationship between the two countries.

Conspiracy theories abound regarding the Kennedy assassination. However, according to the Warren Commission, established on November 29, 1963, Lee Harvey Oswald acted alone in the killing of the American President and the wounding of Texas Governor John Connally. The Commission also concluded that Jack Ruby acted alone in the murder of Oswald. However, these findings have since been viewed in a more contentious light and have been challenged. The Ramsey Clark Panel, the Rockefeller Commission, the Church Committee, and the United States House Select Committee on Assassinations, established in 1976, have all cast doubt on various aspects of the findings of the Warren Commission.

The Dallas Police Department, the Secret Service and the Federal Bureau of Investigation were all found delinquent in their handling of the Kennedy killing. The voluminous amount of evidence that followed has since been studied ad infinitum and the evidence suggests that there was much more to the assassination than was presented to the Warren Commission.

Some of the theories that have been brought forth propose that, at the very least, Castro, who still harbored pent up hostilities, knew that President Kennedy was about to be killed. Author Brian Latell, who had previously been a CIA analyst, wrote in his book *Castro's Secrets* that Fidel Castro had told his staff that he was going to initiate the assassination of Kennedy, in order to prove his allegiance to the Communist cause. It is doubtful that Castro would say this sort of thing, knowing that it would put him at an even greater personal risk. However, if he did say it, it could have been his bravado talking.

For a time following the Bay of Pigs Invasion, the President's relationship with the CIA was strained, primarily because of a number of high profile conflicts he had with the agency. Some theorists have attempted to link this breakdown between the

President and the CIA, with his ultimate assassination. There are also those who believe that Jean Daniel was an inside man for the CIA. That not only did he report on Castro but also Kennedy who was unaware of this ruse.

Author Joan Didion, best known for her novels and her literary journalism, explored the Miami, anti-Castro theory in her 1987 book *Miami*. She claimed that the House Select Committee on Assassinations believed that there was direct evidence linking the Kennedy murder to a number of violent Cuban exiles in South Florida. In 1963, President Kennedy's status had plunged to an all-time low in the eyes of the Conservative Cubans, due to his failure to help Brigade 2506 when he could have.

While venting his hostility at an anti-Castro meeting, Nestor Castellanos, an anti-Kennedy Cuban partisan, was heard to have threatened President Kennedy, with what he called "the works." Castellanos went on to say, "Mister good ol' Kennedy. I would not even call him President Kennedy. He stinks!" An undercover Federal Agent is said to have overheard Castellanos say, "We're waiting for Kennedy on the 22nd. We're going to see him one way or the other."

Evidence was also presented to the House Select Committee on Assassinations, that David Ferrie, an American commercial airline pilot, was alleged by New Orleans District Attorney Jim Garrison, to have been involved in a conspiracy to assassinate President John F. Kennedy. He had flown for Eastern Air Lines until being fired in August 1961, after having being arrested twice on homosexually related morals charges.

Photos have emerged establishing that Ferrie had been in the same Civil Air Patrol unit as Oswald and apparently Ferrie had met with Lee Harvey Oswald during the summer of 1963. Ferrie was extremely against the Communistic philosophy. He was a member of the anti-Castro Cuban Revolutionary group, and was dubbed the master of intrigue. Once when he gave an anti-Kennedy speech to an American veterans' group in New Orleans regarding the Bay of Pigs Invasion, his rant against the President was so belligerent that he was asked to leave the podium. On February 22, 1967, Ferrie mysteriously died of a stroke. The strange part concerning his death was that he left behind two suicide notes and then died of natural causes. In the days preceding his death, he had told friends that he was a dead man. Ferrie was only one of many who were somehow connected to Kennedy's death and who later died in a mysterious way.

Sylvia Meagher in her book, *Accessories After the Fact: The Warren Commission, the Authorities, and the Report After the Fact*, published in 1967, also supported the theory that John F. Kennedy had been killed by Anti-Castro exiles. In her book, she expressed that she was not convinced that Lee Harvey Oswald had been a lone gunman. Her conclusion was that the Warren Commission had attempted to cover-up important details of the actual people behind the assassination. In 1980, Meagher co-authored another book named *Master Index to the John F. Kennedy Assassination Investigations.*

Anthony Summers, the author of *The Kennedy Conspiracy* published in 1980 and again in 1998 as *Not in Your Lifetime*, believes that anti-Castro activists, funded by Mafia mobsters who had been ousted from Cuba, killed Kennedy. Summers believes that members of the CIA took part in this conspiracy and named the people he suspected. Summers also stated in an article published in the *National Enquirer* magazine, on October 25, 2013, that Lee Harvey Oswald didn't act alone. The *National Enquirer* stated that Herminio Diaz, born in Cuba in 1923, had, in 1948, shot Pipi Hernandez, who was a Dominican exile employed at the naval base at Guantanamo. This killing took place at the Cuban Consulate in Mexico. In 1957, he was involved with an assassination attempt against President José Figueres of Costa Rica, who incidentally was a trained Army Ranger and a graduate of the United States Military Academy at West Point.

According to *JFKFacts* published on May 27, 2014, General Fabián Escalante, the historian of Cuban State Security and Castro's former bodyguard, said that the assassin Herminio Diaz, along with Eladio del Valle and three American mobsters: Richard Gaines, Lenny Patrick, and Dave Yara, were the shooters at Dealey Plaza.

Cyril H. Wecht, the renowned forensic pathologist, a consultant in numerous high-profile cases, and who also holds a law degree, confirmed the theory that there were two gunmen involved in the assassination and that the second shooter was most likely behind the picket fence near the top of a prominent grassy knoll.

Even President Lyndon Johnson is said to have implicated the CIA in assassination attempts against Fidel Castro. Some attempts involving the Mafia are said to date back to the Eisenhower years. A 2009 CBS News poll stated that 76% of people believed that Kennedy's death was orchestrated by the Cuban government in retaliation for the CIA's efforts to kill Castro. President Johnson told his former speechwriter, Leo Janos of *Time* magazine, that he "never believed that Oswald acted alone."

The FBI has stated that the investigation relating to Kennedy's assassination is officially closed. The government's position still stands behind the Warren Commission's finding, maintaining that Oswald acted alone. The book *Reclaiming History*, published in 2007 by Vincent Bugliosi, has 1,632 pages that categorically attempt to debunk the conspiracy theories, however human nature will most likely prevail and these theories will probably continue. In addition, there are still findings of relevance that are surfacing. Although there is a smoking gun suggesting a cover-up, no details have appeared with enough definitive evidence to prove that a conspiracy took place. Was the Castro régime involved or was it the anti-Castro faction in South Florida?

There was enough intimidation, witness tampering and foul play to go around. Many books have been published about this subject, witnesses have died, some violently, under very suspicious conditions. Over the years, evidence has been tampered with, and fearing for their lives, most other people have decided to clam up and withdraw into the shadows.

In February 1996, Robert Kennedy, Jr. and his brother, Michael, flew to Havana for a meeting with Fidel Castro. As a gesture of goodwill, they brought with them a file of formerly top-secret U.S. documents. These documents were specifically about the Kennedy administration's attempt to find a peaceful settlement with Cuba. Castro thanked them for the file and shared the impression that it was President Kennedy's desire to normalize relations between the United States and Cuba. "It's unfortunate," Castro said, "that things happened as they did." Castro also indicated that normalization might have been possible, had it not been for President Kennedy's assassination in 1963.

Although numerous attempts at normalization between the two countries have been attempted since this meeting, powerful anti-Castro factions continued to thwart all of these efforts. Fortunately, we are now witnessing the time when ways are being found to improve the relations between the United States and Cuba.

"Forgive your enemies, but never forget their names." President John F. Kennedy, 35th President of the United States

"Che" Guevara in Bolivia

After spending some time in Dar-es-Salaam and Prague where he wrote the rough drafts for two books on economics and philosophy, Guevara returned on a clandestine trip to Cuba to see his wife. He also visited with Castro, who backed his new plans to undertake guerrilla activities in Bolivia, Peru and Argentina. It was during this time that Fidel and "Che" created the "National Liberation Army," known as the *Ejército de Liberación Nacional de Bolivia* (ELN), for a Bolivian operation which would be funded by Cuba and would act as a cover for a small indigenous rebel group consisting of about 80 men.

"I am not a liberator. Liberators do not exist. The people liberate themselves." "Che" Guevara, Communist Activist

Tamara Bunke

Tamara Bunke was the only woman to fight alongside "Che" during his Bolivian campaign. She was an East German national, born in Buenos Aires, Argentina, on November 19, 1937, of Communist activist parents. As a child, her home was frequently used for meetings, hiding weapons and conducting other Communist activities. After World War II, in 1952 she returned to Germany where she attended Humboldt University in Berlin. Tamara met "Che" Guevara when she was an attractive 23-year-old woman in Leipzig, and he was with a Cuban Trade Delegation. The two instantly hit it off as she cozied up to him and, having learned how to fight and use weapons in Pinar del Rio in western Cuba, she joined his expedition to Bolivia.

Becoming a spy for the ELN, she adopted the name "Tania" and posed as a right-wing authority of South-American music and folklore. In disguise, she managed to warm up to and entice Bolivian President René Barrientos. She even went on an intimate vacation to Peru with him.

On a number of occasions, Tamara joined "Che" on his sorties into the Bolivian highlands, without incident. However, on March 24, 1967, a guerrilla fighter who had been captured by the Bolivian army betrayed her by giving away Tamara's location. Although she escaped, the Bolivian soldiers found an address book in her Jeep and came after her in hot pursuit. With no other place to hide, she made her way back to "Che" Guevara's forces. It was considered an open secret that Tamara had been intimate with "Che" but now the troops could not help but notice what was going on. The way they looked into each other's eyes, and whispered sweet nothings, left no doubt in anyone's mind, but that she was his lover....

The Bolivian highlands are notorious for the infestation of the Chigoe flea parasite, which infected Tamara. Having a leg injury and running a high fever, she and 16 other ailing fighters were ordered out of the region by Guevara. On August 31, 1967, up to her waist in the Rio Grande of Bolivia, and holding her M-1 rifle above her head, she and eight men were shot and killed in a hail of gunfire by Bolivian soldiers. Leaving their bodies in the water, it was several days before they were recovered downstream. Piranhas had attacked the bodies and their decomposing carcasses were polluting the water. Since the water was being used for drinking purposes by the people in a nearby village, the soldiers were ordered to clear the bodies out of the river. As they were preparing to bury Tamara's remains in an unmarked grave, a local woman protested what was happening, and demanded that a woman should receive a Christian burial.

When he received the news of what had happened, Guevara was stunned and refused to accept it, thinking it was just a propaganda stunt to demoralize him. In Havana Fidel Castro declared her a "Heroine of the Revolution."

There is always the possibility that Tamara was a double agent, whose mission it was to play up to "Che" when they met in Leipzig and then report back to the DDR (Democratic German Republic), who would in turn inform the USSR of "Che's" activities. The spy game is a little like peeling an onion. Peel off one layer and what you find is yet another layer.

"Che" Guevara's Demise

In spite of the differences that they had, it was a great blow to Fidel when he heard of "Che" Guevara's execution in Bolivia. In the end Mario Terán, a semi-intoxicated Bolivian army sergeant, volunteered to do the job, as pay back, for having lost friends fighting the guerrillas. Bolivian Special Forces had captured "Che" Guevara in the highlands along with three of his compatriots, who were executed immediately. On October 8, 1967, Felix Rodriguez, a Central Intelligence Agency officer known for his involvement in the Bay of Pigs Invasion, was the CIA agent at the scene. He took photos of what was happening. Along with documenting the events, he also photographed the pages of "Che's" diary.

Guevara told Rodriquez, "Tell Fidel that he will soon see a triumphant revolution in America. And tell my wife to remarry and try to be happy." According to Rodriquez, they embraced and "Che" faced his death with courage and grace. The United States wanted Guevara to be brought to Panama alive. However, the Bolivian President Barrientos, feeling that he had been made a fool of by Tamara Bunke, countermanded this and ordered the execution to proceed. On October 9, 1967, although Rodriguez protested, he was outnumbered and on foreign soil. Finally agreeing to the execution, Rodriquez told Sergeant Terán to shoot carefully to make it appear that Guevara was killed in action.

Upon entering the mud schoolhouse where Guevara was being held, Terán hesitated. Guevara was heard to say, "I know you've come to kill me. Shoot coward! You are only going to kill a man." After nervously fumbling, the first volley of rounds that Sergeant Terán fired, hit Guevara in his arms and legs, causing him to writhe in pain. It was the additional rounds fired more accurately moments later, which fatally hit him in his chest and throat. After the botched execution, "Che's" body was airlifted by helicopter to the nearby town of Vallegrande. The small, usually quiet, colonial town in Bolivia, located somewhat over 75 miles southwest of *Santa Cruz de la Sierra*, was where Guevara's body was photographed and put on display before being mutilated. After a heated debate as to how to prove his identity, his hands were cut off and preserved in formaldehyde.

On October 15th, in Havana, Castro, stunned by the atrocious execution, finally acknowledged that Guevara was dead and proclaimed three days of public mourning.

Except for some initial encounters with the Bolivian Army, when the ELN Guerrillas killed some soldiers and inflicted a few casualties, the Bolivian venture was a failure from the start.

It ended with the majority of "Che's" fighting force being killed or captured. Only three Cuban fighters escaped, one of which was Harry Villegas Tamayo, "Che" Guevara's trusted bodyguard. The three Cubans and two Bolivian compatriots managed to hike 125 miles over the Andes on foot, before finally crossing the border into Chile. On February 22, 1968, they turned themselves in, and were held by the Chilean police until being released and given asylum by the then-president of the Chilean senate, Salvador Allende. After considering the consequences of retaining them, Allende on the advice of his staff, decided to have the five survivors expelled from Chile. Not having passports or travel visas, they still had difficulty trying to return to Cuba. Allende helped the survivors by escorting them across the Pacific as far as Tahiti, and from there they were able to fly back to Cuba via New Zealand. For these survivors it was a long arduous journey home. On November 4, 1970, Salvador Allende was elected to the presidency of Chile.

Trail of Death

Sixty years prior to the death of "Che" Guevara and high in the same Bolivian highlands, Butch Cassidy and Harry A. Longabaugh, "the Sundance kid," were holed up and then gunned down by the Bolivian army. It is thought that being mortally wounded, one of them shot the other before shooting himself. Attempts to find any remains that match the DNA of living relatives, has so far failed.

However, Butch Cassidy's sister, Lula Parker Betenson, maintained that her brother returned to the United States and lived in seclusion for years. In 1975, Red Fenwick, the feature writer and columnist at *The Denver Post*, stated that he was acquainted with Cassidy's physician, who continued to treat him for some years after he supposedly was killed in Bolivia.

The likelihood of this account remains extremely doubtful. However, if it were true, Cassidy would certainly have died by now, and any opportunity to determine the truth would be difficult or perhaps even impossible. In addition, if true, it would raise the question of who the two men were that were killed by the Bolivian army....

The road between where the execution of "Che" Guevara took place and where Butch Cassidy and the Sundance kid were shot to death, is called *El rastro de muerte* or "The Trail of Death!"

Ernesto "Che" Guevara, Remembered

In July of 1997 the skeleton of "Che" Guevara was uncovered by a Cuban-Argentine forensic team. On October 17th, his remains were returned to Cuba and publically reinterred with honors, in a specially built mausoleum. In death, he has become an arch villain a martyr or an inspirational leader, depending on your point of view. The one thing that cannot be disputed is that he has become bigger than life. He was an undisputed leader during the Cuban Revolution and the power of his being, continues to this day.

In 1997 Jon Lee Anderson, renown biographer and author of *"Che Guevara: A Revolutionary Life,"* the extensive biography of Guevara's life, interviewed people that were present at the burial of fallen guerrilla fighters, including the separate burial of "Che" Guevara in the Bolivian highlands. Later Tamara Bunke's grave was also located. Because of his quest and perseverance, he gained access to the personal archives held by Guevara's widow, as well as those carefully guarded by the Cuban government. Reconstructing events led Anderson to the gravesites heretofore classified by the Bolivian government.

Lieutenant Colonel Andrés Selich, who had been the officer in charge of the burial, could not be interviewed since he was beaten to death in an unrelated incident while serving as Ambassador to Paraguay. However, his widow told Anderson that the location of Guevara's body, according to her late husband, was in a grave near the Vallegrande airstrip. It was the first time that a truthful account of Guevara's burial was made public.

General Mario Vargas Salinas, retired from Bolivia's Eighth Army Division, was one of the young army officers present at Guevara's burial. It was his duty to accompany an old dump truck carrying the bodies of the six dead rebels, including that of "Che" Guevara, to the airstrip in Vallegrande. Knowing that the facts surrounding the burials were leaking out, decided that after 28 years the world should know what had happened to "Che" Guevara's body. At the time, the then Captain Vargas, who had also led the ambush in which Tamara "Tania" Bunke was shot dead, explained to Anderson that Guevara was buried early on the morning of October 11th. at the end of the town's landing strip. After the gruesome facts became known, the Bolivian government ordered the army to find Guevara's remains for a proper burial.

General Gary Prado Salmón, retired, had been the commander of the unit that had captured Guevara. He confirmed General Vargas' statement and added that the guerrilla fighters had been burned, before dumping their bodies into a mass grave, dug by a bulldozer, at the end of the Vallegrande airstrip. He explained that the body of "Che" Guevara had been buried in a separate gravesite under the runway. The morning after the burials, "Che" Guevara's brother arrived in Vallegrande, hoping to see his brother's remains. Upon asking, he was told by the police that it was too late. Talking to some of the army officers, he was told lies or perhaps just differing accounts of the burial, confusing matters even more. The few peasants that were involved and knew what had happened, were mysteriously unavailable. Having reached a dead end, he left for Buenos Aires not knowing much more than when he arrived.

Canet Sánchez Guevara, "Che's" grandson, reacted to the unraveling of information by saying that he was not sure whether to believe the new revelations or not, that "what is important is not where he is buried, but where his ideas are best understood." Guevara's daughter, Aleida, said that her father believed that: "Wherever a man falls, that's where he remains." Rodolfo Saldaña, one of the combatants who fought with "Che," was interviewed in Cuba, and said that what had been a rumor should now be made public. He said, "It is important now that it has been confirmed by the participants."

Sergeant Bernardino Huanca of the Bolivian Special Forces told Anderson that Guevara, upon his capture, twice wounded and with his gun jammed, shouted, "Do not shoot! I am "Che" Guevara and worth much more to you alive than dead."

Aleida March, "Che" Guevara's widow, blamed Mario Monje Molina, the leader of the Communist Party of Bolivia (PCB), for the death of her husband. In 1966, he had agreed to help Guevara start a revolution in Bolivia, but changed his mind and prematurely withdrew his much-needed support.

"Che" Guevara left a letter for his five children, which was to be opened only after his death. It read:

"Dear Hildita, Aleidita, Camilo, Celia, and Ernesto,

If you ever have to read this letter, it will be because I am no longer with you. You practically will not remember me, and the smaller ones will not remember at all. Your father has been a man who acted on his beliefs and has certainly been loyal to his convictions. Grow up as good revolutionaries. Study hard so that you can master technology, which allows us to master nature. Remember that the revolution is what is important, and each one of us, alone, is worth nothing.

Above all, always be capable of feeling deeply any injustice committed against anyone, anywhere in the world. This is the most beautiful quality in a revolution.

Until forever my children, I still hope to see you.

A great big kiss and a big hug from,

Pap"

No Place to Hide

A high school dropout, Robert Vesco bilked and conned his way to riches. Two times *Forbes* magazine named Vesco as one of the 400 richest Americans. The articles simply stated that he was a thief. As a man continually on the run, he was constantly attempting to buy his way out of the many complicated predicaments he got himself into.

In 1970, Vesco made a successful bid to take over Investors Overseas Services (IOS), an offshore, Geneva-based mutual fund investment firm, worth $1.5 Billion. Employing 25,000 people and selling mutual funds throughout Europe, primarily in Germany, he thought of the company as his own private slush fund. Using the investors' money as his own, he escalated his investment firm into a grand "Ponzi Scheme." During this time he also made an undisclosed $200,000 contribution to Maurice Stans, Finance Chairman for President Nixon's Committee to Re-elect the President, known as CREEP. To make matters worse, the media discovered that his contribution was being used to help finance the infamous Watergate burglary.

In return for his donation, Nixon's Attorney General, John Mitchell, and Maurice Stans, the former Secretary of Commerce, would exercise their influence and intervene in an ongoing investigation by the U.S. Securities and Exchange Commission into Vesco's financial entanglements. For a time things went well. But in 1972, when the economy faltered, the entire house of cards came crashing down. Apparently Vesco was guilty of securities fraud, but instead of facing the music he fled, right after having been indicted in a United States Federal Court. He didn't mind pocketing his investors' money, but he greatly feared going to jail. It seems that he never heard the saying, "Don't do the crime if you can't do the time." The "President's Men," Stans, Mitchell, and Sears, were indicted for perjury and obstruction of justice, however none of this stuck. President Nixon's staffers were acquitted of all the charges.

Vesco, seeing the handwriting on the wall, "beat feet" and fled from the subsequent U.S. Securities and Exchange Commission investigation. He was found hiding in San José, the capital city of Costa Rica. After the dust settled, Maurice Stans, went on to become Nixon's Finance Chairman. Vesco also took care of Nixon's two brothers, Donald and Edward Nixon, and found room on his payroll for Nixon's nephew, also named Donald.

Life on the run was expensive and by now much of the money he had embezzled was gone. But relatively speaking, there still must have been a sizable stash. There was also some question as to how anxious the United States was to get him back. Vesco threatened to tell his side of the story and name names. For his silence, he had expected a full pardon from Nixon. However, with more pressing problems of his own, Nixon didn't deliver and thus betrayed Vesco, who was counting on the promised pardon. At this point in Vesco's saga, it was assumed that he still had $200 million of stolen money, and could easily have returned to the United States. Had he played his cards right, he most likely could have gotten off with a plea bargain.

In 1980, just to keep things even, he also persuaded the Libyan government to pay President Jimmy Carter's brother Billy $220,000 as part of a failed oil deal. Others that he allegedly bribed included the Costa Rican president José Figueres Ferrer and the Bahamas Prime Minister Lynden Pindling.

In 1983, he was still evading prosecution by skipping first to Nassau in the Bahamas and then to the island of Antigua. Vesco thought he could escape the law by buying the Caribbean island Barbuda from Antigua, in order to create an autonomous country having sovereign rights. In 1978, the Costa Rican government under President Rodrigo Carazo's administration prevented him from returning. In 1982, Vesco tried again to return to Costa Rica, but this time the new President Luis A. Monge denied him entry.

Instead, as a fugitive from justice, he had to rely on protection from extradition by constantly massaging his questionable friends in high places. The United States didn't really want to deal with the problems if he returned from these countries. Now, as a man without a country, his final move would be to go to Cuba, where he would have to rely on Fidel Castro to care for him. In 1982 he made the move, believing that Cuba would provide him with medical care for a painful urinary tract infection. At first, Cuban authorities accepted him on the one condition that he would not get involved in any financial entanglements. Happy that he had found a way out of his dilemma, he married Lidia Alfonso Llauger.

In 1989, not one to stay out of trouble, Vesco was charged with drug smuggling, supposedly with Carlos Lehder Rivas, the leader of a Colombian drug cartel. In 1990 he was charged by the Cuban government with "fraud and illicit economic activities." In 1996, he was again indicted on acts prejudicial to the economic plans and contracts of the state. Now 61 years old, Vesco was sentenced to 13 years in a "not so nice" Cuban prison. He was released in 2005 after serving 9 years of his sentence. Robert Vesco's life ended on November 23, 2007, when he succumbed to lung cancer at a hospital in Havana. He was supposedly buried in an unmarked grave. It took the *New York Times* five months after the fact to report his death, leaving many to wonder as to what really happened. Vesco is survived by his wife and five children, all of whom inherited a trust and hold the literary rights to his story. However, it is uncertain as to whether his complete story will ever be told.

Cubana de Aviacion Flight 455

Frequently the CIA was blamed, and perhaps justifiably so, for what partisan individuals did as part of the anti-Castro movement. The bombing of Cuban Airlines Flight 455 is certainly an example of this. On October 6, 1976, a Cuban DC-8-40 was brought down by two bombs made using C-4 military-type explosives with a preset timer. The flight was just leaving Barbados for Jamaica. All 73 passengers, which included 24 members of the Cuban fencing team, plus the 5 crew members on the aircraft, were killed.

At Payne's Bay in Barbados a monument has been erected in recognition of those killed in this airline tragedy. Another monument was dedicated in Georgetown, Guyana.

Of course, Cuba accused the United States of being implicated in this act. Members of the Venezuelan secret police, known as the DISIP, were also allegedly involved. CIA documents that were later released indicated that the details of this planned bombing were known to the CIA four months prior to the incident.

Investigations revealed that two Venezuelan nationals, Freddy Lugo and Hernán Ricardo Lozano, who had been employed by Luis Posada Carriles, planted the bombs that destroyed the Cuban airliner. Posada was known to be an anti-Castro terrorist and a former CIA operative with the code name of "Bambi." Posada apparently worked for the CIA between 1963 and 1964 and was trained in the art of sabotage at Fort Benning, Georgia.

The men admitted to the crime and confessed that they were acting under Posada's orders. During the ensuing investigation, explosives, weapons and a radio transmitter were discovered at Posada's private detective agency, based in Venezuela. Posada and Orlando Bosch Ávila, a Cuban exile who was also a former CIA operative and an accomplice in this crime, were arrested and jailed in Venezuela. In September 1980, a Venezuelan military judge, allegedly influenced by the American Ambassador Otto Reich, acquitted all four men. This ruling however did not stand and was overturned. Posada, Bosch and their two henchmen were remanded to the Venezuelan civilian court system where they were held awaiting trial. Freddy Lugo and Hernán Ricardo Lozano were sentenced to 20-year prison terms to be served in Venezuela. Orlando Bosch was acquitted by the Venezuelan court due to legal technicalities and Posada found himself getting deeper into trouble, having tried to escape from the Venezuelan prison twice. Supposedly, Bosch had the help of Ambassador Otto Reich. So, following his acquittal, he fled to the United States where he was promptly arrested for a parole violation. In spite of being identified as one of the most deadly terrorists in the western hemisphere, Bosch received a pardon from President George H. W. Bush, presumably at the request of his son Jeb Bush, who later became the Governor of Florida.

Apparently, it was later learned that Posada was overheard saying, "We are going to hit a Cuban airplane and Orlando has the details."

Eventually Posada was tried and while awaiting a verdict escaped from prison once again. Apparently a sizeable bribe was paid to his guards and other authorities making it possible to buy his way out dressed as a priest. Once out he fled from Venezuela to Panama and then to the United States. The Venezuelan court promptly issued an arrest warrant, which most likely is still pending. After his return to the United States, he was assigned to Nicaragua, as a deputy to Félix Rodríguez, the CIA Operative who helped capture "Che" Guevara. It is believed that Posada was responsible for 41 bombings during the Contra conflict. By his own admission, he also planned numerous attacks against Cuba. In 1997, Posada was involved in a series of terrorist bombings in Cuba, with the intent of disrupting the country's fledgling tourist industry.

This shadow warfare continues south of the border to this day. Peter Kornbluh, the director of the National Security Archive, has also named Luis Posada Carriles as "one of the most dangerous terrorists in recent history." Both Bosch and Posada have allegedly been involved in many extreme right wing assassinations, bombings and other acts of terror.

It is believed that Luis Posada Carriles, who was born on February 15, 1928, now lives in the Miami area with his wife.

They have two grown children and his pastime is painting. Posada is still politically active and participates in fund raising and protests against Castro and Communism in Cuba. Many in the conservative Cuban community still regard him as a patriot to their cause. Orlando Bosch Ávila resided in Miami, Florida, until, after being hospitalized with several illnesses, he died on April 27, 2011.

Acts of Terror Continue....

It is believed that Bosch and Posada were both members of a group founded in the Dominican Republic named the "Coordination of United Revolutionary Organizations" or "CORU." This group has been implicated in numerous acts of extreme violence. A declassified FBI document describes the bombing of the airliner as an act of war directed against the Castro régime. Additional evidence regarding this and other aggressive efforts to destabilize the government of Cuba are on file at George Washington University's National Security Archives, as a part of the Cuba Documentation Project. In August of 2013, Ambassador Otto Reich and Luis Posada Carriles were accused by Venezuelan President Nicolas Maduro of the "United Socialist Party of Venezuela," of being involved in attempts to assassinate him.

María Corina Machado was the leader of the hardline anti-Hugo Chávez right-wing conservative organization and is also in opposition to Nicolas Maduro. She is a founder and former president of the Venezuelan volunteer civil organization *Súmate*, which claims to be a non-political, election-monitoring group. In February of 2014, with Alejandro Plaz, a fellow founder and activist, she held protest rallies in Caracas and has been involved in recent efforts to overthrow the legitimately elected Maduro government. Being termed non-politically oriented activists, they have benefited from contributions by big businesses in Venezuela and from the United States' "Democracy Assistance Program." The U.S. government supports foreign pro-American programs by using a variety of means, such as the National Endowment for Democracy and the United States Agency for International Development. Assistance is given by what is termed "The Sense of Congress," and although these organizations are stated to be bi-partisan they frequently are not, and their goals are often politically motivated and specifically directed.

Politics in Venezuela have always been problematical. Leopoldo López Mendoza, who comes from one of Venezuela's wealthiest families in Venezuela, was educated at Kenyon College, a private liberal arts college located in Gambier, Ohio. He is known for his "good-boy" looks and has extremely conservative leanings. In February 2006, as the leader of the opposition party, he was shot at, and then held hostage by armed men at the university where he was speaking. In March, his bodyguard was shot to death, while sitting in the passenger seat of the car where he normally sits. López, is the founder and National Coordinator of the Venezuelan political party "*Voluntad Popular*," meaning "Popular Will." Although this party is a self-proclaimed centrist group, its actions are very much right-wing. Under its banner, López led protests against Maduro in Caracas. On February 18, 2014, after one of these protests, López was arrested, and charged with arson, terrorism, and homicide. However, he was released after Amnesty International, and other international human rights groups, challenged his arrest as being politically motivated.

In the year 2000, López was elected mayor of Chacao, which is one of the five political and administrative subdivisions of the capital city of Caracas. He won this election with 51% of the vote and was re-elected in 2004 with 81% of the vote. Although he was in opposition to the popular United Socialist Party and the well-liked President Chávez, by the end of his tenure Lopez had an astounding approval rating of 92%.

A special election was held for the presidency throughout Venezuela on April 14, 2013 and the sitting President Maduro won the contest by a 1.5 percent margin. However, López continues to be actively engaged in his attempts to overthrow the legitimately elected Maduro from the Presidency. Politics in Venezuela is "Hard Ball," and sometimes it is difficult to tell the good guys from the bad guys.

President Maduro fearing the possibility of being ousted in a rebellion, expelled three American diplomats from Venezuela. He accused them of plotting with López and other opposition leaders with the intent of committing terrorist acts. On March 25, 2014, the drama escalated, when President Maduro announced that three Venezuelan Air Force generals had been arrested for their involvement in attempting to get the military to start a coup d'état.

Corruption in Venezuela remains widespread, as it has been for much of its recent history. The oil reserves in Venezuela are the largest in the world, even surpassing those of Saudi Arabia. The discovery of these vast reserves, estimated to continue producing oil for at least another 225 years, have only increased political corruption. In Venezuela, "the Devil's excrement" is a saying frequently heard, as a reference to the extensive corruption brought on by Petroleum.

"When you read about a terrorist attack in which people are killed, does anyone think about the amount of love and treasure and patience parents poured into

bodies no longer suitable for open caskets?" inspired by Jim Bishop, author

More Attempts on Castro's Life

Aside from Marita Lorenz's attempt on Castro's life, there were six other poisoning attempts, purportedly sanctioned by Robert Kennedy, the United States Attorney General. Mostly, they were carried out by the CIA prior to the Bay of Pigs Invasion. Moreover, Johnny Roselli, who is believed by some to have been involved in John F. Kennedy's assassination, also supposedly attempted to poison Fidel Castro.

According to Castro's former bodyguard, Fabián Escalante, and Ramiro Valdés, head of the Cuban G-2 secret service, there were a total of 638 attempts to kill the Cuban leader, including the attempt by Marita Lorenz when she concealed the poison capsules in a jar of cold cream, before bringing them into her hotel room. Another time a fungus-impregnated scuba outfit was prepared, expecting that Fidel would wear it. This was followed by an exploding cigar attempt. Still another time, the CIA supposedly impregnated some of Castro's favorite cigars with botulin, but they never got to him. Cigars as a vehicle to kill Castro were abandoned, when he gave up smoking in 1985.

On November 17, 2000, Fidel Castro was preparing to give a speech at a Panamanian political rally when a security sweep found 200 pounds of high explosives under the very platform Castro was expected to stand on. Once again it apparently was "Bambi's" doing! Luis Posada Carriles had previously worked at the Cuban American National Foundation in Miami. Now, he and three of his co-conspirators were in Panama and had apparently plotted the assassination attempt on the life of Fidel

Castro, who was visiting the country for the first time since 1959.

Although Posada and Gaspar Jiménez were arrested and subsequently convicted for the assassination attempt, on August of 2004 they and their friends were conveniently pardoned by the outgoing Panamanian President Mireya Moscoso of the conservative *Arnulfista* Party. Moscoso, Panama's first woman president, was an outspoken friend of President Bush and didn't want to see Posada and his friends deported to Cuba by her successor Martín Torrijos, a member of the left leaning Democratic Revolutionary Party. Had that happened, Posada, Jiménez and friends would most likely have faced a firing squad. Following his pardon, Posada fled to the United States where he was apprehended in Texas for illegally entering the country. There was always the possibility of extradition to Venezuela, but having the right kind of friends helped. Being released and knowing that he had pushed his luck as far as it would go, Posada retired to the good life among his friends in Florida.

Now that he is an octogenarian, it seems that Fidel's adversaries have finally slowed down with their relentless assassination attempts. However, even now, Cuban security agents still maintain a tight net around him at all times. Fidel reluctantly accepts the bubble he's in with a whimsical sense of humor.

"Thieves, spies and other wise guys are working everywhere... including in branches of the U.S. government." Sherry Morris, Author of Hundred Dollar Bill

The Exciting Story of Cuba.... Part 16

Cuban Foreign Affairs

Cuba's Foreign Policy

After the revolution, Castro envisioned Cuba becoming a socialistically-focused, shining example to other Latin American countries. Fidel may have been able to convince the people of countries in Central and South America that had ruthless dictators at the time, or countries that buckled under the polarization of an economic division between the ultra-wealthy and the unfortunate masses of a poorer peasant class. Because of the disparity behind the scenes, many of these countries were already starting on the path to socialism.

Many Latin American countries, known to cynics as "Banana Republics," had been structured in this manner so that big corporations found it easy to buy political power and appropriate the natural wealth of that country. Cuba, after the revolution, had a visionary foreign policy, although its communistic approach stifled individual incentives. Castro and his administration were praised by many for having stood firmly against the United States, which was considered an imperialistic Goliath. However, since then, Cuba has fallen on hard times, primarily because of the economic hardships they have had to face after the downfall of the Soviet economy.

"The Cuban people have an amazingly strong and unbroken spirit." Wim Wenders, German Filmmaker

Guantánamo as Cuba sees it, and how it really is....

The present government of Cuba believes that the U.S. Naval Station at Guantánamo, originally known as Cumberland Bay when the British seized it in 1741, is disrespectful of Cuba's sovereignty for the following reasons...

- The base was originally taken under duress and has been held by using legal technicalities.

- The base is being maintained under the perceived threat of nuclear force.

- The United States has demanded that Cuba remove defensive weapons, installed by Russia, a Cuban ally. At the same time, the United States was believed by some Cubans, to have weapons of mass destruction to threaten Cuba.

- Starting with the signing of the Cuban-American Treaty in 1903, the United States has exercised complete jurisdiction and control over the U.S. Naval Station at Guantánamo. Although the United States still recognizes that Cuba retains ultimate sovereignty over the territory, it has never negotiated any terms by which Guantánamo would return to Cuban control. Contrary to frequent assertion that the lease is perpetual, the lease for the Naval Base is for a specific but undetermined time related to circumstances. The Cuban government maintains that the treaty was obtained by a threat of force and is therefore illegal and in violation of International Law.

- Cuba claims that weapons are being smuggled into Cuba via the Naval Station and that land belonging to Cuba is being used to shelter murderers and criminals from justice.

- Whereas most provisions of the Platt Amendment were repealed in 1934, Article I of the 1934 treaty with Cuba continues to be in effect. After the "Cuban Missile Crisis," the United States retained the use of the Naval Base and promised not to invade Cuba. However, using the Naval Base as a detention center for prisoners held for alleged terrorist activities, presents a questionable legal issue. The Cuban government has denounced the treaty as a violation of article 52 of the 1969 Vienna Convention on the Law of Treaties, which declares a treaty void if procured by a threat or the use of force. However, continuing, Article 4 of the Vienna Convention states that its provisions shall not be applied retroactively.

- Cuba intends to regain the territory, but does not intend to use force. It is their intention to wait for the right time to exercise their perceived rights through legal means provided by International Law.

- The workers, who are employed at the Naval Base are doing work contrary to the national interests of their country and are paid in pesos, which Cuba believes puts claims upon the wealth of the Cuban Treasury.

Legal Issues

Professor Alfred de Zayas, who was born in Havana, is a naturalized American citizen. He is an attorney, writer, historian and a leading expert in the field of human rights and International Law. Dr. Alfred de Zayas presents the argument that there may be a material or fundamental breach in the present lease regarding Guantánamo, and that the United States remains disrespectful of Cuban sovereignty. He maintains that the present lease could be ruled invalid by International Law.

The legality of the military prison built at Guantánamo to house and permanently detain prisoners is debatable, since the Cuban-American Treaty of Relations of 1934 directly refers to the Platt Amendment and the original 1903 terms of the lease. Article II of the Platt Amendment, states that the United States is generally allowed to do "any and all things necessary" for its use as an American Naval Base.

The key factors regarding the leasing of the Naval Base are that it is available for the time required, referring to an unknown future date at the time of signing, and with the understanding that there could be extenuating circumstances. The time is clearly not "In Perpetuity," or of endless duration, since it is understood that ultimately the sovereignty remains Cuba's, although the lease specifies that it be used temporarily as a Naval and refueling station.

When the Cuban Missile Crisis ended, the United States pledged not to invade Cuba. There was also a partial restoration of the purpose of the Guantánamo lease, and of Article I of the 1934 Treaty of Relations. The American focus regarding the retention of the lease, centers on administrative technicalities. One of these technicalities is that Cuba cashed the first payment it received from the United States in 1959 and, although it refrained from cashing additional checks, the cashing of the first one displayed a willingness on the part of Cuba to accept the terms of the lease.

Of course, being occupied by American troops also makes the legality of the present lease somewhat vague, since reversing the territorial possession and for Cuba to regain the actual sovereignty of Guantánamo would require the good will of the United States, and that does not seem likely without renegotiating new terms to the present lease.

As Cuba complained about the United States being in Guantánamo, in what they perceived to be illegally, they were carrying out clandestine activities themselves. On July 17, 2013, the news media carried the story that a North Korean Ship, the 14,000-ton *Chong Chon Gang*, had departed Cuba and was heading to North Korea carrying missiles as well as other arms and ammunition. As the vessel was attempting to traverse the Panama Canal, the weapons were discovered hidden in containers underneath a cargo of brown sugar. Cuba explained that the hidden cargo consisted of obsolete weaponry from the mid-20th century and that they were being sent to North Korea for repairs. The captain and two of his officers were detained by Panamanian authorities on charges of arms smuggling. All 33 crew members were charged with endangering public security. For the release of the vessel, the North Korean government paid a fine of $666,666.

Attempts to Close the Detention Center

The United States Detention Center on the grounds of the Naval Base was established in January of 2002 by the U.S. Secretary of Defense Donald H. Rumsfeld. It was designated as the site for a prison camp, euphemistically called a detention center, to detain prisoners taken in Afghanistan and to a lesser degree from the battlefields of Iraq, Somalia and Asia. The prison was built to hold extremely dangerous individuals and has the facilities to be able to interrogate these detainees in what was said to be "an optimal setting." Since these prisoners were technically not part of a regular military organization representing a country, the Geneva Conventions did not bind the United States to its rules. The legality of their incarceration is questionable under International Law. This would lead one to the conclusion that this facility was definitely not a country club.

Although, in most cases these prisoners were treated humanely, there were obvious exceptions, when the individuals were thought to have pertinent information. It was also the intent of the U.S. Government not to bring them into the United States, where they would be afforded prescribed legal advantages and a more humane setting. Consequently, to house these prisoners, this spartan prison was constructed at the Guantánamo Bay Naval Base instead of on American soil. Here they were out of sight and far removed from any possible legal entanglements that would undoubtedly regulate their treatment. Many of the detainees reported abuses and torture at the facility, which were categorically denied. In 2005 Amnesty International called the facility the "Gulag of our times."

In 2007 and 2008, during his campaign for the Presidency, Obama pledged to close the Detention Center at Guantánamo Bay. After winning the presidential election, he encouraged Congress to close the detention center, without success. Again, he attempted to close the facility on May 3, 2013. At that time, the Senate stopped him by voting to block the necessary funds for the closure. The Republican House remained adamant in their obstructionistic policies towards the President, showing no signs of relenting. It was not until November of 2014 that any glimmer of hope became apparent.

On June 1, 2013, 100 of the 166 prisoners that were still at the detention center went on a hunger strike. The strike went on for nearly four months, driven largely by the unlimited imprisonment they had to endure. Being incarcerated in an offshore facility, they were held without being charged or brought to trial. An unrelenting core of approximately 30 prisoners had to be force-fed, by placing tubes through their noses, to keep them from dying.

The President expressed his regret regarding the hunger strike and repeated his pledge at the time by emphatically stating, "I continue to believe that we've got to close Guantánamo." President Obama laid the blame for this not happening, squarely on the shoulders of the Republican lawmakers by saying: "Now, Congress determined that they would not let us close it..." Despite Obama's desire to close the detention center he also knew that the Congress, headed by his opposition party, would not revisit this issue any time soon, and if anything were to happen, it would have to be by an executive order.

A total of 779 prisoners have been held at Guantánamo since the facility was opened on January 11, 2002. Of those, 8 have died and 637 have been released or transferred. This left 134 inmates at Guantánamo at the end of 2014, however the number is constantly changing and as of January 2015 the official number of inmates remaining at the Guantánamo detention center was 127. Of these 127 detainees, 55 have been cleared for repatriation and are listed as being eligible to be transferred out. Some of the restrictions regarding the transferring of these prisoners have now been lifted, so they may be sent back to their home countries, provided those countries agree and are able to keep an eye on them. There are still problems regarding some of the more aggressive prisoners from countries that do not want them back. However, recently five of them were sent to the countries of Georgia and Slovakia. Another six detainees were flown to Uruguay over the weekend of December 6, 2014. There still remains a hard core of prisoners left incarcerated at the prison, for whom no release date or destination is scheduled. It is speculated that eventually some of them will come to the United States to face a federal court.

Clifford Sloan, the U.S. State Department's special envoy tasked with closing the prison, said, "We are very grateful to Uruguay for this important humanitarian action, and to President José "Pepe" Mujica, for his strong leadership in providing a home for individuals who cannot return to their own countries." Sloan added, "This transfer is a major milestone in our efforts to close the facility."

Referring to the recent use of the Naval Base, "What has happened at Guantánamo Bay... does not represent the will of the American people. I'm embarrassed about it, I think it's wrong. I think it does give terrorists an unwarranted excuse to use the despicable means to hurt innocent people." Jimmy Carter, the 39th President of the United States

Cuba's Complicated Conundrum

For a small country with limited resources, Cuba is struggling to be as self-sufficient as possible, considering that they no longer receive the sizeable subsidies they had grown accustomed to in the past. Finding their footing with little help from Russia is difficult. However if success is measured in small increments, Cuba is making a respectable comeback. The exotic island nation, with its Caribbean location and pristine beaches, is once again attracting foreign tourists.

However, it is still obvious that Cuba is within the Russian sphere of influence. Havana and Santiago de Cuba remain popular ports of call for Russian vessels. As part of a cruise circumnavigating the island, the Russian ship *Adriana* of Tropicana Cruises, Ltd. stops at the ports of Havana and Santiago de Cuba.

On Wednesday, February 26, 2014, the SSV-175 *Viktor Leonov*, an armed Russian naval intelligence-gathering ship, surreptitiously arrived at Havana's cruise ship terminal. The Russian Defense Minister Sergei Shoigu announced that Russia is seeking to establish several military bases abroad. He also stated that Russia wants to expand its international presence by negotiating for permanent bases in Cuba, Nicaragua, Venezuela, Argentina, Vietnam, Singapore and the Seychelle Islands. In addition, Moscow is planning to have refueling bases for its fleet of strategic bombers. Presently Russia has only the one base, located in Tartus, Syria, that is outside of the boundaries of the former Soviet Union. A Russian naval base in Cuba, although a stick in the eye of the United States, would be a welcome boost to the Cuban economy.

In 1964, after the Cuban Missile Crisis had been defused, Moscow constructed an Intelligence (SIGINT) Base in Lourdes, Cuba. This location, approximately 150 miles from Key West, is just within the *Primer Anillo de La Habana*, the circular highway south of Havana. In 2001, with both Cuba and Russia experiencing financial difficulties, the base was closed.

The problem now is that an agreement was reached to reopen The Russian Intelligence Base during Putin's July 2014 visit to Cuba. This agreement regarding the base was confirmed by a

Russian security source, who told *Reuters*: "A preliminary agreement has been agreed to." Should this actually come into being, the December 17, 2014, agreement between President Obama and the President of Cuba would certainly be at risk.

The United States policy regarding Cuba has been controlled to some extent by the somewhat waning, but still powerful, Russian influence in Cuba. The conservative groups residing in the greater Miami area view this relationship, between the two countries, with skepticism and have remained steadfast to the economic blockade. In contrast, countries such as Canada, England and Germany have long since normalized their relations with Cuba.

A Political Predicament

For some time now, Germany has had cruise ships visiting Cuba, such as the MS *Deutschland*, which can accommodate 513 passengers and has a crew of 260 members. She is known as *das Traumschiff* or the Dream Ship and is Germany's answer to the Love boat. With a displacement of 22,400 GT, the ship brought European tourists with their Euros as stimulus money to Cuba. However, on Monday, February 23, 2015, it was announced, that the operating company has declared bankruptcy. It is expected that finding new investors, and restructuring under the German debtor-in-possession management act, known as *Eigenverwaltung*, would allow the MS *Deutschland* to continue her scheduled visits.

On June 4, 2015, the Carnival Corporation & plc, owner of Carnival Cruise Lines, launched its 10th global brand named "fathom Impact Travel," for the purpose of operating ships from the United States directly to Cuba and the Dominican Republic. Its intent is to provide humanitarian, artistic, cultural and faith-based relations, primarily between American and Cuban citizens. On July 7, 2015, Carnival Corporation announced that the United States government granted approval for the world's largest travel and leisure company to start this operation in May of 2016. It is anticipated that fathom will institute programs that will assist in supporting and aiding the growth and prosperity of the Cuban people. Presently the parent company operates a total of 100 ships with eight new ships under construction, allowing for an expected comprehensive expansion program.

Cuba has encouraged foreign investments in agriculture. The Cuban citrus industry was started during the 1960's to supply the former Soviet Union, as well as other socialist countries in Eastern Europe, with oranges and grapefruit. After the economic crash and the restructuring of the Soviet Union, the demand for citrus crops fell off by about half. In 1994, the National Citrus Corporation was founded in Cuba, and is now known as the "Fruit Trees Enterprise Group." It consists of 13 nationally owned citrus enterprises, a commercial company and 4 processing plants. Cítricos Caribe S.A. has three cold storage facilities and exports to contracted foreign vendors. A Chilean venture and a Greek-British consortium, both affected by the decline of demand, halted their operations in 2014. However an Israel company has successfully developed huge citrus and tropical fruit plantations on the island, with most of their crops being sold in Europe. Israeli orange groves stretch for miles in the Matanzas Province, east of Havana. Known chiefly for its white sandy beaches and resorts, the BM Corporation, which is based in Tel Aviv, operates one of two packinghouses there. Its modern processing factory is located in the middle of 115,000 acres and is the world's largest citrus operation.

The Exciting Story of Cuba

Most countries surrounding Cuba maintain regular air routes, offering their citizens easy and open access to the country. Even the United States usually turned a blind eye towards Americans, using bogus reasons, who traveled to Cuba. Hopefully, the two countries can accelerate their transition to normalized relations.

Charlie Crist, a former Republican governor of Florida, became disenchanted with his party and became a Democrat. As such, he became the Democratic Party's standard-bearer during the 2014 gubernatorial race. On June 24, 2014, the *Tampa Bay Times* headlined the fact that Crist had called off an intended trip to Cuba. The present Republican Lt. Governor of Florida Carlos López-Cantera called Crist's planned visit "disgraceful" and Florida's Governor Rick Scott immediately called Crist's decision a "flip-flop." It became exceedingly obvious that the generally popular Democratic candidate backed off visiting Cuba for political reasons. A poll indicated that approximately 42% of the Miami-Dade Cuban population would be less likely to vote for him if he visited the island. In the final analysis, the Cuban-American vote against Crist played an important part in the outcome of the election. Crist claimed that his limited resources, compared to a last minute infusion of $12.8 million to Scott's campaign, from Scott's personal funds, was the reason he lost the election. Although it is true that Scott outspent Crist on advertising by $30 million, it is also very obvious that the conservative Cuban population in Florida continues to back Republican candidates who support the Cuban embargo.

National polls have shown for some years, that the majority of Americans favor normalizing relations with Cuba, however any continuing attempts to normalize economic dealings with Cuba are expected to be difficult. Dario Moreno, Ph.D., an associate professor of politics at Florida International

University and a well-known political consultant, applauded Crist's decision by saying that, "Crist could have found himself in a politically perilous position." The professor was right and Crist lost the election.

Economic relations with Cuba have been a political predicament for over 5 decades and it is difficult to justify continuing the ongoing embargo when the United States has always been known to quickly resume diplomatic and economic ties with its former enemies. It is also apparent that, although the older generation of Miami Cubans continues to stall progress, some of the younger generation of Cuban-Americans has voiced a more progressive direction concerning the future with our neighbors to the south.

"One of the achievements of which I am most proud was the codification, the writing into U.S. law, of the U.S. embargo on the Castro dictatorship." Lincoln Díaz-Balart, U.S. Representative for Florida's 21st Congressional district from 1993 to 2011

International Mining Operations

Cuba presently ranks ninth in the world in the production of nickel. Cuba also accounts for 8% of the world's cobalt production and although Cuban mining has been off limits to the United States since 1959, a robust mining industry has developed thanks in part to Canadian help. Surprisingly, gold is one of the primary products being extracted. Copper and zinc deposits have also been discovered in the Villa Clara Province, located in the central part of Cuba.

It was always known that a small amount of gold lay beneath the surface in Cuba. However, more of this precious metal has been found and is presently being extracted from a number of active mines. The Oro Castellano mine produces its gold from two heap leach operations. It is a state-operated mining operation located near Havana. The Cobre Mantua mine, also located in the same area near Havana, produces a recorded 15,000 ounces per year. However, it is a 50/50 owned operation between the Northern Orion Company from Canada, and the Ceominera Mining Company S.A., which is also a Cuban state-owned enterprise. This co-op is also re-opening an open pit gold mine at El Cobre, near Santiago de Cuba, that has been closed since 2001. A Venezuelan company is also busy conducting a gold mining operation in the same Santiago area. Finally, there is the Holmer mine, a Canadian silver and gold corporation that conducts its operation under Cuban supervision and authority. Gold is what the state-owned Ceominera Mining Company is seeking, but it happens to be only a byproduct from their lucrative nickel and cobalt mines. Mining has never been a safe endeavor, but Cuba has brought their operations into the 21st Century with updated equipment. Canada, being involved in Cuba mining operations, sells them the required heavy equipment and spare parts. Until conditions between the United States and Cuba become normalized, they will be forced to conduct much of their business via third parties.

Cuba's Involvement in the Middle East

In 1973, during the Yom Kippur War, Cuba sent approximately 4,000 troops and equipment, including 500 tank commanders and helicopter crews, to the Arab States with the Soviets providing the transportation. Tanks and other heavy equipment were sent directly from the Soviet Union. They engaged in combat operations against the Israeli Defense Forces, thus preventing Israel from attacking Syria. In 1974, this led to hostile feelings and the cessation of relations between Cuba and Israel. Another reason for this cessation was Cuba's symbolically retaliating to the close ties between Israel and the United States. Castro persisted in being a thorn in the Soviet Union's side as he expanded his influence on the world stage. Leonid Brezhnev took over the Soviet leadership and attempted to institute an era of détente, primarily with a lessening of tension between the United States and the Soviet Union. However Castro continued to flex his muscles by refusing to sign the Non-Proliferation of Nuclear Weapons Treaty. He pushed his relationship with the Soviet Union as far as he could when he lumped the United States and the Soviets together in May of 1976, as two super powers wanting to dominate Third World countries. His actions brought on a movement by the Soviets to unseat him from power for his advocacy of international armed revolution. Castro proclaimed that Havana, not Moscow, was the leader of Communism in Latin America. However, Brezhnev pressured Castro to fall in line, which Fidel had to do, being dependent on Soviet support for Cuba's daily needs.

Fidel Castro sent medical assistance to the socialist government of Algeria, and in 1965, sent "Che" Guevara to the Congo to train the anti-Mobutu, revolutionary fighters. Castro's alliance with the Soviet Union caused additional tensions between him and "Che" Guevara. Castro had always respected "Che" but sometimes questioned his judgment. He referred to "Che" as "intelligent, daring and an exemplary leader, with great moral authority." Fidel however qualified these accolades by saying that Guevara took too many risks and had a tendency to be foolhardy.

"The essence of government is power; and power, as it must be in human hands, will ever be liable to abuse." James Madison, an American statesman, political theorist and the fourth President of the United States

Namibia, Angola and South Africa

During World War I, German South-West Africa (now called Namibia) was invaded and administered by South African and British forces. Following the war, its administration was taken over by the Union of South Africa, and the territory was governed under a trusteeship granted in 1920 by the League of Nations. A request made by the Union of South Africa that they be able to incorporate the territory of South-West Africa into their sovereign boundaries was countered by the President-General of The African National Congress (ANC), Dr. AB Xuma, who on January 22, 1946, cabled the United Nations with his concerns regarding the absorption of South-West Africa into the Union of South Africa. As a result, the United Nations requested that the Union of South Africa place the territory of South-West Africa under a UN trusteeship, allowing international monitoring. The Union of South Africa rejected this request.

On August 26, 1966, having become the Republic of South Africa, it continued its jurisdiction over South-West Africa and refused to leave. As a result, a conflict began with the first clash occurring between the Republic of South Africa's Police Force and the People's Liberation Army of Namibia. This started what came to be known as the Border War. In 1971 the International Court of Justice, the primary judicial branch of the United Nations, based at the Peace Palace in the Hague, Netherlands, ruled that the Republic of South Africa's jurisdiction over the Namibian Territory was illegal and that they should withdraw.

The war spread to include Angola, where the Portuguese Colonial Forces were in a conflict with the National Front for the Liberation of Angola. When the African National Congress, the largest political party in South Africa, sent a small military unit into Botswana, it inflamed the situation, causing the fighting to escalate even more. On November 11, 1975, the movement that led to the fall of Portugal's Conservative government, called the Carnation Revolution, was settled. The new government withdrew from its colonies, thereby granting independence to Mozambique and Angola. Immediately, there were three rival anti-colonial forces that positioned themselves like vultures for control of the Angolan capital, Luanda. The borders of the countries involved were in dispute, with the United States diplomatically backing the Republic of South Africa and the territories they controlled, versus the Soviet Union and Cuba, which backed the Angolan government.

South Africa was identified by the western media to be the aggressor, thereby justifying Cuba to attack the South African troops. Without consulting the Soviets, Cuba jumped into the fray and fought it out with the South African invaders. Reinforcing its forces, they stopped South Africa's advance, in the largest battle fought in Africa since World War II. Cuban pilots, flying Soviet built MiG fighters, bombed the Calueque hydroelectric plant in Namibia, thereby disabling it. In the process, twelve South African combatants were killed.

The perception was that Cuba won the "Border War." The United Nations negotiations that followed, led to South Africa withdrawing their troops from Angola on August 30, 1988. A United States mediation team brought together negotiators from Angola, Cuba and South Africa who amazingly enough, worked out a peace agreement for the region. The Brazzaville Protocol, an agreement reached in Moscow, decided that the Cuban troops would leave Angola and Soviet military aid would end as soon as South African troops were withdrawn from Namibia. In December 1988, Angola, Cuba and South Africa signed the agreement at the United Nations, with South Africa agreeing to turn control of Namibia over to the UN. It is of interest that Bernt Carlsson, a socialist diplomat and the Assistant-Secretary-General of the United Nations, who had been appointed by the United Nations as Commissioner for Namibia, was not at the signing because he was killed on Pan American Flight 103, which exploded and crashed at Lockerbie, Scotland. If Pik Botha, the South African representative, had not cancelled his delegation's booking on this flight, he and 22 members of his party would also have perished.

From April 1989 to March 1990, the United Nations Transition Assistance Group, UNTAG, maintained the peace in the territory. However, during the elections some hostilities did occur and, out of necessity, a second date was set and the election process was started again. As expected some political problems were encountered, but this time the elections were peaceful and declared free and fair. The Namibian Constitution was adopted in February 1990 and Namibia officially became independent on March 21, 1990.

"The United Nations is designed to make possible lasting freedom and independence for all its members." Harry S. Truman, the 33rd President of the United States

China

Starting in 1847, workers were imported from China to Cuba, to replace the rebelling black slaves in the sugar fields. It was just three years before, in the Year of the Lash, that an uprising of black slaves had been suppressed in what was known as the Conspiracy of the Ladder (*Conspiración de La Escalera*). The abolition of slavery in 1886 left many plantations and industries with a labor shortage. To fill this deficiency during the decades that followed, additional hundreds of thousands of Chinese were brought into Cuba. Since the overwhelming majority of these workers were men, they cohabitated with both white and black women, leaving very few pure Chinese behind. The majority of these workers had eight-year contracts but most of them continued on as settlers. Many moved to *Barrio Chino de La Habana*, Havana's Chinatown, although in recent years the ghetto has diminished in size as its inhabitants continued to intermingle and assimilate with the general Cuban population.

During the early years of the Castro régime, the Soviet Union was Cuba's leading trading partner. Since they suffered an economic decline in the 1990's, leading to the division of the Soviet Bloc Nations and the independence of the Soviet States, the People's Republic of China emerged as the new trade partner for Cuba. Cuba has been able to upgrade its infrastructure by buying diesel-electric locomotives and many other trade items, which the United States incidentally also imports from China. The Chinese have also directly invested in Cuba's economy, building factories and underwriting Cuba's biochemical industry. Economic relations, continue to grow between the two countries, especially now as Cuba looks to China for military assistance, which could possibly lead to their establishing a military base in the Americas. It would also give China a strong military advantage if they sought to control the operation of the Panama Canal. The Chinese government has already helped the Cuban military with electronic surveillance equipment, allowing them to tune in to American specialized broadcasting. Quite possibly Cuba has now installed Chinese technology enabling them to interfere with and jam, commercial and military transmissions. On July 5, 2012, President Raúl Castro flew to Beijing for talks with President Hu Jintao of China. Hu had been to Cuba three times previously, developing Sino-Cuban trade agreements.

"Our government has a firm position to develop trade co-operation between our countries." Liu Yuqin, Chinese Ambassador to Cuba, who described as "excellent" the relations between both nations and governments

Canada, Castro and Carter

Cuba was the first Caribbean country to have a Canadian diplomatic mission. Canada has also been one of the first western countries to normalize relations with Cuba after the Revolution. Prime Minister Pierre Trudeau, a member of the Liberal Party of Canada and having progressive values, paid a visit to Cuba during the 1970's. Although detested by the United States, Trudeau's friendly association with Castro has served both countries well. Presently there are approximately 85 Canadian companies with interests in Cuba. Fidel was appreciative of the new relationship with Canada that gave Cuba a loophole through which they could buy Western goods and deal with the Canadian subsidiaries of American corporations. Trudeau died on September 28, 2000, just short of his 81st birthday. Fidel Castro was invited to be an honorary pallbearer along with Jimmy Carter, the 39th President of the

United States. The two men had an opportunity to talk and, discovering that they had many interests in common, entered into a dialogue. Carter agreed that the Cuban embargo had been a mistake and called the embargo the most stupid law ever passed by the United States. Receiving an invitation from Castro, Carter paid a five-day visit to the Cuban leader starting on May 13, 2002. Castro, who was 75 years old, greeted Jimmy Carter, 78 at the time, and his wife Rosalynn at the Havana airport. He granted Carter the freedom to speak with anyone he wished, regardless of their political leanings. Castro allowed Carter to visit biotechnical institutions to demonstrate that they are not developing biological weapons. Carter also visited members of Cuba's religious and human rights groups.

Nine years later Jimmy Carter returned to the island. He gave an interview on Cuban television after having been able to see Alan Gross, an American subcontractor for the U.S. Agency for International Development, USAID. At that time Gross had already served four years of a fifteen-year sentence in prison for allegedly committing acts against the Independent and Territorial Integrity of the Cuban State. Carter said that he hoped that he would see Gross' freedom. Upon returning to the United States, Carter called upon the State Department to remove Cuba from its list of "State Sponsors of Terror." December 17, 2014, marked a new beginning, with President Obama hoping to roll back this designation, which originally had been enacted on March 1, 1982.

While in Cuba, former President Carter also visited the parents and wives of some of the "Cuban Five," part of the Wasp Network, known as "*La Red Avispa.*" The five Cuban intelligence officers, also known as the "Miami Five," are Gerardo Hernández, Antonio Guerrero, Ramón Labañino, Fernando González, and René González. They were arrested in Miami on

September 12, 1998, on charges of false identification, conspiracy to commit espionage, conspiracy to commit murder and acting as agents of a foreign country and were sentenced to long prison sentences in the United States.

At their trial, substantial evidence was presented that the five had, or intended to, infiltrate several Cuban-American groups including the F4 Commandos, Alpha 66, Brothers to the Rescue (*Hermanos al Rescate*), and the Cuban American National Foundation. Their mission expressively included the infiltration of Cuban exile groups in the Miami area. The five had also been linked to the downing of two American-licensed Cessna aircraft over international waters on February 24, 1996. By monitoring the activities of the anti-Castro organization, Brothers to the Rescue, they gathered information that they then passed along to the Cuban Air Force, who in turn shot the aircraft down over the Straits of Florida. Brothers to the Rescue was known for dropping leaflets over Havana and notifying the U.S. Coast Guard when they spotted Cubans trying to navigate across the treacherous Straits.

The Inter-American Commission on Human Rights stated that weapons of war and combat-trained pilots had been used to attack unarmed civilians, and that it revealed considerable malice and scorn toward the human dignity of the victims. Gerardo Hernández was originally convicted of conspiracy to commit murder, but the conviction was later reversed when the prosecution failed to present evidence that Hernández knew that the Cessnas, in international airspace, would be shot down.

At the time, the trials received much publicity, as well as international criticism. The convictions handed down to the five men were in dispute by the international community from the start. Because of the extreme length of the sentences and the doubts regarding their legitimacy, many questions were asked. More than ten Nobel laureates and many political personalities from around the world asked the United States government for a review of the trial. However, the Republican-dominated U.S. Supreme Court stood firm and refused to hear the case. After thirteen years imprisonment, on October 7, 2011, René González was put on parole for three years. He was released on April 22, 2013, and allowed to return to Cuba for his father's funeral. Fernando González was released the following year, on February 27, 2014, and the remaining three were released on December 17, 2014.

Frequently the proposal was made, by various interest groups, that President Obama grant a pardon to the prisoners, and that Alan Gross be released as a start to the normalizing of U.S. and Cuban relations. Standing firmly against any move that would recognize the Communist government in Cuba is Robert Menendez, born on January 1, 1954 in New York City to Cuban immigrant parents. After serving as the Mayor of Union City, the second largest Cuban-American community in the United States and New Jersey's 13th most populous locality, Menendez was appointed to the United States Senate in January 2006. He was appointed by Governor Jon Corzine to fill the remaining term in the Senate seat that Corzine vacated after being elected Governor of New Jersey. Menendez successfully retained his seat for the following two terms and became chairman of the U.S. Senate Committee on Foreign Relations in January of 2013, a seat he held until the Republican Party took control of the Senate in 2015. Although he is a Democrat, he has consistently blocked the Obama White House regarding Cuban affairs.

The representatives of the conservative Cuban-American constituency have always maintained a hard stand against the presumed enemies of the United States. However, the Council of the Americas and the Cuba Study Group have urged President Obama to use his executive powers to begin lifting the restrictions on trade with Cuba. Many of the younger generation of Cuban-Americans agree with this progressive stance.

In 2012, President Obama eased the embargo, allowing many Americans to travel to Cuba. He directed the Secretaries of State, Treasury and Homeland Security to take a series of steps to continue efforts to reach out to the Cuban people. It was President Obama's aspiration to support the Cubans' desire to freely determine their country's future. He also directed that changes be made regarding travel and people-to-people contact, as well as travel and communications to, from and among the Cuban people. On October 12, 2012, the Cuban government announced reforms in its 52-year-old travel ban. Many in the media claimed that Obama overstepped his authority by restoring diplomatic relations with Cuba; however, the Congress allowed changes to be made by the President. Furthermore, previous presidents have made modifications to the United States' position regarding Cuba without any protests from the Congress.

During the first week of December 2013, Alan Gross sent an open letter to President Obama, expressing his frustration with the U.S. Government for not having negotiated vigorously enough for his release from Cuban prison. Although his futility was recognized by the media and many politicians, much of the blame was assigned to the conservative Cubans in South Florida, who resisted negotiating with Cuba, regardless of the reason.

It was generally believed that Gross was not guilty of any crime, however the fact that both his wife and a daughter are fighting cancer should have been reason enough to have granted him an earlier release based on human compassion. On December 17, 2014, Alan Gross was finally granted his freedom.

"On Cuba, Canada has no choice but to walk Washington's tightrope." Carlo Dade, Columnist for Embassy Newspaper, February 20, 2013

Ideology

Fidel Castro, being an ideologue, has continued his animosity towards the United States, while at the same time attempting to increase his good relationship with many Latin American countries. However, there have been times when he has had a tacit understanding with the United States. On September 11, 2001, Castro offered Cuban airports as emergency landing places, when all American aircraft were diverted from their primary destinations and ordered to land immediately, due to the attack on the Twin Towers in New York City. He also accepted a one-time purchase of food after Category 4 Hurricane Michelle struck the island that same year. At the same time, he declined a U.S. Government offer of humanitarian aid. Castro has continued having close relations with Canada and demonstrated this friendship when he attended Prime Minister Pierre Trudeau's funeral in the fall of the year 2000.

Canada, being one of the first allies of the United States to have opened trade with Cuba, still maintains good relations with Cuba. In 1998, Canadian Prime Minister Jean Chrétien flew to Havana to reinforce the friendship that had been fostered by Prime Minister Pierre Trudeau between their two countries. Relations between Venezuela and Cuba also strengthened during the Presidency of Hugo Chávez; Chávez described Castro as a friend and mentor. The two countries exchange oil for medical assistance and have signed agreements concerning electrical energy, oil, and medical grants. Cuba has also provided training and education to Venezuelan students.

Being now frail himself, Fidel mourned the loss of his friend Chávez who died on March 5, 2013. Fidel's brother Raúl attended the funeral of Chávez where he said, "Most importantly he left this world undefeated." Although the United States did not send any official representation to Chávez' funeral, Sean Penn, a Hollywood actor, and the civil rights leader Rev. Jesse Jackson did attend.

"You have to look at history as an evolution of society." Jean Chrétien, 20th Prime Minister of Canada, from November 4, 1993, to December 12, 2003

Crisis in West Africa

On November 10, 2014, *Time* magazine reported statistics indicating that an Ebola outbreak in West Africa had escalated from 4 cases resulting in 3 deaths in December of 2013, to 13,703 cases resulting in 4,922 deaths by October of 2014. These facts came from WHO (World Health Organization), MSF (*Médecins Sans Frontières*) and *The New England Journal of Medicine*. There is enough finger-pointing to go around, however one of the unfortunate truths is that the epidemic happened in poor countries that were ill equipped to handle the onslaught of the Ebola virus.

While the world watched the catastrophe unfold in silence, very little was done to stem the relentless rising tide of this disease. In March 2014, Doctors without Borders were the first to volunteer assistance in the area. At the end of July 2014, Sierra Leone declared a national emergency. It wasn't until September 16, 2014, that President Obama unilaterally committed $500 million and 3,000 United States troops to Liberia. In all, he requested $6 billion to fight the disease.

Although it was late and the increase in the rate of infection continued to rage, the United States set an example for the rest of the world to follow. Australian heath care workers volunteered, and in November 2014 China allocated $123 million in funds and sent 1,000 medical workers into this battle zone. Other countries also became engaged in this fight.

However, it was 165 Cuban doctors and health workers who arrived in Freetown on October 2, 2014, to fight the Ebola virus in Sierra Leone. Although this act did not receive much attention, Cuba had been preparing for this type of epidemic, calling it "Cuban Medical Internationalism." The Cuban Minister of Health, Roberto Morales Ojeda, called on all countries to "join the struggle against this disease." On October 17, 2014, Fidel Castro wrote an article suggesting that Cuba and the United States cooperate in this challenge, ignoring the political differences between the two countries, pursuing humanitarian aid to save lives and seeking World Peace as the ultimate objective. In the United States the epidemic received additional media attention when it was learned that an American CDC worker went to Cuba for an Ebola briefing.

On May 9, 2015, the deadly outbreak of Ebola in Liberia, which has had the highest number of deaths in West Africa, was declared over by the World Health Organization. From the peak of transmission of the disease, during the months of August and September of 2014, when 300 to 400 cases were reported each week in Liberia alone, the count of new cases of this disease has been reduced to nil. The last official victim in the country was buried on March 28, 2015. After seven weeks without a recurrence of Ebola, another case was reported. The danger of further viral infestations will remain until local wild animals, used as bush meat, are also free of the disease.

Cuba which amongst Latin American countries excels in science, played a significant part in the fight against Ebola in West Africa and should be considered a strong ally and partner regarding medical research in the future.

"This is the way the world ends, not with a bang, but a whimper." T. S. Eliot, Nobel Prize winner in Literature, a poet, publisher, playwright and social critic

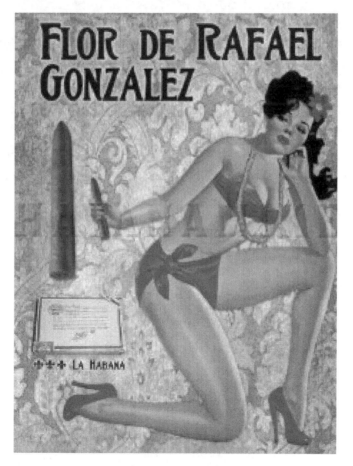

Vintage Cigar Poster

The Exciting Story of Cuba.... Part 17

Cuba's Leadership and Future

Fidel Castro's Personal Life

Fidel Castro always wanted to live in the quiet background. He felt that his personal life was his own and that it should not be privy to the public, and largely he succeeded! Of course, it is always easier when you totally control access and exposure to the media, but in the end, somehow everything does come to light. With the instantaneous flow of information and a 24-hour news cycle, investigative reporters do not miss much.

Fidel's daily routine was frequently out of "sync" with life in the real world. He liked working at night and often had people meet with him during the after-midnight hours, when the rest of the world was asleep. It was common for him to send his driver (he doesn't like the term "chauffer") out to pick up a notable during the wee hours of the morning. Many of his interviews were given during these pre-dawn hours.

During his first marriage to Mirta, he had a mistress, which was not unusual for well-to-do Cuban men. In fact, for many men in Cuba it is part of their culture! Castro's mistress was Natalia Revuelta Clews or "Naty," who was born in Havana in 1925 and was legally married to Orlando Fernández. In the days before the pill, it didn't take long before Castro and Naty had a daughter, Alina Fernández Revuelta, born on March 19, 1956, who, in time, became the public relations director for a Cuban fashion house. Being a model herself, she left Cuba in 1993, supposedly for Spain, but then suddenly reappeared in Columbus, Georgia, before traveling to Miami. Alina has written a book called *Castro's Daughter* about her life in Cuba and now has a radio show, *Simplemente Alina* on WQBA. Seemingly, her relationship is much better with her uncle Raúl than with her father.

Fidel Castro also has a sister Juanita who lives in the United States. Apparently, neither his sister nor his daughter can come to terms with the present communist administration.

Fidel had five sons by his second marriage to Dalia Soto del Valle. In 1993 an American journalist, Ann Louise Bardach, interviewed Fidel. When she asked him how many children he had, his answer with a knowing smile was, "almost a tribe." By one count he had eleven children by seven women, but who's counting?

Although he preferred to live in the shadows, he did have friends that he felt he could trust. His physician, Dr. René Vallejo who had served with the United States Third Army in postwar Germany, died in 1970, and Pepin Naranjo, the former Mayor of Havana who died in 1982, were his closest friends.

Fidel Castro also befriended Gabriel García Márquez, a Colombian novelist, short-story and screenwriter, known affectionately as "Gabo." He was awarded the Nobel Prize in literature and was considered one of the most significant authors and poets of the 20th century. In 1999, Márquez learned that he had lymphatic cancer, however it went into remission upon being successfully treated with chemotherapy. In 2012, his brother divulged that he had developed dementia. García

Márquez died of pneumonia at the age of 87, in Mexico City on April 17, 2014, leaving behind his wife and two sons.

Fidel also enjoyed the wilderness and reminisced about the time he spent in the Sierra Maestra Mountains with his comrades. He satisfied his outdoor spirit on *Cayo Saetía*, a remote man-made island in Nipe Bay, located along the northeastern coast of Cuba. Here he established his own wilderness park stocked with zebra, water buffalo, antelope, deer and wild boar. There are also cattle, horses and one lonely camel, along with some ostriches grazing freely on an open grassy plain. Fidel, his family and special friends would fly in by helicopter to spend a relaxing weekend. It was a great hideaway, which he frequented until 1994. The preserve has now been turned over to the *Grupo de Turismo Gaviota* and belongs to the Mayari municipality of the Holguín Province as a protected Natural Park. The park is open to the public and there is a Cuban Youth Camp, as well as a three-star resort hotel with a small restaurant, on the island. The island is connected to the mainland by an animal restricted bridge, and the closest town is Mayari, 12 miles to the southeast. Now that the park is open to the public, a number of three- or four-star hotels have been built in the area, as well a few more in the nearby city of Holguín.

Fidel has always had a mixed relationship with his brother Raúl. It was always Fidel that was more the idealist, and Raúl the pragmatist. Although basically they now share the same views, Raúl and his friend "Che" Guevara were firm in their beliefs regarding Communism long before Fidel came around to embracing their political concepts.

Fidel's health has been questionable during the past ten years. Prior to his present health problems, he was known to say that he never even had a headache. In 2006, he started to have problems, which the foreign press claimed to be unconfirmed cancer. At the time, he temporarily turned the reins of power over to Raúl and underwent intestinal surgery. The Cuban media was strictly censored regarding Fidel's health and, dutifully, very little leaked out regarding his health problems. However after 18 months, Fidel decided to withdraw from office permanently. In March of 2012, after leaving office, he met with Pope Benedict XVI.

There were also rumors that he suffered from respiratory problems. According to the Venezuelan doctor, Dr. José Rafael Marquina, in statements made to the international press, "Castro had suffered a massive stroke." None of this has ever been substantiated, and on October 22, 2012, when he appeared on Cuban television holding a copy of the newspaper *Granma*, Castro was wearing a straw hat and walking with a cane. Although there was no way of evaluating his mental health, he seemed relatively fit for a man 86 years old.

How much money does a retired Cuban chief executive require, if all of his needs are being met? Most people assume that as the head of a Communist State, money would lose much of its meaning for him and largely that is true. He can do almost anything he wants to, on the island, and can travel to any country he may choose to visit. His needs are totally met, meaning he can order filet mignon, lobster, or for that matter black beans and rice at any time, day or night. He receives the best health care and usually has ten bodyguards and two blood donors standing by. If the aging leader wants for anything, he need only whisper his request and magically his wish will become reality.

Knowing that anything can be his by just snapping his fingers, the fact is that for the most part, Fidel is a modest person who prefers a simple lifestyle. He enjoys conversing with his friends and enjoys their company whenever possible, even though many have passed on in recent years.

One of his personal bodyguards in Cuba, who fled Havana for Miami after completing a prison term, may have been bitter when he wrote that Castro ran the country like it was his own personal fiefdom. He described Fidel as being a combination of medieval overlord and Louis XV of France. He stated that most Cubans have no idea of how Castro lives. Castro has frequently said that he is a dedicated Communist. Furthermore his retirement pay is a mere $36 per month and he claims that his net worth is nil, leaving some to question how it is that his comforts seem to be so well met.

Aside from a relatively modest home in Punto Cero west of Havana, he has the use of the yacht, *Aquarama II*, fitted out with hardwood from Angola and powered by four "PT" style boat engines, donated by former Soviet President Leonid Brezhnev. His aquatic retreat is at Cayo Piedra south of the Bay of Pigs and includes a private island, complete with a turtle and dolphin farm. There is also another boat equipped as a floating hospital, and two commercial fishing vessels utilized to bring in supplies.

One of Castro's visitors, Ignacio Ramonet, a Spanish journalist and writer, interviewed him at length and described his lifestyle as relatively austere. He stated that Castro's lifestyle included reading, exercising and simple meals. The publication *Reporters without Borders*, a non-affiliated organization that promotes and defends freedom of information and freedom of the press, wrote about Ramonet's strong relationship with Fidel Castro, which Ramonet however denied.

Barbara Walters interviewed Fidel Castro both in 1977 and again in 2002. It has been said that she finds him charming and intelligent. In both interviews Barbara and Fidel clashed over the meaning of freedom and how it applies to the media. During her 1977 interview with Fidel Castro, she spent 10 days with him, traveling through the mountains. At one point Barbara actually held his gun in her lap. She said, "People thought we were having a romance, but we never did." During her more recent visit with Castro he tried to compliment her by saying, "You don't look like 25 years have passed; you look exactly the same as you did." I suppose that this accounts for the charming part....

Although most observers consider Castro's lifestyle relatively modest, there are those that are more confrontational and claim that his net worth is over $900 million. *Forbes* magazine has placed Fidel in its "Billionaires edition" as one of the richest rulers in the world. The Cuban government has strongly disputed *Forbes* inclusion of Fidel in their list and Fidel personally denies it, saying that he was considering a lawsuit for libel against the magazine.

The magazine did however admit that it is difficult to estimate the value of privately held companies, lacking creditable financial disclosures. Using a comparative yardstick to appraise the business holdings that they claim Castro has, they come up with $500 million, not counting the possibility of sheltered bank accounts.

Some of the businesses Fidel is said to control includes Cuba's largest commercial corporation, "Cuban Export-Import Corporation" or "CIMEX." Another business is "MEDICUBA," which is an import company supposedly belonging to the health ministry of Cuba. The corporation primarily buys medical devices and equipment from China for use in Cuban hospitals. Other holdings include "The Convention Palace" and a number of resort hotels. Using these facts, his wealth adds up to over $900 million. Very little of this, however, can be accurately verified and Fidel continues to contest *Forbes*. However, testimonies that were given by former insiders support the financial estimates made of these enormous assets, all of which are controlled by Fidel and Raúl.

There is no denying that if power equals wealth, the Castro brothers are extremely wealthy. Considering the form this wealth takes and the sources supplying the information, the actual wealth translated into dollars becomes obscure. This in no way masks the facts, but as was written in the *Preface*, "Ultimately, readers are responsible for interpreting the issues and discerning for themselves, what is factual, or what may be considered conjured." It may be easy to speculate, but regardless, Fidel and his family have more wealth available to them than they can ever spend in their lifetimes, and it has been said that a shroud does not have pockets!

"Writing, as many people know, is an instrument of expression that lacks speed, tone and the intonation of spoken language, and it does not use gestures. It also takes several times our scarce available time. Writing has the advantage that it can be done at any time, day or night, but one doesn't know who will read it...." Fidel Castro, Philosopher

Raúl Modesto Castro Ruz

Born on June 3, 1931, Raúl Castro is Fidel's younger brother. In many ways, the two brothers are very different from each other in both appearance and deportment. Although Ángel Castro is officially listed as the father on Raúl's birth certificate, there have been consistent rumors that his birth father may have been a Cuban Rural Guard commander named Felipe Miraval, a

Batista army loyalist nicknamed "el Chino," for obvious reasons considering his Asian appearance. Raúl was purportedly his mother's favorite child and was endearingly called *"Muso"* by her. Incidentally, *Musou* is an Asian word that means, "The Only One."

Living in his brother's shadow Raúl usually found himself playing second fiddle to Fidel, which made Raúl seem less threatening. However, this was only an illusion. As revolutionaries bivouacking in the Sierra Maestra Mountains, he was always loyal to the mission and knew how to get his thoughts across to his older brother. Although he could, Fidel did not really like to execute anyone, especially one of his own troops. However, when he felt he had to set an example, it was easy enough for Fidel to make the rules, such as capital punishment for rape, but he would call on his younger brother Raúl to carry out the sentence. Fidel ideologically was very liberal, perhaps even to the point of being a Socialist, but he wasn't ready to embrace communism, knowing that the United States, just to their north promised greater rewards, or could become their worst nightmare. It was Raúl's influence that persuaded Fidel to finally accept a communistic form of government.

Raúl was always there for Fidel. They went to the same schools and although Raúl didn't graduate from college with any particular skills, he did take some courses in Business Administration. From the beginning Raúl was involved with his brother in the plans to overthrow the Batista régime. When their attacks on the Moncada and Bayamo barracks failed, both Raúl and Fidel fled to their safe house at the Siboney Farm.

After their successful acquisition of government, Fidel became the Prime Minister and Raúl took over as head of the military. Raúl was designated the Minister of the Revolutionary Armed

Forces, Deputy Prime Minister and First Vice President of the Council of Ministers. Raúl is thought to be homophobic and supposedly even tried to influence Fidel to have homosexuals jailed, during the early years of their régime.

In 1989, Raúl allowed his best friend, Major General Arnaldo T. Ochoa, to be executed. Ochoa was a prominent general who had been with Fidel Castro from the beginning, starting as a member of the 26th of July Movement. He later joined Castro's rebel army in the Sierra Maestra Mountains. In 1984, Fidel even awarded Ochoa the title "Hero of the Revolution."

When Ochoa was chosen to become the head of Cuba's Western Army, close friends accused him of corruption. Opening an internal investigation, it was discovered that Ochoa had been trafficking drugs, which included six tons of cocaine, the sale of diamonds and ivory from Angola, as well as the misappropriation of weapons in Nicaragua. Rumor had it that the CIA had leaked information of Ochoa's illicit activities to the Cuban government. It was speculated that Cuba would be invaded by the United States, using the drug charges as an excuse. Less than a year later the United States invaded Panama in an attempt to overthrow military dictator Manuel Noriega and interestingly, the indictment included drug trafficking charges.

Raúl pleaded with his friend to come clean and explain what had happened so that he could show his friend some compassion. Ochoa refused to cooperate and it was announced by the military that he was under arrest and being investigated for serious acts of corruption, dishonest use of economic resources, and abetting drug trafficking. Ochoa never denied any of these charges but insisted that there were mitigating circumstances that were necessary to carry out his duties. His death sentence was upheld by an appellate court and although it was within Raúl's purview to have the sentence commuted, the popular General Ochoa and three other defendants were executed on July 13, 1989.

Standing before a firing squad, at the military base known as "Tropas Especiales" in Baracoa, West Havana, it is alleged that he requested not to be blindfolded and that he gave the command of execution to the firing squad himself. Gen. José Luis Mesa Delgado, "Head of Special Troops (FAR)," delivered the coup de grâce, by putting a final bullet in Ochoa's head. He was buried at an unmarked site in the *Cementerio de Cristóbal Colón* in Havana.

In October of 1997, the Communist party designated Raúl to become Fidel's successor, and nine years later when Fidel underwent gastrointestinal surgery, he temporarily took over the reins of government. In July of 2006, Fidel turned the leadership of Cuba over to his brother, and then in January of 2008 the 31 member Council of State, elected Raúl to the presidency. There is no doubting the loyalty of Raúl. He was always there when Fidel needed him!

During the time that Raúl headed the military, he introduced a capitalistic idea that could only work in a communistic economy. In Cuba, the armed forces are actively involved, not only in protecting the country, but in protecting and managing its economy. Its involvement with the retail and tourist industry provides the domestic economy a much-needed boost from foreign currency. Raúl was the architect of this unique concept and set it up so that the military owns and operates the country's largest retail chain, *TRD Caribe S.A.* The army-owned retail chain sells from more than 400 locations throughout the island. It caters to tourists and visiting Cubans alike, using the stores as a foreign currency recovery operation. They use Wal-

Mart strategies by offering deep discounts on Chinese made goods that they buy for less in bulk and then make a healthy profit on the resale margin. *Grupo de Turismo Gaviota, S.A.* owns and operates tourist hotels and resorts and *Aerogaviota* is an airline based in Havana that operates domestic passenger charters for foreign tourists who bring in dollars.

Military officers have become the country's business executives and to a great extent enjoy the benefits derived therefrom. Raúl, as part of his crusade to increase efficiency and reduce corruption, has assigned army Colonel Hector Oroza Busutin as the head of Cuba's largest commercial corporation, Cuban Export-Import Corporation "*CIMEX.*" In this strangely unique way, the international business community is learning to accept the Cuban military officers as their counterparts, who are attempting to bring a market economy to the island. As the former head of the military, Raúl has a reputation for delegating authority and demands results from subordinates. Presently there are eight ministries that are headed by career military officers. Of these, three are still on active duty. By some estimates, the military now controls over sixty percent of the Cuban economy.

As "Head of State," Raúl leads a relatively quiet life. As with his brother Fidel, it would be difficult to estimate his personal wealth, though there will always be some that will try. Although his own salary remains modest, on February 23, 2014, he proclaimed a wage increase for employees in the health sector. Most Cubans genuinely like him and his position as president seems to be secure.

There are some who say that he may enjoy his alcoholic drinks a bit too much and that he may even be an alcoholic, but again, this has never really been substantiated. Raúl has close relations and enjoys his friends and family. He and his late wife Vilma Espin had three daughters Déborah, Mariela and Nilsa and a son Alejandro Castro Espín. Mariela Castro Espin, his middle daughter, is active in politics and a member of Cuba's parliament. Mariela is an LGBT rights activist and has taken part in Toronto's World Pride festival as both an attendee and a speaker.

Being Mirta's ex-brother-in-law, Raúl also took care of the arrangements when Mirta requested an occasional visit with her son Fidelito in Havana. There is reason to believe that she may still have feelings for Fidel and, as noted before, she may have visited him as well.

Raúl Castro was considered a competent military leader, and a practical problem solver. On February 24, 2013, Raúl was re-elected to a second five-year term as President of Cuba. As President, it is almost a certainty that he will remain in office until his announced retirement in 2018, at which time he will be 86 years old.

"I was not chosen to be president to restore capitalism to Cuba. I was elected to defend, maintain and continue to perfect socialism, not destroy it." Raúl Castro, President of Cuba since 2008

Looking Ahead to the Future

The new vice president of Cuba is Miguel Díaz-Canel, born on April 20, 1960. He is an electrical engineer who rose out of obscurity in 2013, when he became First Vice President of the Council of State. He has been a loyal member of the Communist Party of Cuba since 2003. Politically he had been a top official in the provinces of Villa Clara and Holguín, and on a national level he served as the Minister of Education from 2009 until 2013. Fidel Castro's son, Fidelito, endorsed him by saying, "I'm certain that he will be well received by the younger generation as well as by the population in general." Díaz hinted that he would reach out and perhaps help the private sector in Cuba rebound. He is said to be accessible to the public, however it is rather doubtful that the Cubans-in-exile will ever accept him. Díaz-Canel took the place of Dr. José Machado Ventura, who was born on October 26, 1930, and is expected to remain in politics, functioning in a lesser role as the Second Secretary of the Communist Party of Cuba. Two others that are ascending in Cuban politics are Mercedes López Acea, born in 1964, who is the president of the Havana Communist Party, and Salvador Valdés Mesa, born on June 13, 1945, the head of the labor federation.

The future is always difficult to predict, but the present attempt at normalizing the relationship between the United States and Cuba seems to be in the best interest for the people of both countries. There are however powerful forces intent on preventing this.

The Helms-Burton Act

The Helms-Burton Act was passed by the 104th United States Congress on March 6, 1996, and enacted into law by President Bill Clinton on March 12, 1996. Its intention was to bolster and continue the United States embargo against Cuba. It also opposes Cuban membership in international institutions, and prohibits commercial television broadcasting from the United States to Cuba. Further, the law provides for the protection of property rights of certain United States nationals.

The Juragua Nuclear Power Plant

The Juragua Nuclear Power Plant on the southern coast of Cuba, just west of Castillo de Jagua near Cienfuegos, was under construction in 1992, but the construction was suspended following the collapse of the Soviet Union. The United States opposition to the project discouraged other countries from assisting Cuba in completing this project. However in the year 2000, on a visit to Cuba Vladimir Putin offered to finish one of the reactors. With estimates regarding the cost to finish this reactor ranging from $300 million to $750 million, Putin offered Cuba a grant of $800 million over a period of 10 years. Because of Cuba's heavy national debt, Castro stated that Cuba was no longer interested in finishing the plant and would be seeking other energy alternatives. In 2004, a turbine was removed from the stalled project, to be used as a replacement for a damaged turbine at the Guiteras thermoelectric plant, thus effectively ending the Juragua project.

For the United States government this was viewed as a successful application of the Helms-Burton Act. It demonstrated that not only did this law prevent American companies from assisting Cuba, but that it also prevented foreign companies from coming to their aid.

Wasted Money

The New York Times has run numerous editorials regarding Cuban-American relations and points out that American initiatives have spent $264 million since the passing of the Helms-Burton Act, with the supposed intention of instigating democratic reforms on the island. In actual fact, the real intention was to destabilize the present Cuban government and, as it turned out, much of this money was misappropriated and found its way into the pockets of outright swindlers. State Department Officials have argued that these programs have failed, are counterproductive, and should be stopped. Legislators representing conservative Cuban-American groups continue to keep these programs alive, without providing the necessary responsible oversight. In 2008, $45 million was appropriated to these initiatives, making it a record amount.

Resistance to Change

One of the major opponents to Castro's government has been Jorge Mas Canosa, who was a self-made businessman in South Florida. He was born on September 21, 1939, in Santiago de Cuba. After coming to the United States he attended the Presbyterian Junior College of North Carolina, before returning to Cuba to pursue a law degree at the Cuban University of the Oriente - Santiago de Cuba. Returning to Miami again, he founded a number of companies, including Church and Tower in Coral Gables, Florida, and the multinational corporation MasTec, which employs over 13,000 people. Recently declassified CIA documents strongly allege a link between Luis Posada Carriles and Jorge Mas Canosa regarding the manufacture of limpet-type bombs. CIA and FBI intelligence documents tie Posada to the bombing of *Cubana* flight 455. Posada's CIA connection was through Grover T. Lythcott who recruited Posada to coordinate several anti-Castro groups including the Cuban Representation in Exile, RECE, headed by Jose M. Bosch who ran the Bacardi Rum Corporation for 32 years until his retirement in 1976. Jorge Mas Canosa was the member charged with Public Relations at the time.

Jorge Mas Canosa is considered a heroic figure among the anti-Castro Cubans in the United States. In 1981, he established the Cuban American National Foundation, and was deemed the

President of the Cuban government in exile. Although it has been denied, there was reason to believe that he would have been ready to assume that role, had the Castro régime faltered. Jorge Mas Canosa died of lung cancer on November 23, 1997. However, he left three sons, Jorge, Juan Carlos and Jose Ramon, to continue his work as active members of the Cuban community in Miami.

The United States quietly began exporting food to Cuba in 2001, following the devastating hurricane Michelle. In 2000, President Clinton authorized the sale of certain humanitarian products and the United States is again the island's primary food supplier. Annual food sales to Cuba peaked at $710 million in 2008. The Latin American Working Group coordinates relief efforts with Cuba in times of need.

There has been a lengthy history binding the two countries, which should not be forgotten. American corporate abuses on the island nation is one of the overwhelming factors deterring Cuba from stabilizing affairs with the United States and the fact that Cuba's government is a dictatorial, communistic régime stands in the way of the United States opening negotiations with them. Guantánamo Naval Base has been held for a long period of time, perhaps too long, and for questionable reasons, whereas Cuba has incarcerated people for political reasons, including some Americans, for far too long. Families have been divided and animosities have continued. Special interest groups, including a very vocal Cuban population in South Florida, continue to block the U.S. Government from initiating reasonable legislature regarding U.S. interests in Cuba, while many other countries carry on normal relations with the country. It would seem that now is a good time for the U.S. and Cuba to become reasonably good neighbors again....

"... big changes appear inevitable in Cuba over the next few years. Cuban-Americans are ramping up investment plans, assuming the U.S. government will finally lift the embargo. But the future may not be all that's expected." Don Ediger, Consortiumnews.com, published on September 19, 2012

Game Changer

At noon on December 17, 2014, President Obama addressed the people of the United States with a message that was seen as a game changer between Cuba and the United States. At the same time, Raúl Castro, as President of the Council of State of Cuba and Council of Ministers, addressed the people of Cuba, regarding the same topic. President Castro attempted to convey the thought that he and his brother Fidel had been willing to hold a respectful dialog between the two countries on many occasions before, but to no avail. However, wearing his four-star revolutionary uniform reminded people that Cuba is a tightly controlled state and that this was an integral part of the same revolution that took place 36 years prior.

Both men informed their constituencies that they had spoken to each other on the previous day and agreed to make headway on topics of mutual interest. Raúl referred to the relationship between the two countries as a long-standing struggle. Obama agreed by saying in Spanish, *"No es fasil,"* "It's not easy." Later in his speech, Obama added, *"Todos somos Americanos,"* "We are all Americans." President Obama mentioned that the United States was in agreement to normalize relations between the two sovereign nations. Both men talked about the prisoner exchange that was taking place as they spoke. They also agreed to cooperate and renew diplomatic relations that had been severed since 1961. President Obama also mentioned that in April 2015 the United States would be prepared to have Cuba join the other nations of the Americas at the Summit of the Americas, which they did. He acknowledged the role Pope Francis played in bringing the two countries together and said, "Going forward, the United States will reestablish an embassy and high ranking officials will visit Cuba." Raúl, referring to the release of the three convicted Cuban prisoners held in the United States, said, "The enormous joy of their families and of all our people, who have relentlessly fought for this goal, is shared by hundreds of solidarity committees and groups, governments, parliaments, organizations, institutions, and personalities, who for the last sixteen years have made tireless efforts demanding their release. We convey our deepest gratitude and commitment to all of them."

Raúl mentioned that the American citizen, Alan Gross, was released for humanitarian reasons. There was also another person released by the Cuban authorities, who was described by President Obama as "an unidentified man." He was said to have been "...one of the most important intelligence agents that the United States has ever had in Cuba." Previously the former U.S. Secretary of State, Hillary Clinton, had told reporters that Gross had been "unjustly jailed for far too long. He needs to be able to leave Cuba and return home." To this, she added that, "This is a great personal pain to his family and concern to the U.S. government."

President Obama, knowing that his unilateral move would bring on a hail of criticism from the conservative right, implored those that have resisted change "...to cut loose the shackles of the past, since it is the right thing to do." Of course some Democrats, but primarily members of the Republican Party, challenged the President for his reconciliatory actions.

Senator Marco Rubio, the junior Senator from Florida, took an angry stance against the President's position, calling him "willfully ignorant and the worst negotiator since Carter." Rubio also took on the Pope, lecturing him on democracy as it pertains to the people of Cuba.

Adam Shaw, a News Editor for *FoxNews.com*, wrote an article headed: *Pope Francis is the Catholic Church's Obama – God help us.* He wrote, "Pope Francis' Vatican just gave Democrats a big boost for 2016." The Speaker of the House John Boehner was somewhat easier on the President, but stood with Rubio's position by saying, "Relations with the Castro régime should not be revisited, let alone normalized, until the Cuban people enjoy freedom – and not one second sooner."

Although most Republicans cannot be seen supporting Obama, Senator Rubio seems to be out of step with most other Republican legislators. The majority of the legislators seem to be in favor of normalizing relations with Cuba. A fellow Republican, Senator Rand Paul of Kentucky, opposed Rubio by saying, "Seems to me, Senator Rubio is acting like an isolationist who wants to retreat to our borders and perhaps build a moat."

The next election cycle in the United States will be in 2016 and lines are now being drawn. The Cuban issue is becoming a "hot button" topic and much of what happens regarding Cuban-American relations will depend on who the next American president will be. Since the United States has found that it is possible to trade with its former enemies, there is very little reason to continue isolating Cuba with an embargo.

On the morning of December 20, 2014, President Obama sent out an email in which he repeated parts of the speech he gave on December 17, 2014. In it, he emphasized what the United

States' new approach will be. First, he has instructed Secretary of State John Kerry to immediately begin discussions with Cuba to re-establish diplomatic relations that have been severed since 1961. Second, he has also instructed Secretary Kerry to review Cuba's designation as a State Sponsor of Terrorism – a review guided by the facts and the law. Third, he wrote that the United States will take steps to increase travel, commerce, and the flow of information to and from Cuba.

President Obama said, "Change is hard – especially so when we carry the heavy weight of history on our shoulders. Our country is cutting that burden loose to reach for a better future." The former Speaker of the U.S. House Tip O'Neill said, "All politics is local," therefore some individuals will benefit by keeping America's relations with Cuba as it is, at arm's length. Others are still so bitter that they, perhaps justifiably so, will never reach an understanding with Cuba.

"Good afternoon, today the United States of America is changing its relationship with the people of Cuba. In the most significant changes in our policy in more than 50 years, we will end an outdated approach that, for decades, has failed to advance our interests. And instead, we will begin to normalize relations between our two countries. Through these changes, we intend to create more opportunities for the American and Cuban people and begin a new chapter among the nations of the Americas." President Barack Hussein Obama II, the 44th President of the United States, at the beginning of a statement made on December 17, 2014

Positive Progress

On Thursday, February 19, 2015, two months after the United States and Cuba announced a willingness to re-establish normal diplomacy, after over 5 decades of hostile relations, the United States House Minority leader and eight fellow Democratic Party lawmakers went to Havana to meet with the Cuban Vice President Miguel Díaz-Canel. On February 27th, Cuban Foreign Ministry Director for North America, Josefina Vidal, and her delegation met at the State Department in Washington, D.C.

Although both Cubans and Americans have a positive view towards improving diplomatic relations, there are legislators in both the U.S. House and Senate that have not joined the administration in promoting the necessary détente and good will in easing the normalization of relations between the two countries. On May 29, 2015, by Executive Order, President Obama took a step by removing Cuba from the list of "State Sponsors of Terrorism."

Freedom in the United States is a word frequently heard, however it should include the right of Americans to travel to Cuba if they so choose. Americans can do more to help the Cuban people by a free interchange of commerce, ideas and friendship than by continuing the embargo initiated over five decades ago.

It remains up to the people of Cuba to bring about a transformation of their government, if that is what they want. A free government is always the responsibility of its citizens and changes are seldom easy. Ultimately, it is up to the Cubans to decide.

The Exciting Story of Cuba

Although the final say regarding the normalization between the two countries is in the hands of politicians representing their various constituencies, pressure is being applied by corporations that, quite frankly, are fed up with the slowness of the process. The idea that everything hinges on the fact the Cuba is a communist country, run by a dictatorship, does not take into account the plight of the Cuban people. The United States may wish for a different government; however it is up to the Cuban people to decide what form of government they will eventually have.

The United States trades with Russia, China and Viet Nam without debilitating interference, and until now hasn't been able to open up an understanding and dialog with one of our closest neighbors. Until Congress acts, most average American citizens are prohibited from visiting Cuba freely, or even from importing and smoking Cuban cigars. Yet for years Americans have been led to believe that they live in a free society.

The First Flight

During the first week of May 2015, the United States government opened trade routes and scheduled flights to Cuba. Almost immediately JetBlue Airlines scheduled a weekly Friday flight from New York City to Havana. Officially the first flight, after travel restrictions were lifted, was an Airbus 150-seat A320, out of New York's Kennedy Airport to Havana on Friday, July 3, 2015. This made JetBlue the first major carrier to fly scheduled flights to Cuba.

United States to Cuba Ferry Service

The U.S. Treasury Department has issued at least four licenses to companies that want to establish ferry service to Cuba from

Key West, Miami, Fort Lauderdale and Tampa. Baleària, a Spanish company, presently owns the Baleària Bahamas Express ferry service from Fort Lauderdale to Freeport, Grand Bahamas, and is now considering a ferry to operate between Florida and Cuba. United Caribbean and Havana Partners have expressed an interest in a service from Tampa to Havana and Mexico. Baja Ferries USA wants to open routes between the Port of Miami and Port Everglades to Cuba.

The details regarding feasibility depends on government restrictions and tariffs placed on them by the countries, as well as the ports involved. Tampa would be a straight run 331 miles due south, but some of the other ports would be closer. In the end it will come down to money, availability of cargo and logistics. Although Miami has declined having a Cuban Consulate in their city, Tampa and The Port of Tampa have expressed their enthusiasm to become fully involved in these new ventures. Bob Rohrlack, President of the Greater Tampa Chamber of Commerce, has been to Cuba several times, taking corporate delegates in preparation for improved, open relations with Cuba.

Prior to December 17, 2014, diplomatic relations between Cuba and the United States were strained, as the following quote illustrates....

"It's unfortunate that President Obama continues to be poorly advised and ill-informed about the Cuban reality, as well as the sentiments of his own people who desire normalization of our relationship." Josefina Vidal, Cuban Foreign Ministry Director of North America, February, 2013

It seems that at the time, Ms. Vidal's quote was deliberately misdirected. Obviously, much has changed during the ensuing two years to temper the diplomatic views of both countries. It clearly showed a desire on the part of Cuba to normalize relations.

Opening of the U.S. and Cuban Embassies

On June 30, 2015, in the Rose Garden of the White House, President Barack Obama, sounding confident, stated that the new policy of reconciliation was "another demonstration we don't have to be imprisoned by the past." The president declared that the United States will reopen its Embassy in Cuba and will restore full diplomatic relations with Cuba for the first time since relations were severed in 1961. Senator Richard Durbin supported the administration by saying: "Five-plus decades of U.S.-Cuba relations being on a Cold War footing haven't worked. Opening the door with Cuba for trade, travel and the exchange of ideas will create a force for positive change in Cuba that more than 50 years of our current policy of exclusion could not achieve." President Obama said that Secretary of State John Kerry would travel to Cuba's capital to celebrate the opening of the American Embassy in Havana and the raising of the U.S. flag there.

Noting that efforts by previous administrations to isolate Cuba have not been successful, Obama called on an adversarial Congress to lift the embargo on the Caribbean island just 90 miles from U.S. shores. "I strongly believe that the best way for America to support our values is through engagement," he said.

On July 20, 2015, the United States and Cuba officially resumed diplomatic relations, with their respective Embassies in both capitals.

Critics of the Cuban government pledged to fight the administration's plan to normalize relations with Havana, letting it be known that they would block any attempts to lift the Cuban embargo. Marco Rubio, the Junior Senator representing Florida and being of Cuban heritage, stated that the White House was being manipulated by the Cuban government into making concessions that wouldn't be met by changes in Havana. "The Cuban government will never allow any changes on the island that will threaten their ability to maintain a grip on power. We've seen that time and time again," Mr. Rubio said. As a member of, and expecting to chair the subcommittee, the Senate Foreign Relations Committee, he pledged that the Congress would prevent funding for the U.S. Embassy in Cuba and would not lift the embargo with Cuba. "This Congress is not going to lift the embargo," Mr. Rubio said. House Speaker John Boehner responded to the President's remarks by describing the steps being taken as "mindless concessions to a dictatorship." Senator Ted Cruz, also of Cuban heritage, supported Senator Rubio by accusing Obama of "continuing his policy of unconditional surrender" to what he called "one of the most violently anti-American régimes on the planet." Other congressional critics included Cuban-American lawmakers like Representative Ileana Ros-Lehtinen of Florida and Senator Bob Menendez, of New Jersey.

However polls indicate that a majority of citizens and many lawmakers on both sides of the isle support Obama's position. Senator Dean Heller of Nevada named "numerous opportunities mutually beneficial to the people of both countries," while Senator Jeff Flake of Arizona, normally a political adversary, said that it was time to abandon "five decades of failure."

"For too long we have let Cuba dictate our policy. We should do what's in our interest, which is to let Americans travel and have better relations. This is the

best chance of spurring good developments in Cuba."
Senator Jeff Flake, of Arizona

Could a Change in Politics help Tourism?
A Vintage Cuban Travel Poster

The Exciting Story of Cuba.... Part 18

Cuba's Five Most Prominent Cities

The Growth of La Habana

In 1592 Diego Velázquez, Cuba's first Governor, founded Havana, replacing Santiago de Cuba as the capital city. At one point in time, Havana was larger than any city on the American Continent. Today the city of Havana has a population of over two million people, still one of the largest metropolitan areas in the West Indies. When the city was conceived, there was some discussion as to which coast it should be located on. The original location on the south shore was swampy and bug infested, but Havana's elevation and natural harbor on the north coast facing the Gulf of Mexico became the determining factors. King Philip II of Spain granted it "city status" and designated it the "Key to the New World" and the "Rampart of the West Indies." Havana's Coat of Arms portrays this, by having three castles and a key on a blue background. During the colonial era, above this crest was the Royal Crown of Spain, which has since been replaced by a golden fortress. The blue background denotes the Gulf of Mexico and the three forts represent the three gates to the city: Fuerza Castle, Morro Castle and Punta Castle. Holly Oak Leaves on both sides, tied together with a small blue ribbon, represent strength, honor and glory.

The Exciting Story of Cuba

The city is comprised of three parts: Old Havana, which is the central part of the city, Vedado where the central part expanded, and the newer outlying suburban districts that now extend beyond the earlier boundaries. Although the epidemic of 1649 killed many and sickened a third of the city's population, during the Colonial years Havana remained larger than either Boston or New York City. During this era, at different times the French and British invaded Havana. The British temporarily occupied and ruled the city, but when Spain regained control in 1763, it took steps to prevent a recurrence, by sturdily fortifying the city with massive stone walls and castles. In the 19th Century, the city prospered and became a center for the arts, fashion and wealth. Theaters, fashion houses and mansions were built and Havana became known as "The Paris of the Antilles."

In 1863, as Havana continued to grow, the need for expansion prompted the removal of the city walls. The Ten Years' War ended with a cease fire from Spain. However, it was followed by the Cuban War of Independence, which lasted from 1895 until 1898 and prompted intervention by the United States. The American occupation of Cuba lasted until 1902. After Cuban Independence came into being, another period of expansion in Havana followed, leading to the construction of beautiful apartment buildings for the new middle class and mansions for the wealthy.

During the 1920's, Cuba developed the largest middle class per total population in all of Latin America, necessitating additional accommodations and amenities in the capital city. As ships and airplanes provided reliable transportation, visitors saw Havana as a refuge from the colder cities in the North. To accommodate the tourists, luxury hotels, including the *Hotel Nacional* and the *Habana Riviera*, were built. In the 1950's gambling and prostitution became widespread and the city became the new playground of the Americas, bringing in more income than Las Vegas. Castro's revolution, with all of its good intentions, put a stop to all of this and 1959 marked the beginning of austerity for this former freewheeling city. The communistic de-privatization of all businesses, along with the embargo imposed by the United States, created a serious decline in Havana's economy. The constant pressure to nationalize, as well as the severe crackdown by the régime to keep people in line, curtailed growth and placed an enormous hardship on the people.

Since the Castro Revolution, the people of Havana have been severely affected, because of the absence of commerce with its former trading partner, the United States, only 90 miles to the north. It has taken a severe toll economically, with its dilapidated houses, and the pre-1959 cars on the streets of the city being a testimony to the bygone era.

For the greatest part, the Port of Havana has also been bypassed, chiefly due to the restrictions placed on them by the United States. However, in recent years the Cuban government has attempted a comeback by attracting tourism from Canada, Mexico, the Bahamas, Latin America, Asia and Europe. The city of Havana has renovated the Sierra Maestra Cruise Port, but only a few cruise companies consider Havana a port of call. Slowly, German and British ships are starting to arrive, including the Fred Olsen Cruises. Canadian affiliates of American hotel corporations are also building new resort areas along the northern beachfront east of the city, now called Blue Havana.

Technically Real Estate Brokers and Automobile Dealers are illegal in Cuba, although real-estate offices and car dealerships are blatantly open for business. The buying and selling of real estate and cars, which was forbidden for many years, can now be done because of changes brought about by Raúl Castro, but only by full-time residents of Cuba. However, gray market sales are thriving through the use of friends and family as proxies.

Havana is also trying to renew and rebuild parts of the old city. Work in Old Havana with its many narrow streets, plazas, overhanging balconies and colonial architecture is proving to be a worthwhile but expensive and formidable task.

The city is also known for its neo-classical architecture introduced by the French in the mid-nineteenth century. In 1925, a master plan was instituted to blend the French neo-classical design with the tropical background. The Art Deco movement, both in Havana and in Miami Beach, took hold during the late 1920's, and is found primarily in the residential section of Miramar. Miramar is where most of the embassies are located, including the massive Russian embassy. The predominant street is Fifth Avenue known as *La Quinta Avenida*, along which is found the church of *Jesus de Miramar*, the *Teatro Miramar* and the Karl Marx Theater. There is also the Old Miramar Yacht Club and the *El Ajibe Restaurant*, recently visited and televised by Anthony Bourdain on his show, "*No Reservations*," on the Travel Channel. Anthony Bourdain is also presently being shown on CNN. The modern five-star *Meliá Habana* hotel, known for its cigar bar, is located opposite the Miramar Trade Centre.

Started in 1772, *el Paseo del Prado*, also known as *el Paseo de Marti*, became the picturesque main street of Havana. It was the first street to be paved in the city and runs north and south, dividing Centro Habana from Old Havana. Having been designed by Jean-Claude Nicolas Forestier, a French landscape architect, it connects the Malecón, the city's coastal esplanade, with a centrally located park, *Parque Central*. Although the streets on either side are in disrepair, the grand pedestrian walkway goes for ten nicely maintained blocks. The promenade has a decorated, inlaid, marble terrazzo pavement with a balustrade of small posts. It is shaded by a tree-lined corridor and has white marble benches for the weary tourist.

Arguably, the Malecón is the most photographed street in Havana. It lies as a bulwark just across the horizon from the United States, which is only 90 treacherous miles away. It is approximately 5 miles long, following the northern coast of the city from east to west. This broad boulevard is ideal for the revelers partaking in parades and is the street used for Fiesta Mardi Gras, known in Cuba as *Los Carnavales*. It has also been used for "spontaneous demonstrations" against the United States. It runs from the entrance to Havana harbor at the Morro Castle, *Castillo del Morro*, alongside the Centro Habana neighborhood to the Vedado neighborhood, past the United States Embassy on the *Calle Calzada*. Since 1977, the renovated Embassy building has housed the United States Interests Section in Havana. The Malecón is also known as a street where both male and female prostitutes ply their trade. At the present time, most of the buildings that line this once magnificent coastal boulevard are in ruins, which doesn't stop it from being a spectacular and popular esplanade for an evening walk by residents and tourists alike.

Modern architecture stands in stark contrast to the older styles that can be found throughout the city, thereby strangely affecting the skyline. It includes some of the relatively newer hotels, such as the four-star Havana Hilton on Calle 23 where Castro stayed upon entering the city in the early days following the revolution. Completed in 1958, it has been renamed the *Habana Libre*. This commercial area has many attractions including the movie theater, *Cine La Rampa*. The Castro government also built a four hundred unit apartment complex with a school, parking facility, restaurant and supermarket, in the modern utilitarian communist style.

Havana, like so many American cities, even has its Chinatown, which is populated by the descendants of workers brought in during the start of the twentieth century, as low paid replacements for the African slaves who had been freed by the end of the Ten Years' War.

The people of Havana have developed a resilience to the adversities imposed upon them and, although they have endured enormous political and economic hardships over the past decades, they have maintained a positive outlook regarding the future.

As the largest cosmopolitan city in Cuba, Havana is also the center for music and the arts. Ernesto Lecuona, born in the Guanabacoa district of Havana on August 6, 1895, was a world-renowned pianist and composer. His compositions include *Canto Siboney*, *Malagueña* and *The Breeze and I*. He frequently went on tour with his sister and mentor, Ernestina Lecuona.

In addition to receiving many other awards, Gloria Estefan was inducted into the Latin Songwriters Hall of Fame on October 20, 2014. She is married to Emilio Estefan, a nineteen-time Grammy Award winning musician and producer, from Santiago de Cuba, who had his start with the *Miami Sound Machine*.

Other stage and motion picture actors originally from Havana include actors Andy Garcia, Daisy Fuentes and Steven Bauer, to name just a few.

"I think that I've tried many times to get Cuba in my writings, especially Havana, which was once a great and fascinating city." Guillermo Cabrera Infante, Cuban Author

Sunny Santiago de Cuba

Of the 57 cities in Cuba, Santiago ranks second in population with not quite a half million people. It is located on the southeast quadrant of the island facing the Caribbean Sea and surrounded by the Sierra Maestra Mountains. Santiago is less than a fifth as large in population as Havana, but is over 7% larger in area.

Santiago de Cuba is known as the city where the Cuban Revolution began on July 26, 1953. The city hosts the Bacardi museum, which has a few paintings left behind by the family when they fled the country after the government takeover on October 15, 1960. The museum also has archeology and history rooms. Other museums in the city include the Isabella Museum, containing farm implements from the French coffee growers. The Museum of Historical Ambiance was once the home of Cuba's first governor Diego Velázquez de Cuéllar. A Piracy Museum and the 26th of July History Museum are also worth seeing. There are numerous concerts presented at the recently remodeled Dolores Hall. Many famous musicians including Desi Arnaz, the late bandleader and actor; Emilio Estefan, a music producer and husband of Gloria Estefan, the singer; as well as the late Compay Segundo, came from Santiago.

Cuba's beloved poet, writer and revolutionary hero, José Martí, is buried in the *Cementerio Santa Ifigenia*, Santiago's cemetery. His cremains are draped with a Cuban flag and a twenty-four hour honor guard stands watch. It is also the final resting place of the first president of Cuba, Tomás Estrada Palma, and Emilio Bacardi y Moreau, a hero of the Cuban War of Independence and whose father started the Bacardi Rum dynasty. Eleven Generals of the War of Independence also rest here.

On June 28, 1514, Cuba's first governor, Diego Velázquez de Cuéllar, founded the city of Santiago de Cuba, and made it chronologically the second capital, after Bayamo, of the island nation. Its geography makes it well suited to be the primary city on the eastern end of the island. It was the home base for the conquistador Juan de Grijalba, who was related to Diego Velázquez. Grijalba explored the southeastern coast of Mexico, and named the Mexican river, *Rio Grijalva*, after himself. Two years after the city was founded, Santiago de Cuba was destroyed by fire.

Hernán Cortés also left from Santiago and took his exploration inland from Veracruz. There is a monument in his honor near Mexico City. In 1519 he had an Indian woman as his interpreter, whom he named Doña Marina, and apparently she also became his mistress, since they had a son.

In 1536, Hernando de Soto was granted the title of Governor of Cuba by King Charles V of the Holy Roman Empire, otherwise known as King Carlos I of Spain. After leaving Santiago with five heavily-laden ships, De Soto trudged through Florida, with a large expedition starting at Piney Point, south of Tampa Bay in Florida, and continuing north to Tallahassee, and then up through Georgia. His expedition continued to Tennessee and the Appalachian Mountains. He followed the sun westward across the Mississippi River into present day Arkansas, where he died on May 21, 1542. His expedition continued south through Louisiana and then along the coast to Mexico. Both Hernando and DeSoto Counties in Florida, as well as a bridge crossing the Mississippi River near Memphis, were named for him. He, like most of the conquistadors, gained a justified reputation for extreme, unbridled abuse and cruelty to the Indians, in his relentless quest for gold and other riches.

In 1553, Santiago was invaded and plundered by the French. They were followed by the British, led by Sir Christopher Myngs in 1662-1663. The British considered him an Admiral, but to the Spanish he was a pirate, when he broke through the strong Spanish defenses to plunder and sack the city. Santiago lost its status as the capital of Cuba when the seat of power was moved to Havana in 1589, but many people to this day, feel it is still the capital city when it comes to culture. Of course, anyone from *La Habana* would vehemently disagree with this! Carnival is the predominant pageant and because it relates to the Afro-Cuban beliefs rather than Christianity, it occurs in July instead of February. The large number of Afro-Cubans in Santiago brought in much of the African culture found in eastern Cuba. Many of these people practice Santería, a religion that emerged from different West African beliefs, and was brought to Cuba from Haiti.

The architectural styles of Santiago's buildings are diverse with a large section of the city having old colonial buildings with balconies and broad open windows. There are numerous parks and hilly streets throughout the city, having some of the first homes built in the Americas. On August 15, 1810, the Cathedral of *Nuestra Señora de la Asuncion* was founded in Santiago. World Heritage Sites in the area include the *San Pedro de la Roca del Morro* Castle and the World Heritage Biosphere Reserve in Baconao Park.

The weather is usually hot and humid with temperatures that remain stable in the high 80's Fahrenheit, dropping only about 10 degrees at night. An occasional hurricane can be expected during the summer and fall months. On October 25, 2012, Hurricane Sandy uprooted trees and damaged 130,000 homes, requiring massive amounts of reconstruction to the city.

Santiago is served by Antonio Maceo Airport, connecting it with the rest of Cuba and the Caribbean. It also has rail and bus service to Havana and the other major cities on the island. Tropicana and Seabourn Cruise ships presently visit the Port of Santiago de Cuba, as well as the Port of Havana.

"Santiago de Cuba is the island's second largest city and a glittering cultural capital in its own right. Anyone with even a passing interest in Cuban literature, music, architecture, politics or ethnology should spend at least a day or two kicking through the myriad of assorted attractions here." Lonely Planet

Historical Santa Clara

Santa Clara is the fifth largest city in Cuba with a population of over 210,000 people. It is the capital of the Province of Villa Clara and was founded by 138 people from only two families on July 15, 1689. As with many Cuban cities during the 17th century, it was constantly attacked and plundered by pirates. Santa Clara has had a number of names since it was founded. Its layout is clearly that of Colonial Spanish origin, having a squared design with a plaza and a church in the center. It is conveniently located along the highway connecting Santiago de Cuba with Havana.

Santa Clara is known as the site of the last battle of the Cuban Revolution. Two columns of rebels attacked the Batista forces on December 31, 1958. One was led by "Che" Guevara and the other by Camilo Cienfuegos. Guevara's troops destroyed the

Trans-Cuban railroad tracks and overturned a train sent by Batista carrying reinforcements. The victory over the city's demoralized defenders was decisive, forcing Batista to leave Cuba and fly to the Dominican Republic. Fleeing into exile, Batista opened the way for the rebel troops to take the capital city of Havana.

In 1987, to commemorate the 20th Anniversary of "Che's" death in Bolivia, a complex of remembrance was constructed at Reparto Raul Sancho, Avenida Liberación, Santa Clara. It is situated on a rolling hilltop overlooking the municipality of Santa Clara and consists of a large tiled plaza with a monumental 20-foot high statue of Guevara made of bronze standing on a pedestal of granite. The statue of "Che" faces south towards Argentina, the place of his birth. The impressive statue is surrounded by four stations with bas-reliefs, showing moments of "Che's" life. One of them is a replica of his farewell letter to Fidel Castro.

The Museum entrance is at the rear of the memorial. It contains Guevara's letters, personal items, his weapons and photos. Guevara is depicted as a guerrilla fighter during the Cuban Revolution, who rose in prominence among the insurgents and was promoted to second-in-command. As a Comandante, he is given credit for playing a pivotal role in the victorious two-year guerrilla campaign that deposed the Batista régime. "Che" is hailed as having been a Comandante in the militia as well as a respected Statesman and Cuban representative.

The Mausoleum was opened in 1997 and became the final resting place for "Che" Guevara and twenty-nine of his fellow comrades, including Haydée Tamara Bunke Bíder, killed while fighting in Bolivia. Inscribed at the base of the monument is his motto: "Hasta la Victoria Siempre," Until the Eternal Victory. Cameras are not allowed in the mausoleum.

The site can be visited Tuesday through Saturday from 9am to 5:30pm. On Sundays, the closing time is 5pm. For information the telephone number is +53 42 205878.

A statue of Marta Abreu stands on one of the corners of the *Parque Vidal* in the center of the city. She is considered Santa Clara's patron for having sponsored the *Teatro La Caridad*, which supports two schools that were also originally built by Marta. There is also a well-known center of dance, which preserves and teaches Cuban folk dances. The University Marta Abreu of Las Villas is a comprehensive school offering Bachelor's, Master's and Doctorate degrees in Engineering, Architecture, Medicine and Agriculture.

People of note from Santa Clara include Rubén González, a pianist; José Bernal, an artist; Moraime Secada, a singer; as well as numerous sports notables including Benny "the Kid" Paret, a boxer.

Camagüey – Looted and Burnt

Camagüey has a population of over 320,000 people and is the capital of Camagüey Province. The old city was designated a UNESCO World Heritage Site in July of 2008. Originally, it was located on the north coast of Cuba and known as *Santa María del Puerto del Príncipe*. At that time, it was constantly attacked by pirates, forcing the population to move inland, where the present city was established in 1528. After Henry Morgan looted and burned the city, it was purposely rebuilt with a maze of winding streets having dead ends and squares leading to only one exit, that only the residents knew existed. The purpose of this maze was to trap and capture the invading pirates.

A friend told me an amusing story that his father had told him... During the mid-1930's his father arrived in Camagüey, looking for work. Being single, he asked some of the locals where he could find a brothel with some "Fun Girls." After getting explicit directions, he started walking along the winding streets of the city, but the maze proved more confusing than he had expected. So, instead of finding the brothel, he wound up staring at the gates of the cemetery. I can only believe that he found the dead center of town!

Camagüey has its own international airport and is also on the direct railroad and bus line between Havana and Santiago de Cuba. Because of the extensive American sugar interests in the surrounding area, until 1959 Camagüey was the only city other than Havana that had a direct flight to Miami. This flight was operated by Pan American World Airways.

The city offers post High School education, including Technical and Military Institutions. It also sponsors the Cuban Major League Baseball Hall of Fame, which includes Atanasio Pérez Rigal who, while with the Cincinnati Reds, won two World Series titles and the 1967 All Star Game. Camagüey was also the home of Nicolás Guillén, a noted poet, and Carlos J. Finley, the physician who discovered the mosquito responsible for spreading Yellow Fever.

Holguín

Cuba's fourth largest city, Holguín was named after Captain García Holguín, a Spanish military officer. Founded in 1545, it is the capital of Holguín Province and has a population of almost 270,000 people. There are several parks and squares including *Parque Martí* and the San José church. It is home to the University of Holguín and has a brewery operated as a joint venture between the Cuban State and Labatt Breweries of Canada. Frank País Airport is named after the hero of the revolution who was murdered in Santiago de Cuba.

Although born in the northern tier of the Oriente Province on July 16, 1943, Reinaldo Arenas moved to Holguín at an early age with the intent of supporting the revolution. In 1963, he moved to Havana and enrolled in the School of Planification, after which he attended the *Universidad de La Habana*, where he majored in literature. As a poet, novelist and playwright his work was immediately recognized by the National Union of Cuban Writers and Artists. However, his overt gay lifestyle brought him into conflict with the powerful Communist régime. In 1992 his autobiography, *Before Night Falls*, was on *The New York Times* list of the ten best books. It was later made into a movie directed by Julian Schnabel staring Javier Bardem, Olivier Martinez, Johnny Deep and Héctor Babenco.

In 1980, as part of the Mariel boatlift, Arenas left Cuba for the United States, settling in New York City, with his friend and lover Lázaro Gómez Carriles. In 1987, Arenas was diagnosed with AIDS from which he died on December 7, 1990.

"With the changes I'm announcing today, it will be easier for Americans to travel to Cuba, and Americans will be able to use American credit and debit cards on the island. Nobody represents America's values better than the American people, and I believe this contact will ultimately do more to empower the Cuban people." President Barack Hussein Obama II, the 44th and current President of the United States, December 17, 2014

We're Keeping an Eye on You!
A Vintage Cuban Travel Poster

A Vintage Postcard

The Exciting Story of Cuba.... Part 19

Cuba's Infrastructure and Transportation

Cuba's Governmental Offices

This list of offices is constantly being changed, and is once again in a state of flux. However, this is the most recent information available from the official Cuban government site www.CubaGob.cu

A more complete index of Cuban documents and information on the Governmental Offices of Cuba can be found in "Cuba City Hall," maintained by Havana Journal, Inc., telephone (508) 744 6790.

When making telephone calls from the United States or Canada, first dial 011, which is the IDD or International Direct Dialing code. This is followed by the country code, which is 53 for Cuba. Next, dial the Area Code, which is, for instance, 7 for Havana and 322 for Camagüay. Finally, dial the 4- to 7-digit telephone number.

- Banco Central De Cuba – Central Bank of Cuba

- Cuban Civil Aviation Institute, Telephone: 33-4949 FAX: 334553, iacvc@avianet.cu

- Cuban Radio and Television Institute

- National Institute of Sports, Physical Education and Recreation
- National Hydraúlic Resources Institute
- Ministry of Agriculture, (537)884-5427, FAX: (537)881-2837
- Ministry of Auditing and Control
- Ministry of Basic Industry
- Ministry of Construction, despacho@micons.cu, FAX: 55-5303
- Ministry of Culture, atencion@min.cult.cu
- Ministry of Economy and Planning, Telephone: 881-8789, mep@ceniai.inf.cu
- Ministry of Education
- Ministry of Finance and Prices, sdinformacion@mfp.gov.cu
- Ministry of the Fishing Industry, Telephone: 209-7930209-7949, 209-7987, 209-7999, FAX: 204-9168, info@fishnavy.inf.cu
- Ministry of the Food Industry
- Ministry of Foreign Affairs
- Ministry of Foreign Investment and Economic Cooperation
- Ministry of Foreign Trade
- Ministry of Higher Education, develop@reduniv.edu.cu Telephone: 55-2314 ext. 29
- Ministry of Informatics and Communication, Telephone: 882-8151, 882-8162, rel_pubicas@mic.cu

- Industry of Iron and Mechanical, Telephone: (537)453911/452435, sime@sime.co.cu

- Ministry of Interior

- Ministry of Justice, minjus@minjus.cu

- Ministry of Labor and Social Security

- Ministry of Light Industry

- Ministry of Public Health

- Ministry of the Revolutionary Armed Forces

- Ministry of Science, Technology and the Environment

- Ministry of Sugar

- Ministry of Tourism

- Ministry of Transportation, Telephone: 55-5047

"You will never understand bureaucracies until you understand that for bureaucrats procedure is everything and outcomes are nothing." Thomas Sowell, economist, social theorist, political philosopher and author

Cuba's Transportation System

Being an island nation Cuba is dependent on ships and aircraft to connect it to the rest of the world. In the early colonial period, the transportation of goods relied on caravels, which were small craft with two or more masts, originally developed by the Portuguese as relatively fast merchant vessels. When carrying passengers, frigates were used, which were over 100 feet in length and about 35 feet wide. Frigates could carry approximately 150 people and were protected with heavy 18-pounder cannons on the main deck, and lighter cannons on the upper and spar decks. Sometimes these ships were referred to as "Treasure Frigates" since they would be used to carry gold and other valuables on their return to Spain. With hurricanes being prevalent in the Caribbean during the summer months and pirates always on the prowl, travel by sea was always plagued by risk. The larger ships were galleons and naos, which were usually merchant vessels with 4 or more masts and over 900 tons. During Spanish colonial rule, the crown maintained a tight control on Cuban commerce and only allowed direct trade with Spain. In time, some of this grip was relaxed but it was not until the Ten Years' War, followed by the Spanish-American War, that Cuba won its independence and could trade with whomever they wished.

Most of the industrial developments occurred during the late nineteenth century and the early twentieth century. Sugar and sugar products became the primary export with tobacco and tropical fruits close behind. Train tracks were laid, ports were developed and aviation came into its own. All of Cuba's industrial and technical imports, as well as agricultural exports, travel by sea or air. An understanding of Cuba's economic history, its international balance of trade, and the island's transportation of people and goods, gives us a better view of its potential.

Cuban Roads and Highways

At the time of the revolution, Cubans were earning close to the average income in the southern sector of the Unites States. The GDP was about half of that of European countries and close to one-third the average in the United States. It was certainly comparable to the highest income levels in Latin America, thus enabling the country to rapidly develop its transportation systems.

The Machado régime can be credited with the construction of the Central Highway, *La Carrentera Central*. Construction of the highway was started in May of 1927 for a total price of $75,870,000 or $107,000 per mile. Two contractors built a distance of over 700 miles of highway on a 20.66-foot wide concrete base. One of these contractors was Cuban and the other American. The surface was paved over with hot asphalt on top of uncompacted Bitulithic. The advantage of this method of construction was that the aggregate of the Bitulithic mixes was not exposed directly to heavy continuous use. Most of the expenses involved in the construction of this road were paid for by a gasoline tax imposed on American tourists who brought their cars across the Florida Straits by ferry. Although there are 37,815 miles of roads in Cuba, most of them are still unpaved.

Cuba has eight toll-free, high-speed highways. *Via Blanca*, or the White Road, links the distance of 86 miles from Havana to Matanzas and Varadero. It is one of the busiest highways in Cuba and includes the country's highest bridge, *El Puente de Bacunayagua*, at the Mayabeque–Matanzas Province border. Although the majority of the road is free, the distance between Matanzas and Varadero is a toll road. In all, Cuba has 569 miles of toll-free highways called *autopistas*, which have a maximum speed limit of about 87 mph. There is also a network of two lane State Highways named *Carreteras*. In general the traffic on these roads is light and they are in reasonably good condition, but there are some potholes near congested areas. However, the maintenance on the open roadways is generally acceptable.

The cars held over from before the revolution are called "Yank Tanks" or *máquinas*. They could only be sold for private use if they have the proper paperwork called "*traspaso*" and had the proper license plates and registration. Laws passed in December of 2013 have finally allowed Cubans to buy and sell cars from each other without government interference. This however also ends the privilege of a select few to profit by bringing in cars and trucks. They must, however, still get government approval to purchase new vehicles. The laws were such that a system of speculation and personal enrichment was in effect, enabling favored individuals to resell newer models for five or six times their original value. The state has now made it easier to buy and sell cars, hoping to eliminate this corruption. There are however still high taxes involved in the sale of vehicles, which have been earmarked to help renew the present rundown public transportation system.

State-owned car rentals are available to tourists at most airports. This mode of transportation is advised if traveling to remote parts of Cuba, especially in the eastern provinces. Most credit cards are accepted, however individual transportation on the popular Viazul bus system is a less expensive option.

"The reason the Romans built their great paved highways was because they had such inconvenient footwear." Charles de Montesquieu, a French social commentator and political thinker of the early 18th century

Cuba's Railroad System

The National Railroad Company of Cuba, known as *Ferrocarriles Nacionales de Cuba*, had its start as *Compania de Camino de Hierro de La Habana* in October 1834, when the Queen Regent of Spain María Cristina approved the construction of the first rail line connecting Bejucal with Havana. Although it was only 17 miles, it was a start that Spain had yet to make. Five years later the tracks were extended to the city of Güines, which is 30 miles southeast of Havana, and soon it spread out to include the cities of San Felipe and then Batabanó on the southern side of the island facing the Caribbean. Ten years later in 1859, Havana had its first street car system. With the help of Sir William Van Horne, a Canadian railroad builder, the Cuban rail system grew to become the largest in tracks per square mile.

The Hershey Railway was founded in 1917 by the Hershey Chocolate Company to transport sugar to the docks in Havana. It was also known as the Hershey Electric Railway and is a standard-gauge electric system that runs from the suburbs of Havana to the town of Matanzas, approximately 57 miles to the east. Presently it runs about four trains per day. However, it now is a part of the nationalized rail system. Eventually other railway companies were founded, but all were merged with the National Railroad Company. During the Batista régime, the Cuban Railroad Company linked in with the United States railroad system via a train ferry service between Havana and Miami.

Four-car, self-propelled, Budd railcars presently connect Santiago de Cuba with Havana on the Central line. The flagship of the system is a 12-coach train originally used between Paris and Amsterdam. Although buses competed with the railroad, they all became nationalized after the revolution. Attempting to prevent the decay of the Cuban system, British Rail helped during the 1960's by supplying new locomotives. However, this slowed and eventually came to a halt after the Bay of Pigs Invasion and the Cuban Missile Crisis. Eastern Bloc and countries that continued to be friendly with Cuba, such as Canada, Spain and Mexico, took over. During the past decade China, Iran and Venezuela became Cuba's primary benefactors and suppliers. Cuba has had long-range plans to update and modernize its railroad system. These plans are presently being realized and the upgrading and modernizing of the country's

26,000 miles of track and replacing older locomotives, including some steam engines, with powerful and modern diesel-fueled locomotives are becoming a reality.

"As a child I found railroad stations exciting, mysterious, and even beautiful, as indeed they often were." Paul Johnson, an English journalist, historian, and author

History of Airports in Cuba

Cuba's history of aviation dates back to the presidential administration of Mario García Menocal, who was a strong supporter of business. During Menocal's second term in office, and with Cuba, at the time, becoming involved in World War I, the concept of constructing an airport near Havana became a reality.

In 1919, having a safe elevation of about 98 feet above sea level, Havana's Columbia Airport (MULB) opened for traffic. It was located approximately 15 miles west of the city center, next to the beach in the borough of Playa. The Columbia Airport was formally known as *Aeropuerto de Columbia* and was part of the *Base Militar de Columbia*. The Columbia airport has since been renamed as the *Ciudad Libertad* Airport. The Columbia airport was Cuba's main airport until 1930, when it became secondary to the new José Martí International Airport (MUHA).

Whereas the Columbia Airport was once exclusively for the military, during the mid-1950's two airlines, "*Aerovías* Q" and "*Cuba Aeropostal,*" operated there until the Castro takeover in 1959. These two airlines had been owned in part by Batista and by people of high privilege in his administration.

The *Ciudad Libertad* Airport is now home to Cuba's Air Defense Command, and continues to be operated as a government, executive transportation facility. *Ciudad Libertad* Airport is presently used by both the military and for general aviation.

In March of 1929, commercial aviation came to Cuba when the *Aeropuerto de Rancho-Boyeros*, or the Rancho-Boyeros Airport, located 9 miles southwest of Havana, was built as an alternate to the smaller Columbia Airport. It started operations in February of 1930, at which time it became Havana's primary airport. In January of 1943, this airport had the first control tower in Cuba. In the 1950's its name was changed to the José Martí International Airport (MUHA).

On April 15, 1961, the airport was said to be bombed by B-26 aircraft from Brigade 2506. However, it is on good authority that the only airports attacked by the insurgents with ties to the CIA were the *Ciudad Libertad* Airport in Havana, the main Cuban Air Force Base at San Antonio, *San Antonio de los Baños Airfield* (MUSA), and Antonio Maceo Airport (MUCU/SCU) in Santiago de Cuba.

There are currently four passenger terminals in use at José Martí International Airport, plus a freight terminal. Although there are many American charter flights to Havana, next to *Cubana*, the Cuban national carrier, Copa Airlines is the most active foreign company using the airport. As a Panamanian-owned carrier, Copa operates 34 flights a week to Havana from Panama City and Bogotá. The airport is operated by *Empresa Cubana de Aeropuertos y Servicios Aeronáuticos*, which is a Cuban government-owned cooperation that operates 22 airports in the country. It almost goes without saying that Cubans are not allowed to own aircraft, or use the airport for either private or commercial flights. Only government-owned or foreign-owned aircraft are allowed to use the airport or the ground facilities.

There are other major airports in Cuba, including Ignacio Agramonte International Airport (MUCM), which serves the central Camagüey Province. From April 13, 1942, until August 1944, this site was used by the United States as a military airfield. During World War II it housed the 417th Bomber Squadron, which flew Douglas-built B-18 Bolo Bombers, on anti-submarine missions over the northern Caribbean. The base also had the 1st Rescue Squadron, as an air-sea rescue support group. Ignacio Agramonte International Airport is also an inactive Cuban Revolutionary Armed Forces air base.

There is also Carlos Manuel de Céspedes Airport (MUBY), a regional airport serving the city of Bayamo, in the Granma Province of Cuba.

Santiago de Cuba has the Antonio Maceo Airport (MUCU/SCU), which was home to the Cuban Revolutionary Armed Forces. The airport is essentially a turboprop hub, however it can also accommodate mid-sized jet aircraft. There are about twenty international flights each week, but most arrivals are by domestic airlines. The eastern location and the international status of MUCU/SCU has spurred the interest of foreign airlines as a promising future destination.

All in all, Cuba now has ten international airports, capable of serving long-range flights.

There are also five military airbases on the island, one of which is used by the United States Navy. Leeward Point Field NBW, also known as Leeward Airfield, at Guantánamo Bay (MUGM) or *Bahía de Guantánamo*, is owned by the U.S. Government and has restricted arrivals.

Curtiss Aviation

Glenn Hammond Curtiss was a bicycle enthusiast before he started building motorcycles. Although he only attended grammar school to the 8th grade, his interests motivated him to move on to greater things. In 1904, as a self-taught engineer, he began to manufacture engines for airships. During this time, Curtiss became known for having won a number of international air races and for making the first long-distance flight in the United States. On September 30, 1907, Curtiss was invited to join a non-profit pioneering research program named the "Aerial Experimental Association," founded under the leadership of Dr. Alexander Graham Bell, to develop flying machines. The organization was established having a fixed time period, which ended in March of 1909. During this time, the members produced several different aircraft in a cooperative, rather than a competitive, spirit.

In 1910 Curtiss started the Curtiss Aeroplane Company of Hammondsport, New York, which later in the year he named the Curtiss Motor Company. That same year he took on the Burgess Company of Marblehead, Massachusetts, as a subsidiary.

On January 12, 1912, Curtiss developed a utility flying boat that he sold to the U.S., Russian and Italian navies. The following year he designated these as the Model F series aircraft, some having transatlantic capabilities. The first Model F saw service with the United States Navy, having the designations C-2 through C-5. These aircraft were later reclassified to AB-2 through AB-5. In October of 1913, Curtiss met John Cyril Porte, a British pioneer in aviation who shared his interest in flying boats and helped design the improved Model F-5-L flying boat. These aircraft became known as "Seagulls" in the postwar civilian market.

In January of 1916, Curtiss brought his holdings together under the name "Curtiss Aeroplane and Motor Company." During World War I the company built aircraft for the U.S. Army and Navy. With military orders rapidly increasing, the Curtiss' manufacturing facilities needed to expand, thus he moved his company to Buffalo, New York. It was here that Curtiss helped the U.S. Navy advance naval aviation by providing flying boats that did not depend on land-based runways. Curtiss also founded flying schools in competition with the Wright Schools of Aviation. In 1912 he opened the first one in San Diego, California, and two years later, one in Miami, Florida. In the next few years, other Curtiss flying schools were opened in Hammondsport, New York, Newport News, Virginia, and Toronto, Canada. These schools played an important part in the training of pilots in the U.S. Military, along with civilian pilots from Canada, Cuba, Italy and Russia.

The Curtiss Company helped create the training and groundwork necessary for the Cuban military and the emergence of a Cuban Airline.

Agustín Parlá, Father of Cuban Aviation

Agustín Parlá Orduña was among the early Cuban aviation aces. He was born in Key West, Florida, on October 10, 1887, and received his early education there. After Cuba was liberated from Spain, the family returned to Havana, where he continued his education. On April 20, 1912, he received his pilot's license at the Curtiss School of Aviation in Miami. On July 5, 1913, when the Cuban Army Air Corps was formed, Agustín Parlá was commissioned as a captain in the Cuban Armed Forces.

On May 17, 1913, Domingo Rosillo and Agustín Parlá attempted the first international flights to Latin America, by trying to fly their airplanes from Key West to Havana. At 5:10 a.m., Rosillo departed from Key West and flew for 2 hours, 30 minutes and 40 seconds before running out of gas. He had planned to land at the airfield at Camp Columbia in Havana, but instead managed to squeak in at the shooting range, thereby still satisfactorily completing the flight.

Parlá left Key West at 5:57 in the morning. Just four minutes later, at 6:01 a.m., he had to carefully turn back to the airstrip he had just left, since the aircraft didn't properly respond to his controls. Parlá said, "It would not let me compensate for the wind that blew." When he returned to Key West, he discovered that two of the tension wires to the elevator were broken.

On May 19, 1913, Parlá tried again and left Key West, carrying the Cuban Flag his father had received from José Martí. This time he fell short and had to land at sea off the Cuban coast near Mariel, where sailors rescued him from his seaplane.

Being adventuresome, while attending the Curtiss School of Aviation in 1916, Parlá flew over Niagara Falls. In his honor, the Cuban flag was hoisted and the Cuban national anthem was played. The famous Cuban composer, pianist, and bandleader, Antonio M. Romeu, composed a song in his honor named "*Parlá over the Niagara.*" Agustín Parlá became known as the "Father of Cuban Aviation." However, in August of 1918, Parlá resigned from the Army.

In 1919, Parlá, being one of the founders of *Compañía Aérea Cubana*, was appointed its manager. On May 29, 1919, he and the American pilot Johnny Green flew a Curtiss flying boat, the "Sunshine," on the first commercial flight from Havana to Key West. Then on May 7, 1920, Parlá became the first person to fly over Havana by night. The following August, he was commissioned "Chief of Instructors" in the newly formed Cuban Army Air Corps.

In 1921, due to a downturn in the economy, the company foundered and went out of business. Because of name recognition and close ties with financial backers, the Curtiss Aircraft Manufacturing Company started the "*Compañía Nacional Cubana de Aviación Curtiss*," at first as a charter carrier and a flying school. This company became the forerunner of the Cuban airline "*Cubana de Aviación S.A.*" For years, many Cuban's simply called the airline "Curtiss."

Remembering history, on July 4, 1957, a bust in Agustín Parlá's likeness was dedicated at the Key West International Airport (EYW), commemorating his achievements. Some of the memorabilia of his achievements can be seen at the San Carlos Museum in Key West.

The Early Years of *Cubana de Aviación S.A.*

Cubana de Aviación S.A., Cuba's international airline, was founded on October 8, 1929, as one of the first airlines to be established in Latin America. It was a founder, and is still a member, of the International Air Transport Association. Although other airlines were started in Cuba during that same era, they only existed for a relatively short time, primarily because of the Great Depression. *Cubana's* first airplane was a Curtiss Robin C-1, followed by Ford Trimotors and Sikorsky S-38 seaplanes. *Cubana de Aviación's* first flight was from Havana to Santiago de Cuba via Santa Clara, Moron and Camagüey, thereby starting the country's airmail service.

It was in 1932 that Pan American Airways (PAA) acquired *Cubana Curtiss* and was responsible for dropping *Curtiss* from the name and changing it to *Compañía Cubana de Aviación S.A.*, known to all as just *"Cubana."* Lockheed Model 10 Electras were purchased in 1934, allowing *Cubana* to extend its domestic routes. Ten years later in 1944, 58% of the airline was sold to Cuban investors with Pan American Airways still holding a narrow controlling 42% stake. In the years that followed, *Cubana* inaugurated scheduled flights to Port-au-Prince, Haiti and Spain. In 1954, the airline became fully Cuban-owned when Pan American Airways sold its remaining shares.

Antonio Menéndez Peláez's Flight to Spain

On January 9, 1936, Captain Antonio Menéndez Peláez flew a wood and fabric Lockheed 8A Sirius aircraft, with an open cockpit. Owned by the Cuban Navy, it was named the "4th of September" in reference to the "Revolt of the Sergeants," started by Fulgencio Batista on September 4, 1933. Menéndez flew the aircraft on the first 2-hour, 309-mile leg, from Havana to Camagüey, Cuba. The airplane had a 550 HP engine, giving it a cruising speed of 180 mph. It was fitted out with larger fuel tanks and at the same time, some of the superfluous equipment was removed to lighten the load.

From Camagüey he flew across the Caribbean Sea to Caracas, Venezuela. Then flying east along the northern coast of South America, he landed in French Guiana, with its notorious penal colony *Île du Diable* or "Devil's Island." It is now the site of the European Space Agency's activities, founded in 1964 by French President Charles de Gaulle. Captain Menéndez then continued over the treacherous Amazon, before making a few more stops at coastal cities in Brazil: Belém, São Luís and

Fortaleza, known for their old colonial buildings and cobblestone streets. The beaches along this northeastern coast of Brazil are spectacular and the Atlantic waters are always warm. Having a constant and pleasant breeze, this coastline presented excellent conditions for flying. Although São Luís was originally founded by the French in 1612, and occupied by the Dutch, São Luís remains predominately Portuguese in appearance. The buildings with beautiful *azulejo* tiled walls and the cobblestone streets of its well-preserved historic center, have been listed as a "World Heritage Site" by UNESCO.

Captain Menéndez reached Natal, Brazil on February 2, 1916, 585 years after Amerigo Vespucci discovered this part of South America. In the mid-16th Century, French pirates led by Jacques Riffault, started trading with the local Indians. The 9th Portuguese Governor-General of Brazil Francisco de Sousa, who took part in military expeditions in North Africa where he fought the Moors, now expelled the French buccaneers from Brazil. He didn't do this out of the goodness of his heart, rather he did it because he was really a slave merchant, who also traded in commodities such as palm oil and gold. Known for his extravagant hedonism, he had at least 80 children with the many women he kept in his harem. De Sousa wanted to retain the local market for himself, as he continued to market slaves even after the trade in human traffic became illegal.

Waiting for better weather, Menéndez remained in Natal, the capital city of Rio Grande do Norte, a state of Brazil, for a week. Although the weather at the time was far from perfect, he grew anxious to continue on his epic journey. Calculating his probable arrival time, he took off in the middle of the night for the dangerous trans-Atlantic leg. The first three hours were worse than he had anticipated as he flew through a blinding rainstorm, before encountering better conditions. After 1,964 miles across the Atlantic Ocean, he landed at an airstrip in Bathurst, Gambia, now known as Banjul, located just south of Dakar the capital of Senegal. In his flight north, he encountered a sand storm as he crossed into the Spanish Sahara, forcing him to land at Villa Bens, in the colony of Cabo Juby, now known as the Tarfaya Province of Morocco. His last leg north was to the Tablada airfield in Seville, Spain, bringing the 7,833-mile flight to a historic conclusion. He was hailed a hero, as the people of many Spanish cities celebrated his brilliant feat. The Principality of Asturias, the region of his birth, was especially proud and welcomed Captain Antonio Menéndez with a parade in his honor.

On April 27, 1933, he embarked on the S/S *Cristóbal Colon* in Santander, Spain for the transatlantic voyage to Havana, where he was again received as a hero. With this flight, Captain Antonio Menéndez Peláez became the first Hispanic aviator to fly from America to Europe. The first to cross the North Atlantic on a solo non-stop flight was Charles Lindbergh, who took off on May 20, 1927, from Roosevelt Field, on New York's Long Island. He landed the next day at Le Bourget Field, in Paris, France, covering a distance of nearly 3,600 miles. Their flights opened trans-Atlantic aviation to the airlines, which rapidly developed scheduled routes across the ocean.

On October 25, 1936, the S/S *Cristóbal Colon*, which was built in 1923, ran aground on a northern reef of Bermuda and now is scattered across 100,000 square feet of ocean floor, lying in 55 feet of water where she has become an artificial reef for fish. The *Cristóbal Colon* is unique as being one of the few ships that was built with rectangular portholes.

"Aviation is proof that, given the will, we have the capacity to achieve the impossible."   Eddie

Rickenbacker, American Medal of Honor recipient and a fighter ace in World War I

Compañía Cubana de Aviación after World War II

The first *Cubana* international commercial flight after World War II was in 1945 when a *Cubana* DC-3 flew from Havana to Miami. By 1948 the "Route of the Stars" from Havana to Madrid was inaugurated using the newer and larger DC-4. Later, for a limited time this route was extended to Rome.

Right after World War II *Cubana's* inventory included six DC-3's and two DC-4's. Both of the original DC-4's crashed, but were quickly replaced.

In the early 1950's, *Cubana* purchased several Lockheed Super Constellations L-1049E and L-1049G from the United States and 3 turboprop Vickers Viscount VV-755 aircraft from Britain, updating its fleet.

By March of 1953, *Cubana* had 11 aircraft, with more on order. In 1953, still controlled by Pan American, *Cubana* augmented its fleet with three Super Constellations, expanding its operations to Mexico, the Caribbean and Latin America.

In 1954 when Pan American sold the last of its shares, *Cubana* was on its own. At the time, *Cubana* sold some of the C-46's, thereby removing them from their inventory. With Mexico City added to their routes, the now entirely Cuban-owned airline bought two long range Bristol Britannia 318's and four Vickers Super Viscount turboprop aircraft VV-818, to accommodate its expansion.

By 1956, the first of three Viscount 755's arrived in Cuba. In 1958 one crashed as a result of a botched hijacking and two were then sold. Later, in 1958, *Cubana* took delivery of its first Bristol Britannia CU-T668, providing faster more competitive turboprop flights to Cuba from New York City.

Prior to the Revolution, *Cubana* became the first Latin American airline to fly only turboprop aircraft on all of its international routes. *Cubana* became the most experienced Latin American Airline, flying modern American Super Constellations and British-built turboprop aircraft.

Aerovías Q

During the Grau Presidency, *Aerovías* Q was founded by Colonel Manuel Quevedo and a few of his choice friends, with $1,110,000 backing him. From the time it was founded in 1945, *Aerovías* Q operated from the *Ciudad Libertad* Airport, which at the time was the Camp Columbia Airfield. In September of 1946, *Aerovías* Q scheduled flights using DC-3's and some Curtiss C-46's, to Key West and West Palm Beach.

After taking over the presidency on March 10, 1952, Batista took a keen interest in the airline, as did the Mafia. With his backing, *Aerovías* Q felt free to use fuel, parts, staff and pilots from the Cuban Air Force. Although it was never proven, it was rumored that drugs, including cocaine, were clandestinely transported by the airline.

"Aviation is the branch of engineering that is least forgiving of mistakes." Freeman Dyson, theoretical physicist and mathematician

Vintage Airline Poster

Aerovías Cuba Internacional

Aerovías Cuba Internacional was a small, separately owned airline, sometimes confused with *Aerovías* Q or *Cubana*. Two months after its origin, the company attempted to expand its flights to Spain, naming it the "Route of Columbus," *Ruta de Colón.*

The Cuban-owned four-engine DC-4 carried the American registration N44567 and required five people in the cockpit to fly it. Flying the shared Havana-Madrid route, it crashed on February 6, 1947, at an altitude of 4,593 feet in the "Sierra de Gredos," a mountain range in central Spain that is located in the Province of Ávila, approximately 100 miles west of Madrid. All 12 people aboard were instantly killed. It was shortly thereafter that *Aerovías Cuba Internacional* went out of business.

Cuba Aeropostal

On August 16, 1948, *Cuba Aeropostal* was founded with $400,000 in start-up capital. It started flying cargo and mail flights with six airplanes, including war surplus C-47's and a Curtiss C-46, which was rated as a high altitude transport aircraft. The company began operations on May 3, 1949, flying from Camp Columbia military field on routes between Havana and Miami, as well as New Gerona, *Nueva Gerona*, on the Isle of Pines, *Isla de Pinos.*

The Cuban Ministry of Defense operates *Aerogaviota*, the newest airline in Cuba and flies from *Playa Baracoa Airport*, 26 miles southwest of Havana. It operates scheduled flights domestically, and to nearby islands including Jamaica.

Terrorists and Tourism

During the post-war years as tourism grew in Cuba, so did *Cubana*, and as a marketing tool they offered packages which included the flight from Miami to Havana, a hotel room and ground transportation. Flying modern aircraft, its international service included Madrid, Mexico City, Nassau, Port-au-Prince, as well as Miami and New York in the United States. Had there not been a revolution spreading throughout Cuba, things would have been much different. However revolutionary activists were intent on bringing the Batista régime down. The world finally took notice that a revolution was taking place on the Island. Ft. Lauderdale was just being introduced into *Aerovías* Q's flight schedule, when Fidel Castro overthrew the Batista régime.

Cuban Aircraft are Seized

During the early 1960's Erwin Harris sought to collect $429,000 in unpaid bills from the Cuban government, for an advertising campaign promoting Cuban tourism. Holding a court order from a judge and accompanied by local sheriff's deputies, he searched the East Coast of the United States for Cuban property. In September 1960, while Fidel was at the United Nations on an official visit, Harris found the Britannia that Castro had flown in to New York. That day the front page of *The Daily News* headlined, "Cuban Airliner Seized Here."

Erwin Harris continued by seizing a C-46, which was originally owned by *Cuba Aeropostal* and was now owned by *Cubana*, as well as other cargo airplanes. He seized a Cuban Naval vessel, plus 1.2 million Cuban cigars that were brought into Tampa, Florida, by ship. In Key West, Harris also confiscated railroad cars carrying 3.5 million pounds of cooking lard destined for

Havana. All of these things, excepting the Britannia, were sold at auction.

Nikita S. Khrushchev, the Soviet premier, replaced the airplane that had been confiscated. On September 28th, Castro boarded the Soviet aircraft at Idlewild Airport smiling, most likely because he knew that his Britannia airplane would be returned to Cuba due to diplomatic immunity.

Cuban Aviation after the Revolution

After January 1, 1959, the Castro Revolution changed the way business was done in Cuba. Abruptly, supplies for *Cubana* were no longer available, most routes were altered or suspended, and many of the pilots deserted their jobs or were exiled. In May of 1960, the new Castro administration merged all of the existing Cuban airlines and nationalized them under a drastically restructured *Cubana* management. At the time, many of *Cubana's* experienced personnel took advantage of their foreign connections, and left for employment with other airlines.

During the Bay of Pigs Invasion in April of 1961, two of the remaining *Cubana* DC-3's were destroyed in the selective bombing of Cuba's airports. Actually the only civil aviation airport that was proven to be bombed was the Antonio Maceo Airport in Santiago de Cuba.

During the following years, the number of hijackings increased and some aircraft were abandoned at American airports, as the flight crews sought asylum in the United States. This corporate instability, as well as political unrest, resulted in a drastic reduction of passengers willing to fly with *Cubana*. Of course, this resulted in a severe reduction in revenue, making the airline less competitive. The Castro régime reacted by blaming the CIA for many of *Cubana's* problems. However, slowly, except to the United States, most of the scheduled flights were restored. Not being able to replace their aging fleet with American manufactured aircraft, they turned to the Soviet Union.

Currently *Cubana's* fleet includes Ukrainian designed and built Antonov An-148's and An-158's. The *Cubana* fleet also has Soviet designed and built Illyushin Il-96's and Tupolev TU-204's built in Kazan, Russia. Despite daunting difficulties, primarily due to the United States' imposed embargo and the lack of sufficient assistance from Canada, efforts to expand and improve operations during the 1990's proved successful.

"*AeroCaribbean*" originally named "*Empresa Aero*" was established in 1982 to serve as Cuba's domestic airline. It also supported *Cubana's* operations and undertook its maintenance. Today *Cubana's* scheduled service includes many Caribbean, European, South and Central American destinations. In North America, the airline flies to Mexico and Canada.

With Cuban tourism increasing, *Cubana* has positioned itself to be relatively competitive. However much depends on Cuba's future relations with the United States. The embargo imposed in February of 1962 continues and is the longest on record. However, *Cubana* has continued to expand, helping to make Cuba one of the most important tourist destinations in Latin America.

The little known fact is that although *Cubana*, as expected, is wholly owned by the Cuban government, the other Cuban airlines are technically not. Instead, they are held, operated and maintained by the Cuban military, having been created by Raúl Castro during his tenure as the Minister of the Revolutionary Armed Forces.

"What the history of aviation has brought in the 20th century should inspire us to be inventors and explorers ourselves in the new century."   Bertrand Piccard, a Swiss psychiatrist and balloonist who was the first to fly a balloon around the world

The History of Agriculture and Industry

Although sugar cane was grown in Cuba prior to 1760, the Spanish trade regulations prevented the Cuban growers from trading with foreign countries. Sugar was labor intensive and Spain prevented Cuba from having access to the slave market unless they paid the crown an exorbitant 20% fee. Although this fee was originally intended to insure a 20% income from the slaves brought in to work the lucrative gold mines, it was applied to all slaves who came into the country. The turning point came on July 30, 1762, when the British invaded Havana during the Seven Years' War. It freed the planters from the high tariffs, and allowed them to bring in thousands of slaves without having to pay the charges formerly imposed by the Spanish crown. Since the British occupation lasted for less than a year, these benefits to the planters were limited.

The Haitian Revolution, otherwise known as the Haitian Slave Rebellion, forced many of the French population in Haiti to flee to Cuba. At the time, the country was named Saint-Domingue, under the rule of the French. Now renamed Haiti, it is an independent country, but at the time its sugar production suffered from the mass exodus and the Haitian economy drastically declined. It was in 1793 that the first of 30,000 white refugees fled from Haiti to Cuba, bringing with them their knowledge of sugar refinement. Soon the coffee industry followed, bringing with it additional slaves. From that time on, the coffee and sugar industries grew and Cuba soon took the world's lead in the production of sugar. Slavery was accepted with mixed emotions, and although the profits made from sugar were welcome, the concept was abhorrent. It was not until 1886 that slavery was finally abolished.

When the Planters fled from Haiti, they established coffee farms or *cafetales*, as part of their newly formed Plantation. Generally, coffee profits were about 5%, whereas sugar gave them a 10% return, but much was dependent on the economy and local conditions. *Cafetales* were easier to start and with as little as 10 slaves, a planter could begin his enterprise. Most of the French plantation owners took great pride in their holdings and beautified their plantations with magnificent palms lining grand entryways and spectacular wrought iron gates. The eastern end of Cuba was still available for development and many big plantations started in this modest way, but eventually the coffee plants were replaced with sugar cane due to the greater profit margin. Though blamed by many as the sole cause for the decline of Cuba's coffee industry, the U.S. Import Tariff of 1835 was only partially to blame for the fall in coffee production.

From the beginning, the prices of sugar fluctuated and prevented the Cuban economy from ever becoming stable. The first time was when the prices reached a high, during the Peace of Amiens in 1802. The treaty only survived for a year and shortly thereafter prices plunged, when the supply exceeded demand. During the French Revolution and the Napoleonic Wars, the price of sugar soared again, until the British conquest of Martinique and Guadeloupe brought the price tumbling down. The following year during the War of 1812 prices rose again, and by 1814 they reached another all-time high. This continued into modern times, creating a feast or famine economy.

New technology helped with production and much of the profits went into developing Cuba's infrastructure. Railroads were constructed during the turn of the twentieth century and allowed faster shipment of perishable commodities. With sugar being processed within a few days of being harvested, crystallized sucrose sugar was easier and faster to produce, thus preventing it from degrading into a less recoverable product. During the 1920's under Machado's administration, port facilities, as well as the trans-Cuba highway were built.

In 1914, at the beginning of World War I the demand for sugar escalated, encouraging the formation of American sugar cartels that burned and destroyed virgin forests in order to create agricultural land. In 1920, shortly after the War, the economic bubble that had formed burst, creating a sudden crash in sugar prices. Until the Cuban revolution in 1959, American corporations owned the majority of the Cuban sugar industry, and the United States imported a third of its sugar from the island nation, thus tying Cuba's economy to the economy of the United States. During World War II and in the two years following hostilities, the price of sugar in Cuba skyrocketed from 4 cents a pound to over 20 cents a pound. It was a bubble that could not be sustained, and as competition increased, the prices fell back to their pre-war levels. During the late 1940's the United States agreed on fixed prices and the number of tons per year to stabilize the cost of sugar. This was known as the "Cuban Sugar Quota.". By the 1950's, statistics confirm that the general economy was growing in great part due to the tourist industry established by Batista and the Mafia. The relative impact on the economy by sugar prices was therefore waning. After the revolution, the sugar treaties Cuba signed with the

Soviet Bloc countries, prevented Cuba from being able to compete on the open market, thus bringing their production down to 40% of their pre-revolution levels.

Pinar del Rio, the far western province of Cuba, is where most of the tobacco farms are located. Between 1830 and 1850 the export of tobacco products to Europe and Britain increased three-fold. Cuba exported tobacco products to Spain during the colonial period, however, the concept of tobacco as a product that could be freely traded did not occur until after Cuban independence in 1898. In the following years, production stabilized, making Cuba the second largest producer of tobacco. Cuban cigars became famous and in demand worldwide. Nearly all of the cigars are for the export market, which now accounts for a third of Cuba's income.

Cuba has always grown citrus for their domestic market. In 1991, Cuba invited foreign investors to start citrus groves. Israel came in and developed the market, using the name *Cubanita* for the European export market. Approximately one-third of their harvest is grapefruits and two-thirds is oranges.

Other agricultural products grown for the domestic and export market include potatoes, cassava, rice, and cotton, although sometimes even these staples have to be imported to supplement Cuba's domestic production.

After the revolution in 1959, it took some time for Castro to nationalize all the industries, businesses and corporations in Cuba. By 1968, the great majority of agriculture and industry had been taken over by the government. Cuba had over 150 sugar mills in the mid-1990's, with most of the machinery for the mills coming from the Soviet Union. In recent years with the Russian economy suffering and their buying power diminished, sugar prices fell and many of the sugar mills were forced to close.

Other domestic products consist of dairy products, preserved fruits and vegetables, flour, pasta, rum and soft drinks. Manufactured goods include textiles, shoes, petroleum and biochemical products, chemicals, cement and cardboard boxes. Antillana de Acero, the Cuban iron and steel company located in Havana, has recently installed new equipment to increase its production.

The Cuban economy has been improving with an increase in tourism, which has taken first place ahead of the sugar industry. Many of the newer resorts are subsidiaries of Canadian and Spanish companies. A persistent problem Cuba has had is that since the 1960's, trained people were replaced by political appointees. Competition, rather than a top-down controlled economy by the communist state, is promoting new growth. Presently there is a noticeable shift away from this dogmatic approach, as Cuba looks to China as a model for their new semi-capitalistic approach.

Cuba's Threatened Agricultural Balance

Understanding how the people thought and lived in Cuba, especially in the eastern Oriente Province, was essential to the success of Castro's campaign. Fidel's older brother, Ramón Eusebio Castro Ruz, was the quartermaster in charge of procuring food and supplies. Although he was not an active member of the rebel forces, he was interested in agriculture and understood the needs involved in feeding an army, which later helped to make the nation relatively self-sufficient.

As the U.S. trade embargo is lifted, it may become a threat to Cuba's ecosystem and wildlife. Some predict that the end of the embargo will have distressing results for the agricultural balance. Tourism and other industries are certain to affect the economic and agricultural development, and could change what was once a nearly pristine bio-network. On the other hand, if handled correctly, Cuba could become an example for the world to follow, by the considered development and conservation of its natural resources.

Commercial Agriculture

In Cuba sugar cane is still the most important commercial crop, followed by root plants such as cassava. Their famous tobacco, native to the island, is internationally known for its robust flavor, fuller body, and spicy aromas. It is extremely difficult to grow anywhere else, although some varieties are now grown with reasonable success in the Dominican Republic and Nicaragua. Nat Sherman in his 1996 primer "*A Passion for Cigars*" stated that the cigars coming out of Honduras, Mexico and the Dominican Republic today are superior to Cuban cigars. Obviously, many cigar aficionados are prepared to dispute this.

H. Upmann Cuban Cigars

"When you concentrate on agriculture and industry and are frugal in expenditures, Heaven cannot impoverish your state." *Xunzi, a Chinese Confucian philosopher*

Animals found in Cuba's Wilderness

The Trogon is Cuba's national bird. Hutias or *Jutias*, hawks, cuckoos, boas, finches, bees, hummingbirds, parakeets, kites, bulldog bats, solenodons, mongooses, pallid bats, crocodiles, ground iguanas and the Cuban Finch are among the many native animals. Cuba has seven species of snakes of which the threatened Cuban Boa, sometimes known as a Tree Boa, is the largest. Although it spends a lot of its time up in trees, it can also be found in woodlands or rocky habitats.

El Almiquí, a Cuban solenodon, is a rare, long-nosed animal with small eyes, and dark brown or black fur. The Cuban solenodon is sometimes compared to a shrew, although it more closely resembles members of the Tenrecidae family of Madagascar. It is from 16 to 22 inches long, from nose to tail-tip, and looks like a large brown rat with an extremely elongated snout and a long hairless tail. The German naturalist Wilhelm Peters first discovered the animal in 1861. Its saliva is venomous and only 36 have ever been caught. For years, it was thought to be extinct, since none had been found since 1890. Three were captured in the mid 1970's, and ensuing studies showed that although rare, they still exist in the eastern end of Cuba. Out of concern for its continuing existence, it has now been placed on the endangered species list.

Hutias or *Jutía Conga* are mid-sized rodents sometimes called "Tree Rats" and are from 12 to 24 inches in length, with stout bodies and large heads, looking a bit like squirrels. These rodents are Cuba's largest endemic land mammal. Most species are herbivorous, though some may consume small animals. They nest in trees or rock crevices. They are common and widespread throughout Cuba and the Caribbean, however some subspecies have become extinct or are extremely rare and are on the endangered species list. In the Guantánamo Bay Naval Base, the rodents are known as "Banana Rats" and are generally considered a vermin.

Another animal commonly found on the U.S. Naval base is the Cuban Ground Iguana. This species of iguana is listed as vulnerable in the rest of Cuba, as they were frequently poached for food.

There are 59 species of Cuban Bats, which are unique to the island, five of which are endangered. They include the Little Goblin Bat, endangered due to a shrinking environment, the Cuban Greater Funnel-eared Bat, which is also found in Colombia, the Dominican Republic, Haiti and Jamaica, and finally the Cuban Red Bat, which is used as the "Red Bat" Bacardi Logo. With so many caves in Cuba, the large number of bat species is to be expected.

There are many species of frogs in Cuba, however the island is best known for its native Cuban Tree Frog, which can also be found in Florida. There is also the small nocturnal Monte Iberia Dwarf Eleuth, which is extremely rare.

Cuba's Zoos

Cuba has several zoos, the largest of which are in Havana and Santiago de Cuba. The Havana National Zoo is dedicated to going beyond the mere display of animals and attempts to maintain a more natural habitat, supporting and promoting breeding programs for various species with follow-up scientific research programs.

The once neglected zoo has recently received a facelift. So far, $1.5 million has been invested into the park, replacing dilapidated fences and repairing buildings. A quarantine facility has been initiated to house incoming animals for a period of 40 days. Prior to this, the last animals that came to Cuba arrived from Africa 32 years ago, but all that has now changed with the guidance and encouragement of Namibia. The ambitious project named "Operation Noah's Ark," included 146 animals that came with both food and medication. Most of the animals, including 10 rhinos, 5 elephants, 4 lions, and some leopards and buffalo, were airlifted to Cuba. In spite of the concerns of the NSPCA of South Africa, things have gone well and Cuba's government is committed to investing an additional $1.5 million.

Supposedly there is still work to be done around the crocodile and flamingo pool, but the progress is evident, with even the children remarking that the animals appear to be healthier. The old rusty bus that had been donated to the zoo by Spain years ago is still in use. Visitors are informed that "Ada," the zoo's only elephant, will now have five young companions. The number of people visiting the zoo has dramatically increased, with as many as 2,000 attending on any given day. Things are currently looking up.

The second largest zoo in Cuba is a theme park in Santiago de Cuba. It has giraffes, elephants, hippopotami, gorillas, pythons, brown bears and what is called a *"cebrasna,"* which is a zebra crossed with a donkey. Overall, it is considered an informative and pleasant place to visit.

Zoo animals are ambassadors for their cousins in the wild. Jack Hanna, an American zookeeper who is the Director Emeritus of the Columbus Zoo and Aquarium

Flora

There are about 3,000 plant species native or endemic to Cuba. The island nation has the most species of palms in the Caribbean. Some rare native plants of Cuba include the swamp buttercup, nodding trillium, big leaf aster, and spring chickweed.

The Botanical Gardens in Havana are located outside the downtown area near Lenin Park, *"Parque Lenin,"* which is just east of the zoo. It has also suffered through the years for the same reason, however it offers tranquility and is a wonderful place to go in an otherwise busy city. The greenhouses have everything from arid cacti to tropical plants. The Japanese garden is not to be missed, being beautiful and is supposedly the place where you can get the best luncheon deal in Havana.

Invasive Plants

Ramona Oviedo, a botanist with the Ecology and Systematics Institute of Havana, has covered the countryside of Cuba to observe and help control the spread of aggressively invasive foreign plant species. She maintains that it is a serious problem, which has been further aggravated by changes in the weather. Hurricanes and global warming can worsen the impact of invasive plant species, which are frequently more resilient to local conditions than Cuba's native flora. There are presently over 550 alien plant species in Cuba that tend to threaten the native plant population, thus upsetting the balance of nature.

Botany programs have been initiated in Cuba, to make children aware of the dangers created by invasive plant species. On field trips they are encouraged to identify these plants and make adults alert to the dangers these plants can cause. The Marabú tree is one such plant, and it covers vast areas on the island. However since these trees tend to improve the soil, provide firewood and are used to make furniture, they are not classified as being hostile. Like with most things, there are two sides to a story.

In my lifetime, we've gone from Eisenhower to George W. Bush. We've gone from John F. Kennedy to Al Gore. If this is evolution, I believe that in twelve years, we'll be voting for plants. Lewis Black, Comedian, author & playwright

The Exciting Story of Cuba.... Part 20

Cuban Flags, Coat of Arms and National Anthem

Cuban Flags

The Céspedes Flag

On October 10, 1868, when Carlos Manuel de Céspedes del Castillo proclaimed Cuba's freedom from Spain, he showed his defiance of the occupying Spanish troops, by unfurling and raising a flag, uniquely made by his lover, Candelaria (Cambula) Acosta Fontaigne, using material from a blue dress, a piece of white fabric, and part of some red mosquito netting.

This flag became known as the Céspedes flag and today it hangs in the Room of the Flags in the Museum of the City of Havana. It shows a white, five-pointed star on a red background and has a broad white stripe over a blue stripe.

The Cuban Flag

The current Cuban flag was created by Narciso López in June 25, 1848, and first sewn by Emilia Teurbe Tolón. It consists of five blue and white alternating stripes, with a streaming, equilateral, red triangle having a 5-pointed white star at its center. As a symbol of Cuba's independence and sovereignty, this flag replaced the American flag on May 20, 1902.

The Cuban Crest

The Cuban Coat of Arms

The Cuban crest, as printed at the beginning of each chapter of this book, has been the official Coat of Arms for Cuba since April 24, 1906. It was created by Miguel Teurbe Tolón and consists of a shield, crowned by a soft conical cap known as a Phrygian Cap, signifying freedom and the pursuit of liberty. The star in the middle of the cap denotes Cuba's Independence. The same symbol is used on the seal of the United States Senate and the United States Department of the Army. The shield, supported by oak leaves on one side and laurel leaves on the other, is divided into three sections. At the top of the shield is the sun rising over Cuba, the key to the Gulf of Mexico and the Caribbean Sea. The diagonal blue and white stripes represent the Cuban flag, and the royal palm, with the Sierra Maestra Mountains looming in the background, represents the country's abundance.

El Himno de Bayamo

Céspedes del Castillo's comrade, Pedro Figueredo, known to most as just *"Perucho,"* was also an activist and organizer of the Cuban uprising against the Spanish. It was said that he wrote the rousing lyrics to *El Himno de Bayamo* while on horseback. What started out to be a military rallying song became the popular Cuban National Anthem. Two years later Figueredo was captured by the Spaniards and executed, but not before shouting out some words of his anthem, *"Morir por la Patria es vivir!"* (To die for the country is to live!)

El Himno de Bayamo was officially adopted as the National Anthem of Cuba in 1902. Since some of the lyrics were deemed to be too insulting, after the final resolution with Spain, the six original stanzas were reduced to two stanzas. Both the flag and the anthem were retained by the Castro government after the revolution of 1959.

The arrangement commonly used is that by José Norman, the author of *Cuban Pete*, a Cuban rumba song made popular by Desi Arnaz. Antonio Rodriguez-Ferrer, a professor of music known for his symphonies, *Preludio Tematico* and *Fantasia*, was responsible for the musical introductory notes to this anthem.

The National Anthem

El Himno de Bayamo

Al combate corred bayameses
que la patria os comtempla orgullosa
no temais una muerte gloriosa
que morir por la patria es vivir

En cadenas vivir es vivir
En afrenta y oprobio sumido,
Del clarín escuchad el sonido;
¡A las armas, valientes, corred!

English Translation

Hasten to battle, men of Bayamo,
For the homeland looks proudly to you!
You do not fear a glorious death,
Because to die for the country is to live!

To live in chains
Is to live in dishonour and disgrace.
Hear the clarion call,
Hasten, brave ones, to battle!

The Exciting Story of Cuba.... Part 21

A Taste of Cuba

Cuban Cuisine

The History of Cuban cuisine includes the culinary skills that many of the Spaniards, who came as settlers or explorers looking for gold, brought with them. Africans that were brought to the island as slaves, had their own way of cooking, as did the French colonists who arrived as refugees from Haiti.

Cuban cuisine comes to us as a delightful combination of Spanish, Portuguese, African, and Taíno or Caribbean cuisines. Authentic Cuban recipes are mild compared to most other Caribbean foods, but do include a variety of spices generally used in Spanish and African cooking. For the more adventurous, the hotter Caribbean spices may be included. The result creates a flavorful merger of the various cultural influences and in some aspects makes Cuban cooking similar to Dominican and Puerto Rican cuisine. Considering the number of Chinese *mestizos* in Cuba, there is little wonder that a subtle hint of Asian influence is found in Cuban cuisine, primarily in the proximity of Havana.

In colonial times wild boar, free ranging poultry and the abundant seafood surrounding the island, provided for the essential nutritional requirements of the early Cubans. Cuban cuisine is also greatly influenced by the fact that the island lies in the tropical zone. A tropical climate yields magnificent fruits and the starchy root vegetables that are generally part of most Cuban dishes.

Generally speaking, eating out is for tourists. Since all businesses have been nationalized in Cuba, the only restaurants with a full menu are those owned by the State. There are, however, some very small, family-operated restaurants called *"paladares,"* taken from the Spanish word *"paladar."* However, delicacies such as fish and lobster still remain reserved for the State-operated restaurants. *Paladares* that violate the rules, or "fish laws" as they are called, can cause serious problems for their owners. The experience of eating at one of these restaurants is reminiscent of the Prohibition days in Chicago, back in the roaring 1920's. The only small difference is that now it's Caribbean lobster and fish, not alcohol, that is being served behind closed doors. To avoid a tempest in a teapot, most Cubans eat at home.

"Food for the body is not enough. There must be food for the soul." Dorothy Day, an American journalist and social activist. A convert to Catholicism, she sponsored aid for the poor and homeless.

The Wonderful Cuban Sandwich

Unknown to most, is that the real Cuban sandwich had its origin in Tampa, Florida. Of course, the boiled ham sandwiches found in Havana were the basic inspiration for the Cuban sandwich; however, they did not come into their own until the concept arrived in Tampa, Florida. It is somewhat similar to a ham and cheese sandwich, but with some remarkable twists, that makes it special.

Long before the Cuban Revolution, immigrants from the island nation came to the United States and worked in various professions, but most frequently as cigar makers in Tampa's Ybor City, known for the manufacturing of premium cigars. These skilled craftsmen also worked in Key West, where hand rolled cigars were lovingly made for a selective market of discerning American aficionados.

The cafes catering primarily to these workers created these delicious sandwiches and they soon became a favorite luncheon meal that could be obtained in all of the immigrant Cuban communities. In more recent times, Cuban refugees and exiles took the concept of this sandwich to Miami, where it is very popular with tourists and the large Cuban population alike.

Of course, anything as tasty as a Cuban sandwich, much the same as Italian Pizza or Chinese Chop Suey, soon spreads into the general population. One of the better Cuban sandwiches made in the Tampa Bay area is on the menu at Central Park Family Restaurant on State Route 54, in New Port Richey, Florida. It is owned by a Greek-American family, and is run by their son Chris Michael. The restaurant also features a dish not to be missed, called "A Taste of Cuba."

The Columbia Restaurant is known by visitors to Tampa's Ybor City as the oldest restaurant in Florida. It is also the largest Spanish restaurant in the world and specializes in Cuban food including their famous Cuban sandwich. Of course there is always competition and La Teresita Restaurant at 3248 West Columbus Drive claims to be the best Cuban restaurant and Banquet hall in Tampa. I'll have to leave it up to the reader to decide.

In April of 2012, the Cuban sandwich was chosen by Tampa's City Council as the official sandwich of the City of Tampa.

The Exciting Story of Cuba

Although there are many subtle variations to the Cuban sandwich, this should work well as a delightful *"imbiss"* or *"tomar un tentempié"* as you read this book.

Basically, the sandwich is made with ham, roast pork, Swiss cheese, pickles, mustard, and sometimes salami, on Cuban bread.

Your ingredients should include:

1. A 7-inch loaf of Cuban bread. If this is not available, Italian or French bread can be substituted. In fact, you could even use a hoagie roll.

2. 1/2 pound of cooked Deli, Virginia or Boiled Ham.

3. Several slices of Salami, Sausage and / or Mortadella.

4. ¼ pound of sliced, thinly handcut roast pork, for a country-style, homemade flavor.

5. Several slices of Swiss cheese. Provolone cheese may also be used.

6. Dill pickles, tomatoes and lettuce.

7. 1 tbsp. of butter, mayonnaise and yellow mustard for moisture and taste.

8. Dried plantain chips or potato chips.

Directions:

1. Cutting lengthwise, slice the bread deep enough so that you can open it.

2. Evenly spread the bread with the butter, mayonnaise and yellow mustard.

3. Starting with the ham, layer in the ingredients, finishing up with the cheese and pickles. You may be tempted to add sliced tomatoes and onions and perhaps even some sliced olives, but then you will have a different kind of delicious sandwich. However, it will not be a "Cuban!"

4. Cut several slices of dill pickles into flat rings, and then cut the rest lengthwise into spears. Place the cut rings on the top of the layered ingredients of the sandwich.

5. Now, for one of the twists mentioned before, close the sandwich and butter the crust before grilling it in a hot press or a pan. It should take about 5 minutes to get it toasty brown and crispy. Be Careful! The cheese should have melted and the sandwich should be hot to the touch.

6. Placing the prepared "Cuban" on a cutting board, slice it lengthwise, at a long, oblique angle, with a sharp bread knife.

7. Arrange tomato wedges and dill spears on lettuce leaves, along with plantain chips, placed on the side of the "Cuban" as a delightful complement to the sandwich.

8. Beware! These sandwiches may be habit forming and are definitely dangerous to your waistline.

Cuban Chicken, Black Beans and Rice with Plantains – *Arroz con Pollo Cubano*

Lining up your ingredients:

1. A good-sized (6 to 8 pound) whole chicken should be cut into about eight pieces. If you prefer, pre-cut chicken parts, with or without bones, will do very nicely.

2. Spices, including salt, pepper, cumin, dried oregano flakes, freshly chopped garlic or garlic flakes, and paprika. Use 4 to 6 squashed or minced garlic cloves, or the equivalent. If you like garlic, feel free to add more according to your taste.

3. Regular Olive oil. Extra virgin olive oil can be used, if you prefer a milder olive oil taste, along with orange or lime juice. If unavailable, or if you prefer a little more pucker power, 1 tbsp. white vinegar can be added.

4. ¼ to ½ cup of chopped fresh onions or the equivalent in flakes.

5. Two or three cups of cooked white or brown rice.

6. Two or more ripe Sweet Plantains. When they are so black that you begin thinking of throwing them out, don't! This is the time they are just perfect! Butter for frying.

7. Additional spices could include a hint of cinnamon, chili powder and coriander.

8. Black beans prepared from scratch or from a can.

Directions:

1. Rub the chicken with the olive oil and sprinkle on the spices. Roll the chicken around, covering the pieces. Heat and

brown the chicken using a cast iron or enameled kettle, or brown the pieces separately in a deep frying pan.

2. Leave the chicken parts in the kettle, or place the browned pieces into a slow cooker, or whatever will comfortably hold them. Combine the spices with some orange or lime juice and add additional vinegar, if you prefer, into the pot with the browned chicken. Don't forget to salt and pepper the pieces to taste.

3. If you have the time, leave the chicken in the marinade for at least an hour. If you're keeping the chicken in the marinade for over an hour it's best to refrigerate it. Better safe than sorry!

4. When you're ready, turn up the heat to a simmer and leave it for at least an hour. If you wish, heat the oven to about 450 degrees and leave it for an hour. Add water as necessary to maintain about one inch of liquid in the pot, and don't forget to baste the chicken from time to time. At the end, sprinkle and spread the chicken with just enough paprika to give it some color. Being made from the ground dried fruits of the chili pepper family, paprika can also add heat, so be cautious. A little goes a long way! Also, don't let the pot burn. It takes oven cleaner and a lot of scrubbing to clean a burnt pot!

5. Cook the rice as per the instructions on the box, and heat the prepared beans to a simmer. When the rice is ready, add the black beans, along with an appropriate amount of juices, and mix them to a uniform blend. For extra flavor, add some garlic.

6. Slice the black peel of your plantains a number of times lengthwise. They are not at all like bananas, and it takes a bit of doing to peel them. Cut the plantains into generous pieces

diagonally. (If you wish, you may cut and flatten them on a cutting board with the broad part of a knife. However, that is not the traditional way.) Pick up the pieces of the plantains with a spatula and fry them in a frying pan using the butter. Wash your hands after working with the plantains, to prevent them from turning black. When they are golden brown in appearance, they are ready.

7. Using a large dinner plate, present your Cuban masterpiece with the chicken, rice and beans combination, and plantains, all presented separately. It is easy to make and will readily forgive any errors.

8. I understand that a White or Pink Moscato wine, with a sweet, crisp taste, makes a wonderful selection to enhance this delightful meal. Of course if you're like me and don't drink, an Iced Tea will suffice just fine.

"If you really want to make a friend, go to someone's house and eat with him... the people who give you their food give you their heart." Cesar Chavez, An American farm worker, labor leader and civil rights activist

The Exciting Story of Cuba....Part 22

People Who Shaped Cuba

Listed in Historical Order

Guanahatabcy Indians – The name "Ciboney" has also mistakenly been given to the Indian population in Cuba. They are thought to be the earliest inhabitants of Cuba, who came up the chain of islands from South America.

Ciboney Indians – were pre-Columbian indigenous people of the Greater Antilles. Ciboney comes from the Taíno word meaning cave dwellers. A relatively short time after the Spaniards arrived, the Ciboney's were integrated or annihilated.

Taíno Indians – Were the first people Columbus encountered in 1492. They were peaceful Indians who occupied the Lesser Antilles and the Bahamas. There were five Taíno tribes as a part of the Arawak peoples. Most of the Arawak were killed off or assimilated by the Carib Indians. In a recent survey there were only about 3,000 Caribs remaining.

Queen Isabella of Spain – Born on April 22, 1451, also known as Isabella I of Castile. Spanish Queen who sponsored Columbus' voyages. She was against slavery and did not pay Columbus until after his fourth voyage. Her son Prince John died in 1497, which was the beginning of her failing health, leading to her death on November 26, 1504.

King Ferdinand of Spain – Born on March 10, 1452, as Ferdinand of Aragón. Sos del Rey Católico, where he was born, is a historic town located in the province of Zaragoza, Aragón, Spain. He influenced his wife Isabella to sponsor Columbus and negotiated the Treaty of Tordesillas. He ruled Spain after Isabella's death in 1504. His son-in-law was Henry the VII of Britain. Ferdinand died on January 23, 1516.

Christopher Columbus – Cristoforo Colombo, born in Genoa, Italy, sometime before October 31, 1451. Named Cristóbal Colón by the Spanish, whose monarchs backed his endeavor to find a trade route to India. Landed in Cuba on October 1492 and returned in 1494. He had four brothers and two sons by different women, Diego and Ferdinand. Among other titles, he was appointed the first Viceroy of the Indies, which included Cuba. Almost two years after his fourth voyage and suffering from arthritis, he died in Valladolid, Spain, on May 20, 1506, at 54 years of age.

Juan Rodríguez Bermejo – also known as Rodrigo de Triana, was the lookout on the Pinta and first to see America since the Vikings. He saw lights on the island of San Salvador at 2:00 on the morning of October 12, 1492. Columbus cheated him out of a lifetime pension, by claiming he saw a light 3 hours before.

Michele de Cuneo – Member of Columbus' crew, who documented some of the atrocities committed by the admiral. Cuneo took a teenaged girl for himself, documenting that he had thrashed and raped her.

Francisco de Bobadilla – Was a member of the Order of Calatrava, which was the first military order of Castile. After Columbus was relieved of his duties as first Viceroy, he was appointed the first governor of the Indies. In 1500 as governor, he arrested Columbus and sent him back to Spain in irons. He died on July 11, 1502, when his ship *El Dorado* sank in the Mona Passage as the result of a hurricane.

Sebastián de Ocampo – discovered that Cuba was an island in 1508. Also given credit for discovering the Gulf of Mexico.

Fray Nicolás de Ovando y Cáceres – Born c 1460, was a Knight of the Order of Alcántara and became the second governor of the Indies in 1502, His administration was the most brutal towards the Indians. He died in Madrid on May 29, 1518.

Pope Alexander VI – Was born January 1, 1431. He was married and had numerous mistresses as well as 11 documented children. In 1494 he sanctioned the Treaty of Tordesillas. On Friday, August 18, 1503, he died at 72 years of age. It is speculated that his son, who intended to kill Cardinal Adriano, had poisoned his father accidentally. It is documented that the poison caused his body to decompose quickly and turned his body grotesquely black.

King John III of Portugal – Born June 7, 1502, son of Manuel I of Portugal, and Maria of Aragón, the third daughter of Queen Isabella I of Castile and King Ferdinand II of Aragón. He ascended the throne of Portugal at 19 years of age and opened up trade with China and Japan. He signed the Treaty of Zaragoza and claimed the Maluku Islands "Spice Islands" on April 22, 1529. John III was 55 years old, on June 11, 1557, when he died of internal bleeding at the Ribeira Palace in Lisbon. His only heir was his three-year-old grandson, Sebastian. His body rests at the Monastery of Jerónimos in Lisbon, Portugal.

Diego Columbus – Born c 1479. He was the 2nd Admiral, 2nd Viceroy and 3rd Governor of the Indies. He spent much of his time trying to get the titles reinstated that his father was stripped of in 1500. He was helped in this endeavor when he married into the royal family. Diego died on February 23, 1526, in Montalban, Spain, leaving his heirs a litigational mess regarding their inheritance. His son Luis Colón de Toledo was commissioned "Admiral of the Indies."

Juan de la Costa – Known as Juan de Vizcaya or Juan the Biscay. Born c 1450. Was the captain and owner of the Santa María. He drew the oldest surviving chart, showing America. It also showed Cuba as an island. He was killed on February 28, 1510, by a poisoned dart propelled by hostile Indians in Turbaco, Colombia.

Piri Reis – Born c 1465. Was known as Captain Piri, a Turkish military officer and cartographer. He was also a member of the Order of Assassins. He rose to the rank of an Ottoman Admiral, and was known for his sense of humor and accurate charts of the Mediterranean Sea, as well as early maps of America that are still in existence. He died in 1553.

Diego Velázquez de Cuéllar – Born c 1465. A conquistador who came to the Indies on Columbus' second voyage in 1465. Ambitious First Governor of Cuba in 1518, and was the first to bring black slaves into the country. He lost the riches of Mexico to Hernando de Soto and died a bitter man on June 12, 1524, in Santiago de Cuba.

Chief Hatuey – Was born on the Island of Hispaniola. Led the Indians to fight the Spaniards. He was burned at the stake on February2, 1512, and is considered Cuba's first national hero.

Don Francisco de Contreras – In 1598, the cousin of the Spanish queen, he was sent to Cuba by King Philip V as the Chief Justice, with a commission to stop smuggling. He confiscated jewelry, silver and gold, a percentage of which he handed down, thus creating the present day controversy with the Bank of England.

Pope Innocent XIII – Born near Rome, Italy on May 13, 1655, the son of Carlos II, Duke of Poli, and named Michelangelo dei Conti. Pope Innocent XIII made lasting changes to the behavior of the papacy by ending the practice of nepotism. He also imposed new standards of frugality, abolishing excessive spending. He was one of two men who authorized the University of Havana, at first called *Real y Pontificia Universidad de San Gerónimo de la Habana*, which was founded in 1728. Unfortunately, he never saw the founding of the University, due to his death on March 7, 1724, from an inflamed hernia.

King Philip V of Spain – Born December 9, 1683, and was the first member of the House of Bourbon to rule Spain. He co-founded the University of Havana in 1728. He suffered from depression and during his second ascension to the throne, died on July 9, 1746.

Sir George Keppel – The 3rd Earl of Albemarle was born April 8, 1724. He fought in the European-American Seven Years' War. Keppel was appointed Knight of the Garter in 1765. He held the rank of Commander in Chief of British forces, during the invasion and occupation of Havana. On May 26, 1772, he was promoted to the rank of General, prior to his death on October 13, 1772.

Carlos Manuel de Céspedes del Castillo – Born on April 18, 1819, in Bayamo, Cuba. Hero of the Cuban War of Independence. A Cuban planter and sugar mill owner who freed his slaves and on October 10, 1868, declared his country's independence from Spain, thus starting the Ten Years' War. Céspedes was killed on February 27, 1874, by a patrol of Spanish soldiers.

Nicolás Morales – A free black man who led a revolt of white and black people to wrest the island from Spain in 1795. He is considered a national hero.

José Antonio Aponte – In 1812, a free black carpenter became an officer in Cuba's black militia and led an uprising, with the objective of freeing black slaves.

Narciso López – Was born in Caracas, Venezuela, on November 2, 1797. He was only twenty-one years of age when he was promoted to the rank of Colonel in the Spanish army. Later he joined the existing anti-Spanish movement in Cuba. On September 1, 1851, he was executed in Havana, along with many of his followers.

William McKinley – Born January 29, 1843, and was the 25th President of the United States. He sent the USS *Maine* into Havana harbor and signed the declaration of war against Spain, on February 15, 1897. McKinley was shot on September 6, 1901, and died September 14, 1901.

José Martí – Revered Cuban Journalist, Poet and Activist for human rights. Born January 28, 1853, in Havana. His death on May 19, 1895, happened during one of the first skirmishes in the War of Independence. He is hailed as the founder of modern day Cuba. Cubans everywhere celebrate his birthday.

Pascual Cervera – Born February 18, 1839, Admiral of the Spanish Caribbean Fleet which was lost coming out of Santiago de Cuba harbor to U.S. firepower. He remains a hero to this day in Spain.

Theodore Roosevelt – 26th President of the United States, born October 27, 1858. Was a Lieutenant Colonel of the First U.S. Volunteer Cavalry Regiment known as the Rough Riders. Awarded the Medal of Honor posthumously for his actions during the battle of San Juan Hill. He died in his sleep of a heart attack on January 6, 1919.

Leonard Wood – An army officer and physician, born October 9, 1860. He was the commander of the Rough Riders during the battle of San Juan Hill and was awarded the Medal of Honor. He was appointed the Military Governor of Santiago in 1898, and Cuba from 1899 until 1902. Unsuccessful Republican candidate for the presidency of the United States in 1920. He died on August 7, 1927, at 66 years of age. He is buried in Arlington National Cemetery but his brain is at Yale University.

Tomás Estrada Palma – Born July 9, 1832. Moderate Party President of Cuba 1902 until 1906. He died in Santiago de Cuba on November 4, 1908, at 76 years of age.

José Antonio de la Caridad Maceo y Grajales – Antonio Maceo, the "Bronze Titan" was born in Santiago de Cuba. He became a Lt. General and was second in command of the Cuban Army of Independence under Major General Máximo Gómez. He reached the westernmost part of Cuba when he led the "Invasion of the West." He was killed in battle on December 7, 1896.

William Howard Taft – Born in 1857, On September 29, 1906, Secretary Taft initiated the Second Occupation of Cuba when he established the Provisional Government of Cuba under the terms of the 1903 Platt Amendment. As the United States Secretary of War, he declared himself Provisional Governor of Cuba from September 29 until October 13, 1906, and later became the 27th President of the United States. He died on March 8, 1930.

Charles Magoon – Born December 5, 1861. Appointed the Occupational Governor of Cuba following Taft, from 1906 until

1909. He was 58 years old when he died in Washington, D.C. on June 13, 1921.

José Miguel Gómez – Born July 6, 1858. Liberal Party President of Cuba 1909 until 1913. He died when he was 62 years of age in New York City, on June 13, 1921. His remains were brought back to Cuba and he is buried in the Colon Cemetery in Havana.

Mario García Menocal – Born December 17, 1866. Conservative Party President of Cuba 1913 until 1921. He died in Santiago de Cuba at 74 years of age on September 7, 1941.

Agustín Parlá – Born in Key West, Florida, October 10, 1887. On May 19, 1913, Augustin Parlá was the first Cuban/American to fly from Key West, Florida, to Havana, Cuba. He and American aviator Johnny Green flew a Curtiss flying boat, the "Sunshine," on the first commercial flight from Havana to Key West. Agustín Parlá died in Havana on July 31, 1946.

Alfredo Zayas – Born February 21, 1861. Popular Party President of Cuba from 1921 until 1925. He died in Havana at 73 years of age on April 11, 1934.

Gerardo Machado – Born September 28, 1871. Cattle rustler and General during the Cuban War of Independence. Liberal Party President of Cuba 1925 until 1933. He died at 67 years of age in Miami Beach, on March 29, 1939.

Alberto Herrera y Franchi – Military Provisional, one-day President, August 12, 1933, until August 13, 1933. He died at 79 years of age on March 18, 1954, in Havana.

Julio Antonio Mella – Born March 25, 1903. While a law student at the University of Havana, he founded the Cuban

Communist Party. He was assassinated in Mexico City on January 10, 1929. He is a present-day hero in Cuba.

Tina Modotti – Born in Italy c August 16, 1896. An uninhibited photographer, movie starlet, model and communist activist. She was the girlfriend that was with Julio Antonio Mella, when he was assassinated on the streets of Mexico City. An autopsy indicated that she died of congestive heart failure on January 5, 1942, in Mexico City.

Vittorio Vidali – Born in 1900, a Soviet RSFSR and MVD agent. After 1934 he was an NKVD agent. Most likely assassin of Julio Antonio Mella and 400 others. He died in 1983.

Carlos Manuel de Céspedes y Quesada – Born in New York City on August 12, 1871, the son of Carlos Manuel de Céspedes del Castillo, hero of the Ten Years' War. Member of the political party, ABC Revolutionary Society. President of Cuba from August 13, 1933, until September 5, 1933. He died at 67 years of age on March 28, 1939, in Havana.

Pentarchy of 1933 – All of the following were members of the Executive Commission of the Provisional Government of Cuba (Pentarchy of 1933) from September 5, 1933, until September 10, 1933. **Ramón Grau San Martín,** Cuban Revolutionary Party; **Guillermo Portela y Moller,** Liberal Party; **José Miguel Irisari y Gamio,** Conservative Party; **Sergio Carbó y Morera,** Cuban Popular Party & National League; **Porfirio Franca y Alvarez de la Campa,** Liberal Party.

Ramón Grau – Born on September 13, 1887. Was a physician and Revolutionary Party Cuban President from September 10, 1933, until January 15, 1934, and again from 1944 until 1948. He died at 81 years of age on July 28, 1969, in Havana.

Manuel Márquez Sterling – Born in 1872. Independent. Was the Provisional President of Cuba for one day, January 18, 1934. Died at 62 years of age on December 9, 1934, in Washington, D.C.

Carlos Mendieta – Born in 1873. National Union Party Provisional President of Cuba from January 18, 1934, until December 11, 1934.

José Agripino Barnet – Born June 23, 1864 in Spain. He graduated from the University of Havana, School of Law. National Union Party President of Cuba from December 11, 1935, until May 20, 1936. Died on September 18, 1945, in Barcelona, Spain.

Miguel Maríano Gómez – Born in 1886. National Union Party President from May 20, 1936, until December 24, 1936. He died at 61 years of age on October 26, 1950, in Havana.

Federico Laredo Brú – Born in 1875. National Union Party President from December 24, 1936, until October 10, 1940. He died at 71 years of age on July 7, 1946, in Havana.

Fulgencio Batista – Born Rubén Zaldivar on January 16, 1901. The Democratic Socialist Coalition Party, President of Cuba from 1940 until 1944. Military coup with the help of the army made him the Dictator from 1952 until 1959. He died at 72 years of age on August 6, 1973, in Guadalmina, Spain.

Anselmo Alliegro y Mila – Born March 16, 1899. Progressive Party. Acting President of Cuba for one day, January 1, 1959. Was the Prime Minister in 1944. He died on July 15, 1961, in New York City.

Carlos Hevia – Born in 1900. Revolutionary Party Provisional President for three days from January 15, 1934, until January 18,

1934. He died at 64 years of age on April 2, 1964, in Lantana, Florida.

Eduardo René Chibás Ribas – Born in 1907. A well-liked senator who tried to clean up corruption in Cuba. He formed the *Ortodoxo* Party and failed in his attempt to become president. Mortally shot himself on August 5, 1951.

Carlos Manuel Piedra – Born in 1895. Independent. Was the president of Cuba for one day, January 2, 1959. Died in 1988 at 93 years of age.

Manuel Urrutia Lleó – Born December 8, 1901. He was a liberal lawyer and politician, and was the independent president of Cuba from January 3, 1959, until July 18, 1959. He died in Queens, New York on July 5, 1981.

Osvaldo Dorticós Torrado – Born April 17, 1919. United Party of Cuban Socialist Revolution, Communist Party of Cuba. Was the president of Cuba from July 18, 1959, until December 2, 1976. He committed suicide on June 23, 1983, in Havana, after losing his wife.

Fidel Castro – Born Fidel Alejandro Castro Ruz on August 13, 1926. Founder of the M-26-7 Movement. Became the Prime Minister and later the 15th President of Cuba. A charismatic, Marxist, Leninist, who led the Cuban Revolution and became the First Secretary of the newly-founded Communist Party of Cuba.

Ernesto "Che" Guevara – Was born on June 14, 1928, in Rosario, Santa Fe, Argentina He was an idealized Argentinian medical doctor, who became a communist guerilla fighter advocating revolution. As an activist, he served as a Revolutionary Commander during the Cuban Revolution, and later headed the Cuban overseas campaigns. "Che" was executed in the Bolivian highlands by being shot nine times by an incompetent Sergeant Mario Terán, who had volunteered for the job. Dying on October 9, 1967, he left instructions for his wife to remarry and be happy.

Camilo Cienfuegos – Born February 6, 1932. A Revolutionary Commander. Described by Castro as "a very, very brave man, an eminent leader, very daring, very humane." Went missing on a flight from Camagüey to Havana on October 28, 1959.

Juan Almeida Bosque – Born February 17, 1927, of a poor family in old Havana. An original Revolutionary Commander and Hero of the Republic of Cuba. Died of a heart attack on September 13, 2009.

Frank País – Born on December 7, 1934. Was shot in the back of the head by Santiago de Cuba police on July 30, 1957, causing his death and a subsequent workers' rebellion in Santiago. Out of respect, Batista allowed him to be buried in his M-26-7 uniform.

Reinaldo Arenas – A poet and author, he was born on July 16, 1943, in the Oriente Province. Persecuted for being homosexual, he left Cuba for New York. His awards included the Guggenheim Fellowship for Creative Arts in Latin America and the Caribbean. After a lengthy illness, he died on December 7, 1990, in New York City.

Frank Sturgis – Born December 9, 1924. Probable CIA operative who helped train Castro's guerrillas. Later helped with the planning of the failed Fidel Castro's assassination by the Mafia and the CIA. He was also one of the Watergate burglars. He died December 4, 1993.

Marita Lorenz – Born August 18, 1939. Had an affair with Castro and was later involved in a plan to assassinate him. She was enlisted, supposedly, as a CIA operative by Sturgis. She presently lives in New York City.

Raúl Castro – Born June 3, 1931. Co-founder of the M-26-7 Movement. Brother of Fidel Castro. Acting President of Cuba 2006 until 2011. President of Cuba from April 19, 2011, until the present. He married Vilma Espin in January 1959.

Miguel Díaz-Canel Bermúdez – The 52-year-old Vice President of Cuba. He came from being the top Communist Party official in Villa Clara and Holguín. With an 81-year-old President there is a reasonable likelihood of him ascending to the presidency.

"They say, best men are molded out of faults, And, for the most, become much more the better... For being a little bad." William Shakespeare, an English poet, playwright and actor

Havana
A Vintage Cuban Travel Poster

The Exciting Story of Cuba.... Part 23

Chronology of Cuban History

Year   Event

Pre-Columbian Era

c 3500 BC   The first Indians arrive in Cuba from South America and Florida.

c 48 BC   The Library of Alexandria is destroyed by fire.

313 AD   Edict of 313 allowed Christianity to flourish in Rome.

711   Moors and Berbers invade Spain.

c 982   The Vikings start their voyages of discovery.

c 1000   Leif Ericson discovers America.

1139   January 2. Portugal becomes a nation.

1469   Spain becomes a nation and the Moors are defeated.

1478   King Ferdinand and Queen Isabella request permission from the Pope to start the Spanish Inquisition.

1483	The Inquisition begins with Tomás de Torquemada, the Inquisitor General. Over the next 15 years, two thousand people are killed.

Era of Discovery & Exploration

1492	October 12. Christopher Columbus discovers San Salvador.
	October 29. He sets foot on Cuban soil and claims it for Spain.
1493	January 15. He departs for Spain.
	May 4. Pope Alexander VI issues Papal Bulls decreeing lands west of a line of demarcation, 100 leagues to the west of the Cape Verde islands, belong to Spain. The territories east of this line belong to Portugal.
1494	April 24. Columbus returns to explore the south coast of Cuba.
	June 7. The Treaty of Tordesillas gives Spain all territorial rights 370 leagues or 1,110 nautical miles west of Cape Verde.
	September 22. Pope Alexander VI rescinds the Treaty of Tordesillas, giving Spain the rights to all territories.
1496	March 10. Columbus departs from La Isabela for Spain.
	June 8. Columbus reaches Portugal on the *Niña*.
1498	May 30. Columbus departs from Spain for the Canary Islands.

June 19. He arrives at Gomera where he divides his ships, with three heading straight to the West Indies. He sails for Cape Verde.

July 4. With three ships, Columbus departs from the Cape Verde Islands.

July 31. Columbus arrives at Trinidad.

August 13. Columbus leaves Gulf of Paria for Isla Margarita.

August 19. Columbus arrives at Santo Domingo, Hispaniola.

1500	Columbus and his brothers are arrested. Columbus is removed from office and returned to Spain in chains.
1502	May 11. Columbus sails from Spain with four ships.

June 29. Columbus is refused entry into Santo Domingo and anchors in the mouth of Rio Jaina instead.

July 1. Worst hurricane Columbus ever recorded! Sank 29 gold-bearing ships and 500 lives are lost. Columbus' gold is spared.

July 30. Columbus arrives to explore the Central American coast from the Mosquito Coast to Panama. He hears about the Pacific Ocean.

1503	June 25. Columbus runs storm-damaged ship aground in Jamaica.

1504	June 29. Columbus and his men are rescued from Jamaica and returned to Santo Domingo.
	November 7. Columbus and his crew are returned to Spain.
1506	May 20. Columbus, 54 years old, dies at Valladolid, Spain.
1511	Diego Columbus, the Governor of the West Indies, appoints Diego Velázquez the governor of Cuba for the Spanish Crown.
1512	Taíno Indian Chief Hatuey stood up to the brutal Spanish invaders and is burned at the stake for it.
1513	Ferdinand II of Aragón decreed a land settlement system that was used throughout the Spanish territorial holdings.
	Diego Velázquez relocates the capital of Cuba from Baracoa to Santiago de Cuba.
	Ponce de Leon discovers and explores south and east coast of Florida. On April 2, he names it *La Florida*.
	The first documented slave ownership in Cuba.
1514	Havana, known as *San Cristóbal de la Habana*, is founded.
1520	300 slaves arrive from Hispaniola to work in the Jaguar gold mine.
1523	Emperor Charles V had the first cotton mill built in Cuba.

1526	The first slaves that were shipped directly from Africa arrive in Cuba.
1529	The Treaty of Zaragoza divides the land claims in the Pacific between Spain and Portugal 297.5 leagues east of the Maluku Islands, formerly the Spice Islands.
1532	Slave rebellion at the Jaguar mine is put down and four are killed.
1537	The French fleet attacks and briefly occupies Havana.
1538	French pirates burn Havana.
	The governor, Hernando de Soto, moves his advanced base to Havana.
1539	Hernando de Soto sails from Cuba to explore Florida.
1542	The land settlement plan is abolished by the Spanish crown.
1553	Gonzalo de Mazariegos, the governor of Cuba, moves the seat of government to Havana.
1554	The French pirate "Peg Leg LeClerc" attacks Santiago de Cuba.
1555	Jacques de Sores, another pirate, sacks Havana.
1578	The French plunder Baracoa.
1586	English privateer Sir Francis Drake lands at Cape Antonio.

The Crown regulates sale of tobacco.

1597   Morro Castle is built overlooking the eastern entrance of Havana harbor to protect the city.

Colonial Cuba

1607   Havana officially becomes the capital of Cuba.

1628   The Dutch pirate Piet Heyn captures the Spanish fleet near Havana.

1646   An epidemic kills a third of Cuba's population.

1662   English Captain Christopher Myngs captures Santiago de Cuba with the intention of opening trade with Jamaica.

1670   English leave Cuba after Spain accepts England's sovereignty over Jamaica.

1697   The Treaty of Ryswick outlaws piracy, ending many of the raids.

1708   By Royal Decree, slaves can buy their freedom. Those who do are named *cortados*.

1715   *Factoria* is created, allowing the government to purchase all tobacco grown in Cuba at a fixed price. They in turn sell it for a profit.

1717   All Cuban tobacco is regulated creating a government monopoly, which leads to a revolt. This reoccurs in 1920 and 1923.

1727   A slave rebellion takes place at a sugar mill near Havana. Troops are brought in to quell it.

1728	The University of Havana is founded.
1740	The concept of *Factoria* spreads to include all import and export trade.
1741	British Admiral Edward Vernon captures Guantánamo Bay. He is forced to withdraw due to fevers and guerrilla resistance.
1748	The construction of the Cathedral in Havana is completed.
	The University of Jeronimo is founded in Havana.
	October 12th. British and Spanish flotillas fight the battle of Havana.
1762	King George III declares war on Spain. In June British forces capture and occupy Havana during the Seven Years' War.
	Starting under British rule, over 390,000 slaves come to Cuba during the next 50 years.
1763	The British suffer great losses due to illness, and agree to trade Cuba for Florida. Havana reverts back to Spanish rule.
1790	First newspaper established in Cuba.
1793	The Haitian revolution causes 30,000 white refugees to flee to Cuba.
1808	Napoleon overthrew King Ferdinand VII and held him under guard, replacing him with his brother Joseph Bonaparte.

1809	The first movement towards Cuban independence was organized by Joaquin Infante.
1813	December 11th. Ferdinand VII is restored to the Spanish throne.
1817	England and Spain agree to end the trading of slaves starting in 1820.
1818	The Spanish Crown opens Cuba to international trade. Epidemic of smallpox infests the island.
1823	The United States invokes the Monroe Doctrine.
1828	A second epidemic of smallpox hits Cuba.
1835	U.S. Import Tariff of 1835, which was blamed by many as the reason for the decline of Cuba's coffee industry.
1837	The Cuban Railroad commences operations.
1844	An uprising of slaves, called the Conspiracy of the Ladder, is suppressed. This brutality makes 1844 the "Year of the Lash."
1845	Spain ends the trading of slaves. June 14th. Antonio Maceo is born in Santiago de Cuba.
1853	January 28th. José Martí is born in Havana.
1868	October 10th. Céspedes del Castillo declares Cuban Independence. Beginning of the "Ten Years' War." Also known by Cubans as "The Great War."

1870	March 4th. Accused of treason for his opposition to colonial rule, Martí is sentenced to six years in prison.
1874	January 3rd. End of the "First Spanish Republic."
1878	Ten Years' War ends with the "Pact of Zanjón."
1886	Spain abolishes slavery.
1892	José Martí starts the Cuban Revolutionary Party.
1895	February 24th. The beginning of the Cuban War of Independence.
	May 19th. Cuban patriot José Martí is killed in the battle of Dos Rios after he and General Máximo Gómez y Báez fought in a resumption of the Cuban Revolution.
1896	Successful battles by the rebels. However Antonio Maceo y Grajales is killed in action at Punta Brava.
1898	February 15th. USS Battleship *Maine* explodes in Havana harbor, starting the Spanish-American War with the war chant, "Remember the Maine, to hell with Spain."
	July 1st. The 9th and 10th U.S. Cavalry take San Juan Hill.
	December 10th. The Spanish-American War ends with the Treaty of Paris. Spain relinquishes sovereignty over Cuba.

United States Occupation of Cuba

1899	January 1st. U.S. General Brooke in command of the troops in Cuba tried to establish a legal system. He inadvertently insults the Cubans.
	December 20th. Leonard Wood takes over control of Cuba as the Military Governor and establishes his cabinet using Cuban nationals.
1901	March 2nd. The Platt Amendment is imposed as a condition of U.S. troop withdrawal. It allows U.S. control over Cuban affairs.
1902	May 20th. United States intervention ends. Tomás Estrada Palma becomes the first elected president of Cuba.
1903	Cuban-American Treaty grants the United States a lease over the southern portion of Guantánamo Bay.
1906	September 29th. William Howard Taft is appointed governor in the second intervention of Cuba.
	October 13th. Charles Edward Magoon is appointed governor.

Republic of Cuba

1908	José Miguel Gómez wins the Cuban presidency as the Liberal candidate. He takes office January 28, 1909.
1913	Due to corruption in the prior administration, Mario García Menocal, a conservative, is elected to the presidency on May 20.

1917	April 7th. Cuba joins World War I, formally declaring war against Germany and siding with the Allies.
1919	May 19th. Agustín Parlá flew a Curtiss flying boat, the "Sunshine," on the first commercial flight from Key West to Havana.
1920	Sugar prices drop between June and November ending the "Sugar Boom."
1921	May 20th. Alfredo Zayas y Alfonso becomes president of Cuba, having been elected in 1920. A member of the Cuban Popular Party, he was known as "El Chino."
1925	May 20th. Gerardo Machado, a popular hero of the Cuban war of Independence, becomes president. Julio Antonio Mella and other Havana University students found the Cuban Communist Party. It was later renamed "The People's Socialist Party."
1926	August 13th. Fidel Castro is born on his father's farm in Birán, Oriente Province.
1928	January 10th. Julio Antonio Mella, founder of the Cuban Communist Party, is assassinated in Mexico City. June 14th. "Che" Guevara is born in Rosario, Argentina.
1933	August 24th. Sumner Welles representing the U.S. government mediates the political truce

forcing Machado out of office. Machado goes into exile in Miami, Florida. Carlos Manuel de Céspedes y Quesada becomes Provisional President.

September 4th. "Sergeants' Revolt" puts Fulgencio Batista in power.

Ramón Grau becomes president of the revolutionary government.

1934   On January 15th Batista overthrows Ramón Grau and appoints Carlos Hevia y de los Reyes-Gavilan to be president.

On January 18th Carlos Hevia is replaced as president by Manuel Márquez Sterling, who in turn is replaced on the same date by Carlos Mendieta.

May 29th. The Platt Amendment is renegotiated. Everything in the document is abolished except for the Guantánamo provisions.

December 9th. Manuel Márquez Sterling, the 6-hour president, died in Washington, D.C., at 62 years of age.

1936   On January 9th.to February 2nd. Captain Antonio Menéndez Peláez, of the Cuban Navy, flew a Lockheed 8A Sirius aircraft from Cuba to Spain.

January 10th. Miguel Maríano Gómez becomes the elected president.

December 24th. Federico Laredo Brú becomes president. He refused entry of 930 Jewish refugees from Germany on the M/S *Saint Louis*.

1938	Communist Party is legalized.
1940	Constitution is drafted. October 10th. Batista is elected to the presidency.
1941	December 8th. Cuba declares war on Japan. December 11th. Cuba declares war on Germany and Italy.
1943	First Soviet Embassy is established in Havana.
1951	August 5th. Eduardo Chibás predicts that Batista is about to attempt a military coup.
1952	March 10th. Batista cancels the elections and seizes the presidency as a dictator, with the help of the army. Batista suspends constitutional guarantees and uses heavy-handed tactics to intimidate the Cuban people.
1953	July 26th. Fidel Castro launches an attack on the Moncada Barracks.
1954	November. Batista is elected president using intimidation, terror and fraud.
1955	June. "Che" Guevara joins Fidel and the Cuban Revolutionary Movement in Mexico.
1956	March 22nd. María Teresa is born in Havana. She became Grand Duchess of Luxembourg by marriage on March 4, 1981. Her family fled Cuba along with many others, leaving their holdings behind in October 1959. She was related to King Ferdinand I.
	December 2nd. The yacht *Granma* lands Fidel's rebel forces in Cuba.

1957   March 13th. University students attack the
              Presidential Palace and are defeated.

              In May, Batista launches an all-out offensive in
              the Sierra Maestra Mountains. By August, the
              rebels defeat the attackers and acquire many
              additional weapons.

              July 30th. The Santiago police assassinated
              Cuban revolutionaries, Frank Pais and Rául
              Pujol.

1958   March 13th. U.S. supplies and arms to Batista are
              halted.

              December 28th. Rebels seize Santa Clara, in the
              final deciding battle of the revolution.

1959   January 1st. Batista flees Cuba with $300 million
              plus another $700 million in art and cash, along
              with approximately 180 of his supporters.
              Batista flies to the Dominican Republic. Anselmo
              Alliegro y Mila becomes Acting President for a
              day. Castro gives orders to his M-26-7 loyalists
              to prevent looting.

The Castro Brothers

1959   January 1st. Rebel troops from Fidel Castro's
              army enter Santiago de Cuba. Carlos Manuel
              Piedra, eldest judge of the Cuban Supreme
              Court, becomes president (in name only) for a
              few hours. Rául Castro starts to execute
              Batista's loyalists. Members of the urban
              resistance forces secure Havana.

              January 2nd. Camilo Cienfuegos and "Che"
              Guevara lead their troops into Havana, as Fidel

Castro accepts the surrender of the Moncada Barracks in Santiago, and enters the city. Castro declares a general strike against the "provisional" government and proclaims Manuel Urrutia Lleó to be president.

January 8th. Camilo Cienfuegos meets Fidel Castro and his army as they enter Havana. Castro speaks to crowds at Camp Columbia, and sets up his headquarters in the penthouse of the Havana Hilton Hotel.

January. Raúl Castro marries Vilma Espin Guillois, the revolution's poster girl.

February 16th. Fidel Castro becomes Prime Minister.

April 15th. Castro makes his first official visit to the United States. President Eisenhower avoids him. Fidel Castro dislikes Vice President Richard Nixon when they meet. Leaving, he travels to Canada and South America.

May 17th. The first Agrarian Reform Law is enacted.

July 17th. Manuel Urrutia is forced out of office by Fidel Castro and Osvaldo Dorticós Torrado is appointed president.

September 15th. Fidel goes to New York with a large entourage and talks at the Council on Foreign Affairs. Nixon considers Castro naïve regarding communism. Castro's airplane is impounded in Miami so he uses a borrowed Soviet airliner to return to Cuba.

October 28th. Camilo Cienfuegos disappears on a flight from Camagüey to Havana. He is never found and is assumed to be dead.

1960   March 4th. The French ship *La Coubre* carrying munitions, explodes in Havana harbor, killing 75 and wounding 200 people. It is believed by Cuban authorities to be the work of the CIA.

July 5th. Major U.S. and other foreign businesses, except for some Canadian banks, are nationalized.

March 17th. President Eisenhower gives the order for the CIA to train Cuban exiles for an invasion of Cuba.

September 18th. Castro arrives in the United States. On September 26, he gives a blistering four hour and 29 minute speech against the U.S., calling it Imperialistic and an aggressor. It was the longest speech in UN history.

September 19th. Nikita Khrushchev is prevented from visiting Disneyland, but sees Castro in New York City instead.

October 19th. The United States imposes a U.S. embargo on Cuba except for food and medical supplies.

October 26th. The Cuban government impounds all U.S. property.

1961   April 15th. Bay of Pigs Invasion.

April 20th. 1,189 men surrender, ending the Bay of Pigs Invasion.

December. Castro proclaims that he is a Marxist-Leninist. His son Fidelito attended school in Moscow.

1962   January 31st. Cuba is expelled from the OAS (Organization of American States).

August 29th. A U-2 mission over Cuba confirms missile installations in Cuba. U.S. President Kennedy addresses the American public on October 22nd.

October 23rd. The United States warns the Soviet Union, and threatens to invade Cuba unless the missiles are removed. Concessions are made to remove U.S. missiles from Italy and Turkey and not to invade Cuba.

November 21st. The Cuban blockade ends.

1963   February. Fidel receives a letter from Khrushchev explaining why he reached an agreement with the United States. Castro visits the USSR.

October. The second Agrarian Reform Law is enacted.

The newspapers *Hoy* and *Revolución* are combined to become the *Granma*.

November 22nd. John F, Kennedy, 35th President of the United States is assassinated.

1964   Castro goes on a second trip to the Soviet Union and signs a trade agreement including a provision to supply sugar at a fixed price.

1965	October 3rd. The Integrated Revolutionary Organization officially changes its name to the Cuban Communist Party.
	Castro allows thousands of Cubans, including convicts, to leave Cuba.
1966	Relations between Cuba and China become strained.
1967	October 9th. "Che" Guevara is killed in the Bolivian highlands.
1968	All remaining small businesses become nationalized.
1972	Cuba joins COMECON, the Soviet Bloc economic alliance.
1974	Cuba sends military support to Syria during the Yom Kippur War.
1975	Cuba sends troops to Angola.
	July. The OAS lifts the trade embargo. The U.S. retains most conditions of the embargo.
1976	South African troops withdraw from Angola giving Cuba the victory. Cuba keeps troops in Angola.
	December 2nd. Castro becomes the President of Cuba replacing Manuel Urrutia. Castro accuses Urrutia of treason.
1977	COMECON announces its intention to build a nuclear power plant.

May. Cuba sends troops to Ethiopia. Cuban advisers are expelled from Syria.

1980   April. The "Mariel Boatlift" - Cuba allows anyone who wishes to leave the country to depart by boat. This brings 125,000 new refugees to Florida; included among them are criminals. U.S. President Jimmy Carter orders the return of some of the worst criminals.

1983   October 25th. The United States invades Grenada, clashing with Cuban troops.

1984   Cuba reduces its troop levels in Ethiopia to 3,000.

1989   September 17th. The last Cuban troops leave Ethiopia.

1990   March 23rd. "TV Martí" broadcasting to Cuba is started.

1991   The economic collapse of the Soviet Union hurts Cuba.

Czechoslovakia stops representing Cuba in Washington.

May. Cuba removes all troops from Angola.

Cuba allows foreign travel for adults if they can get a visa from the host country.

1993   November 6th. Cuban-owned enterprises are opened to foreign investments.

Alina Fernández, Fidel's daughter, leaves Cuba for Spain. She now lives in Miami and has an anti-Castro radio show.

1996	Cuban fighter jets shoot down U.S. civilian aircraft over International waters near Havana, killing four men.
1999	Hugo Chávez is elected to the presidency of Venezuela. He becomes a good friend of Fidel Castro.
2000	Fidel Castro comes to the UN in New York and denounces the U.S. embargo on Cuba.
	December 14th. Russian President Vladimir Putin pledges to strengthen their ties.
2001	The U.S. releases $96.7 million to the families of the pilots shot down by the Cubans in 1996.
2006	July 31st. Fidel temporarily delegates the presidential duties to his brother Raúl.
2008	Raúl Castro assumes the presidency due to Fidel's illness.
2011	Fidel Castro resigns as the chairman of the Communist Party due to illness.
2012	October 21st. Raúl is elected to the presidency for a five year term by the National Assembly.
2013	February 2nd. President Hugo Chávez of Venezuela dies after treatment in Cuba. Raúl Castro is the official Cuban representative to attend his funeral.
2014	December 17th, President Obama and President Raúl break the ice and publically agree to reinstate relations.

December 17th, Alan Gross was granted his freedom.

2015   Diplomatic discussions are initiated to reopen their respective Embassies.

The Exciting Story of Cuba

The Exciting Story of Cuba.... Part 24

Recommended Research Material

Books

Cuba – A History by Hugh Thomas is a detailed text called "brilliant" by *The New York Times*. The author gives a detailed account of Cuban history from the British capture of Havana, to the Cuban revolution led by Fidel Castro. If you are interested in a complete, in-depth study of Cuban history, this is the reference book to have.

Cuba – The Pursuit of Freedom by Hugh Thomas is a readable historical text that starts with the first Anglo-Saxon capture of Havana in 1862. The first half of *The Pursuit of Freedom* is the detailed story of the early colonial years of Cuba, but the second half deals with the contempoary politics imposed upon the Cuban people. Hugh Thomas attempts to maintain a neutral view of Cuba's contemporary history, but recognizes that this history-in-the-making must be preserved.

Cuba – From Columbus to Castro and Beyond by Jaime Suchlicki (1967) is an academic look at the island nation by Jaime Suchlicki, Ph.D, Texas Christian University, Professor of Latin American History. He has also written a similar book on Mexico and is a renowned consultant on Cuban and Mexican affairs.

Havana Before Castro – When Cuba was a Tropical Playground by Peter Moruzzi features hundreds of vintage photographs, postcards and brochures.

Cuba Confidential – Love and Vengeance in Miami and Havana by Ann Louise Bardach is told in a refreshingly new way and does not pull any punches.

Cuba – A New History by Richard Gott is an acute and profoundly engaging exploration of Cuban history.

Che Guevara: A Revolutionary Life by Jon Lee Anderson. An in-depth, informative biography of "Che" Guevara. It is the most complete documentation of the life of "Che" Guevara's life and death, by the man who uncovered the location of his body. Acclaimed by *The Los Angeles Times*, *The Boston Globe* and countless other newspapers and magazines, it was a best seller and *The New York Times* notable "Book of the Year."

The Cuban Insurrection 1952-1959 by Ramón L. Bonachea and Marta San Martín. An in-depth study of the first stage of the Cuban Revolution, the years from 1952 to 1959.

Tina Modotti: Photographs by Caronia María and Vittorio Vidali includes a biography focusing on Modotti's life. Included is a selection of her work.

Tina Modotti: A Fragile Life by Mildred Constantine features over 100 striking photographs and a meticulously researched text.

Tina Modotti (Aperture Masters of Photograpy) by Margaret Hooks is a multi-language 95-page book of photographs taken by Tina Modotti during the first half of the twentieth century.

Voyage of the Damned by Gordon Thomas and Max Morgan-Witts. The voyage of the M/S *Saint Louis* is detailed in this book, published in 1974. It was adapted and released as a film of the same title in 1976.

Havana Nocturne: How the Mob Owned Cuba... and Then Lost It to the Revolution by T. J. English, "A juicy mix of true crime and political intrigue, all set against the sexy sizzle of Havana nightlife." – San Francisco Chronicle.

The Moncada Attack: Birth of the Cuban Revolution by Antonio Rafael de la Cova. "A comprehensive assessment of the assault that set the Cuban Revolution into motion and for which the 26th of July Movement was named." To understand present Cuban history, this book is a must read. "The Cuban Revolution was born at Moncada." – Celia Sánchez, a founder of the 26th of July Movement.

The Cuban Connection: Drug Trafficking, Smuggling, and Gambling in Cuba from the 1920's to the Revolution by Eduardo Sáenz Rovner – Translated by Russ Davidson. "A fascinating look at how the drug trafficking and related activities helped shape Cuban identity from the early twentieth century through the rise of Fidel Castro."

This is Cuba: An Outlaw Culture Survives by Ben Corbett "...offering an insight into the lifestyles of average Cubans..." *Seattle Times.* "Offers a picture of the complex, contradictory, and chaotic island that remains the final battleground of the Cold War." *The Rocky Mountain News.*

Cinema

The Lost City (2005): In the late 1950's, a wealthy family living in Havana are caught up in the complexities of the Cuban Revolution. After the violent overthrow of Batista's régime, one of their sons, a prominent night-club owner, flees to New York City to start a new life. Stars Andy Garcia, Inés Sastre, Dustin Hoffman and Bill Murry. Directed by Andy Garcia.

Frida (2002): Is about the life and times in the 1920's Mexico of Diego Rivera and his wife Frida. This movie portrays Communism in Mexico and the bohemian lifestyle of these characters and their friends. It includes Ashley Judd as Tina Modotti.

Havana (1990): Shows both sides of the Cuban Revolution. Set during the last days of the Batista régime and shows the personal dangers people faced. Stars Robert Redford, Alan Arkin, Rául Julia and Lena Olin.

Cuba (1979): A soldier of fortune is sent to Havana during the last days of the Batista régime to train Batista's army. Stars Sean Connery and Brooke Adams.

Before Night Falls (2000): The biography of Cuban poet and author Reinaldo Arenas. The dramatic occurrences of Arenas' life in post-revolutionary Cuba are brought to life in this compelling film directed by Julian Schnabel and staring Javier Bardem, Olivier Martinez, Johnny Depp, Sean Penn and Héctor Babenco.

Las Doce Sillas, The Twelve Chairs (1962): When her country is taken over during the revolution, a wealthy woman can't bear to give up all her wealth and possessions to the new government. She hides her treasures in the 12 chairs of a dining room set. After her death her nephew finds out what she had done and, since the chairs had been "nationalized," they are now in the possession of different people. He sets out to find them and get the wealth he believes to belong to him. (Comedy) Subtitles: English Stars: Enrique Santiesteban, Reynaldo Miravalles, René Sánchez. Director:Tomás Gutiérrez Alea.

Habana Eva (2010): A funny Romantic comedy. Eva works as a seamstress in a sweatshop where she dreams of becoming a fashion designer with her own a room. Her love is her longtime partner Angel, a charming yet lazy islander. Her dream of marrying Angel fades when she meets Jorge, a handsome and wealthy Cuban raised in Venezuela who returns to Cuba, with a more ambitious project than taking photos of Eva for a book. Eva who has been living with her aunts falls for him and has to decide which of the two men she will want to marry. Directed by Fina Torres, starring Prakriti Maduro as Eva and Juan Carlos García as Jorge and Carlos Enrique Almirante as Angel. Venezuelan produced and filmed in La Habana, Cuba. *Habana Eva* film won the Best Picture award at the New York International Latino Film Festival on August 2, 2010.

Vampiros en la Habana (1985): Joseph Amadeus von Dracula, known as *Pepito* to his friends, is a trumpet player in Havana during the 1930s. Pepito schemes a quasi-terrorist plot to overthrow the Cuban government of dictator, Gerardo Machado. Unaware that he is a vampire, and that his uncle, Werner Amadeus von Dracula, is the son of Count Dracula, has been using him to test a way of countering the usually fatal effects of sunlight on a vampire. Animated film directed by Juan Pedron. (See the advertising poster for this movie, which follows.) A sequel to this film is *Más vampiros en La Habana(2003).*

"The length of a film should be directly related to the endurance of the human bladder." Alfred Hitchcock, *"Sir Alfred Joseph Hitchcock, KBE,"* an English film director and producer. Often thought of as *"The Master of Suspense."*

About the Author

Captain Hank Bracker is a graduate of Admiral Farragut Academy which was in Pine Beach, New Jersey, and Maine Maritime Academy in Castine, Maine. His graduate studies were in education at the State of Connecticut University System, as well as language studies at Brigham Young University in Provo, Utah, and the S.U.N.Y. University in New Paltz, New York. Hank was involved in teachers' labor relations as the President of The Connecticut State Instructors' Organization. He is presently the President of CSEA/SEIU Chapter 425 of the Connecticut State Employees Association Retiree Chapter, in the Tampa Bay area of Florida. Captain Hank is also a member of the Propeller Club of America, and The Council of American Master Mariners in Tampa, Florida.

Working in the Maritime Industry, Captain Hank was a Harbor Pilot for the Port of Monrovia, Liberia. He was also the Captain of coastal cargo vessels in West Africa and in the United States, where he piloted coastal tankers from Eastport, Maine, to the Chesapeake Bay. With the U.S. Navy in New York, he served as the head of the Navigation Department and was the Navy Port Captain for the Military Sea Transport Service.

His military career spanned over forty years, first as a Commissioned Officer in the United States Naval Reserve and later in the United States Army Reserve, where he was an Officer with the Military Intelligence Corps.

For twenty-four years, he was employed by the State of Connecticut, both as a teacher and administrator. He is also a recognized contributor to Wikipedia, the online encyclopedia.

The Exciting Story of Cuba

Captain Hank's career took him to Cuba during the years of the Castro Revolution, creating a long-lasting interest in the history of this Island Nation.

"Being a unique superpower undermines the military intelligence of strategy. To think strategically, one has to imagine oneself in the enemy's place. If one cannot do this, it is impossible to foresee, to take by surprise, to outflank. Misinterpreting an enemy can lead to defeat. This is how empires fall." John Peter Berger, an English novelist, painter and poet. He won the 1972 Booker Prize for his novel "G" which was followed by the essay "Ways of Seeing."

Raconteur

Stories as told by Captain Hank become exciting, as he weaves vignettes of historical events into them. This book is best read casually, using dates only as a reference as to its continuity. It brings to life Cuban history, as he editorializes on why things happened the way they did, and who the people behind the events were. Follow in the footsteps of the heroes, beautiful movie stars and sinister villains, who influenced the course of a country that is much bigger than its size.

The Exciting Story of Cuba

Other Books by the Author

Suppressed I Rise – The life of Adeline Perry edited by Hank Bracker. The true story of a courageous mother from South Africa caught in the horrors of World War II in Nazi Germany. Available from the publisher. The second edition of this book is pending.

Seawater One – Sea stories based primarily on the life of the author. It's an exciting journey starting with the Great Depression in Jersey City, New Jersey, and continuing on to his graduation from Maine Maritime Academy in the mid 1950's. It is very factual with no holds barred.

Seawater Two – An exciting adventure that starts with the author arriving in politically torn Liberia, and takes the reader through West, South and East Africa. This book is in the works and should be available by end-of-year 2015.

Seawater Three – Is being planned to take the reader through the years when the author was active in the military having retired first from the U.S. Naval Reserve and then the U.S. Army Reserve, with over twenty years in each. It will also cover his time as an educator and bring his ongoing ventures into the 21st Century.

Vintage The Highway Traveler *Poster*

A Final Thought

"Hope for the Best. Expect the worst. Life is a play. We're unrehearsed..." Encouraged by his wife Anne Bancroft, Mel Brooks wrote the music and lyrics to this song for his movie, The Twelve Chairs *(1970).*

≈ *El Fin* ≈

12/2015

DATE DUE

PRINTED IN U.S.A.

45371906R00338

Made in the USA
Charleston, SC
19 August 2015

"The Exciting Story of Cuba"

Stories as told by Captain Hank become exciting, as he weaves vignettes of historical events into them. This book brings to life the history of Cuba, as he clarifies why things happened the way they did, and who the people were behind the events. Follow in the footsteps of the heroes, beautiful movie stars and sinister villains, who influenced the course of a country that is much bigger than its size.

Captain Hank Bracker is a graduate of Maine Maritime Academy, and enjoyed the adventurous life most people only read about. Look for his "Seawater" series of books.

ISBN 9781484809457

90000

9 781484 809457